HISTORIC PHOTOS OF
DENVER

TEXT AND CAPTIONS BY MYRON VALLIER

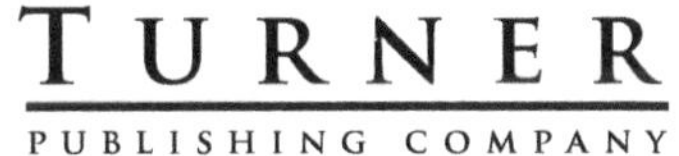

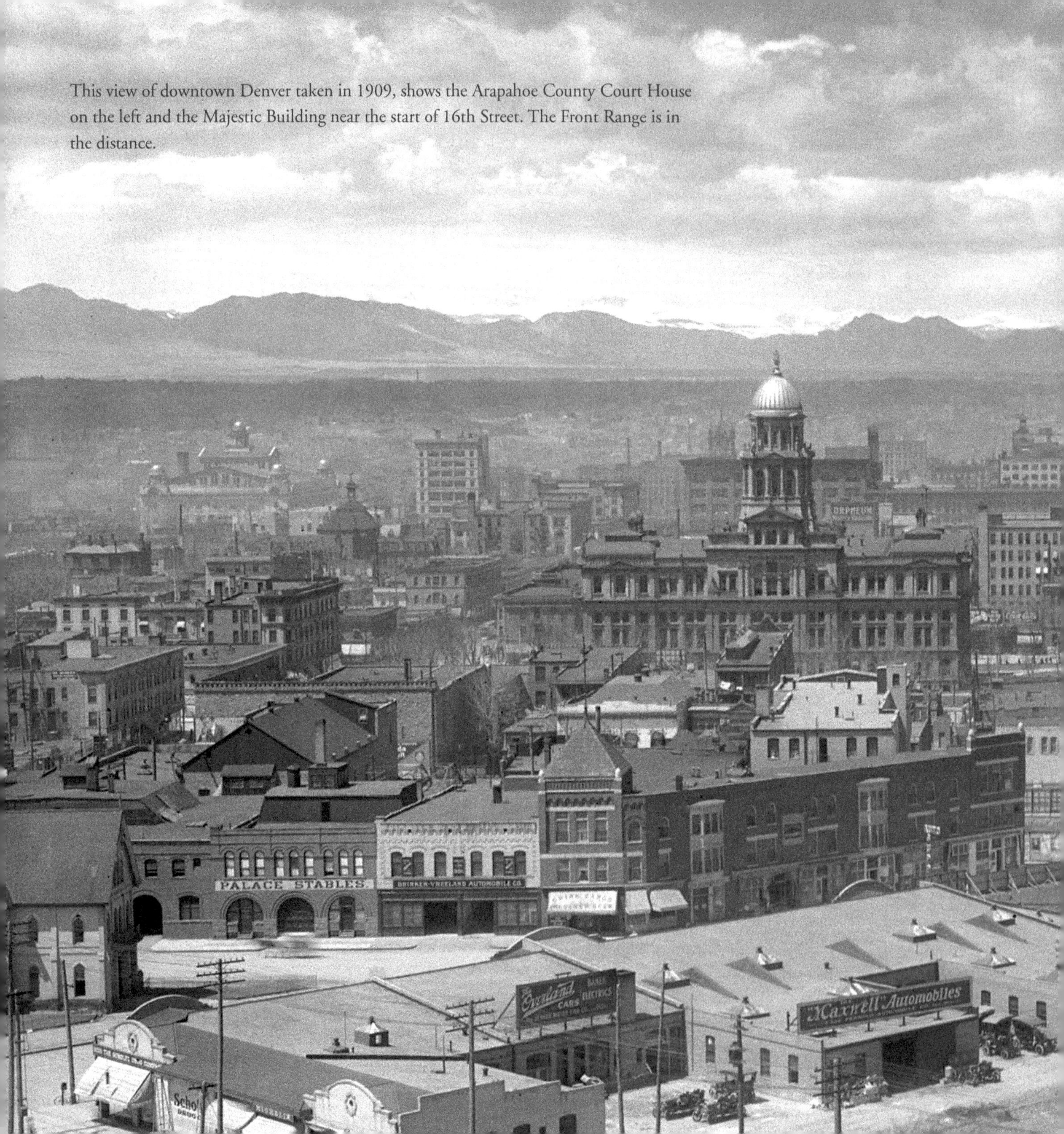

This view of downtown Denver taken in 1909, shows the Arapahoe County Court House on the left and the Majestic Building near the start of 16th Street. The Front Range is in the distance.

HISTORIC PHOTOS OF
DENVER

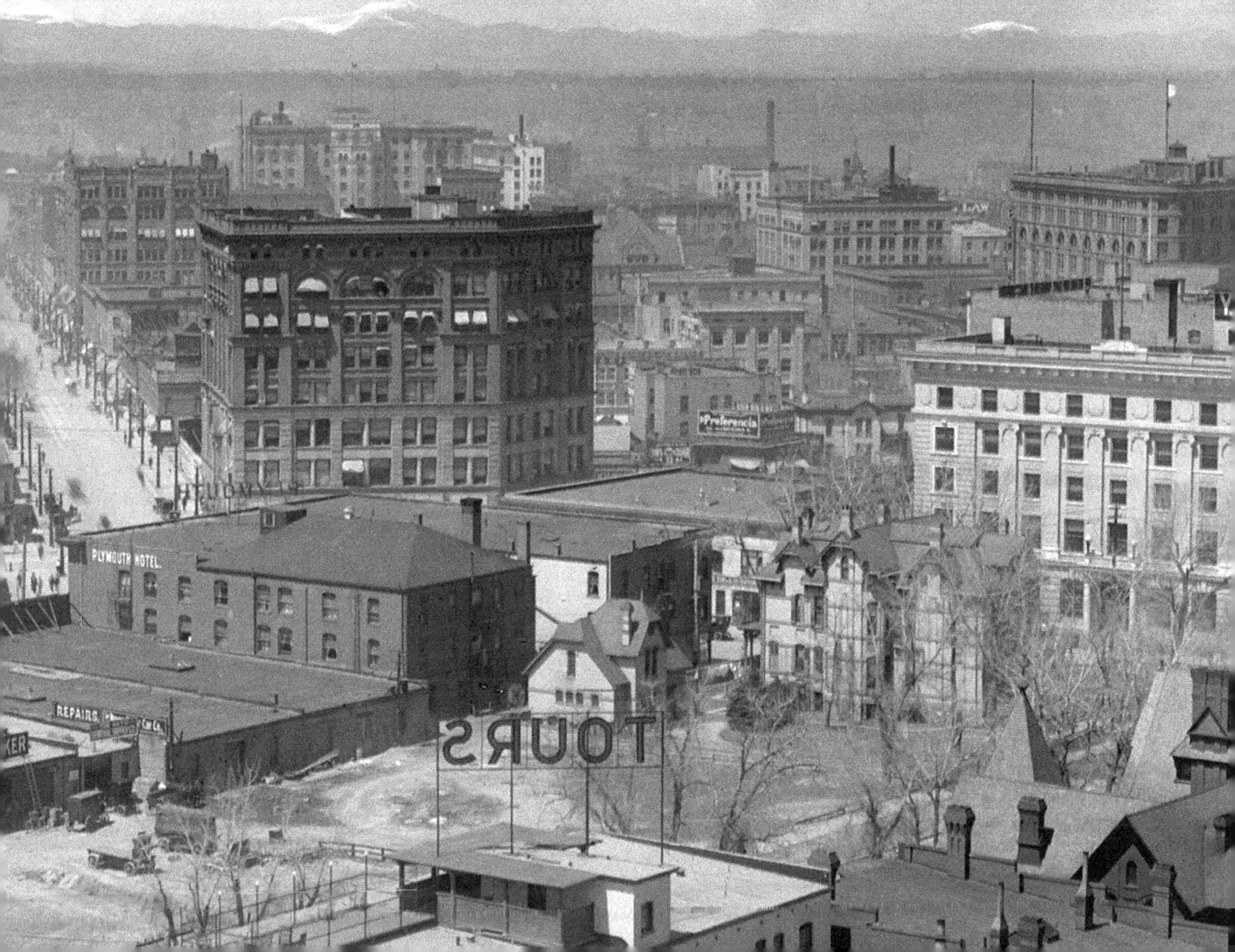

Turner Publishing Company
www.turnerpublishing.com

Historic Photos of Denver

Library of Congress Control Number: 2006937077

ISBN-13: 978-1-59652-319-7
ISBN: 1-59652-319-0

Printed in the United States of America

ISBN 978-1-68336-934-9 (hc)

CONTENTS

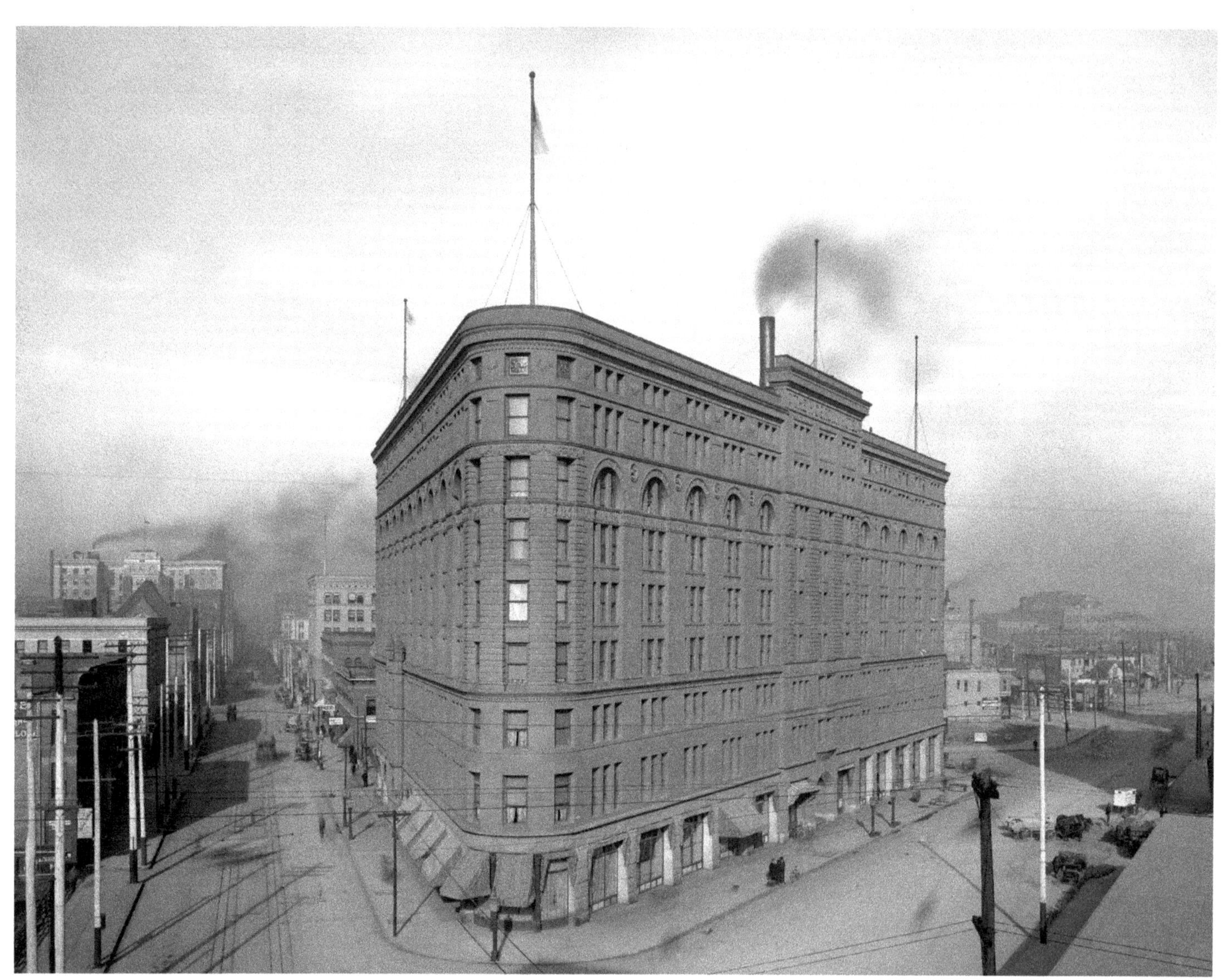

The Brown Palace Hotel, located at the intersection of Broadway and Tremont Place, was designed by Frank E. Edbrooke, for Henry C. Brown, and opened in 1892. It is still one of the great hotels of the world.

ACKNOWLEDGMENTS

This volume, *Historic Photos of Denver*, is the result of the cooperation and efforts of many individuals and organizations. It takes a community to preserve local history, especially visual history. The photographs featured in this book come from the Denver Public Library Western History/Genealogy Department's Western History Photograph Collection. This archive contains more than 600,000 photographs and negatives that document the history of Colorado and the trans-Mississippi West.

The library's photo database contains more than 110,000 images and catalog records of North American Indians, pioneer life, railroads, mining, Denver, Colorado towns, city, farm, and ranch life, recreation, landscape, as well as numerous other subjects.

Most of the digitized material on the website is from the Denver Public Library's Western History Photograph Collection; however, there is also a significant amount of material from the Colorado Historical Society photograph collection. The library sells high-resolution photographic prints, transparencies, and digital files of any of Denver Public Library's images on the website. To view or find more information about the collection or to order images, visit the library's website at

www.photoswest.org

This volume would not have been possible without the professional and amateur historians devoted to preserving the past, including the dedicated staff—past and present—of the Denver Public Library.

Coi Drummond-Gehrig
Linda Running Bently
Bruce Hanson

The publisher would also like to thank Myron Vallier, the author, for his valuable contributions and assistance in making this work possible.

Preface

Denver has thousands of historic photographs that reside in archives, both locally and nationally. This book began with the observation that, while those photographs are of great interest to many, they are not easily accessible. During a time when Denver is looking ahead and evaluating its future course, many people are asking, How do we treat the past? These decisions affect every aspect of the city—architecture, public spaces, commerce, infrastructure—and these, in turn, affect the way that people live their lives. This book seeks to provide easy access to a valuable, objective look into the history of Denver.

The power of photographs is that they are less subjective than words in their treatment of history. Although the photographer can make decisions regarding subject matter and how to capture and present it, photographs do not provide the breadth of interpretation that text does. For this reason, they offer an original, untainted perspective that allows the viewer to interpret and observe.

This project represents countless hours of review and research. The researchers and writer have reviewed thousands of photographs in numerous archives. We greatly appreciate the generous assistance of those listed in the acknowledgments of this work, without whom this project could not have been completed.

The goal in publishing this work is to provide broader access to this set of extraordinary photographs which seek to inspire, provide perspective, and evoke insight that might assist people who are responsible for determining Denver's future. In addition, the book seeks to preserve the past with adequate respect and reverence.

With the exception of touching up imperfections caused by the damage of time and cropping where necessary, no other changes have been made. The focus and clarity of many images is limited to the technology and the ability of the photographer at the time they were taken.

The work is divided into eras. Beginning with some of the earliest known photographs of Denver, the first section records photographs from before the Civil War through the late nineteenth century. The second section spans the early years of the twentieth century through the World War I era. Section Three moves to the twenties and thirties. The last section covers the post World War II era up to recent times.

In each of these sections we have made an effort to capture various aspects of life through our selection of photographs. People, commerce, transportation, infrastructure, religious institutions, and educational institutions have been included to provide a broad perspective.

We encourage readers to reflect as they go walking in Denver, strolling through the city, its parks, and its neighborhoods. It is the publisher's hope that in utilizing this work, longtime residents will learn something new and that new residents will gain a perspective on where Denver has been, so that each can contribute to its future.

Todd Bottorff, Publisher

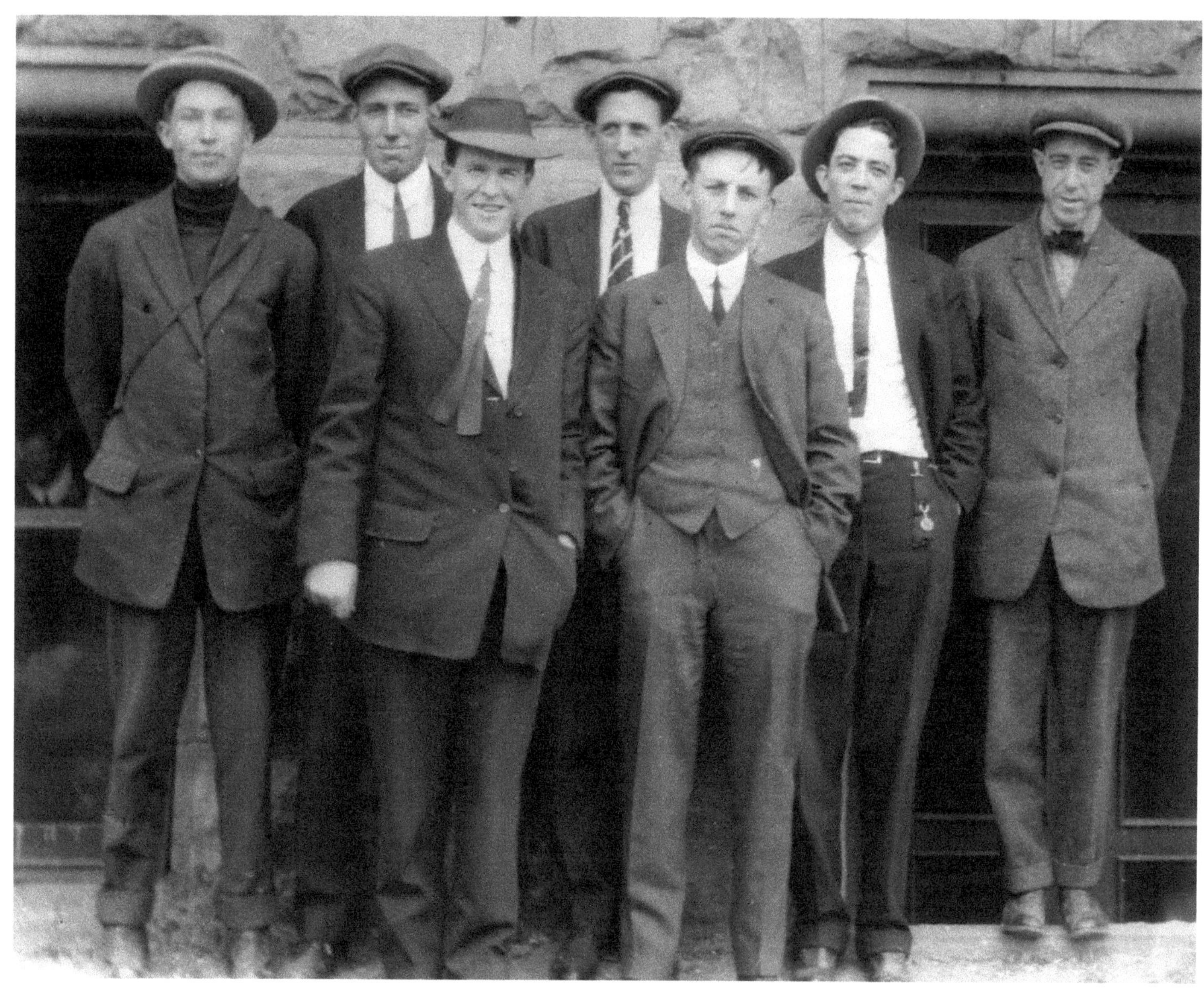

Denver newspaper police reporters pose in front of the old Denver City Hall. The men are identified as George Flanagan and Mudge Ransom, in the front row, and George Minot, Walter Lovelace, an unidentified reporter, Johnny Day, and Joe Satterthwaite, in the back row.

From Gold Camp to "Queen City of the Plains"
1858–1899

For centuries the mountains and plains of Colorado were hunting grounds for North American Indians. The Arapaho regularly camped at the confluence of the South Platte River and Cherry Creek on the site of what is now Denver. Auraria, the first European settlement in the area, came about as a result of an 1858 gold strike on Cherry Creek, made by William Green Russell. Soon after, William Larimer established another settlement across Cherry Creek, Denver City, named after the first territorial governor of Kansas, James Denver. By 1860 the two towns would merge as Denver.

In 1863 Denver's business district was destroyed by fire and in 1864 a flood on Cherry Creek devastated parts of Auraria. But the city quickly recovered, and by 1865 it had become the capital of the Colorado territory. Growth, however, eluded the city and the 1870 census counted fewer than 5,000 residents. The first railroad arrived in Denver in 1870; soon others followed and brought much-needed diversity to the Denver economy.

In 1881 Denver was named capital of the state of Colorado, and by the 1880s and 1890s silver mining in the nearby mountains brought rapid growth and prosperity to the city. In 1885, the Denver Electric and Cable Company began the city's first cable railroad service, and in that same year, the Denver Tramway Company started the city's first electric streetcar service using an underground conduit.

Education was very important to early Denver residents. Two private schools, St. Mary's Academy (Catholic) and Wolfe Hall (Episcopalian) were opened in the 1860s, and the first Denver public school, Arapahoe School, was opened in 1873. Three private colleges were opened between 1864 and 1887, the University of Denver, Regis College, and Loretto Heights College.

By 1890 the city had grown to 108,000, making it the second largest city in the West. However the silver panic of 1893 put an end to Denver's first boom. By the end of the century, Denver had become a center for transportation, agriculture, and industry, but economic prosperity once again eluded the "Queen City of the Plains."

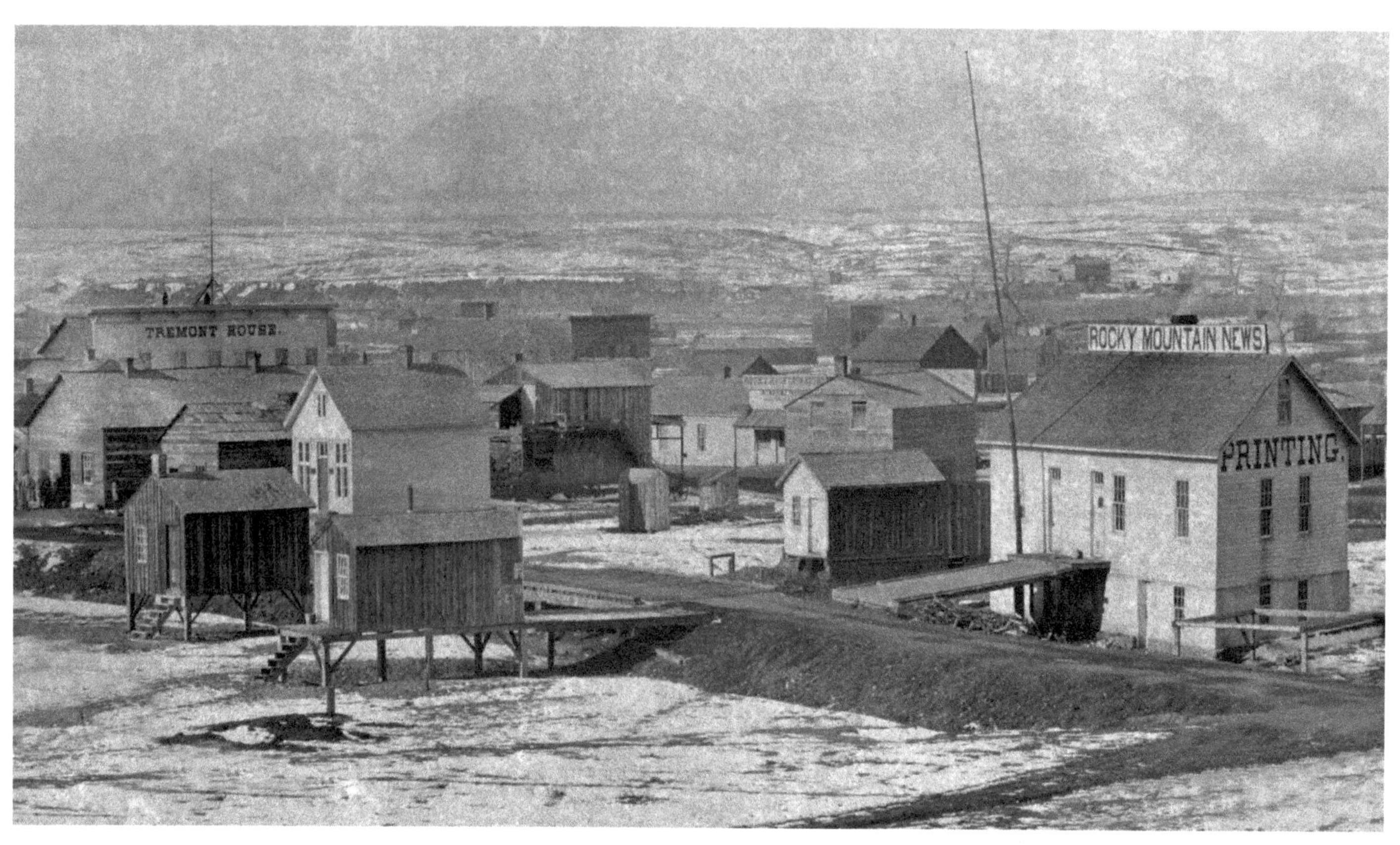

The Rocky Mountain News office, built in 1860, was destroyed by the Cherry Creek flood in 1864. The newspaper, founded by William Newton Byers, is still in existence.

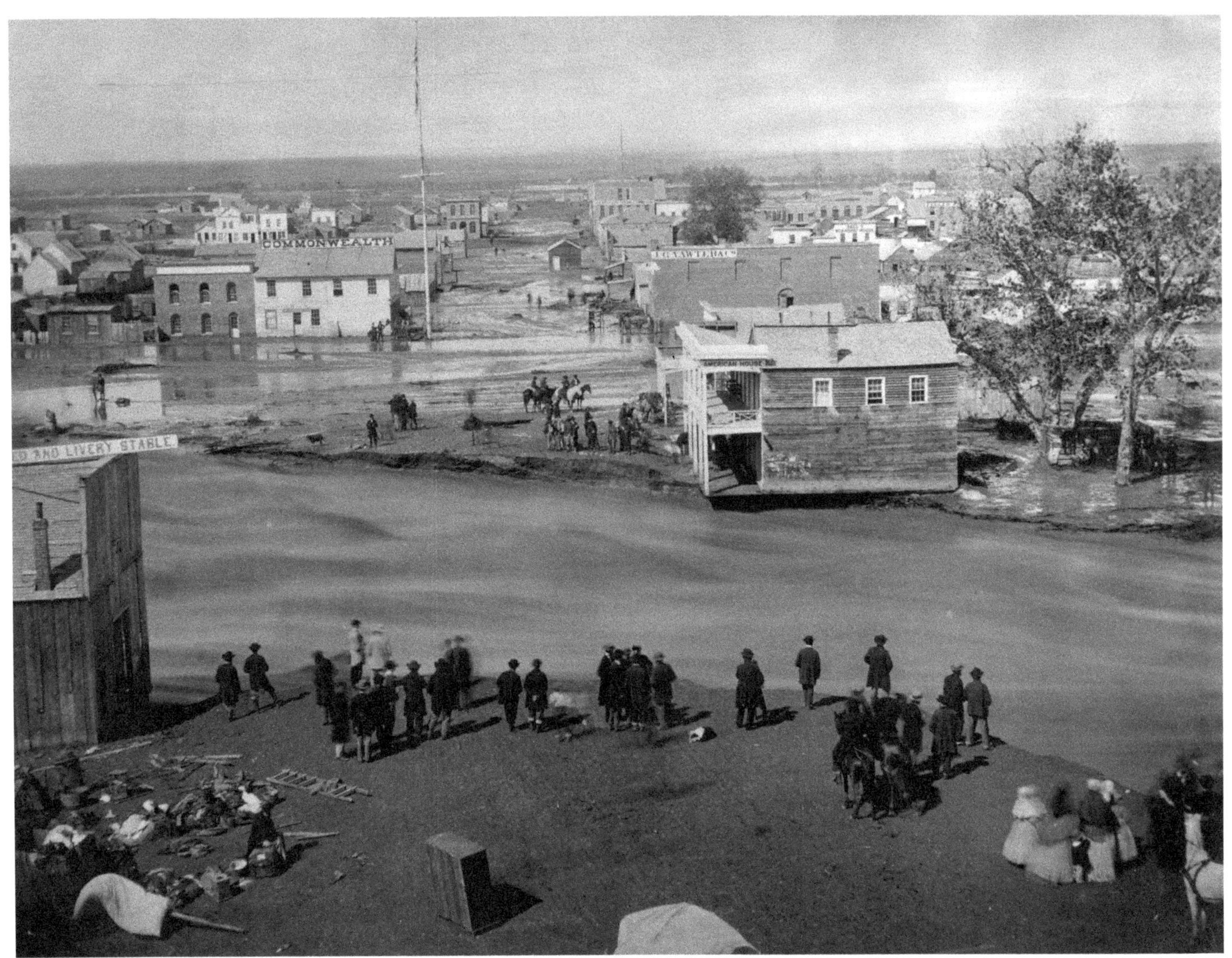

The early city of Denver suffered great damage, and the city of Auraria was wiped out, when Cherry Creek flooded in 1864. Despite warnings of the potential hazard, the settlers had built near the river. Here we see well-dressed residents surveying the damage from both sides of the creek.

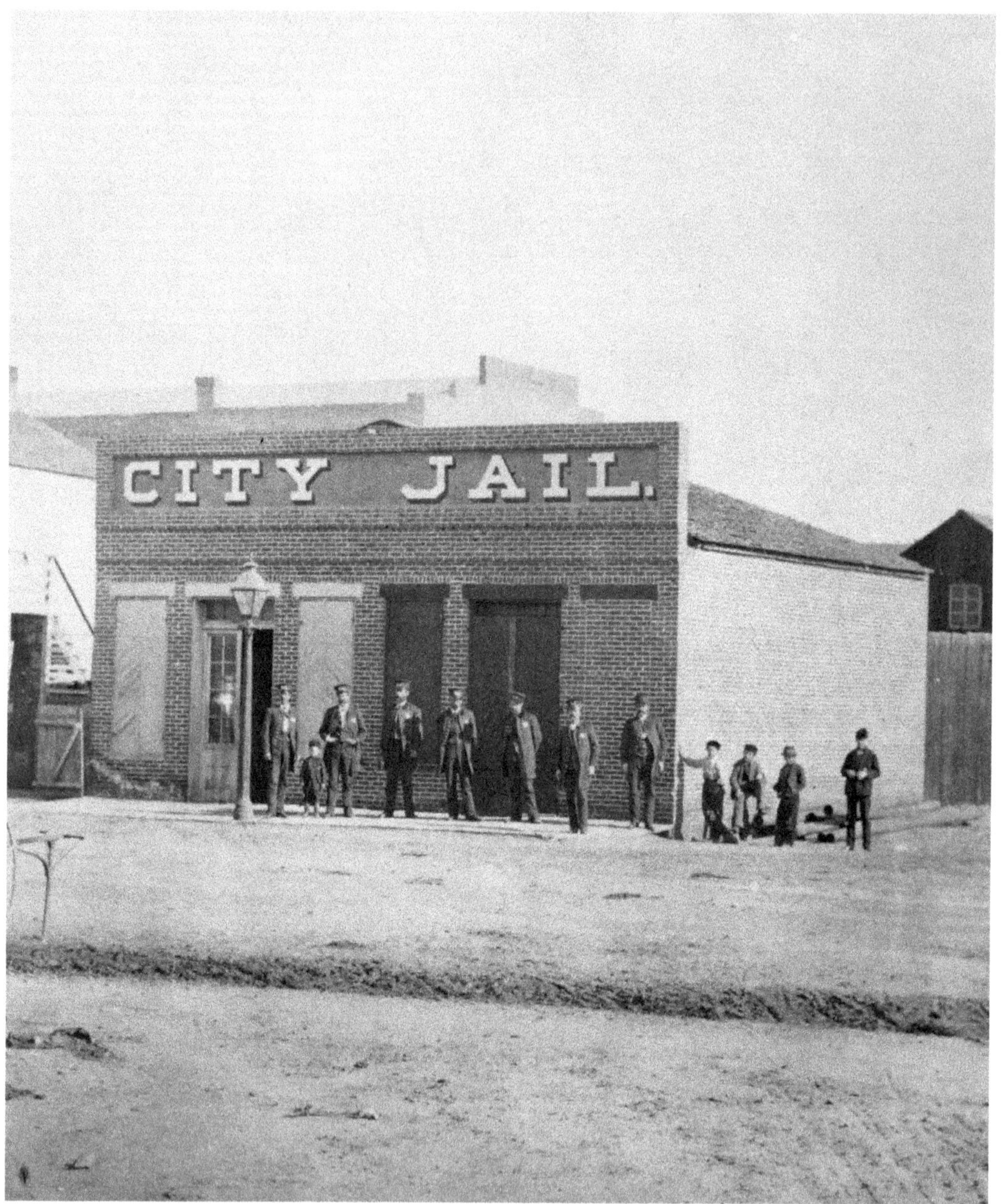

City policemen dressed in uniform and young boys pose in front of the City Jail located in the former Butterick Meat Market building at 1355 13th Street. One of Denver's earliest jails, it was located here from 1866 through 1883.

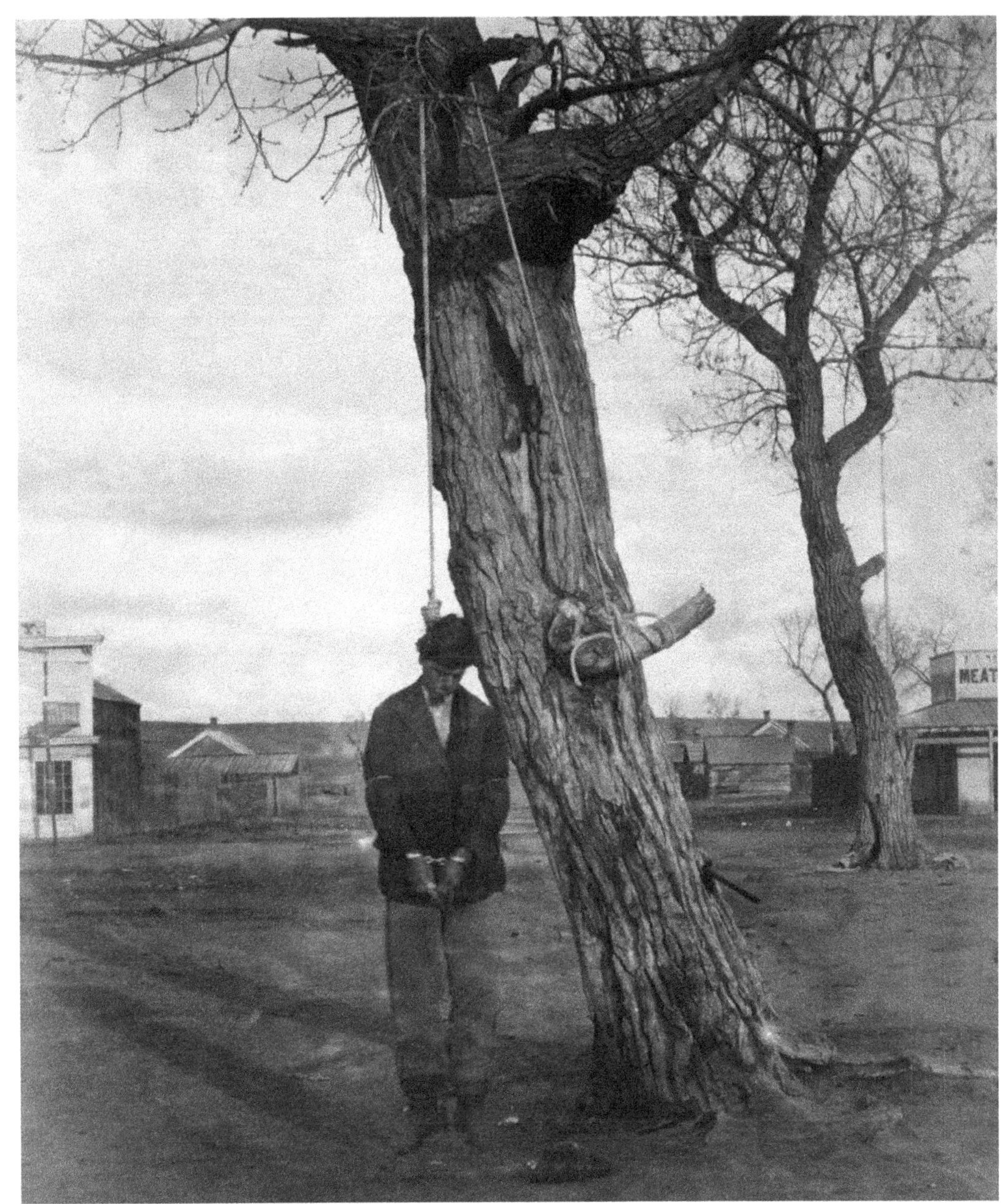

Frontier justice could be swift. Sanford Dougan, accused of murder, was hanged by a mob in Denver on December 2, 1868.

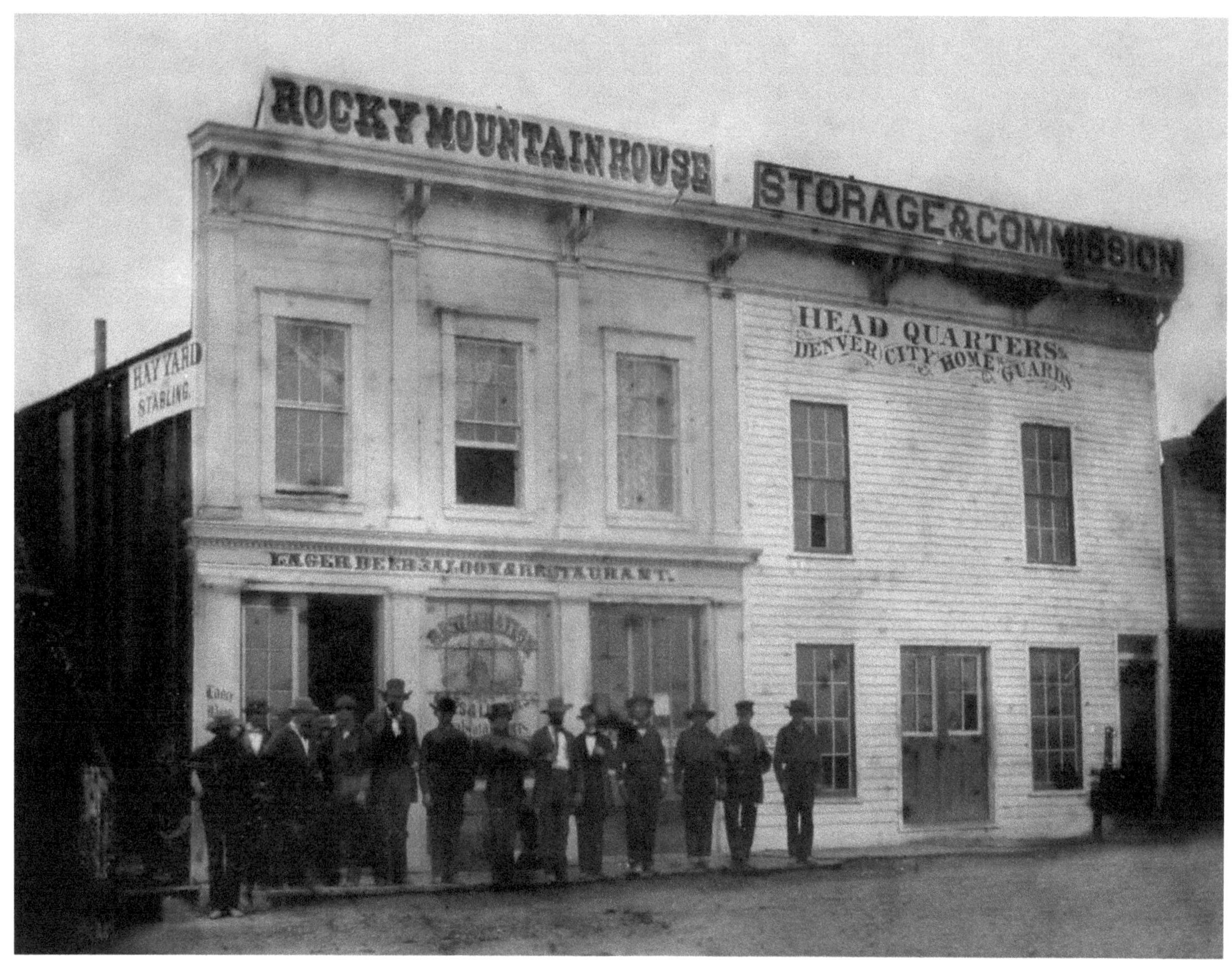

The Denver City Home Guard was organized in 1861 to fight in the Civil War and attached to the District of Colorado. The guard marched to New Mexico and engaged Confederate troops on February 21, 1862, at Valverde, south of Socorro. The guard was mustered out on April 1, 1862.

Originally the U.S. Branch Mint, located near the corner of 16th and Holladay (later Market) streets, was the Clark, Gruber & Co. bank and mint. The business was sold to the government in 1863. The original building was then incorporated into the building pictured here.

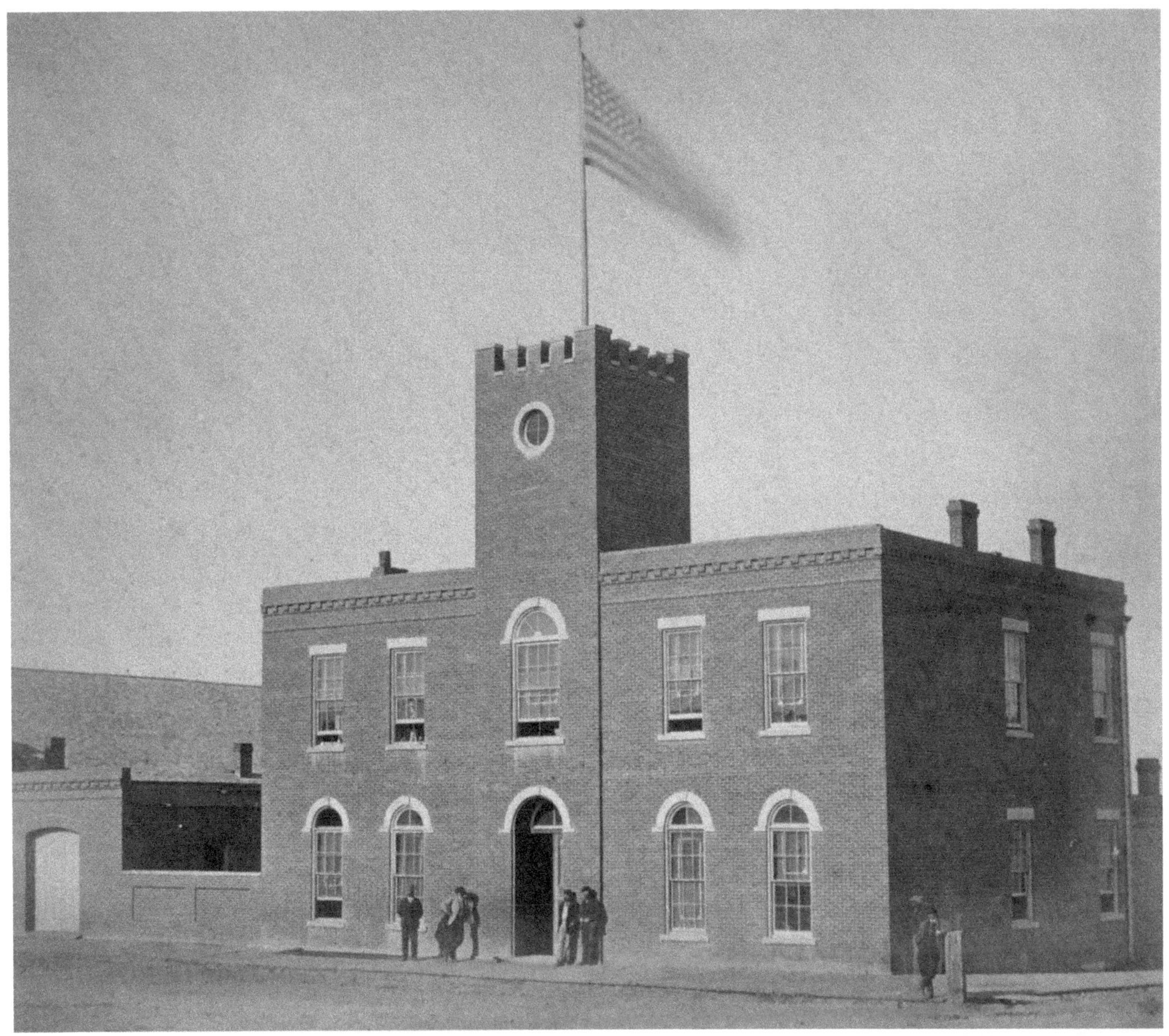

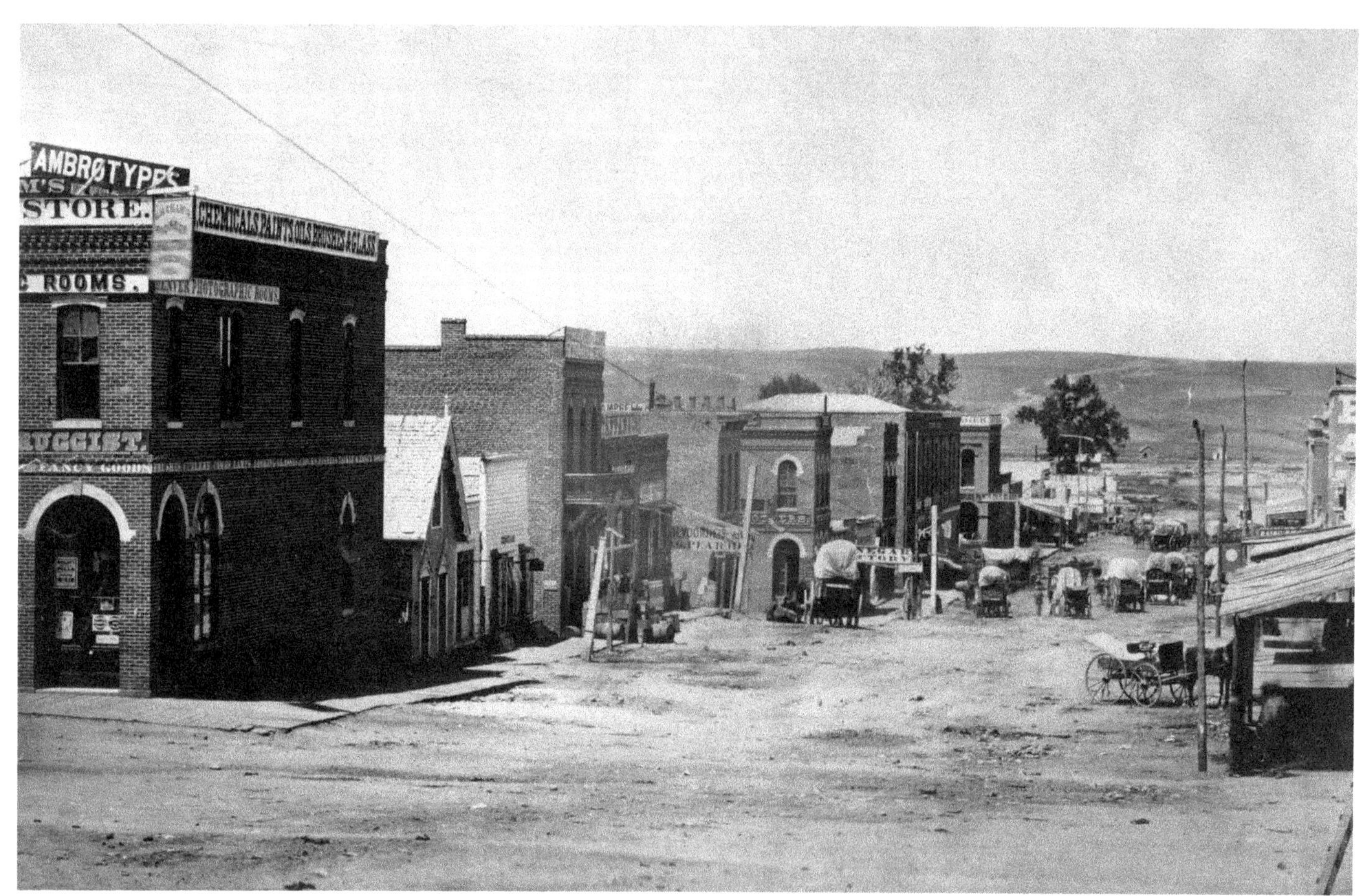

Covered wagons crowd 15th Street in this photo taken in 1865. The photographic studio of William G. Chamberlain is on the corner of Larimer Street.

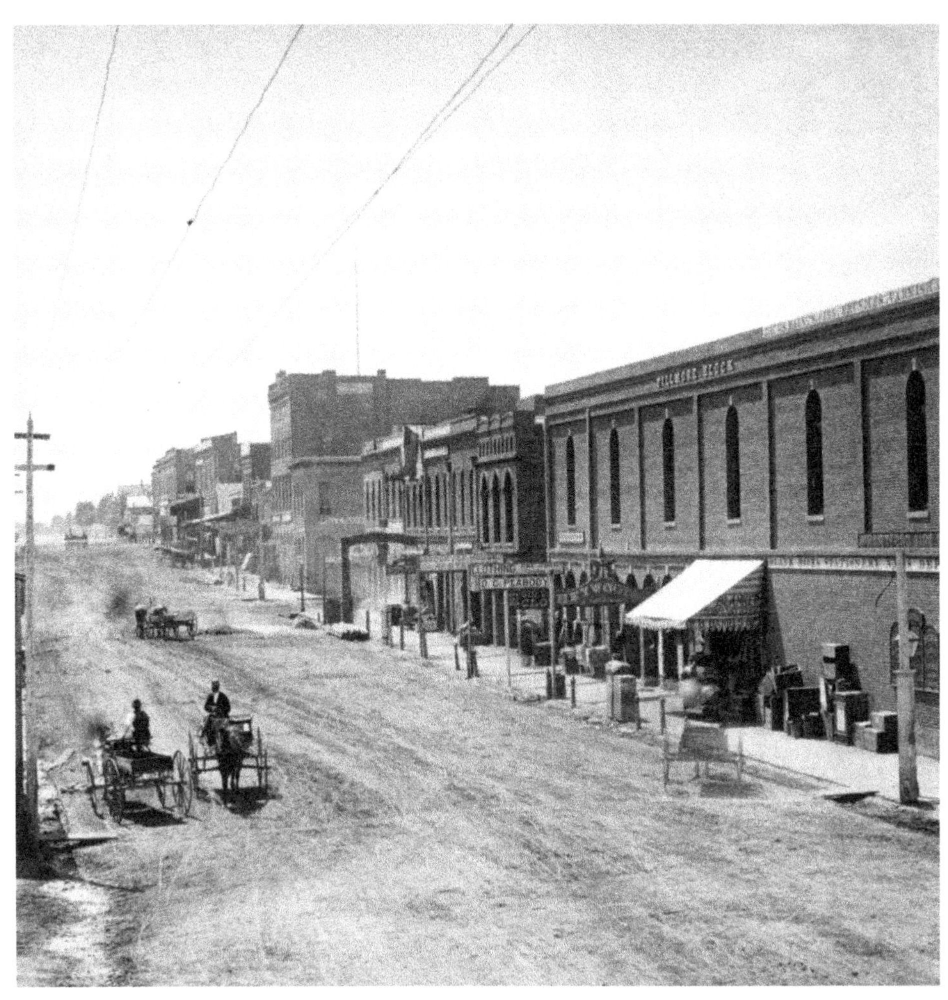

A view of 15th Street in the 1860s. The Filmore Block is on the corner.

The First National Bank building on the corner of 15th and Blake streets was built in the mid 1860s. The third story was added in the early 1870s. The building was the site of the Colorado Constitutional Convention held between December 1875 and March 1876.

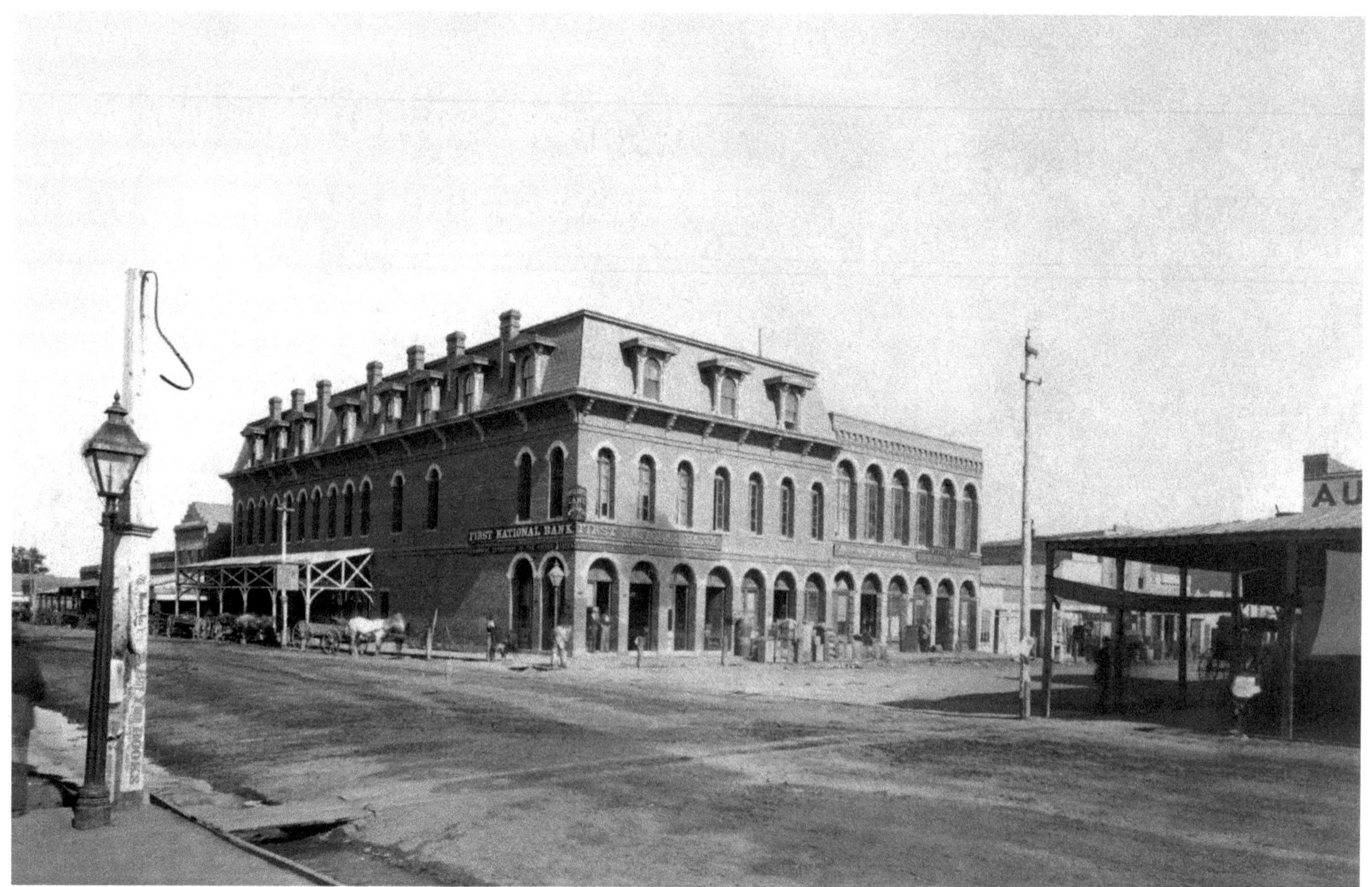

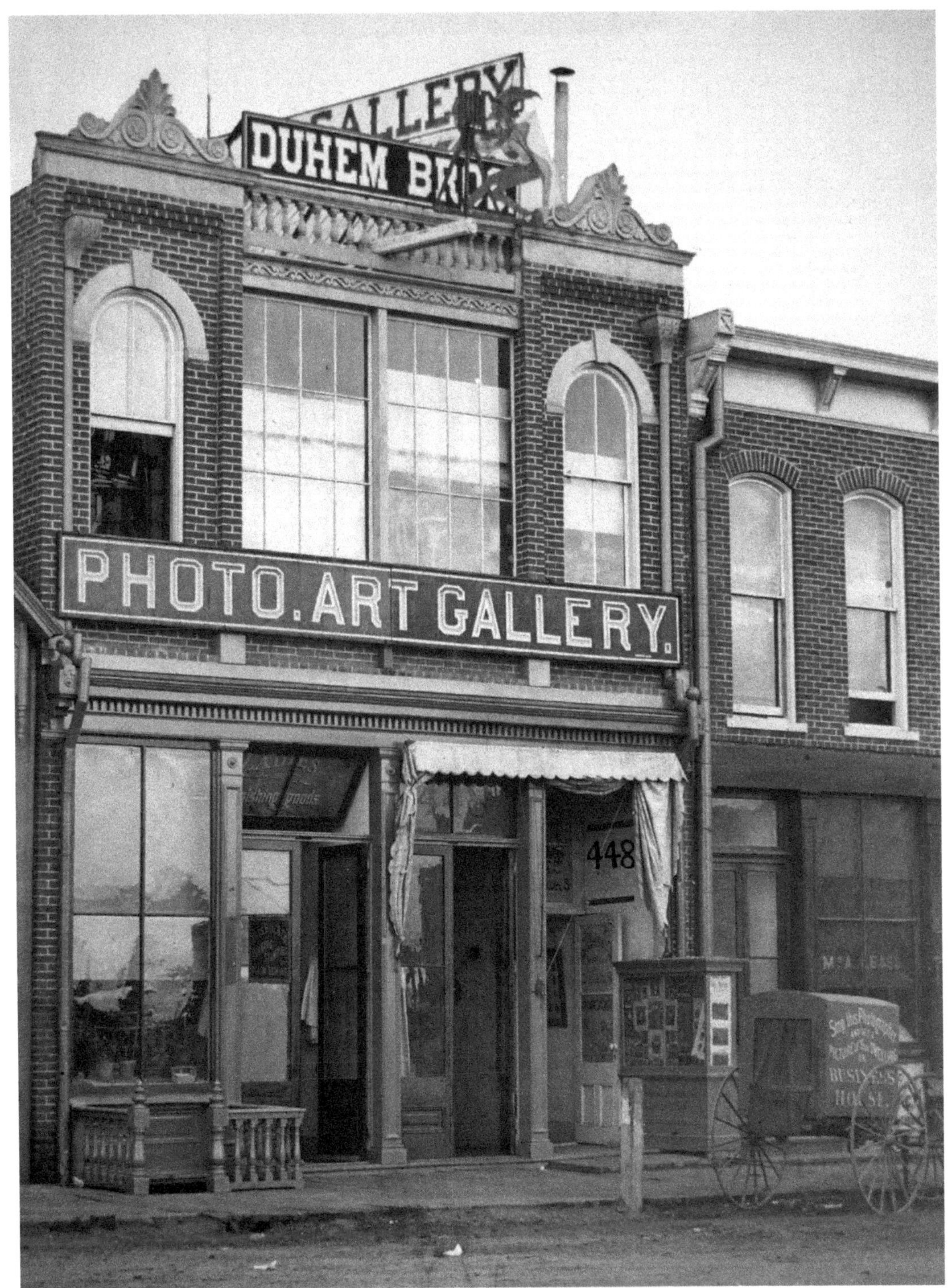

The Duhem Brothers, noted Denver photographers, had a studio located at 448 Larimer Street. The carriage parked in front of the building at right holds a portable darkroom.

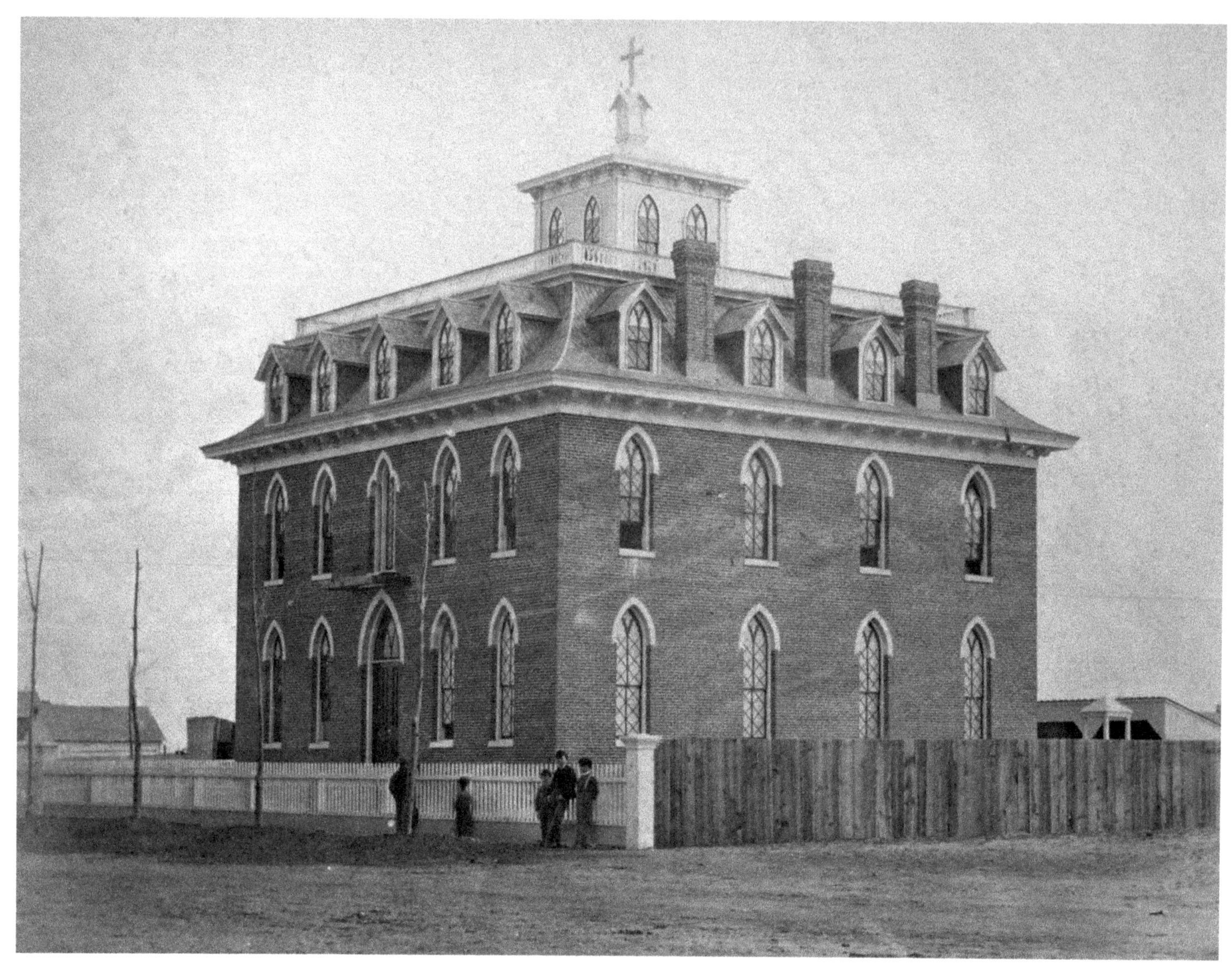

A view of Wolfe Hall, an Episcopalian women's seminary school at 17th and Champa streets. Built in 1867, this was one of Denver's earliest private schools. It was founded by Denver's first Episcopal Bishop, George Randall.

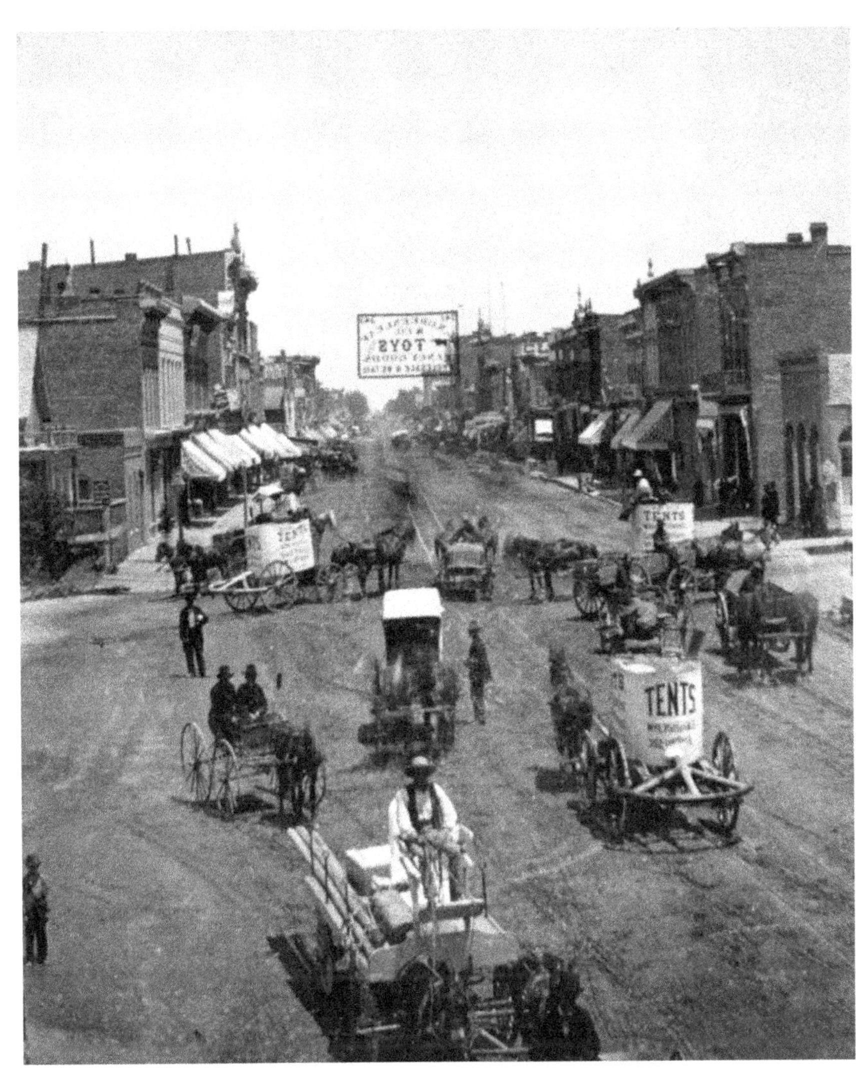

Larimer Street was the first business district in Denver. It served as the center of commercial activity for the "Queen City of the Plains." The businesses in this area supplied the goods for surrounding communities as well as for the many gold camps in the mountains to the west of the city.

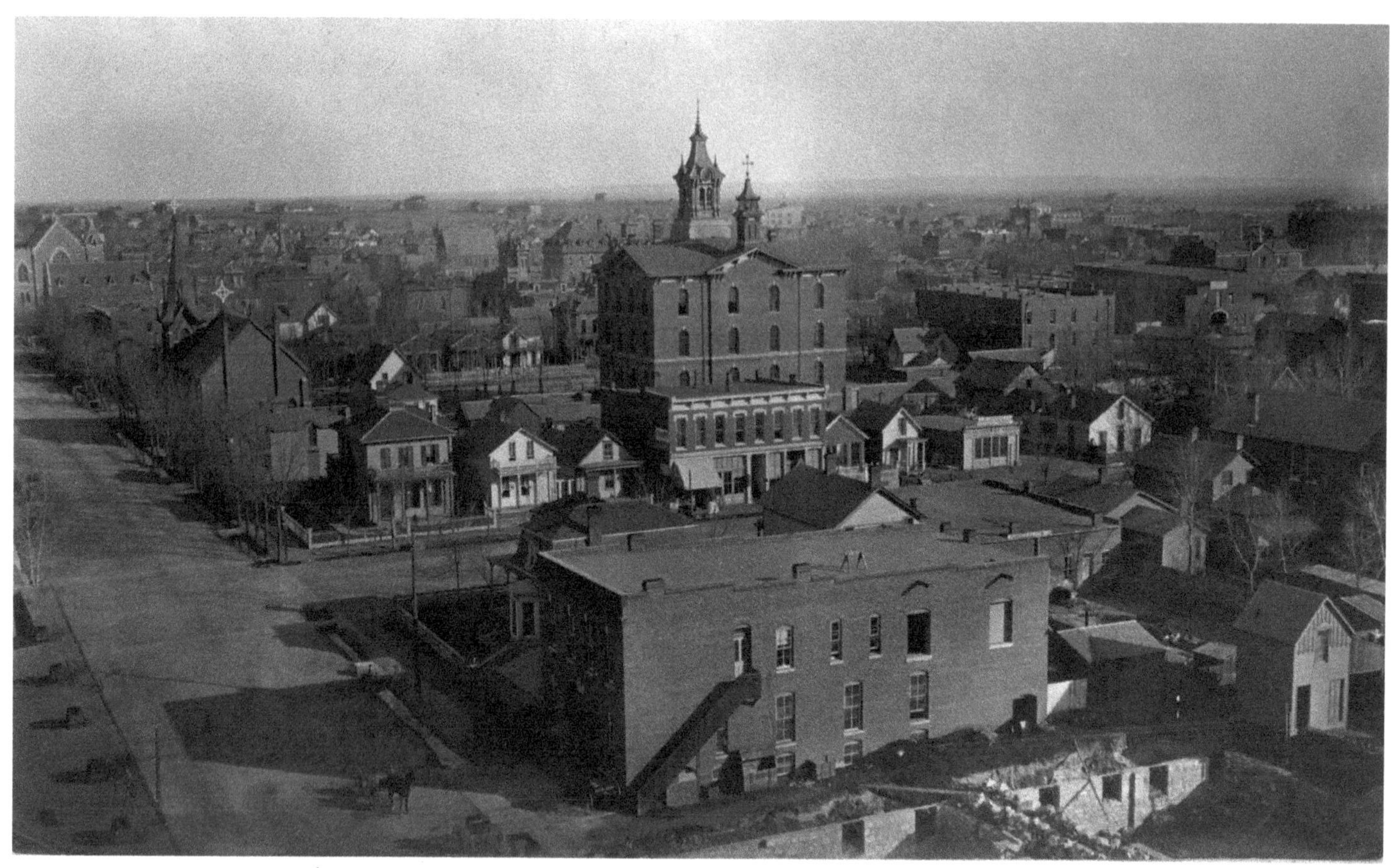

Central Denver was rapidly changing by the middle of the 1870s. Arapahoe School, built in 1872, was Denver's first public school; it is shown in the center of this image with a tile roof and cupola. By 1882 the area had been engulfed by the city's growing business district, and the school was closed.

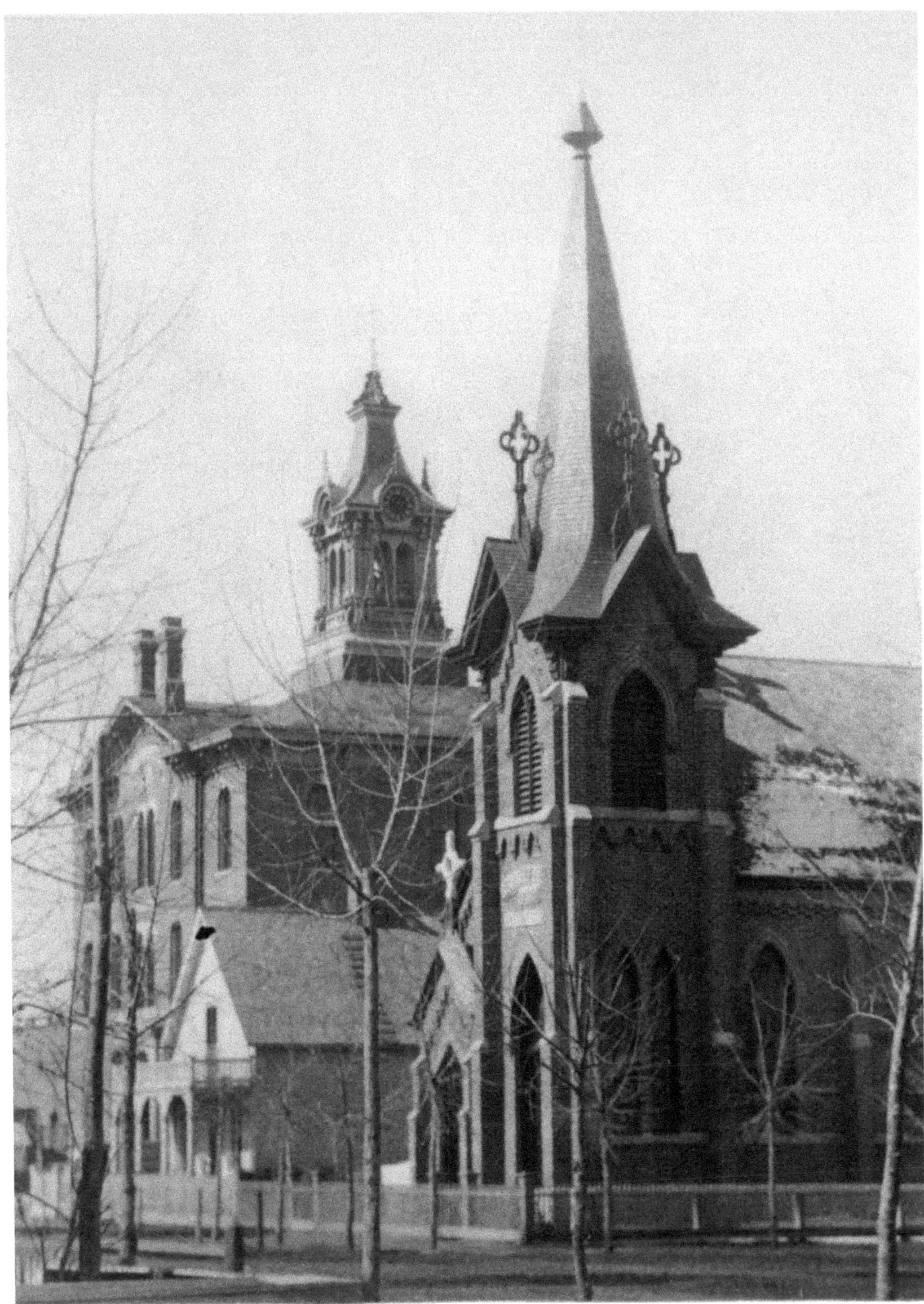

This is a view of the German Methodist Episcopal Church located on 18th and Arapahoe streets. The church was built by members of Denver's thriving German community.

The Inter-Ocean Hotel built by Barney Frank, an African American entrepreneur, opened on October 29, 1873, and was one of the city's leading hotels. It was located at the corner of 16th and Blake streets.

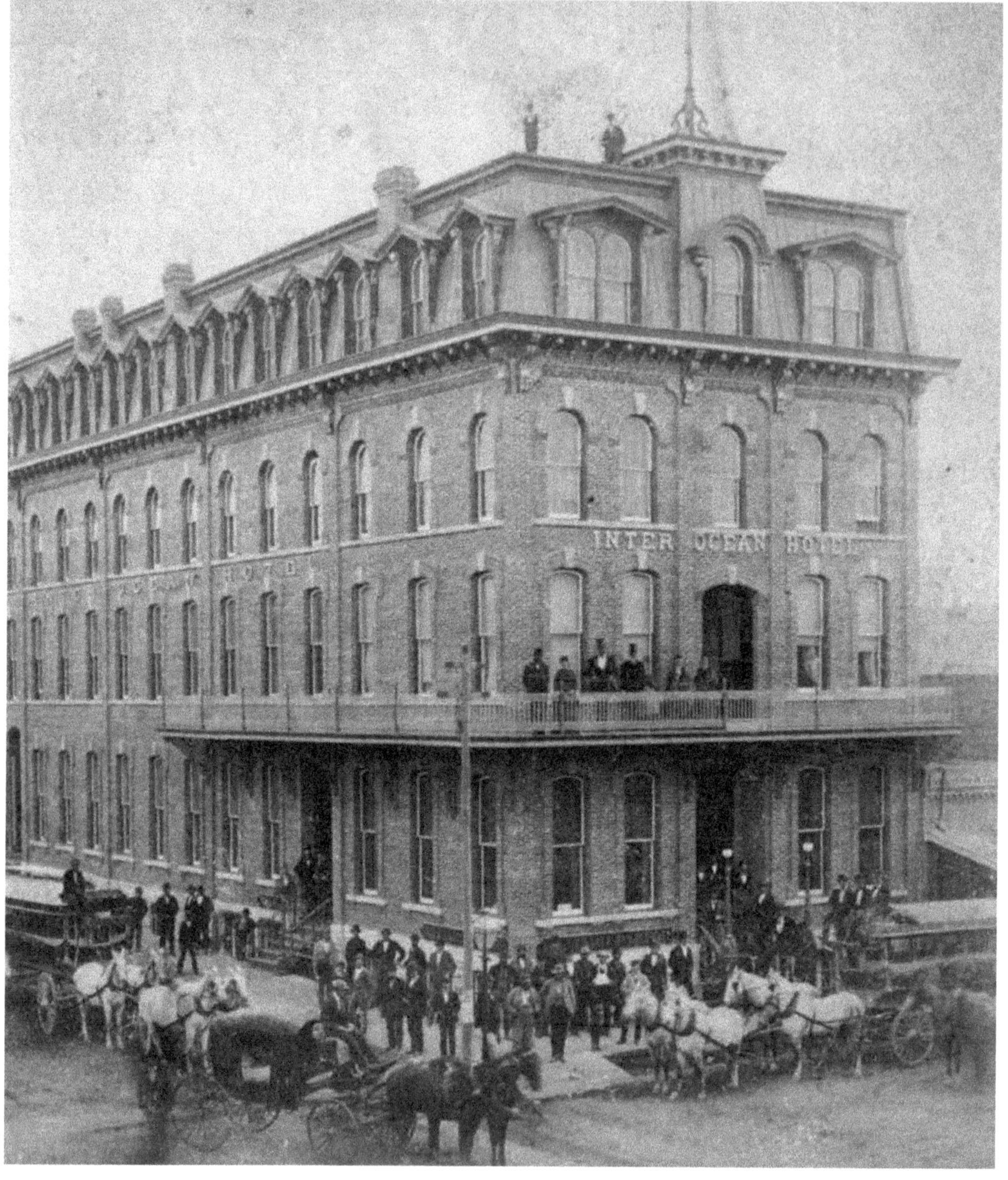

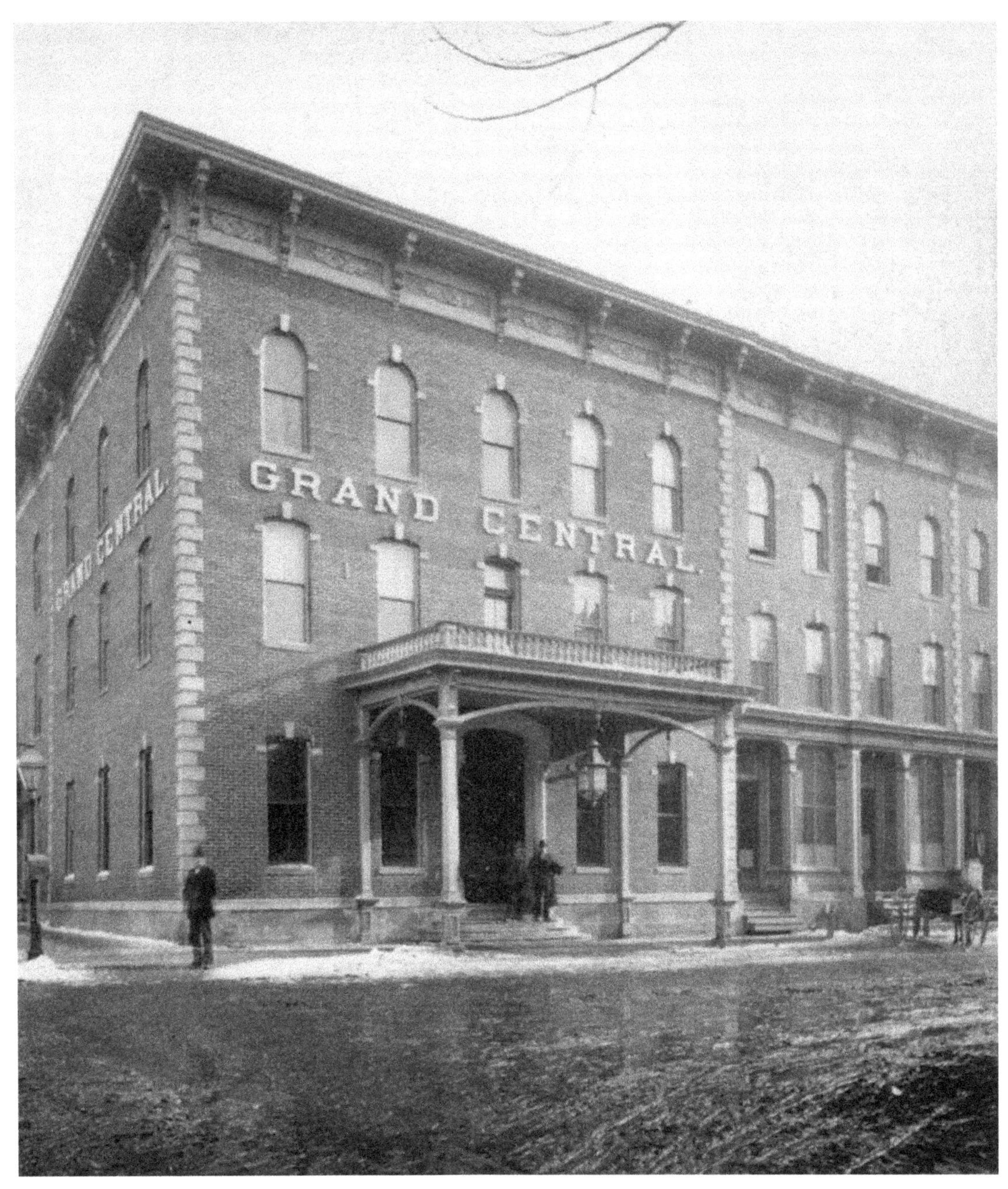

Located on the corner of 17th and Lawrence, the Grand Central Hotel opened in 1872. After being sold in 1882 and extensively remodeled, the enlarged facility reopened as the Markham Hotel.

The First Baptist Church of Denver was established in 1864 and is the oldest Baptist Congregation in Denver and Colorado. The original building, shown here, was built in 1873 at the corner of Larimer and 15th streets.

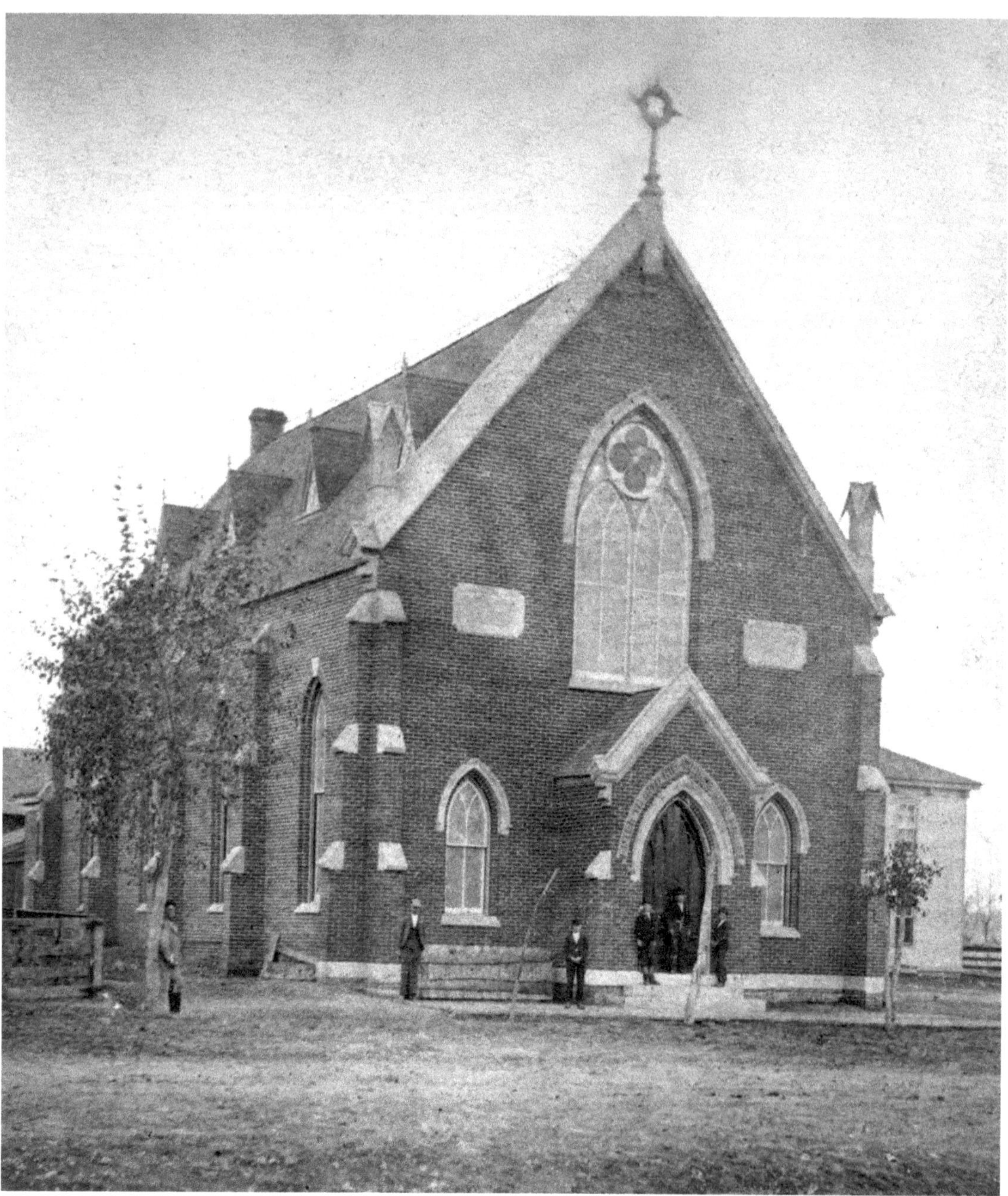

The first Daniels and Fisher store was located at 390 Larimer Street. It became Denver's premier department store and lasted well into the twentieth century.

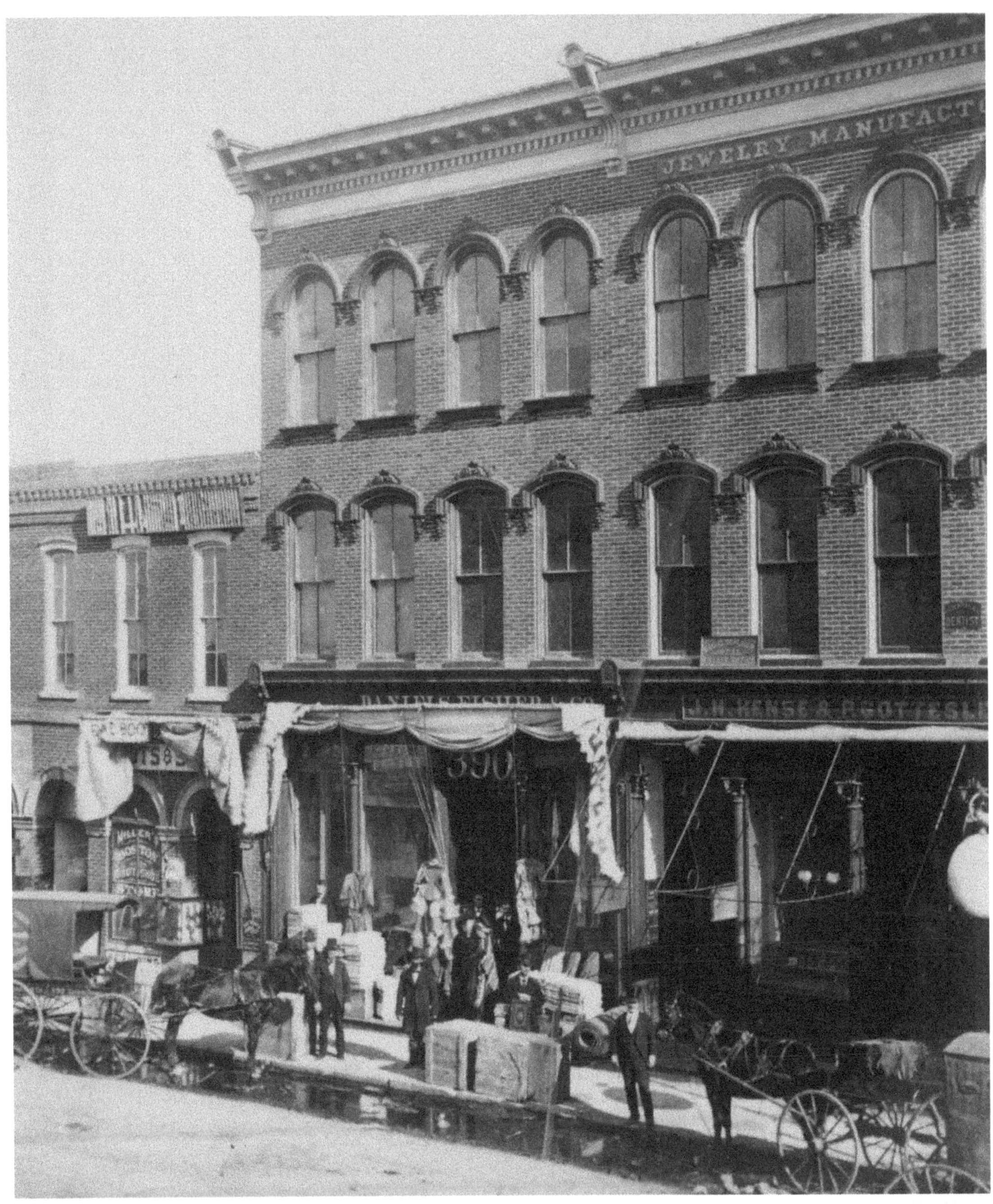

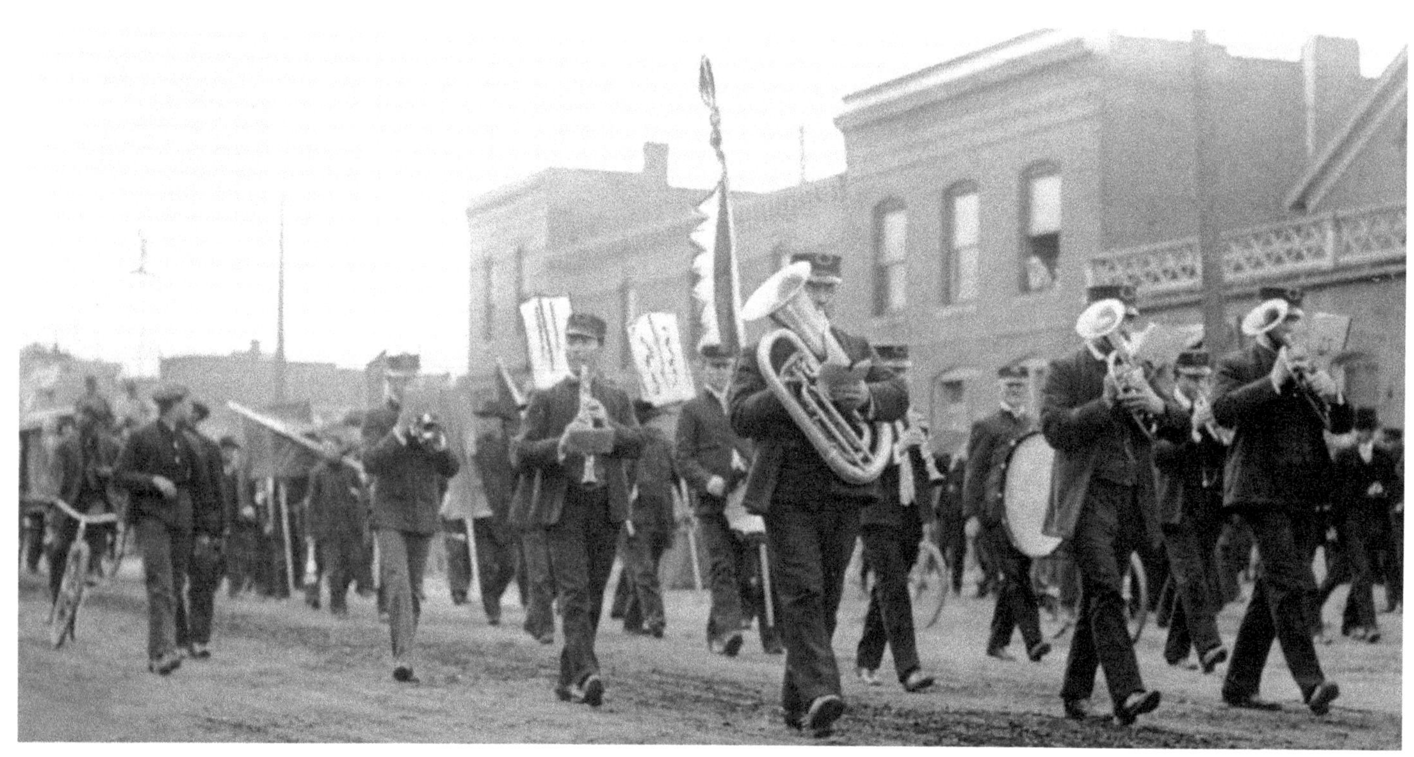

A Chinese band leads a funeral procession near Hop Alley, a neighborhood of Chinese laborers settled in 1870 by laid-off railroad workers. The area was located between Blake and Wazee streets near 20th Street. In 1880 an anti-Chinese riot started in Hop Alley and much of the area was destroyed.

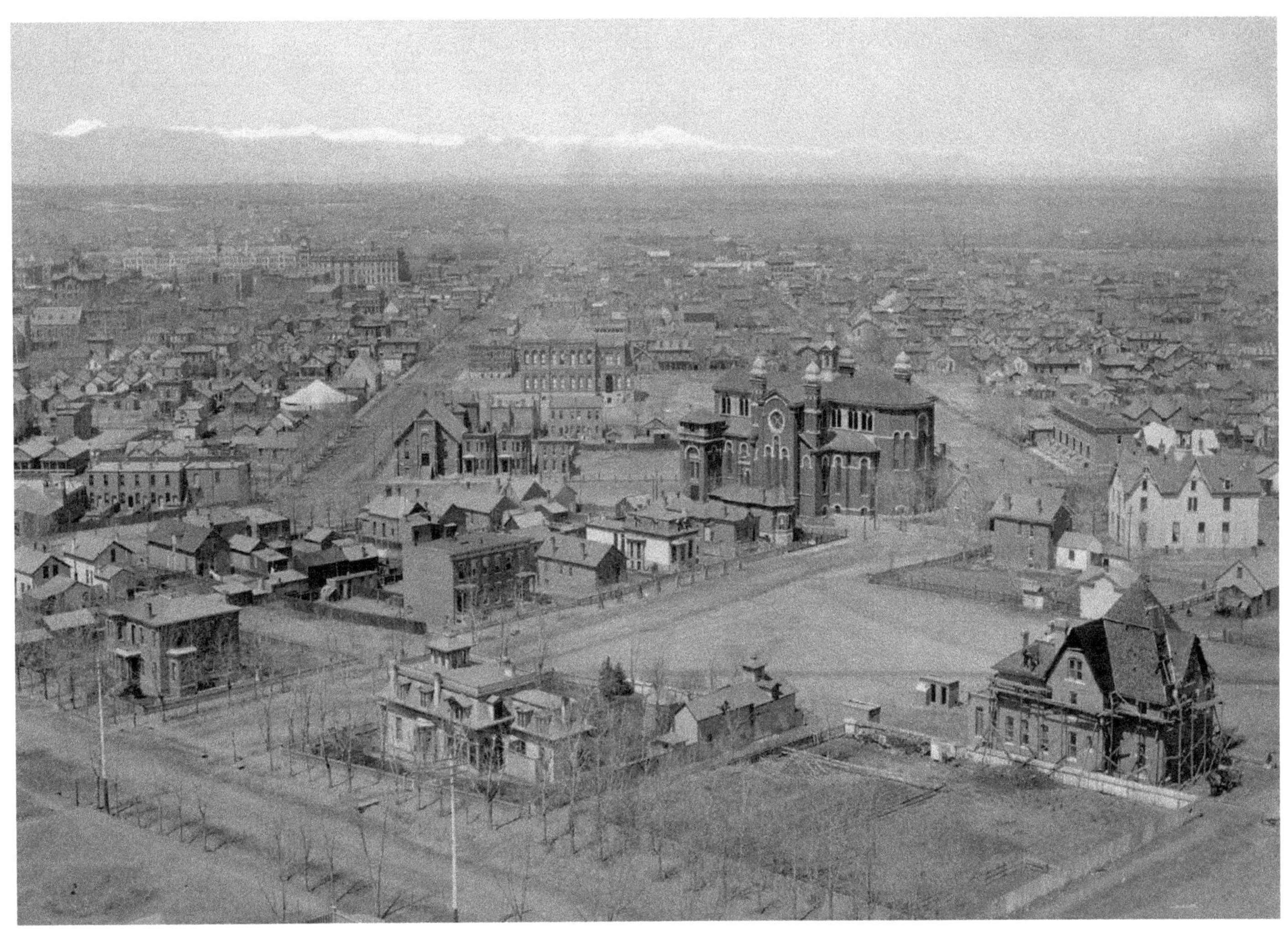

This aerial view of Denver, taken in the early 1880s, is dominated by the Episcopal Cathedral of Saint John the Evangelist. The church was located on the corner of 20th and Welton streets.

This view taken at the corner of 16th and Larimer streets shows two well-dressed women walking through the intersection behind a horse-drawn streetcar. The five-story Italianate Tabor Block, designed by Frank E. and Willoughby J. Edbrooke, is on the corner.

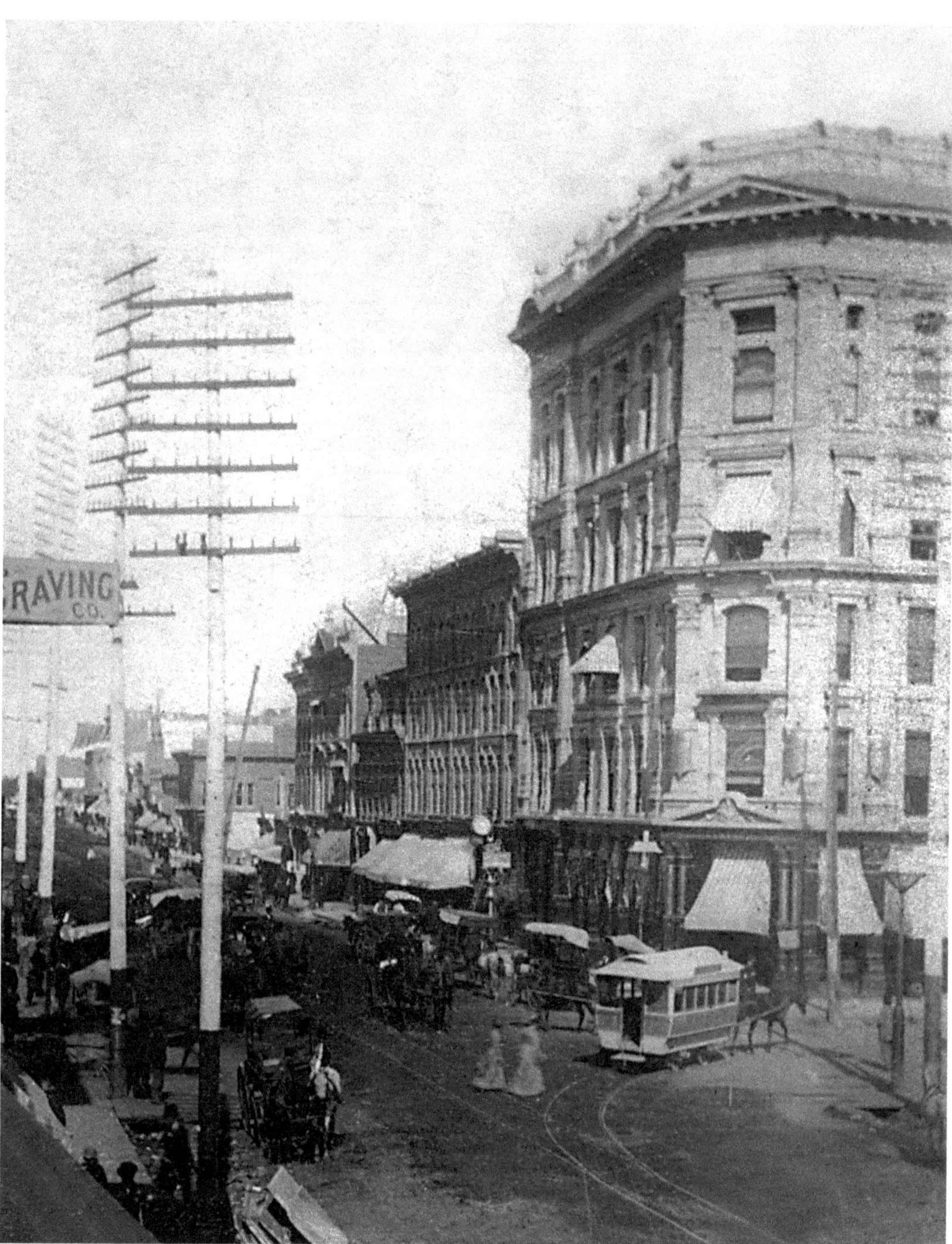

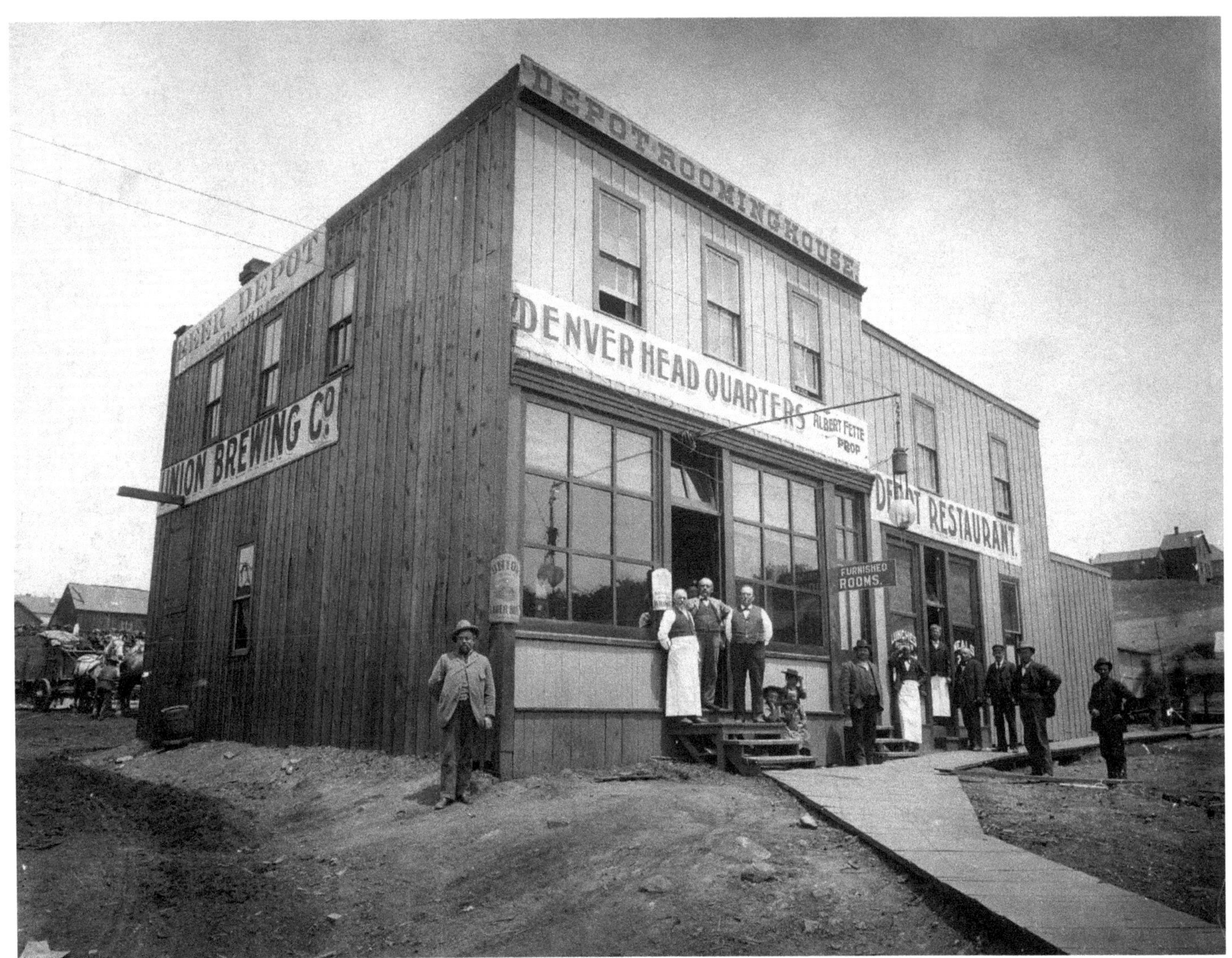

Bartenders stand on the steps of the Beer Depot of the Union Brewing Company located at 2433 Sixteenth Street in Denver, Colorado. Waiters pose next door at the Depot Restaurant. In 1900, the Union Brewery merged with the Tivoli Brewing Company to form the Tivoli Union Brewing Company, which remained in business until 1969.

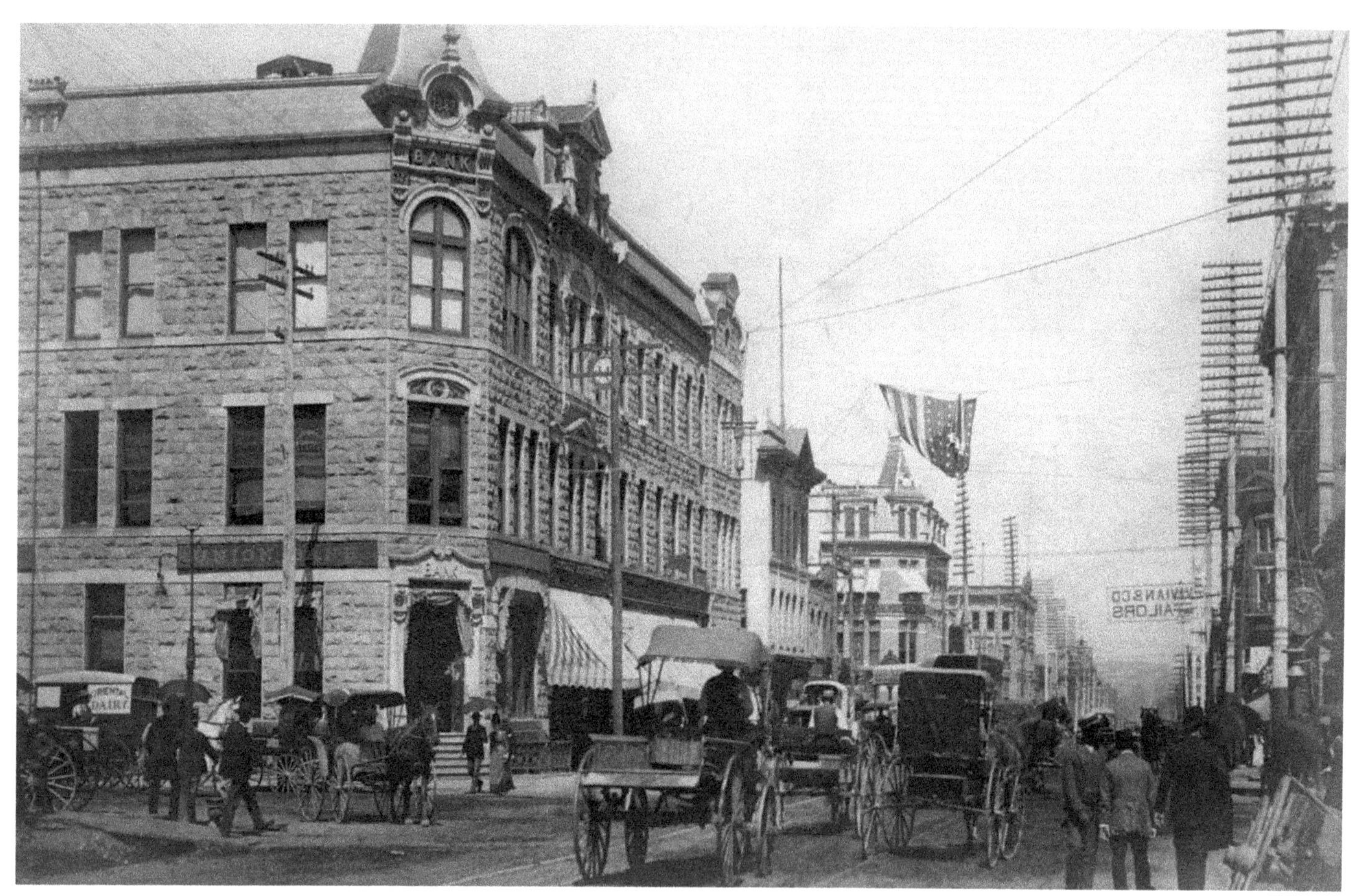

Horse-drawn carriages, wagons, and delivery vans crowd the intersection of 16th Street and Arapahoe Street. The Union Bank, a three-story stone building, is on the corner. Well-dressed men and women sport umbrellas to shade themselves from the sun.

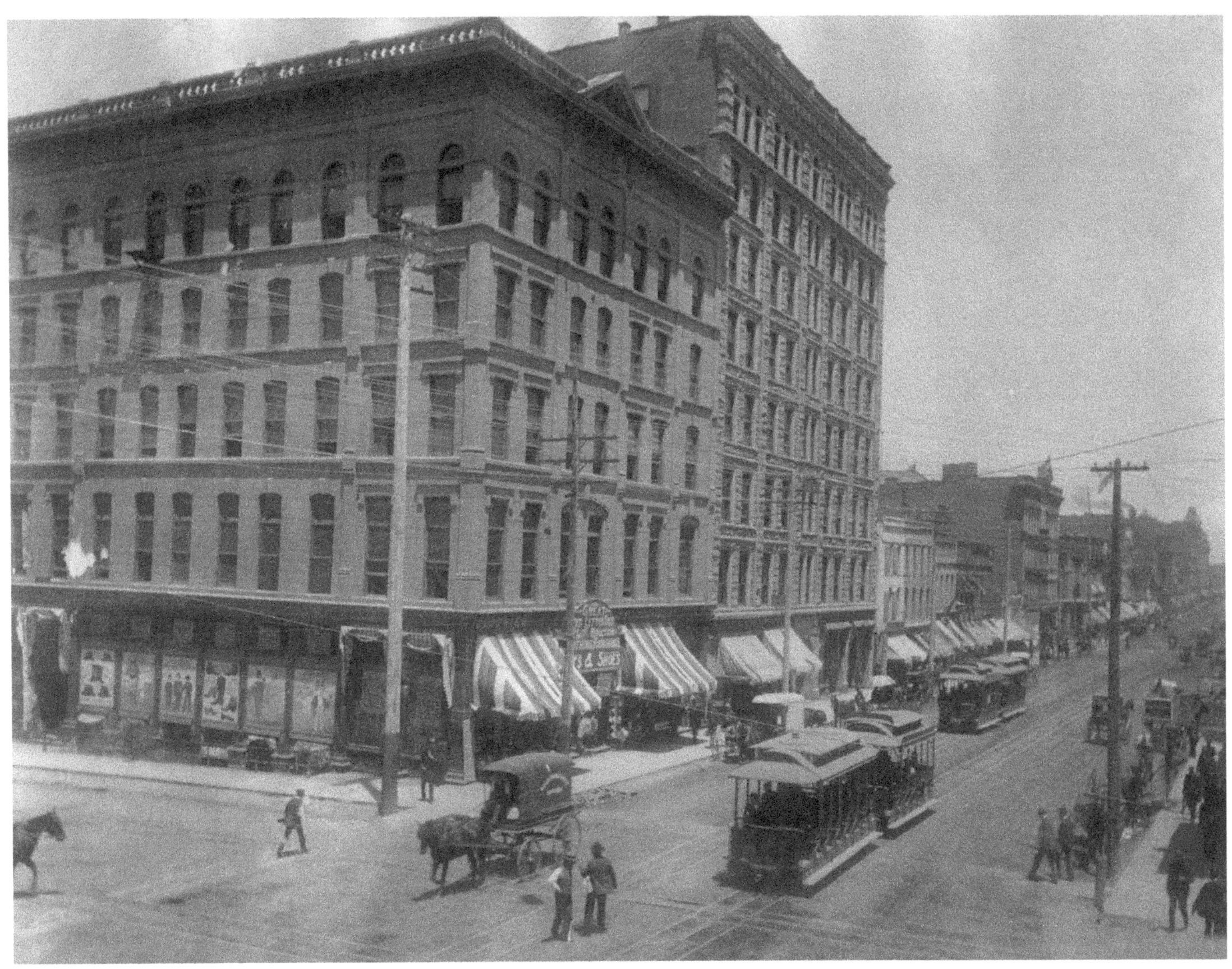

A view of the Italianate McClintock Block located on the corner of 16th and Larimer streets. The Dewey Hotel, an eight-story stone building, is next door. Denver Tramway trolley cars travel down Larimer Street.

The Tabor Opera House, designed by Frank E. and Willoughby J. Edbrooke, was built by silver magnate Horace A. W. Tabor at a cost of more than $850,000. Opening in 1881, it was one of the most ornate and magnificent structures west of the Mississippi. Tabor would meet Elizabeth Bonduel McCourt in 1880. Although he was married to Augusta Tabor, he and "Baby Doe" would begin a liaison that would eventually lead to his divorce. After their marriage, Tabor lost his considerable fortune in the silver crash of 1893. He died in 1899 leaving his wife and children impoverished. Baby Doe would die in 1935 frozen to the floor of a cabin at a former Tabor mine, the Matchless.

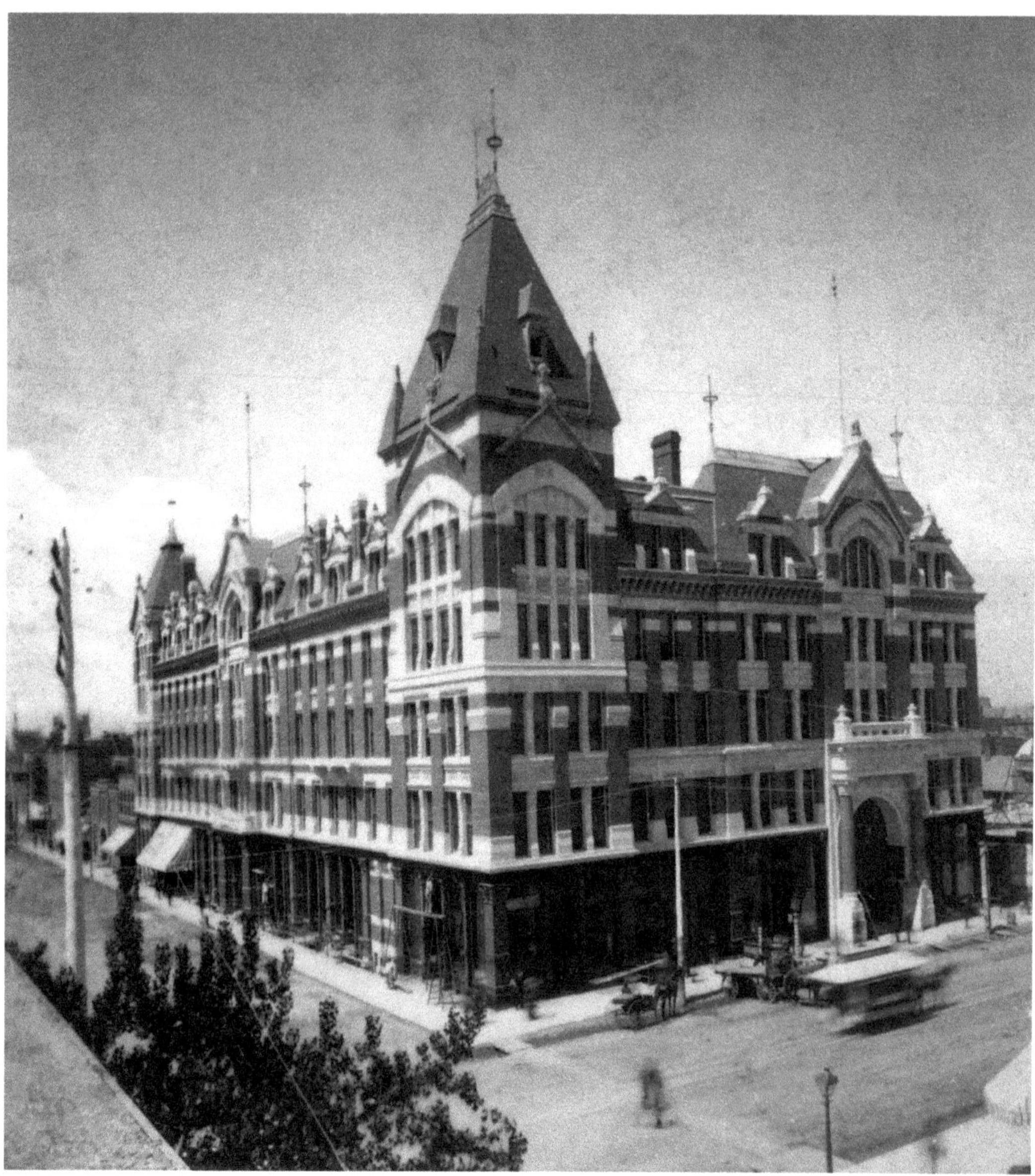

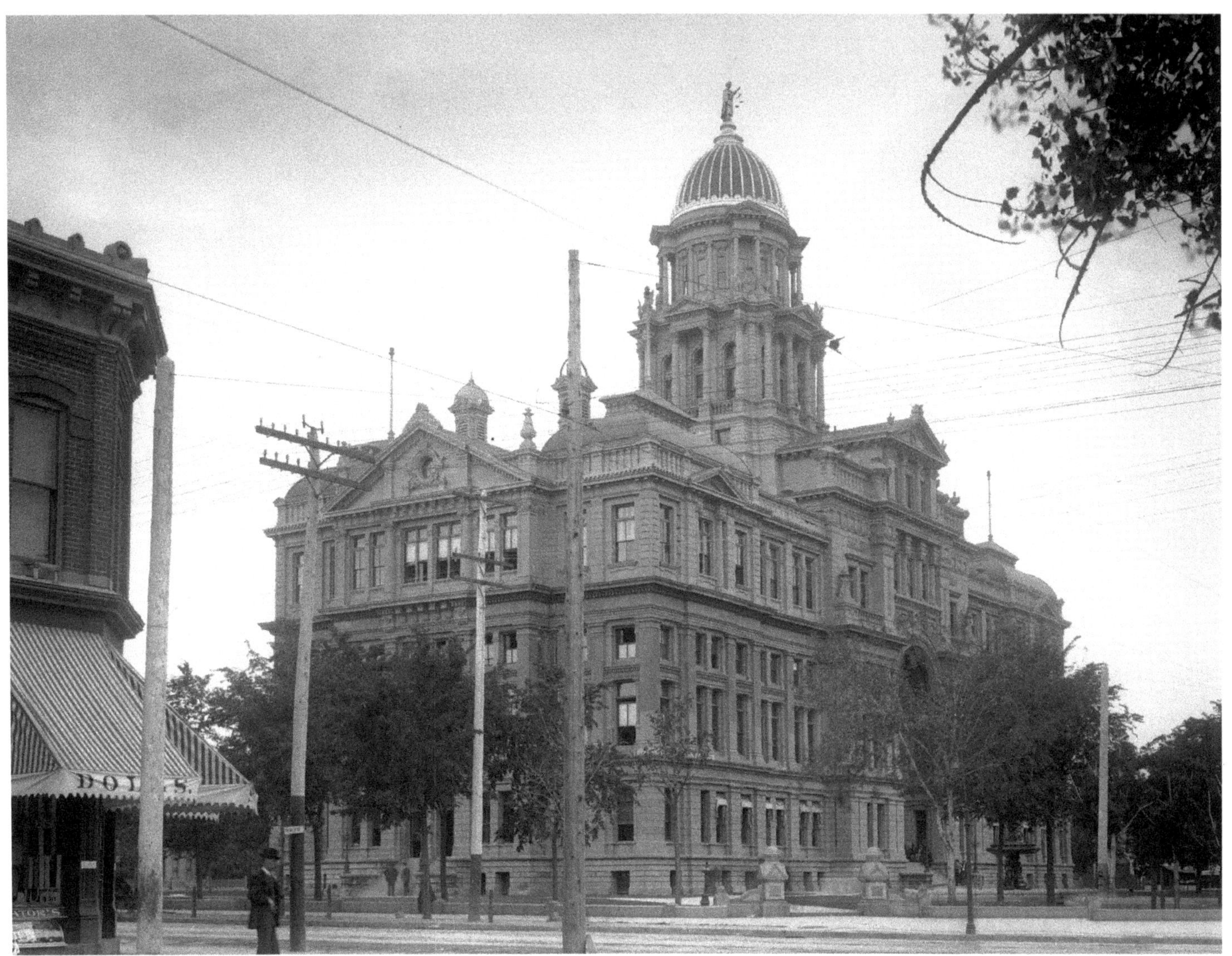

The Arapahoe County courthouse, built in 1883, was located at 16th and Tremont streets. Originally, Denver was part of Arapahoe County. When the City and County of Denver were incorporated in 1902, it became the Denver County Courthouse. It remained in use until the early 1930s when it was demolished.

This 1884 view of a thriving Larimer Street reflects the city's growth driven by mining and railroads. During the 1880s Denver's population of 106,000 people made it the second largest city in the West.

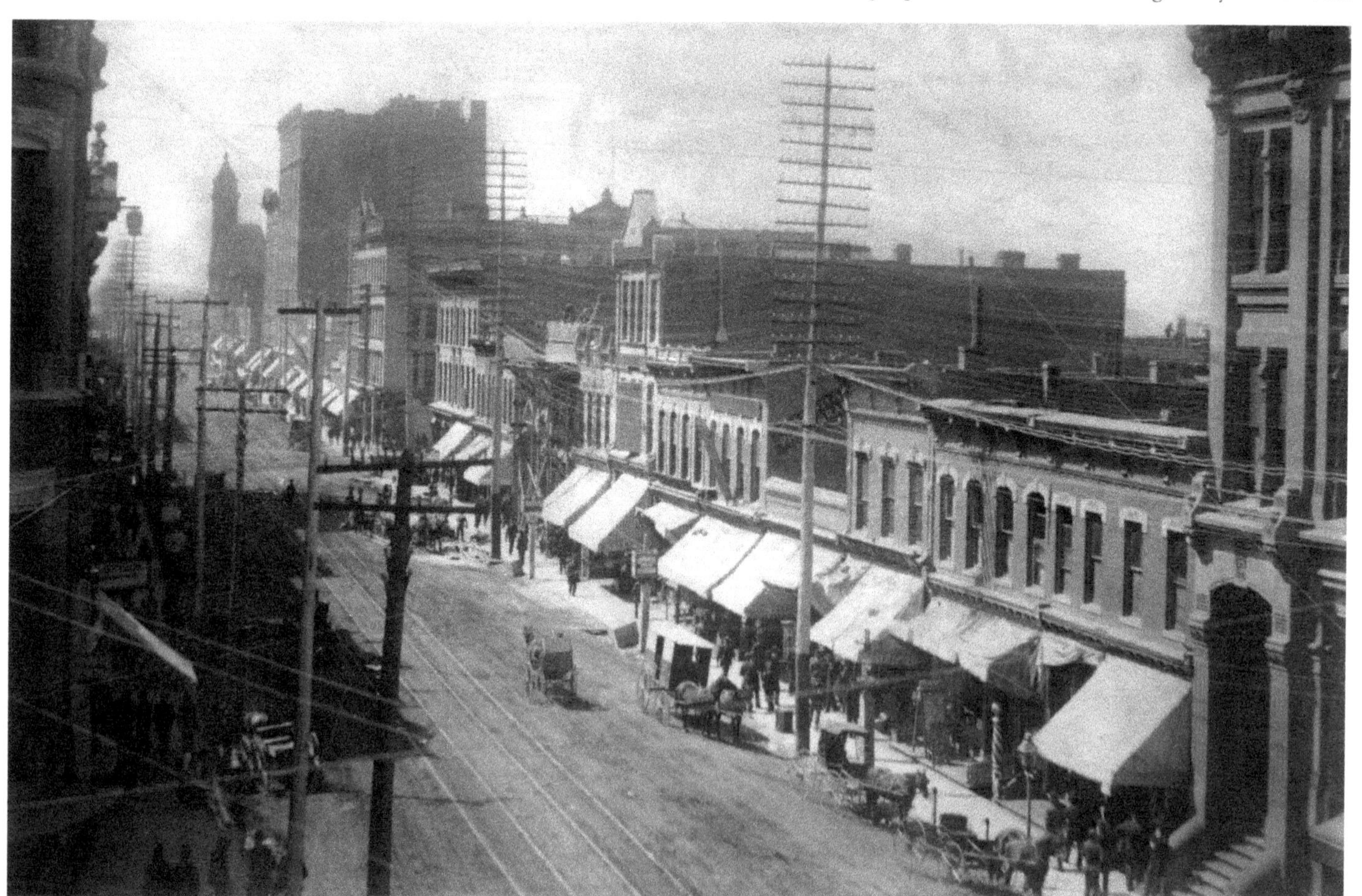

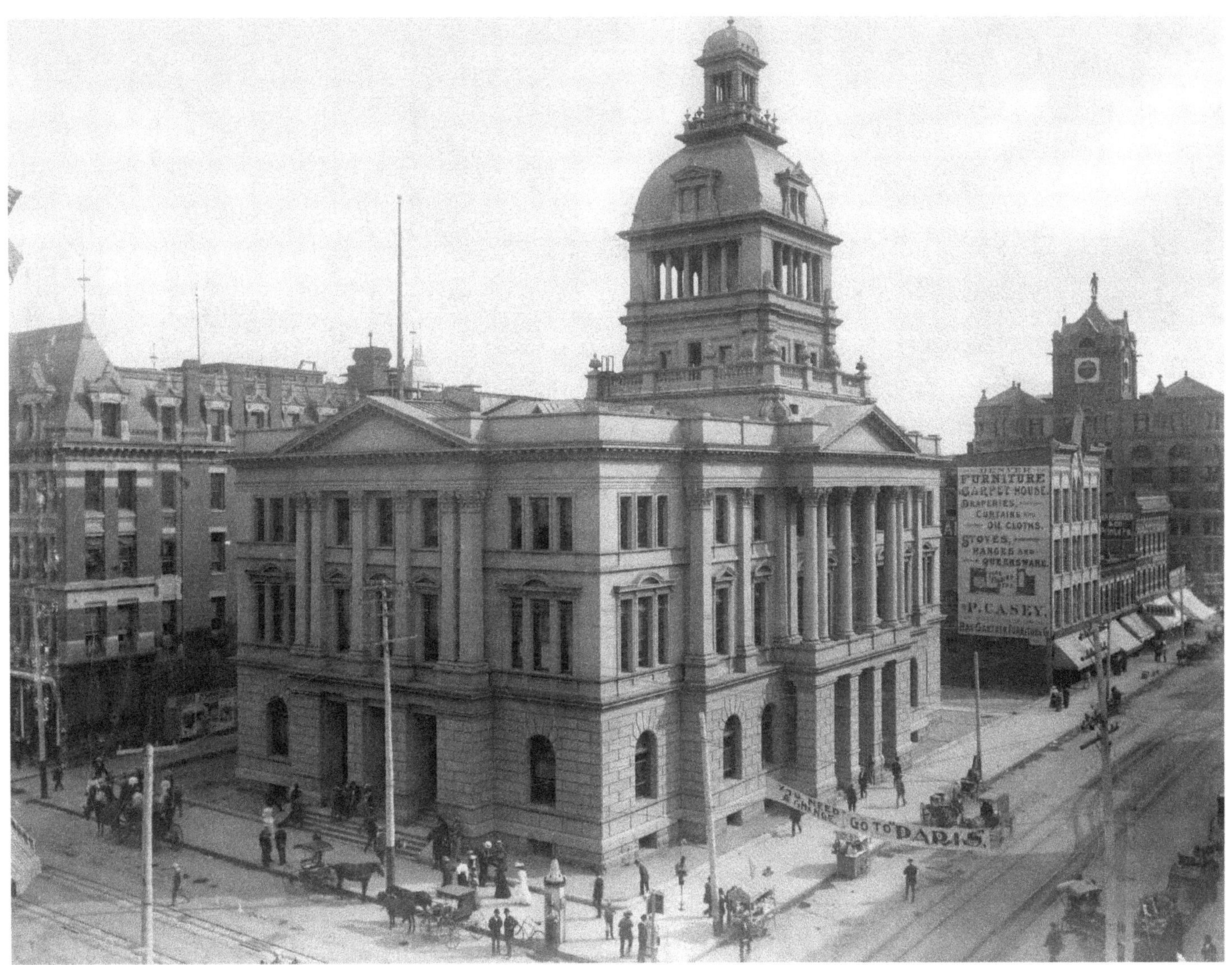

This view of the old United States Post Office located at 16th and Arapahoe streets was inadequate for postal services when it opened in the 1880s. A new post office was built in 1916, and this building served as the U.S. Customs House until it was demolished in 1965.

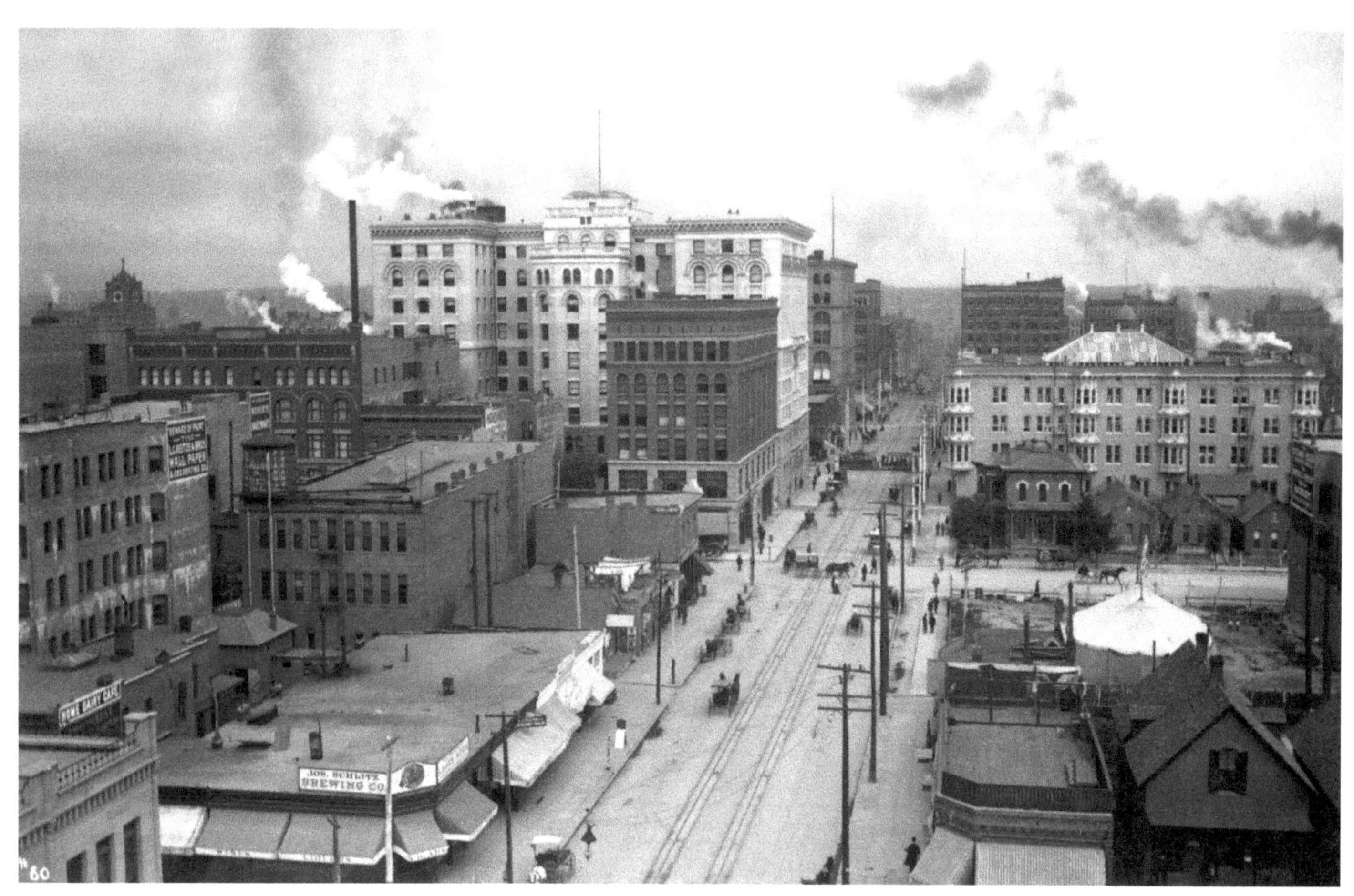

This panoramic view of 17th Street shows how the city prospered during the boom of the 1880s. The large Renaissance Revival building in the distance is the Equitable Building, Denver's first high rise when it was completed in 1892, just before the depression of 1893.

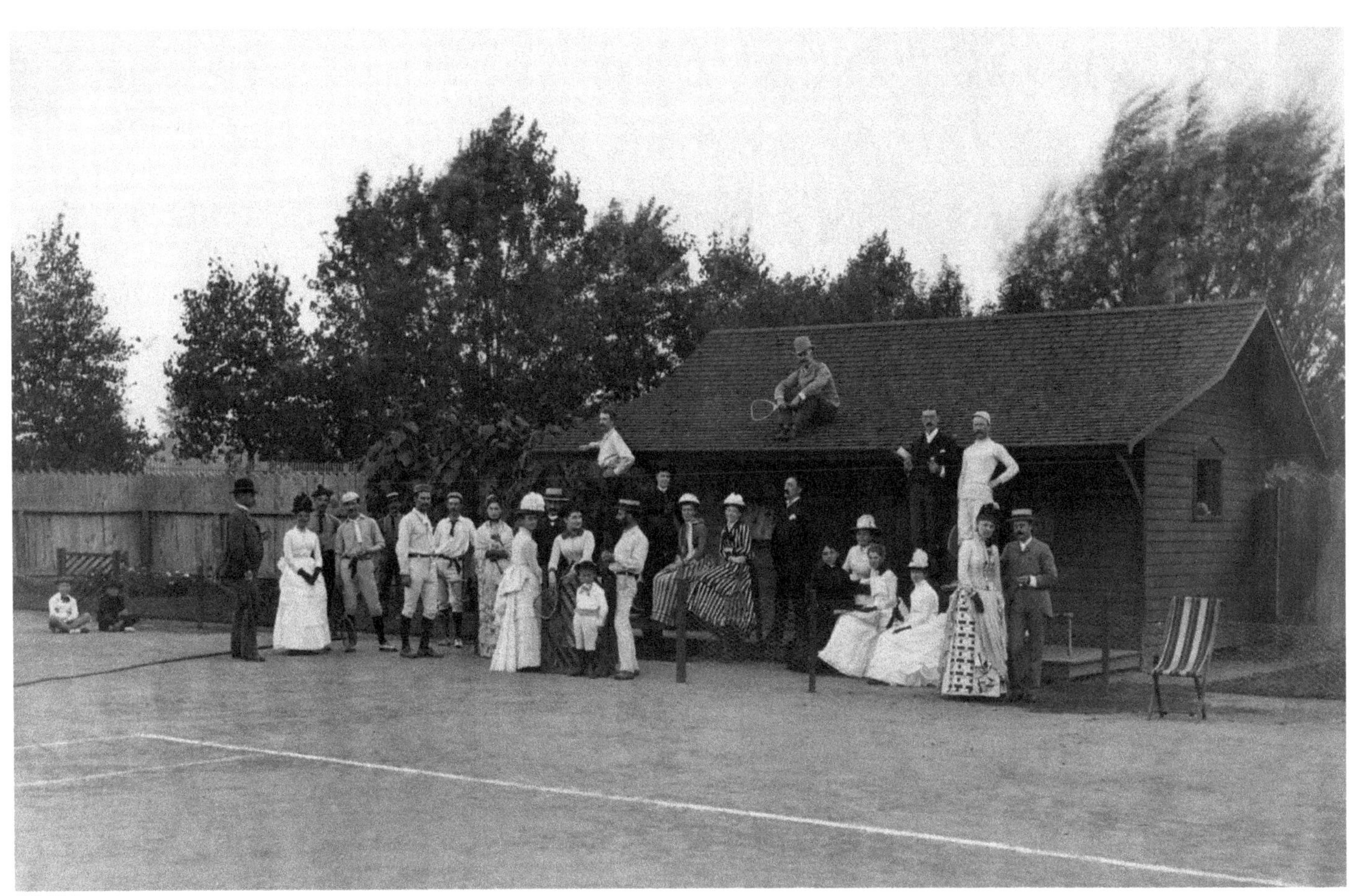

Members of a tennis club pose on a tennis court in front of their clubhouse. Florence Ward (Holland) wears a dress with a light bodice and striped skirt; she holds a tennis racket. Edward Wolcott, later U.S. senator from Colorado, stands at the extreme right.

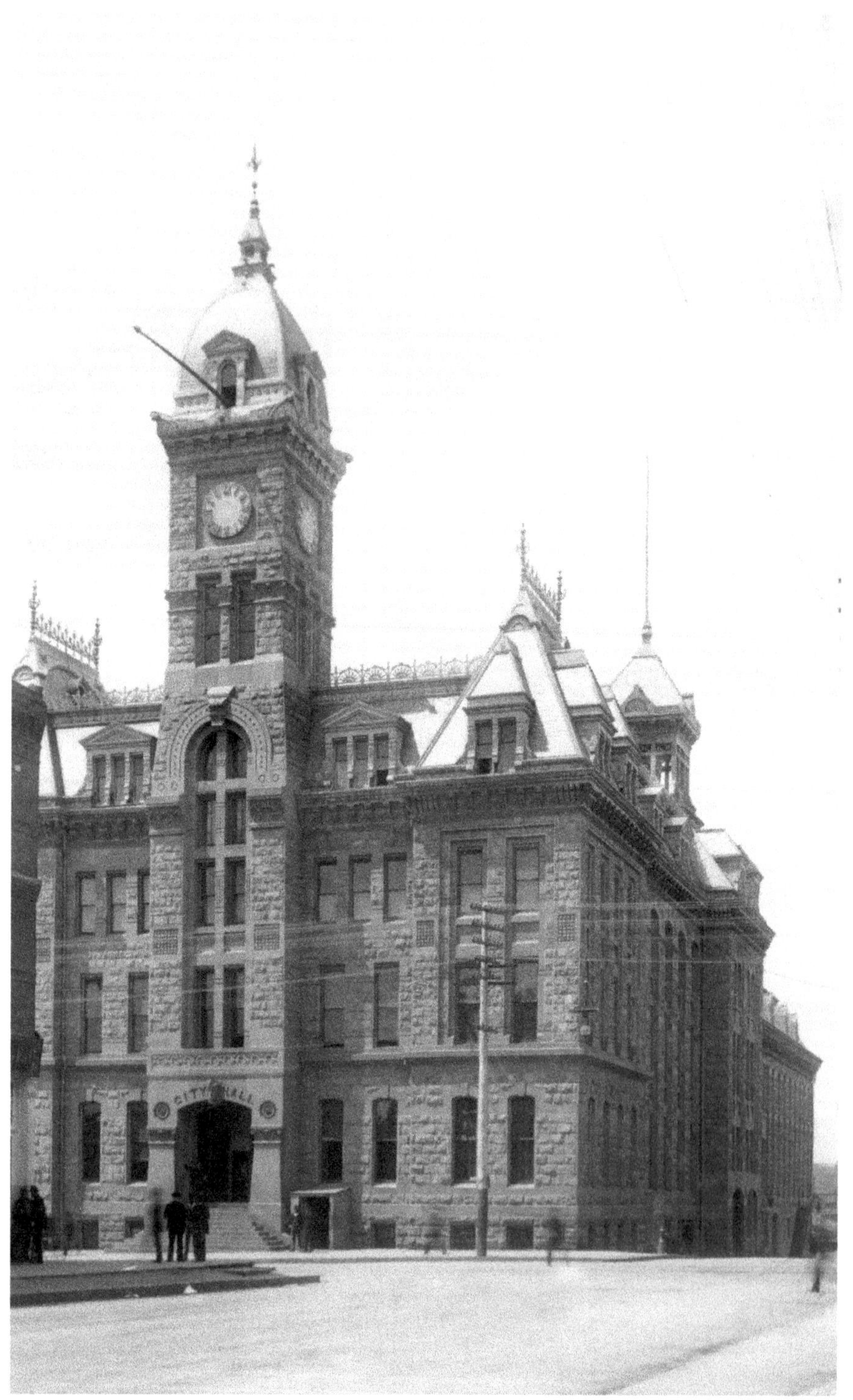

A view of the old City Hall located at 14th Street and Larimer. The stone and granite building was built in 1886 and was later used by the fire department and the police department before being razed in 1945.

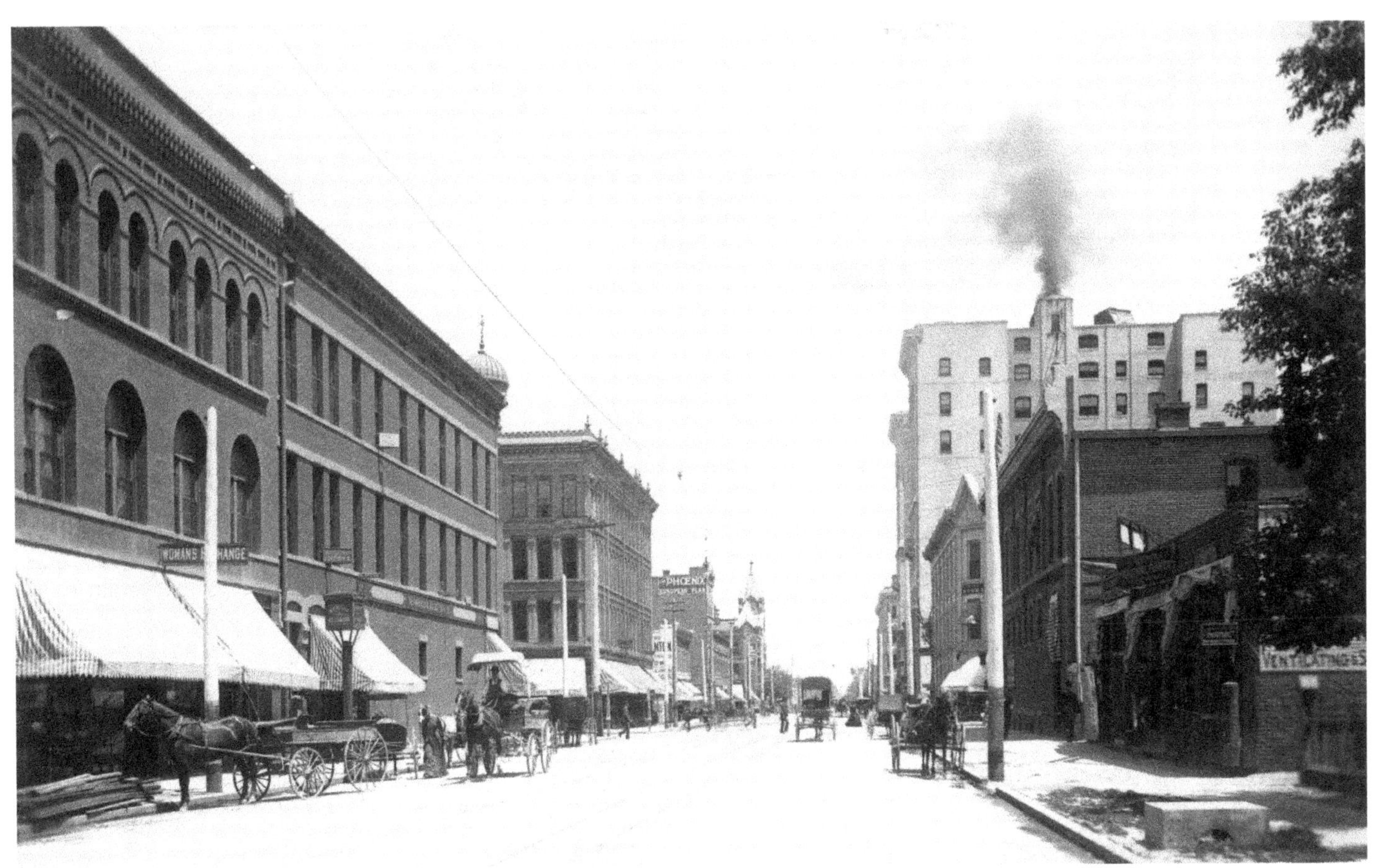

This view of Stout Street shows how the commercial heart of Denver was beginning to grow in the 1880s and 1890s. The building on the left houses the Women's Exchange, a benevolent organization for needy women. The First Baptist Church is visible in the distance.

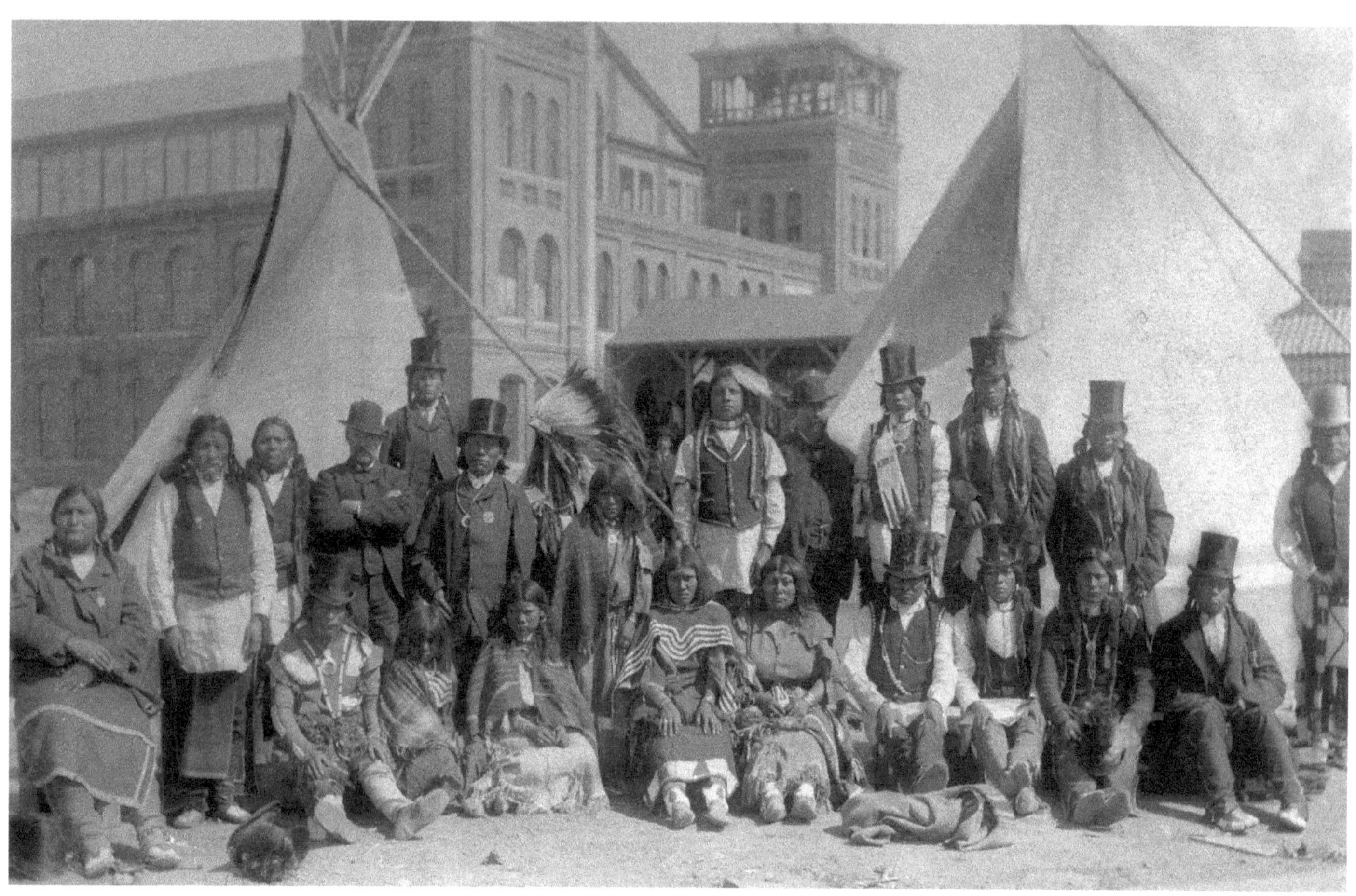

Ute Indians camp at the 1884 National Mining and Industrial Exposition. The building in view in the background, located in South Denver just East of Broadway, was built specifically to house expositions. The 1884 exposition, however, turned out to be a financial failure and it was discontinued. The building was sold and later razed.

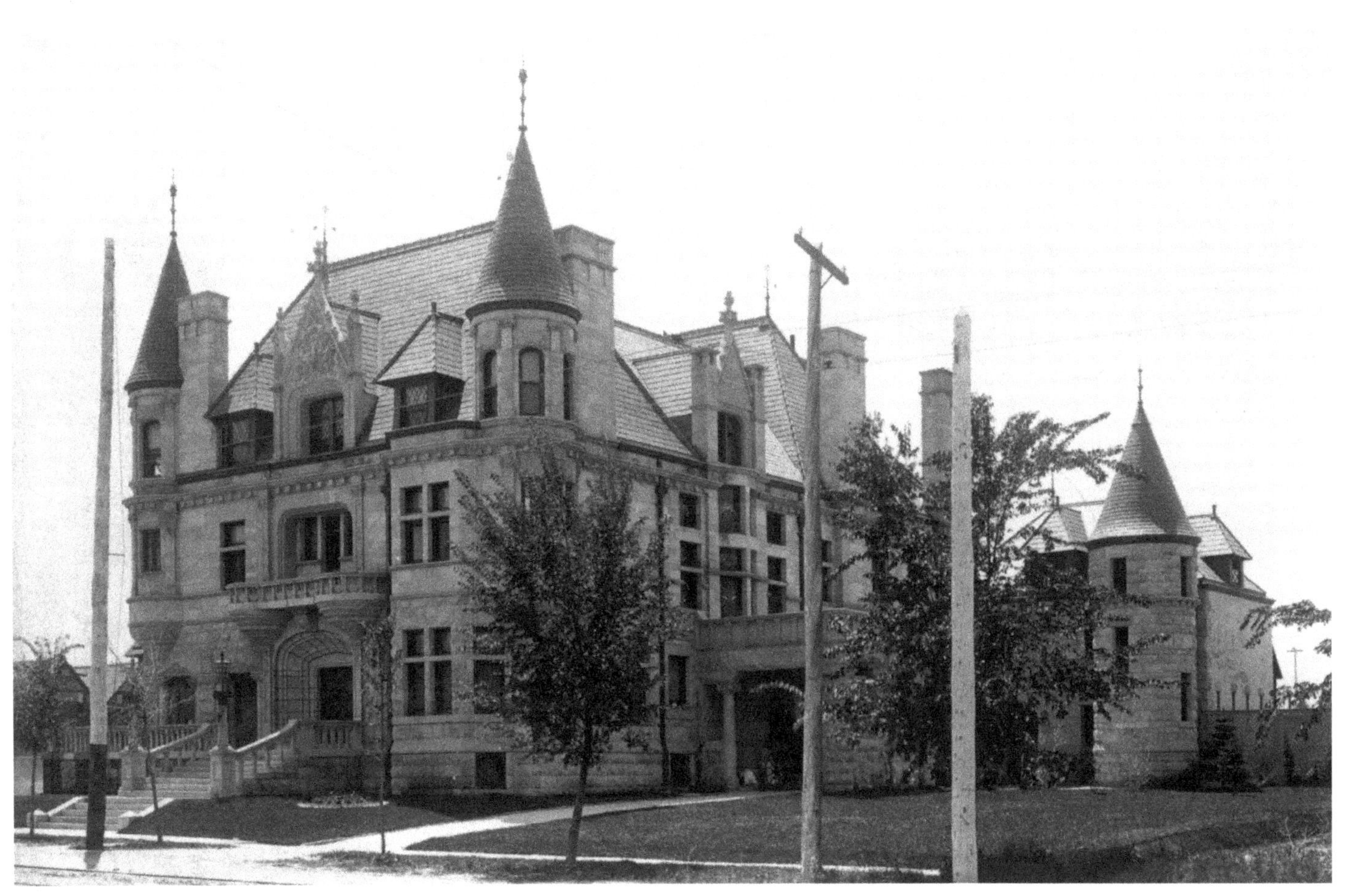

This French Chateau–style house was designed by architect Theodore Davis Boal, for Captain Decatur Bethel. It was located at the corner of Colfax Avenue and Marion Street.

Denver City Cable Railway Company cable car number 31 is stopped near the corner of 15th Street and Lawrence in the Central Business District. The seven street-railway cables extended over nearly 30 miles and were powered by a single power plant.

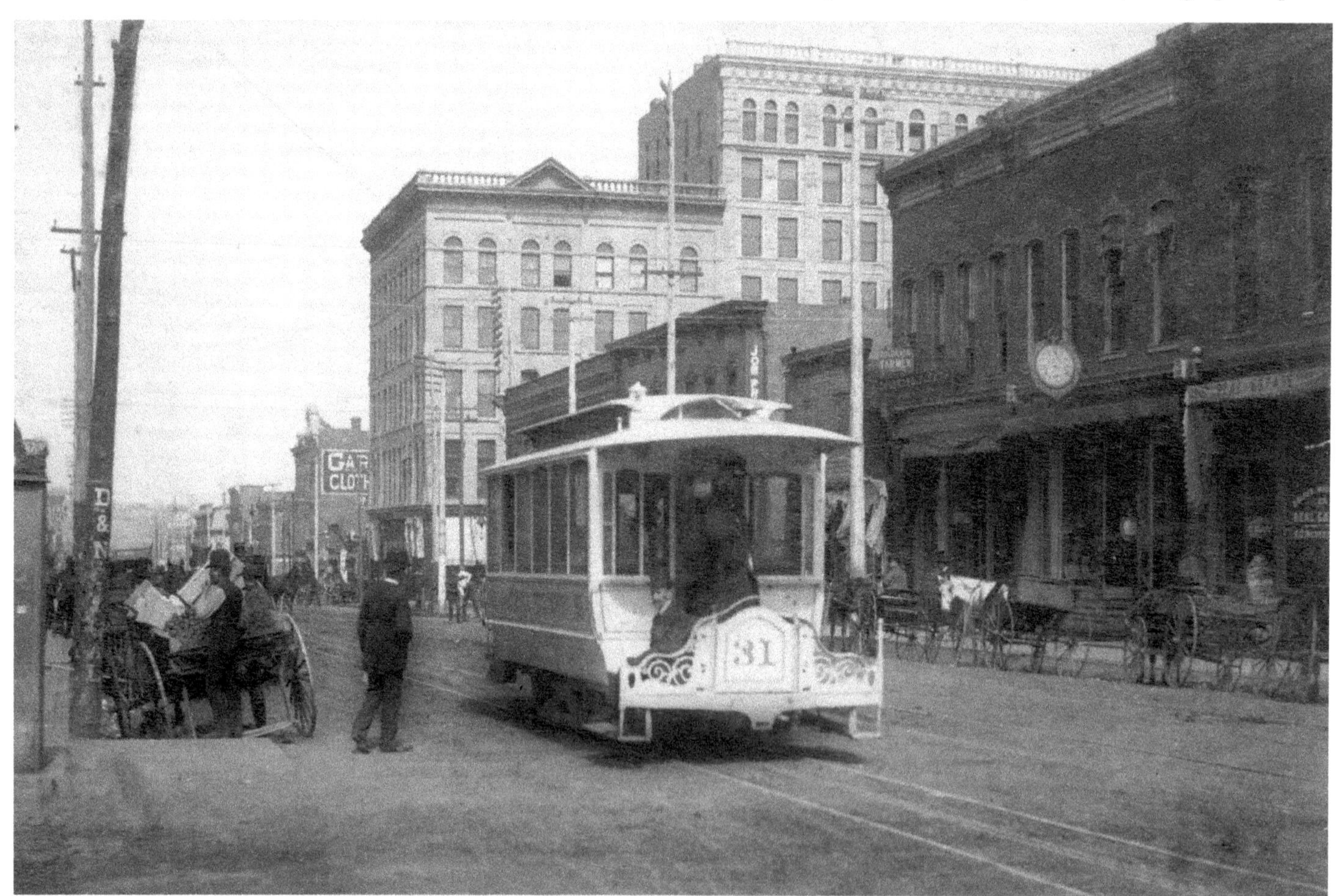

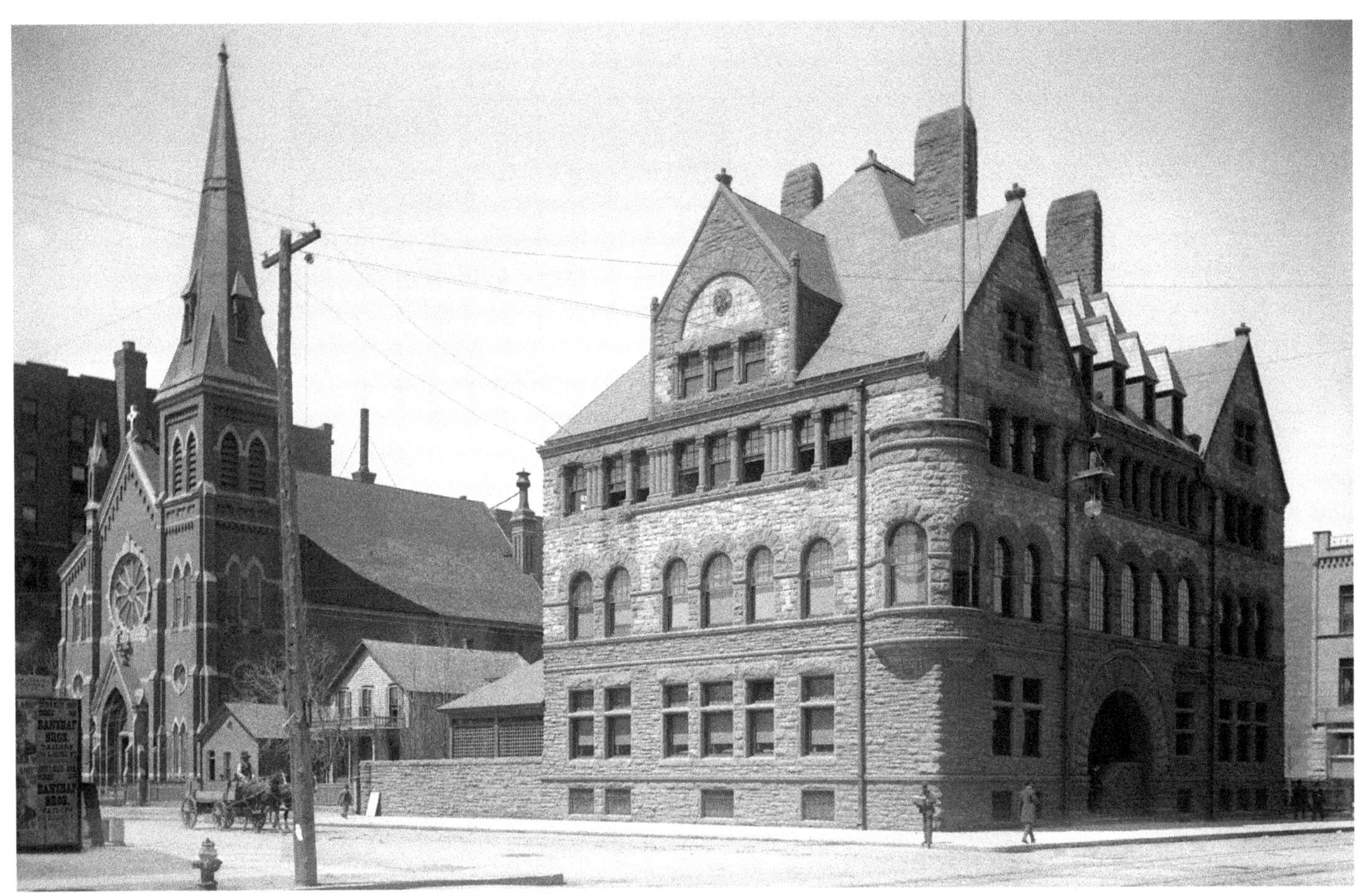

The Denver Club, a private men's club, was organized in 1880 by some of the city's most illustrious civic leaders, including David Moffat, Walter Cheesman, and Henry Wolcott. The Victorian Romanesque–style building, designed by Frederick Junius Sterner, opened in 1888 and continued in use until 1953. The First Congregational Church is next door.

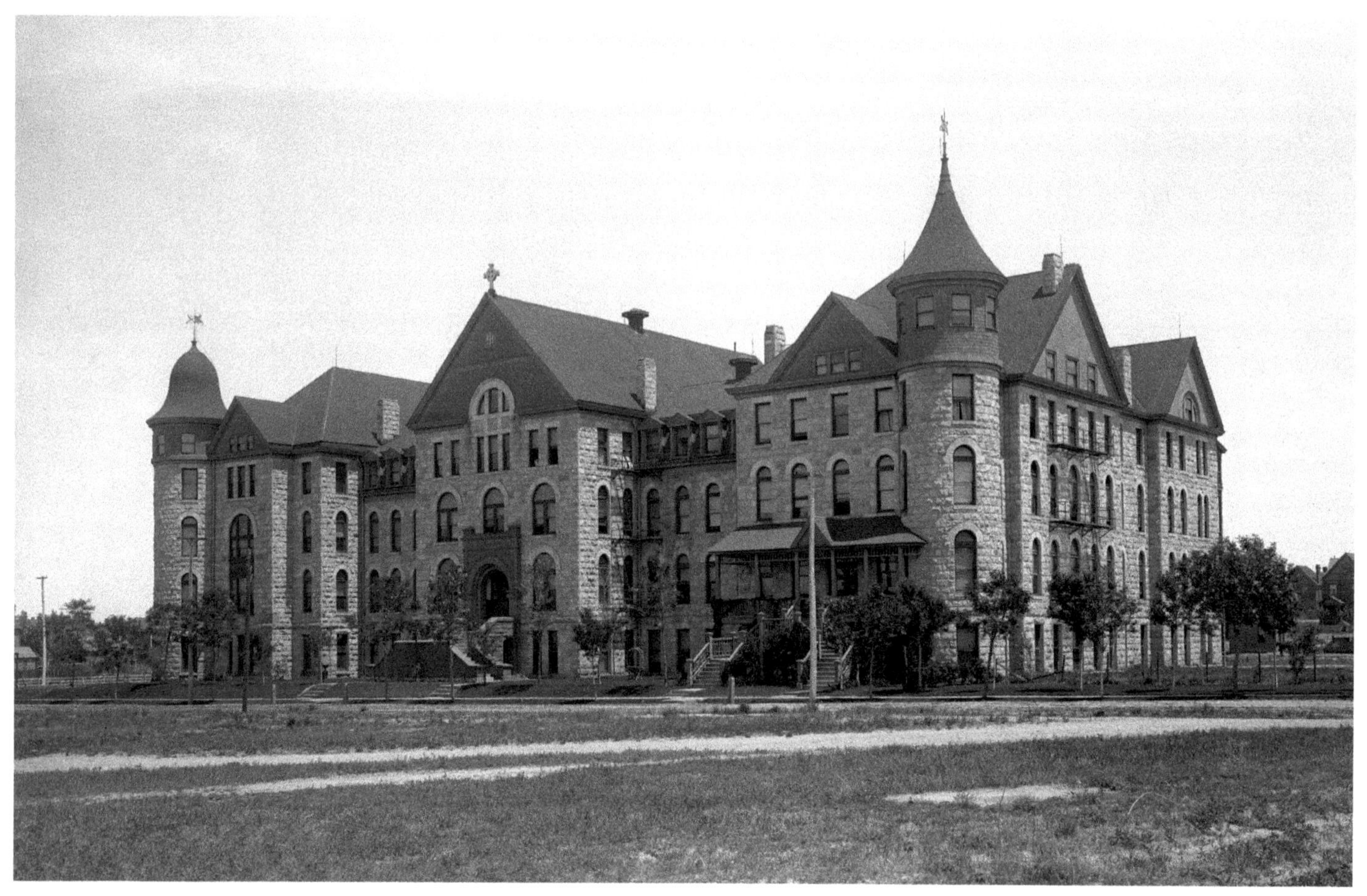

Wolfe Hall, an Episcopalian seminary for young ladies, was located between 13th and 14th avenues on Clarkson Street. The school moved to this building, designed by John W. Roberts, in 1889. The chateau-style building was razed in 1920.

The railroad gothic-style Union Depot opened in 1881.

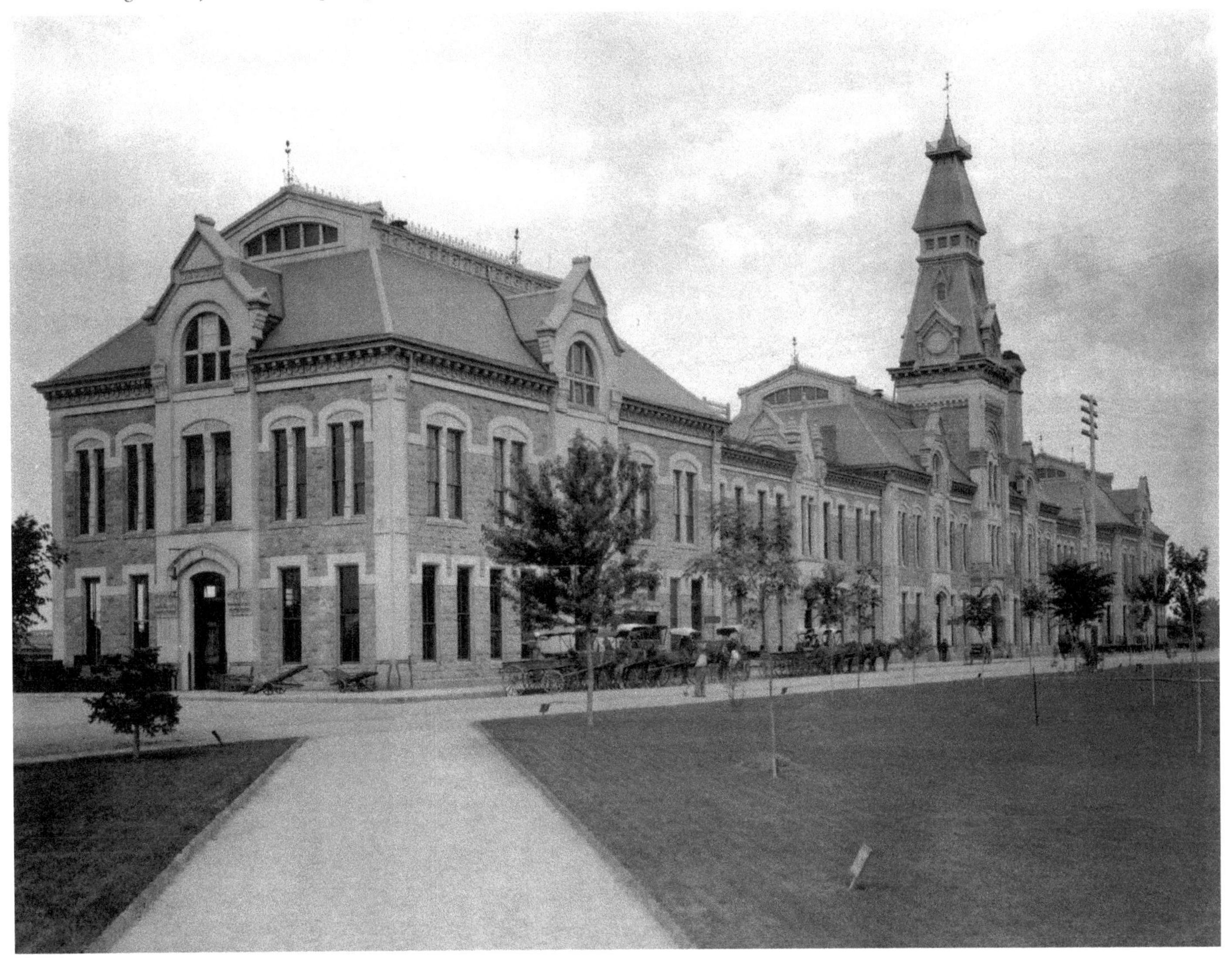

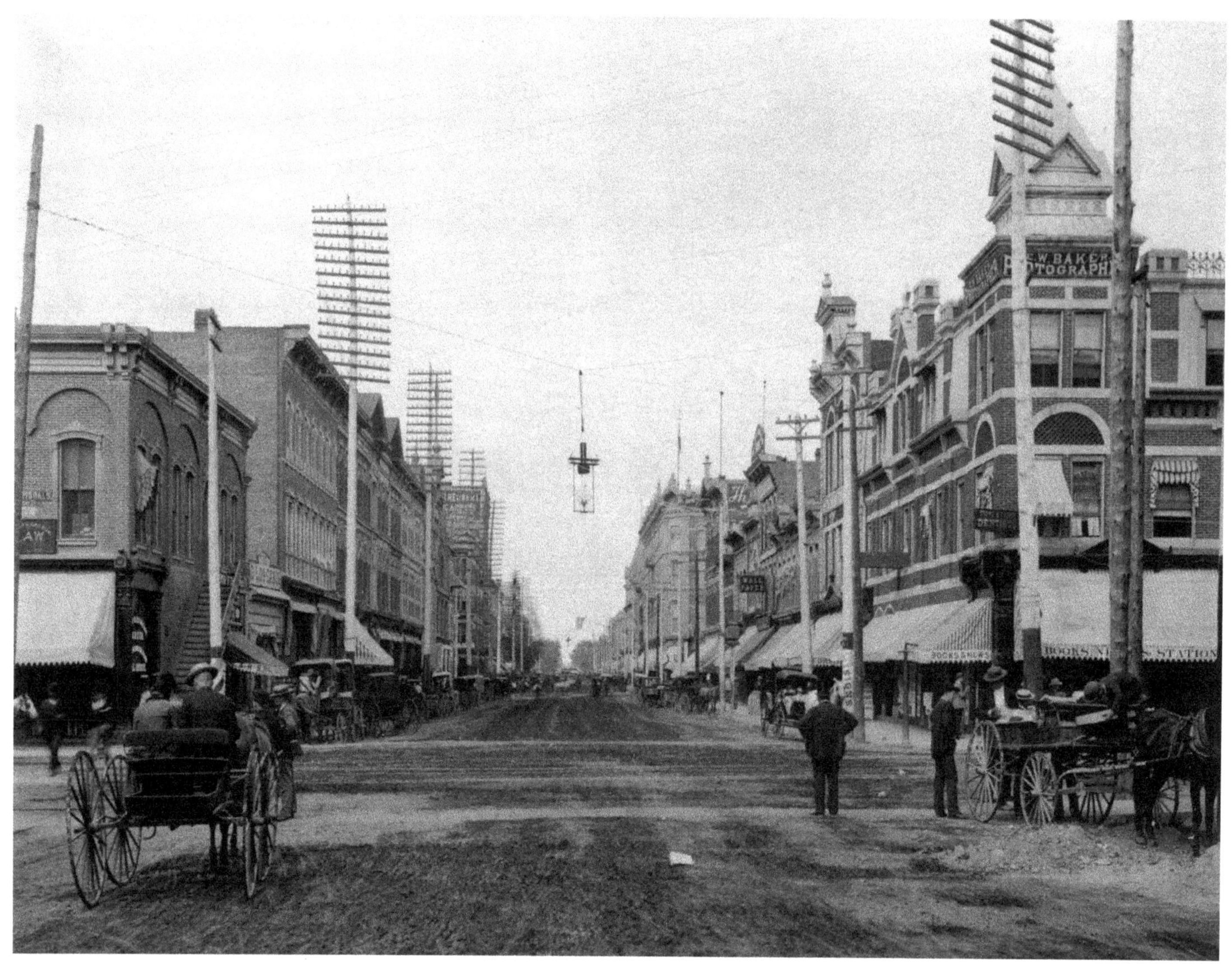

Horse-drawn wagons are parked on both sides of North Lawrence in the Central Business District in the mid 1880s. A large incandescent street light hangs in the intersection of 15th and Lawrence streets.

Studio portrait of John Bill, a police officer in the Denver city police department in the mid 1880s.

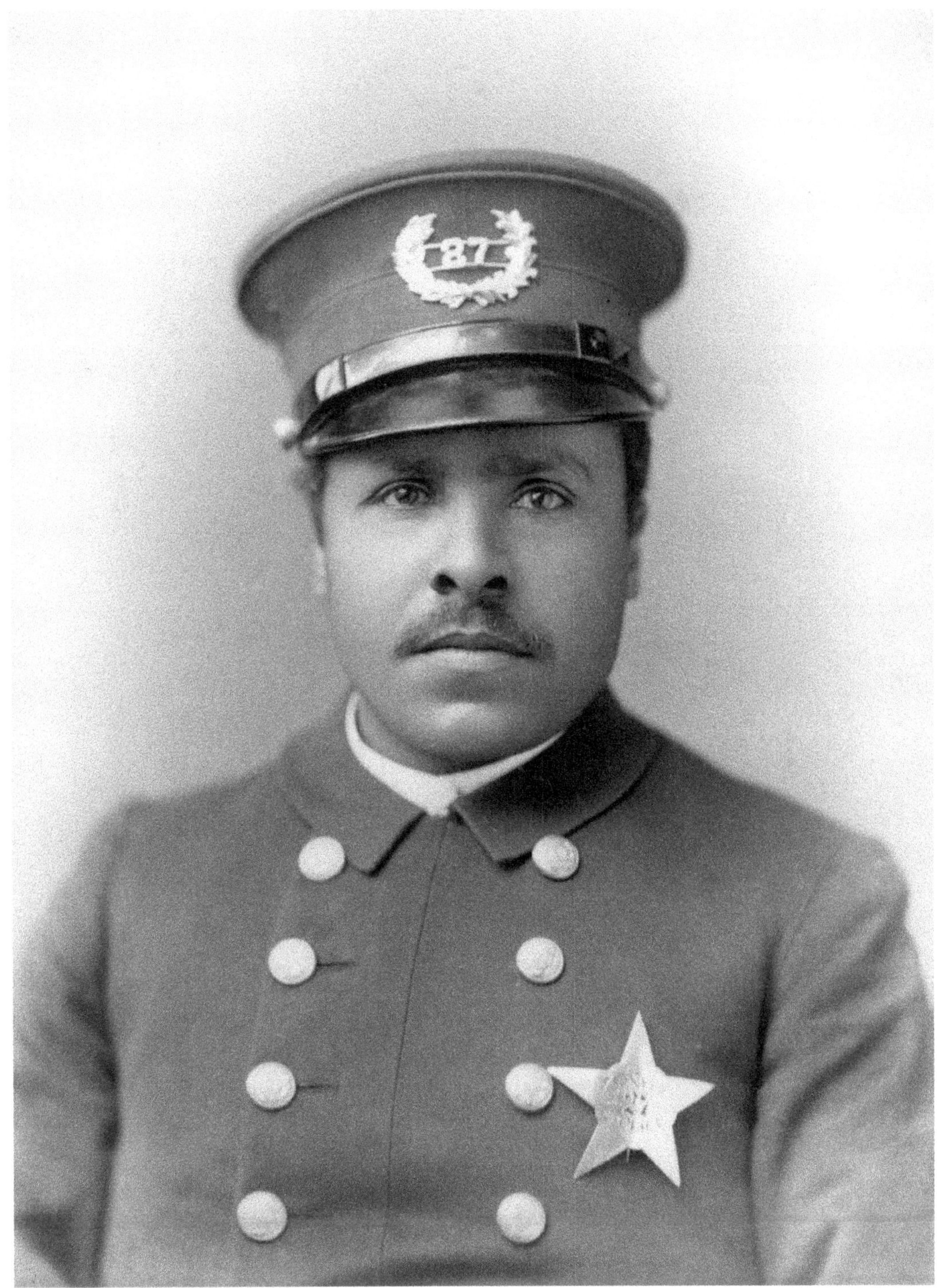

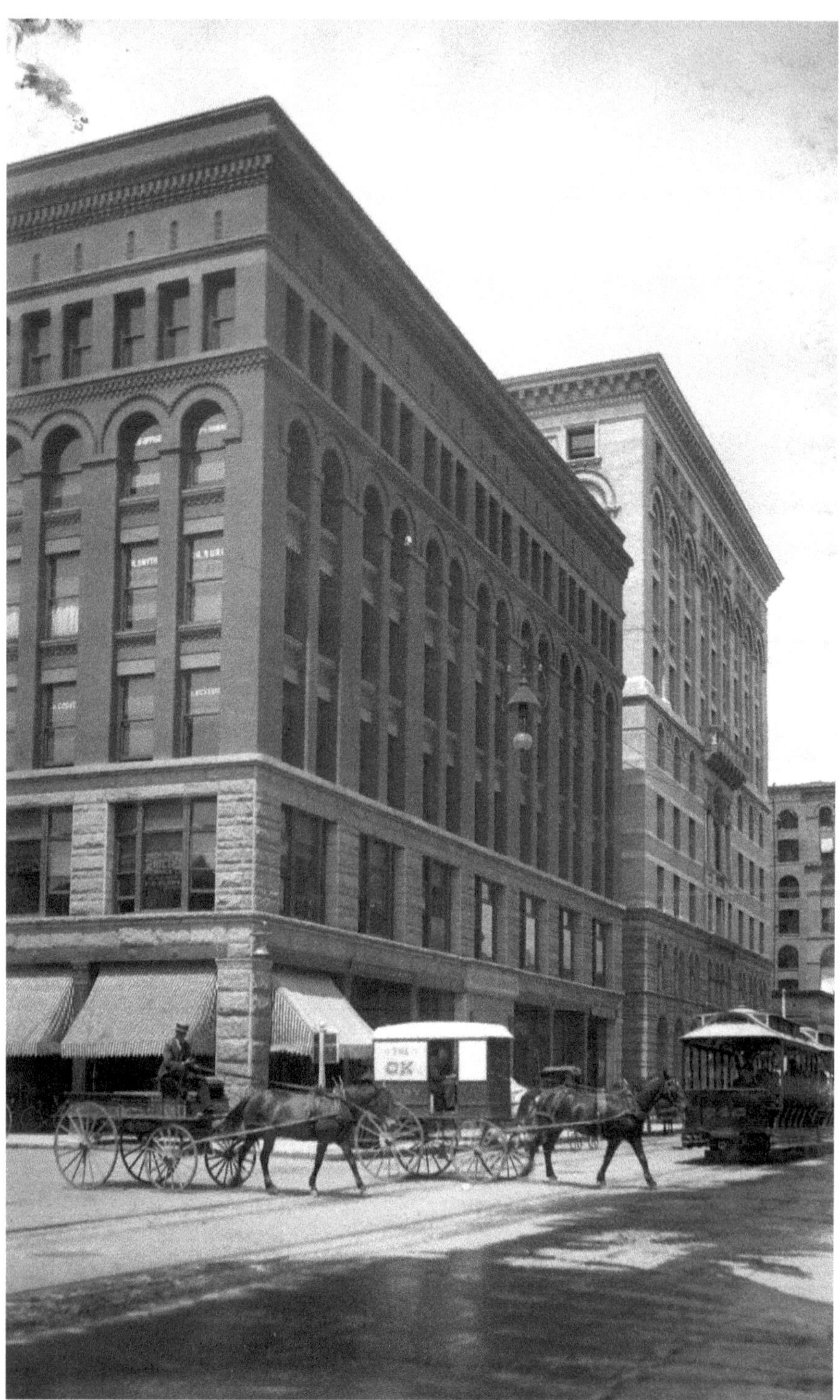

Here are two of Denver's early office buildings, both built in 1892. The California Building at 17th and California streets, and the Equitable Building located at 17th and Stout streets. A delivery wagon, milk wagon, and cable car are rolling into the intersection.

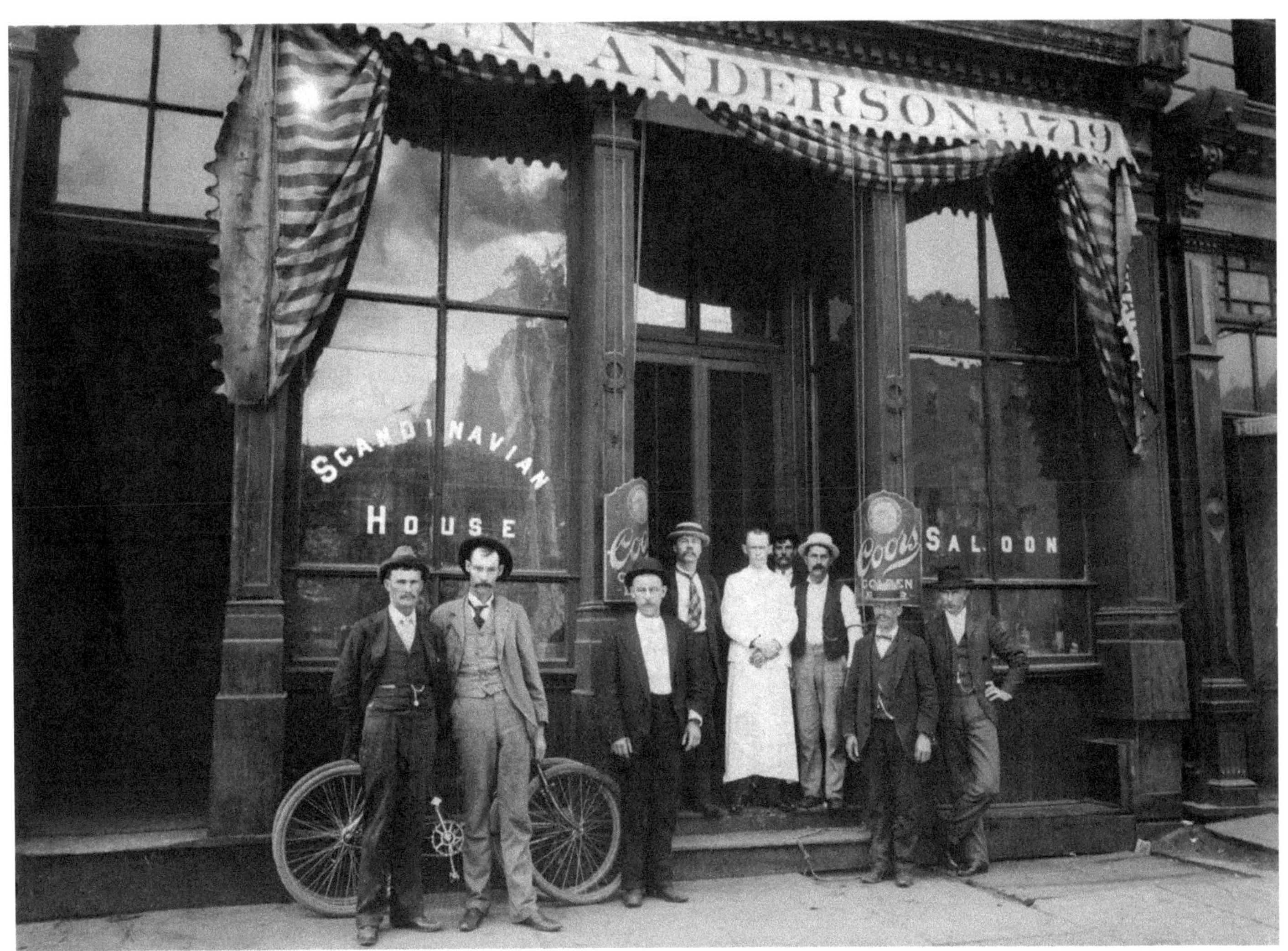

Early in the 1890s these men pose in front of the Scandinavian Saloon at 1719 Blake Street. The bartender stands in the center of the group in a white coat and apron. A pair of safety bicycles are parked behind the two men at left.

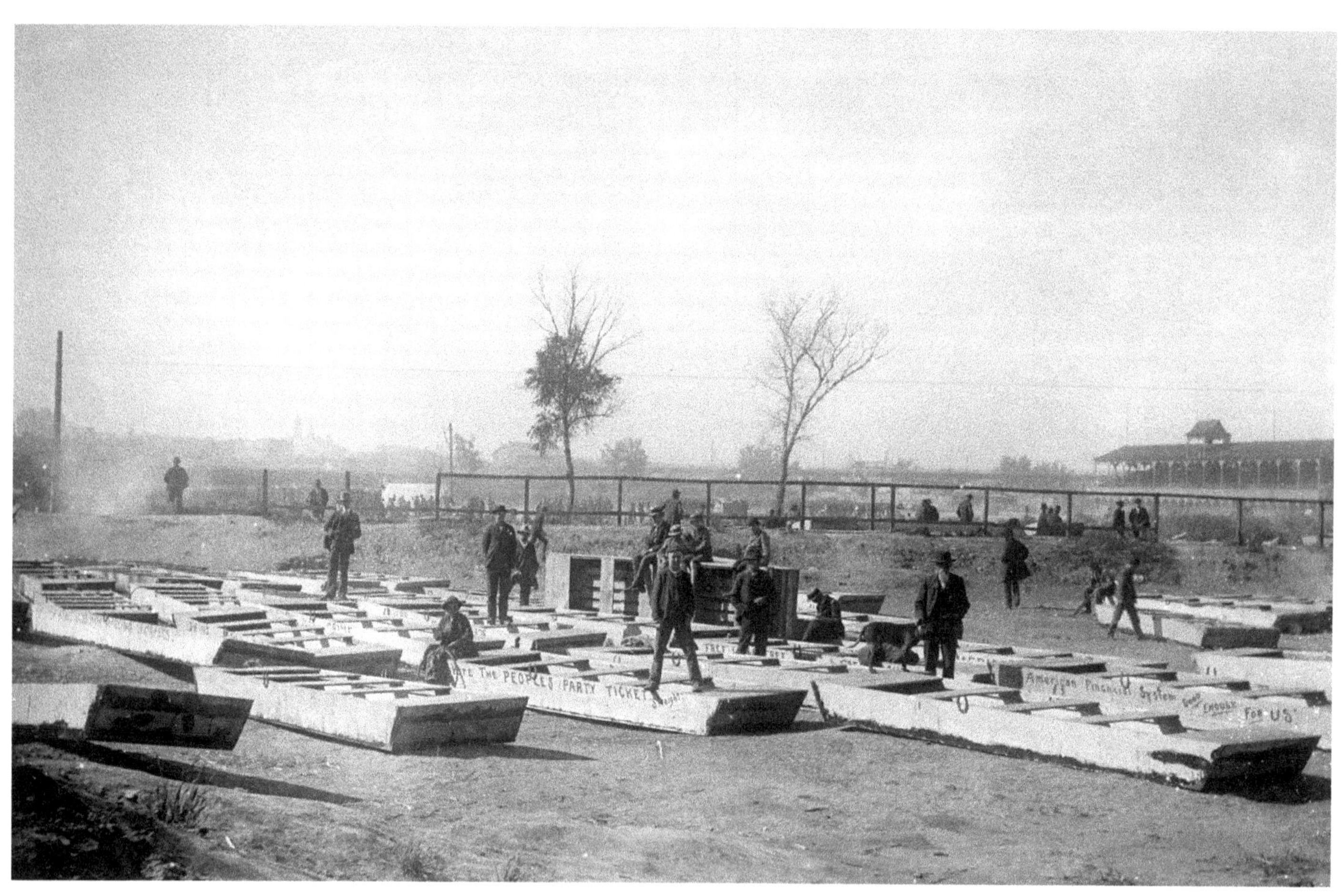

Following the depression of 1893, Ohio businessman Jacob Coxey organized an "Industrial Army" of the unemployed. "Coxey's Army" was created to protest the government's failure to deal with the economic crisis. In this picture, probably from 1894, unemployed men stand near boats that they have built near Riverside Park. They are preparing for a journey over water and land to attend a demonstration organized by Coxey in Washington, D.C. The park's racecourse grandstand is visible in the distance.

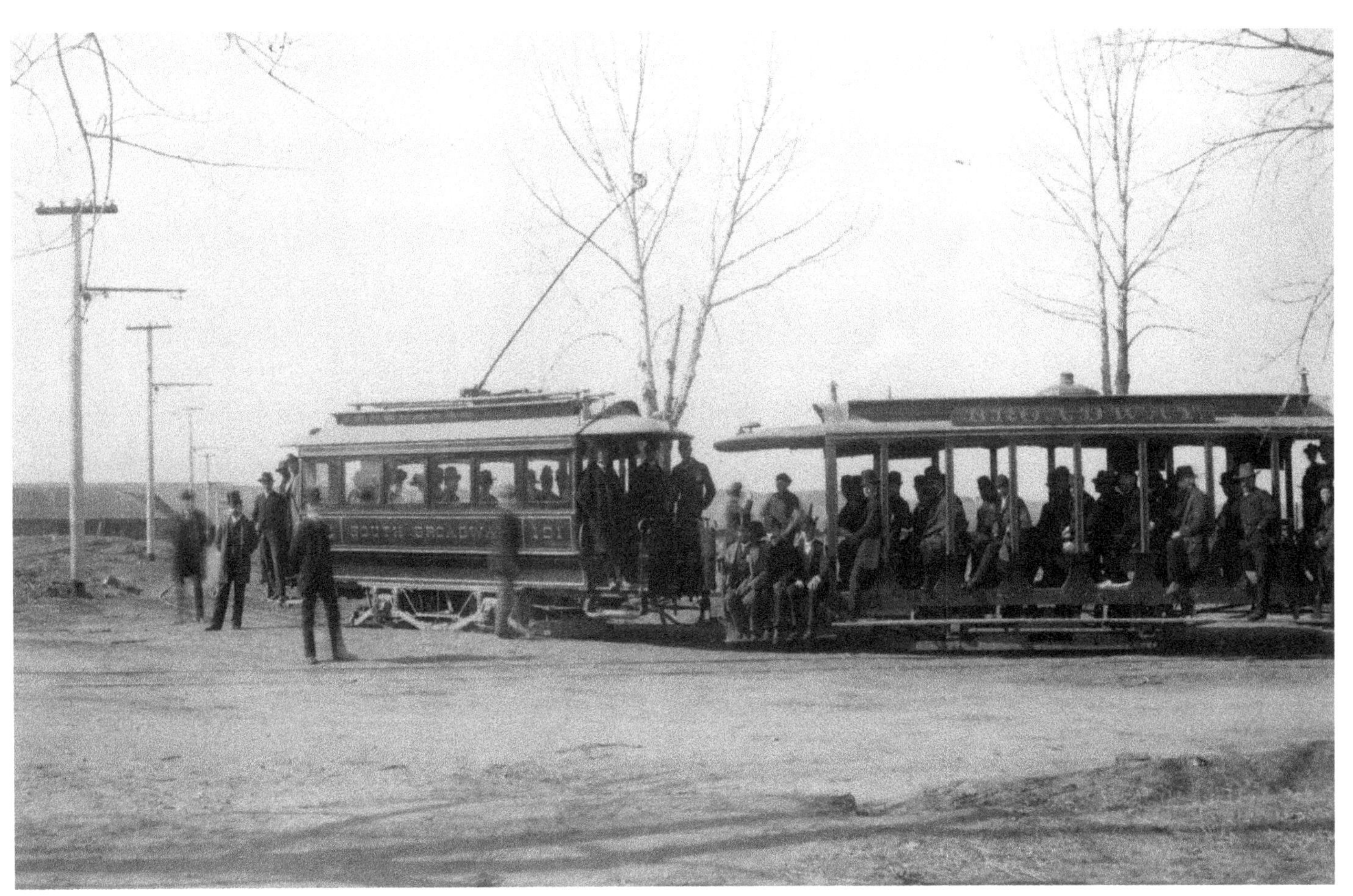

Men pose on and near a streetcar and an observation car at the corner of Colorado Avenue and South Broadway on the newly constructed South Denver Cable Railway Line on December 25, 1889. The electric streetcar service began in January 1890.

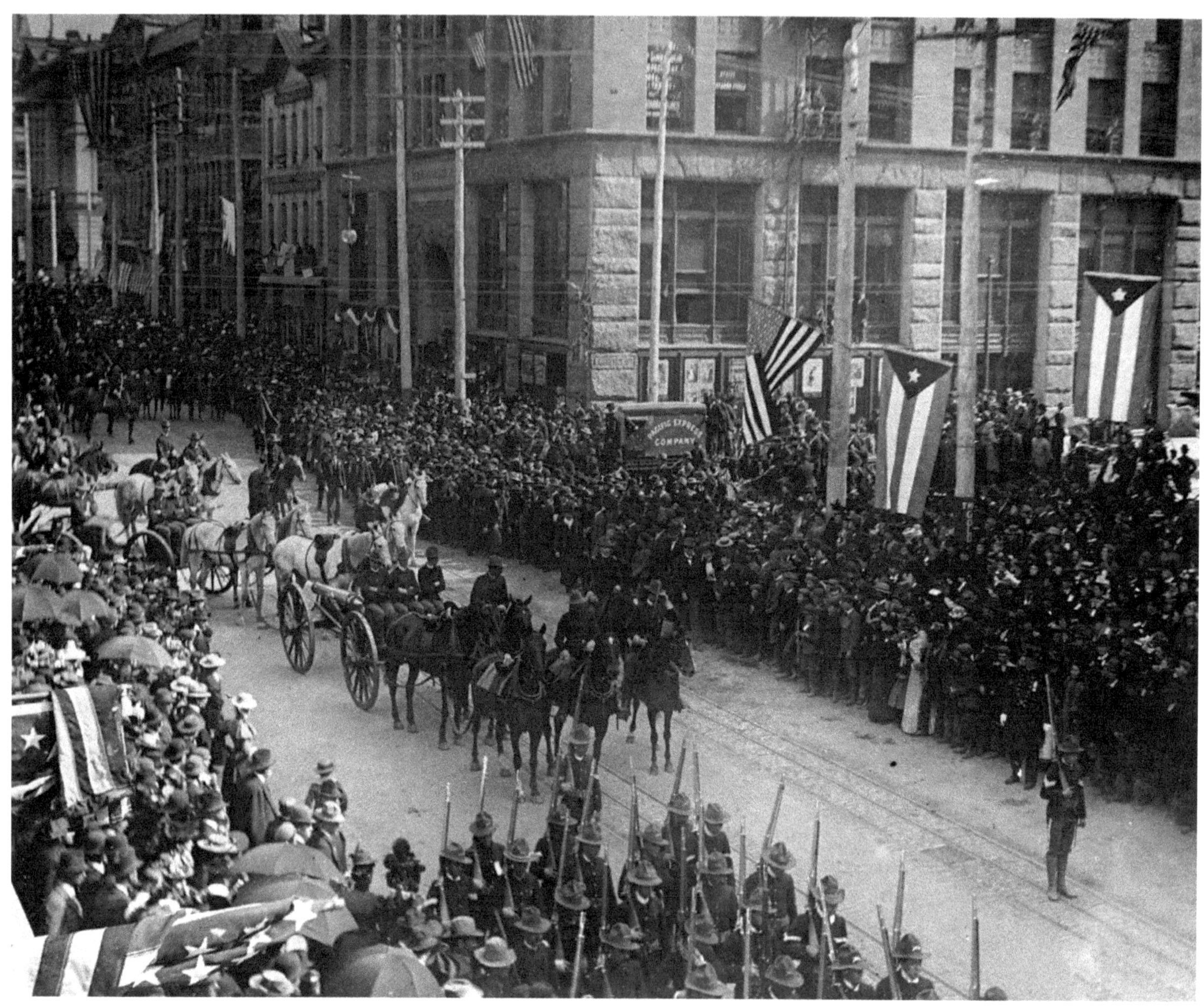

Members of the 1st Colorado Infantry Volunteers ride past City Hall bound for the Philippines in the Spanish American War. The horse-drawn wagons carry cannon and soldiers.

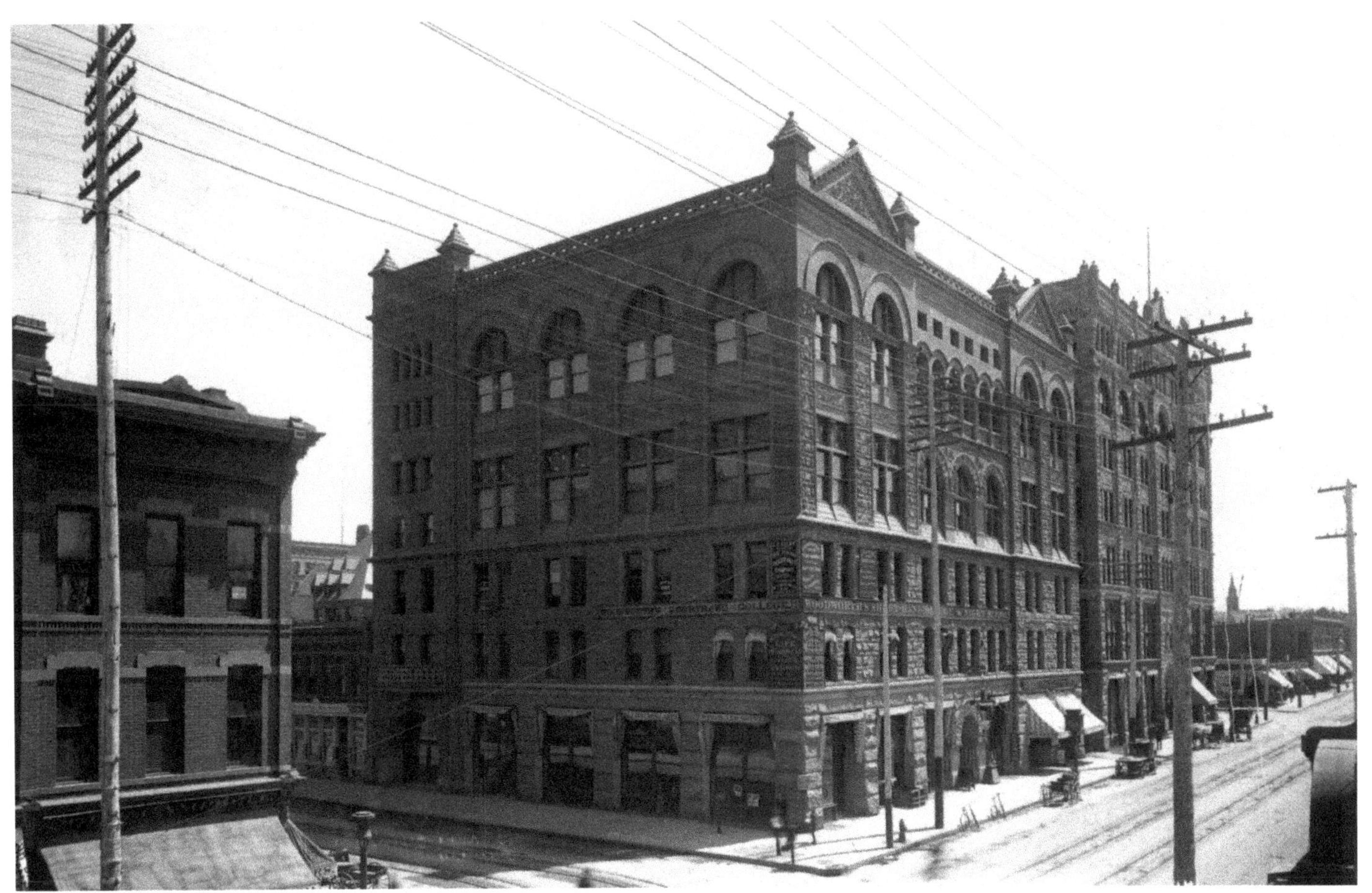

The Romanesque Revival–style Masonic Building located at 16th and Welton streets was built in 1890 by F. E. Edbrooke & Company. For many years it served as the center for the activities of the Masonic Order in Colorado. The bottom floors were rented out for business.

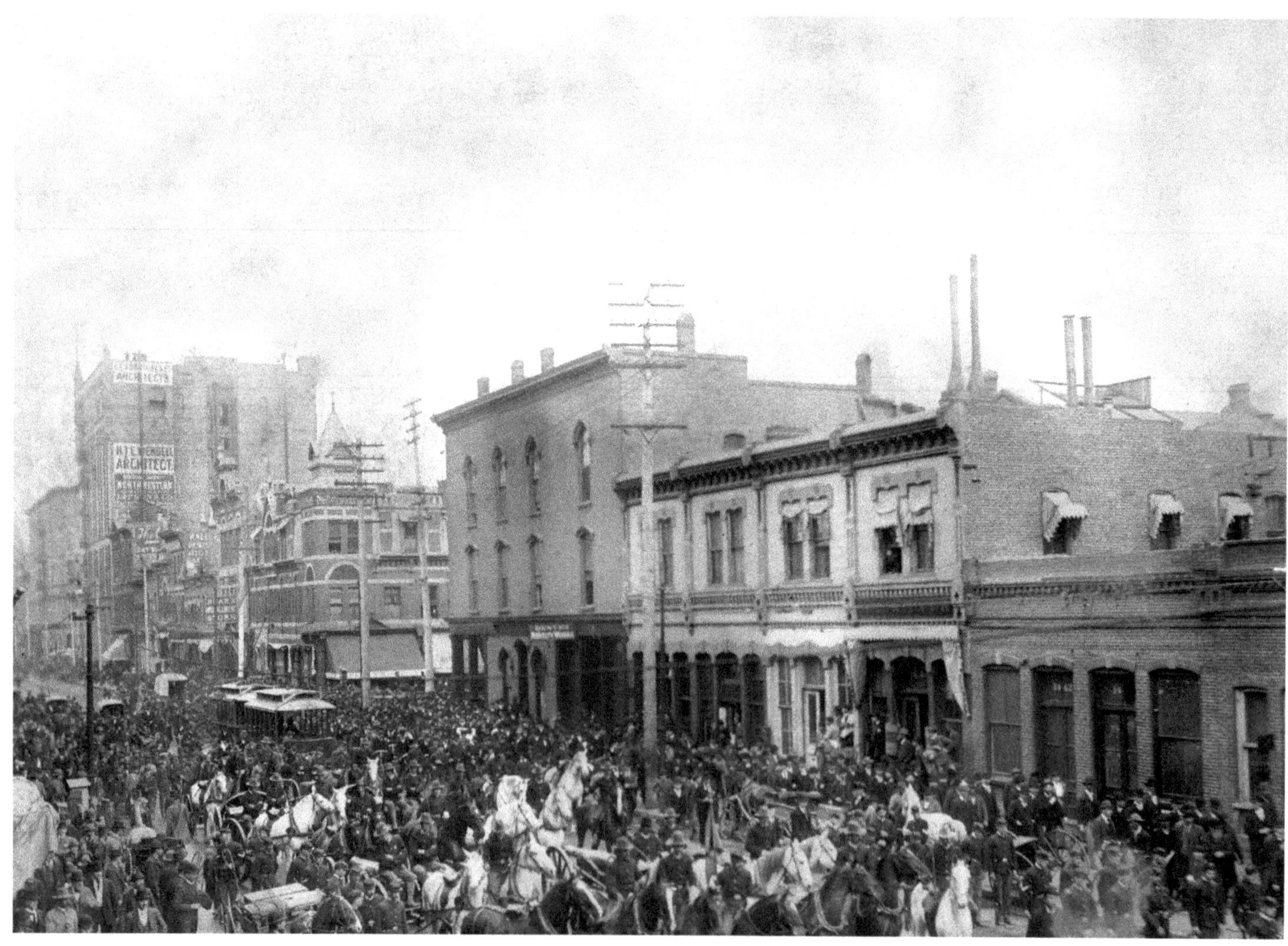
ARCHITECT

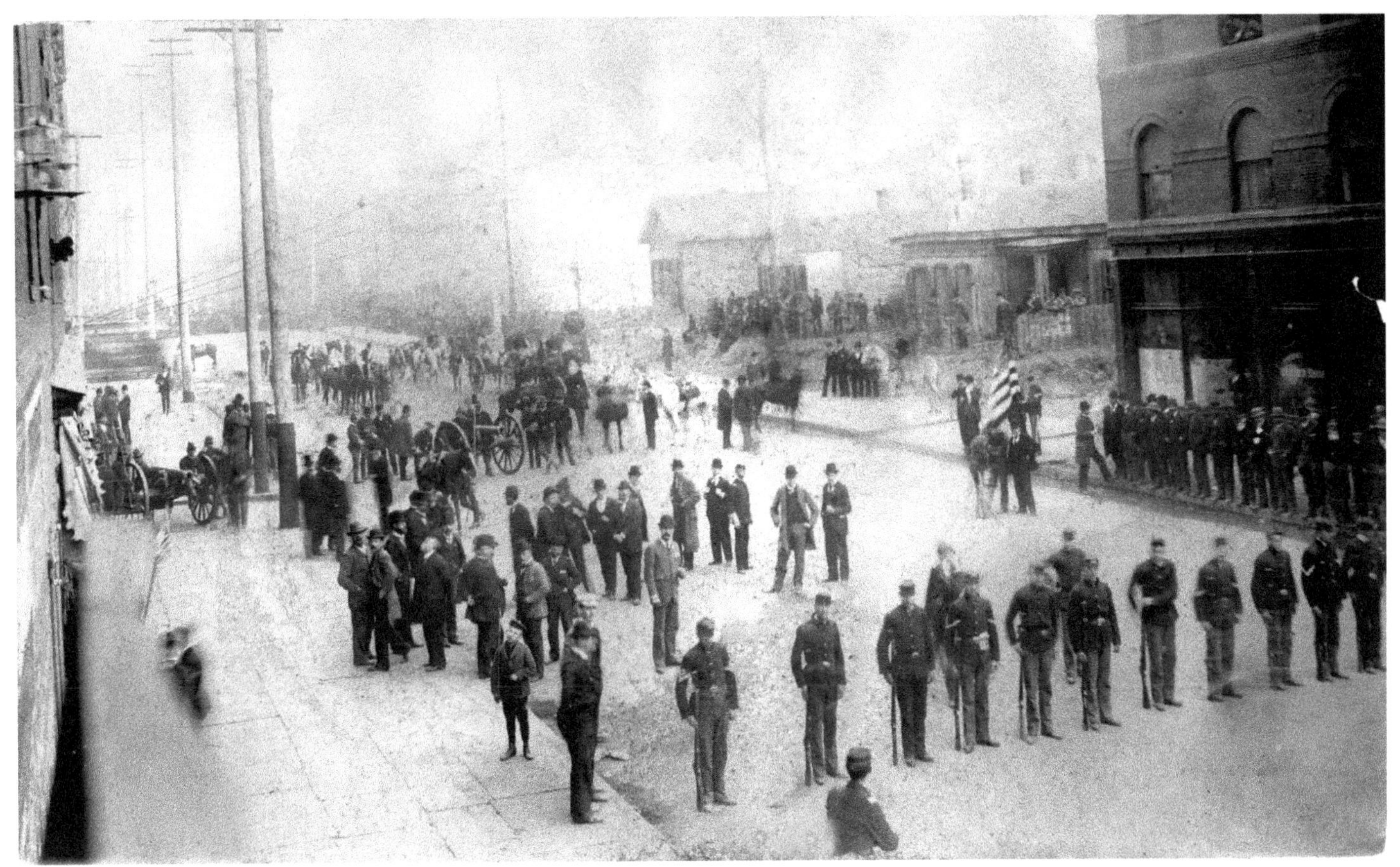

This Page and Preceding: Members of the Colorado Infantry stand in formation on Lawrence Street during the "City Hall War," a dispute between Governor Davis Waite and two of his appointees to Denver's police and fire boards. Waite attempted to forcibly remove these men as well as some of his other appointees from office. When City Hall employees learned of this, they barricaded themselves inside City Hall. The entire Denver police department and many sheriffs' deputies were later to join them outside the building. Finally the court ordered board members to give up their seats, but ruled that the governor had exceeded his authority in calling out the infantry.

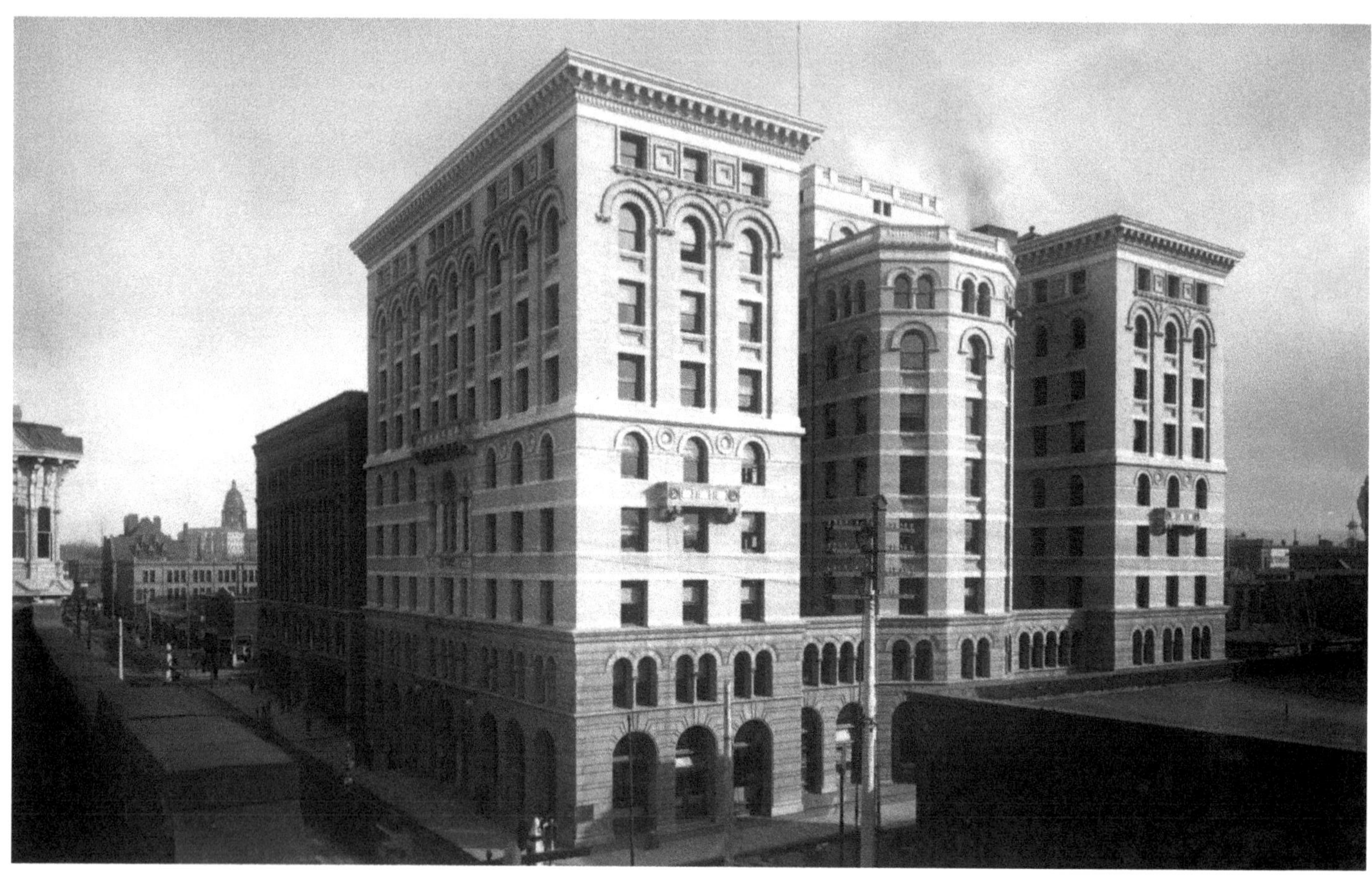

The Italian Renaissance–style Equitable Building, built by the Equitable Life Insurance Company, was located at 17th and Stout streets. It was Denver's first high rise when completed in 1892.

This man in his suit and top hat rides a bicycle adapted as a velocipede for the tracks in the railroad yards near 20th Street.

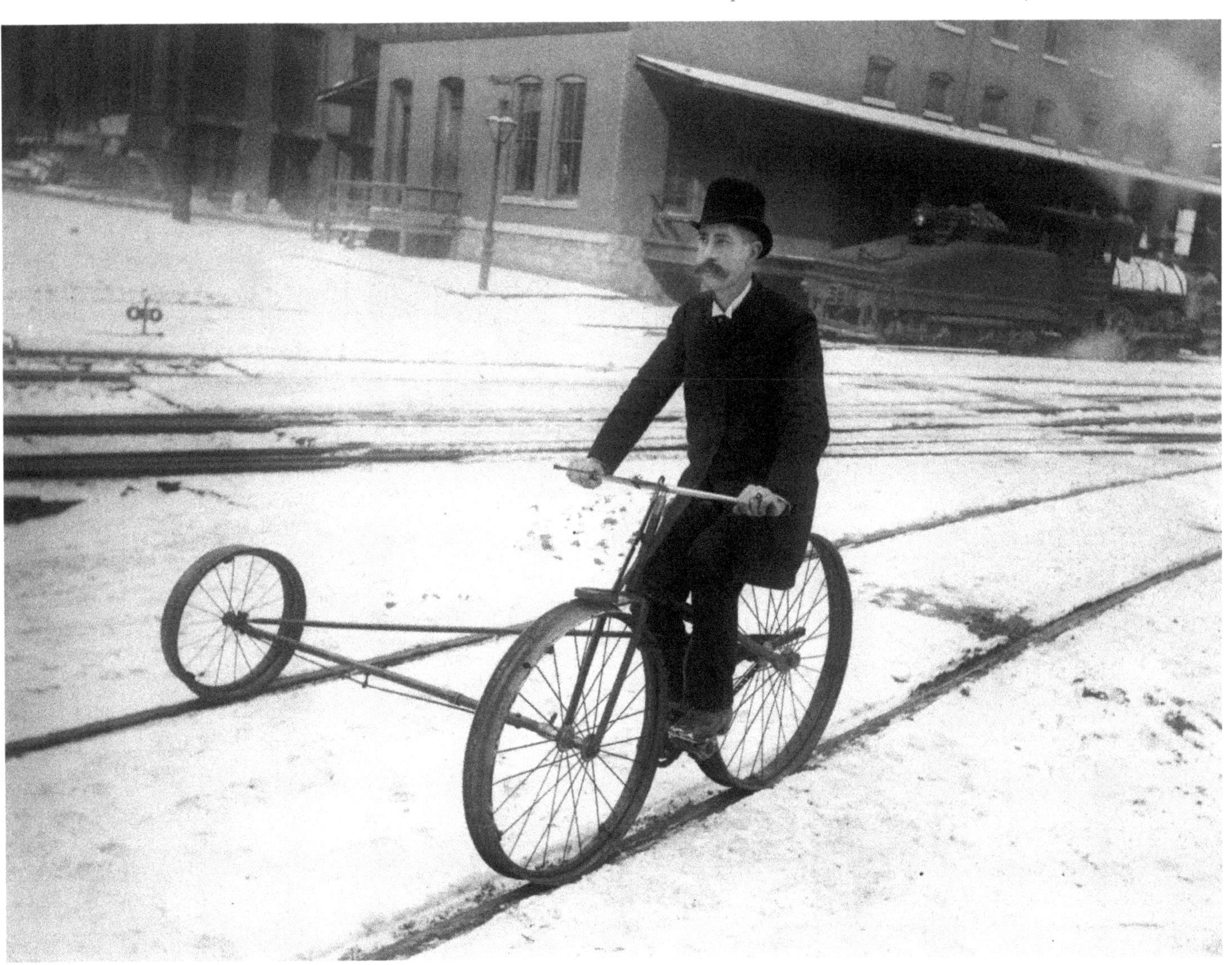

Turner Moving & Storage Company horse-drawn moving vans are lined up on 16th Street in front of the Denver Republican Newspaper building. The large merchant wagons are pulled by four-horse teams.

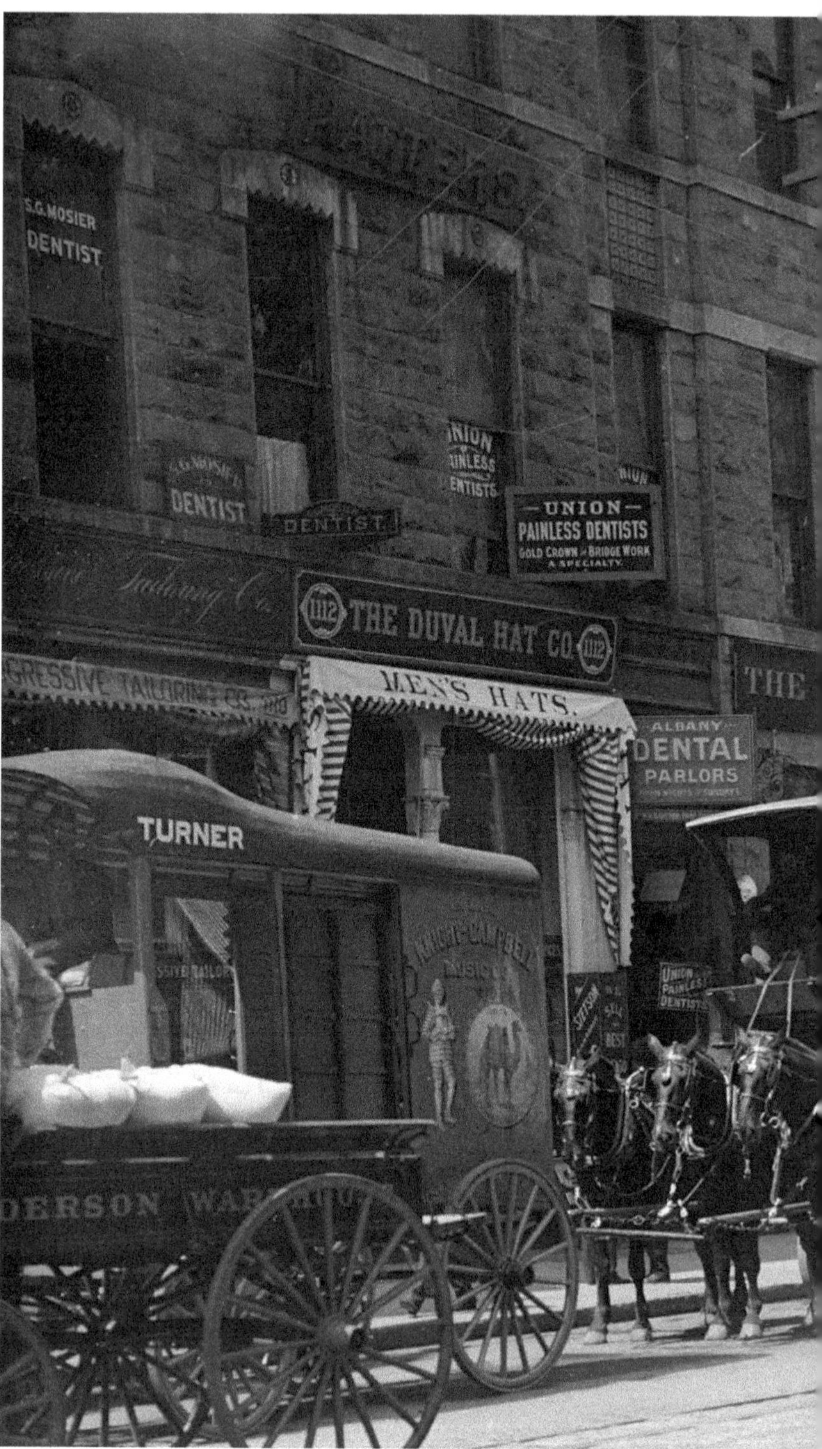

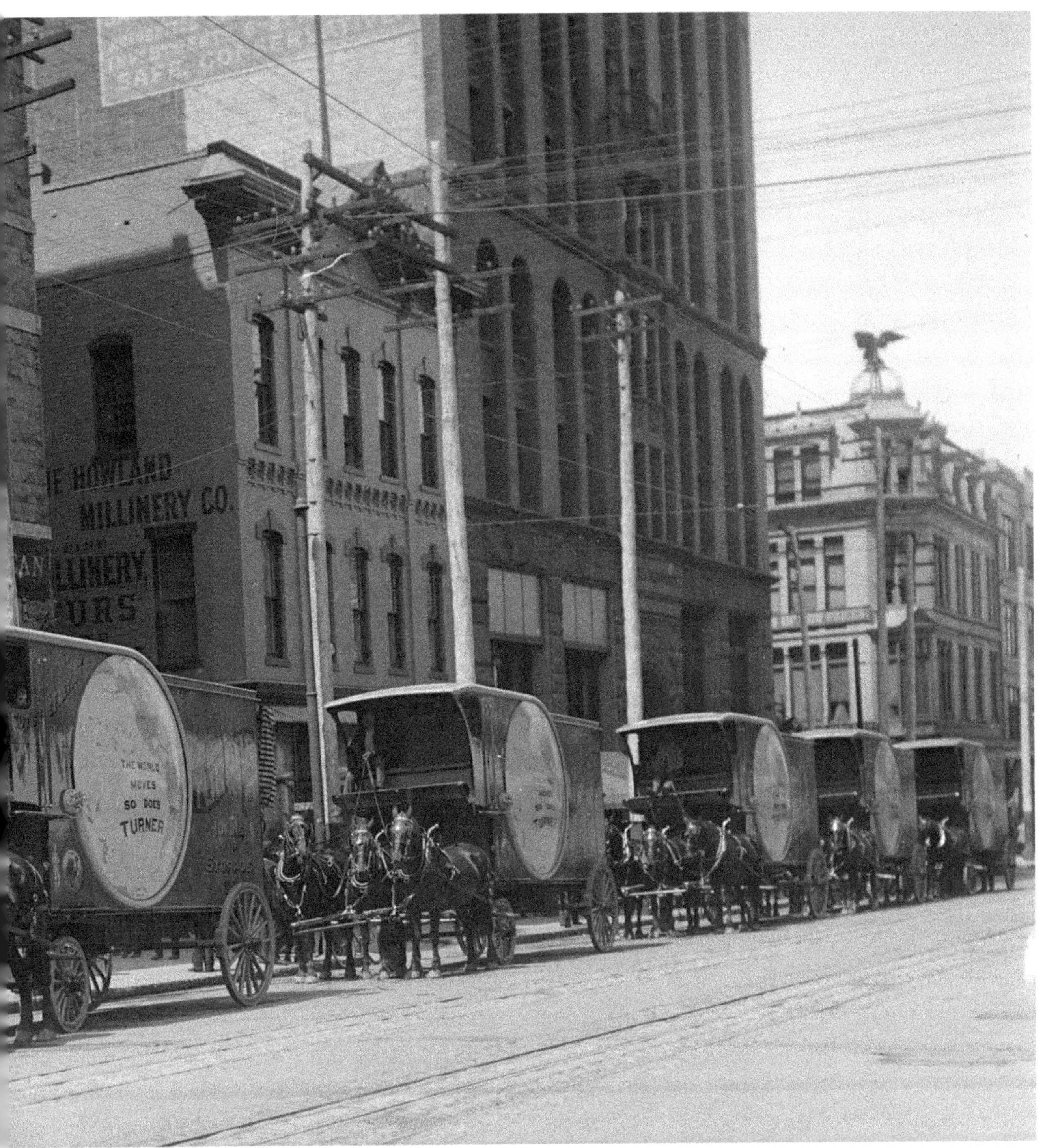
E HOWLAND
MILLINERY CO.
LLINERY
URS
THE WORLD
MOVES
SO DOES
TURNER

Horse-drawn freight and merchant wagons crowd this panoramic view of the Turner Moving & Storage Company warehouse.

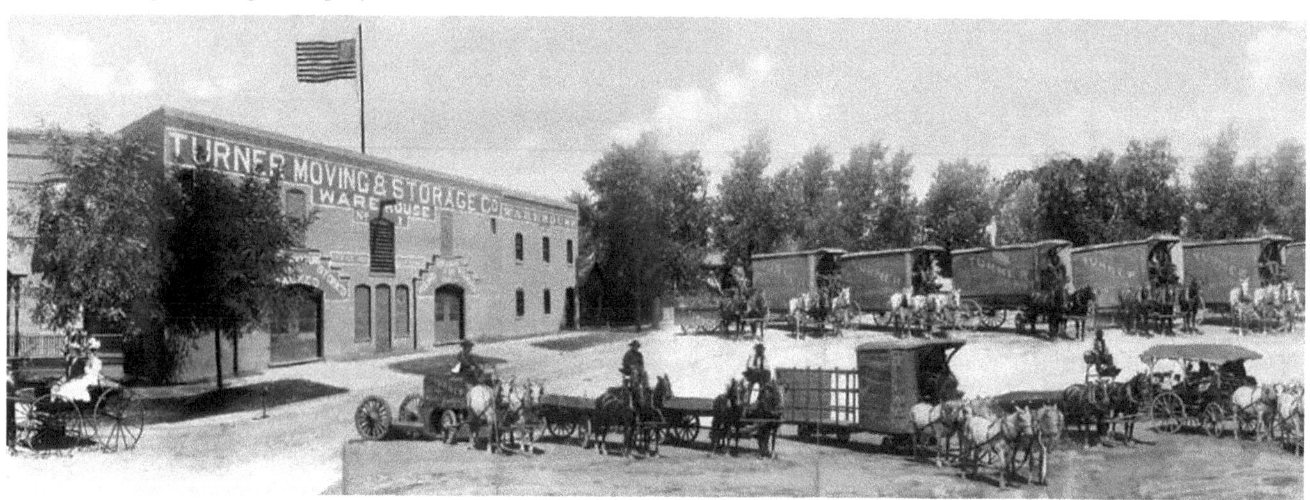

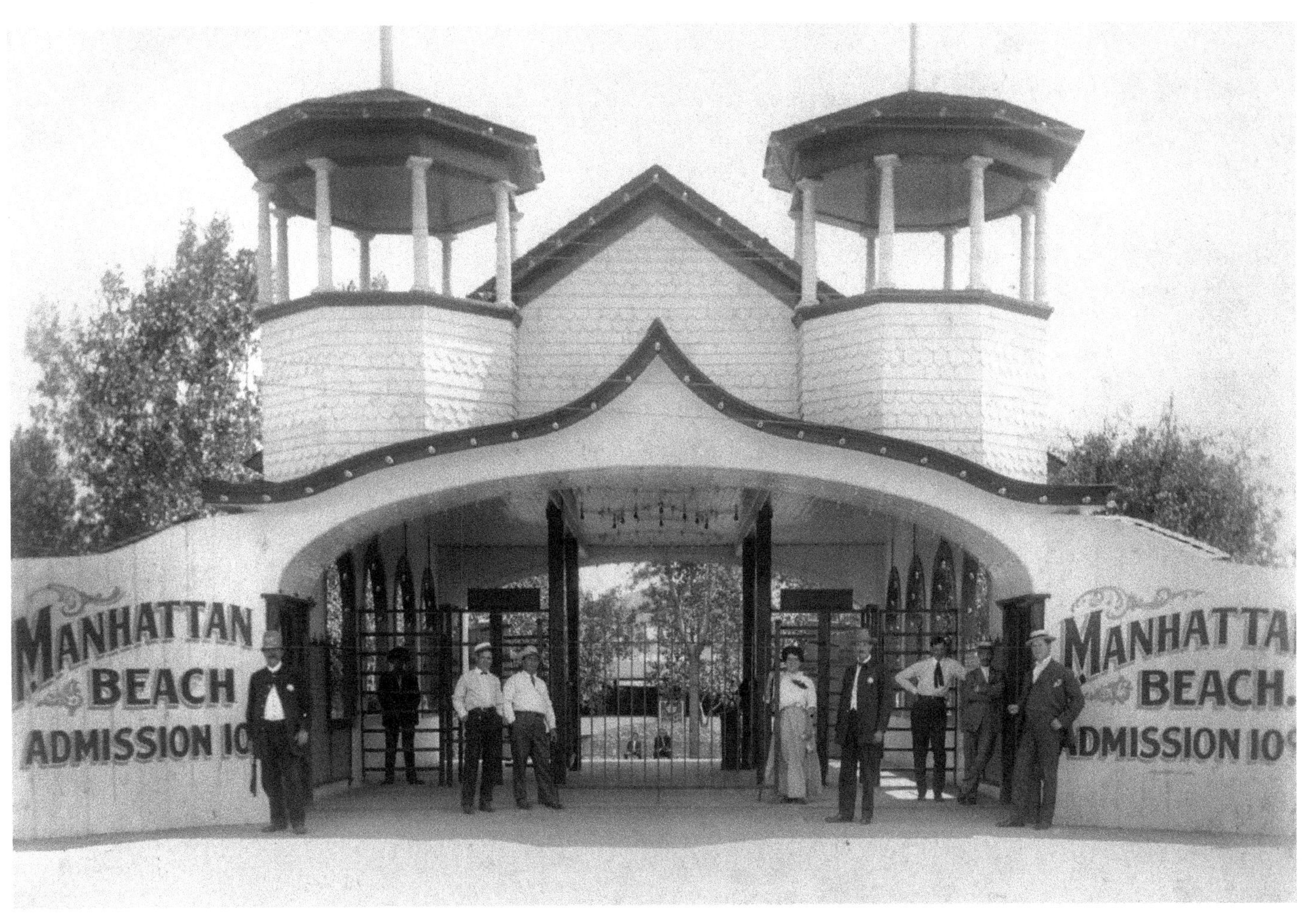

The Manhattan Beach amusement park, located on the northwestern shore of Sloan's Lake, opened in 1891. The park featured a summer stock theater and a large roller coaster. In 1906 a fire destroyed the theater; soon after the park's steamboat, *City of Denver,* sank. The Manhattan Beach park closed and was reopened as Luna Park.

The Ernest & Cranmer Building was located at 17th and Curtis streets. Designed by architect Frank E. Edbrooke and Company, it opened in 1891. The first two floors of the building were constructed using Colorado red sandstone; the upper part was built of brown brick.

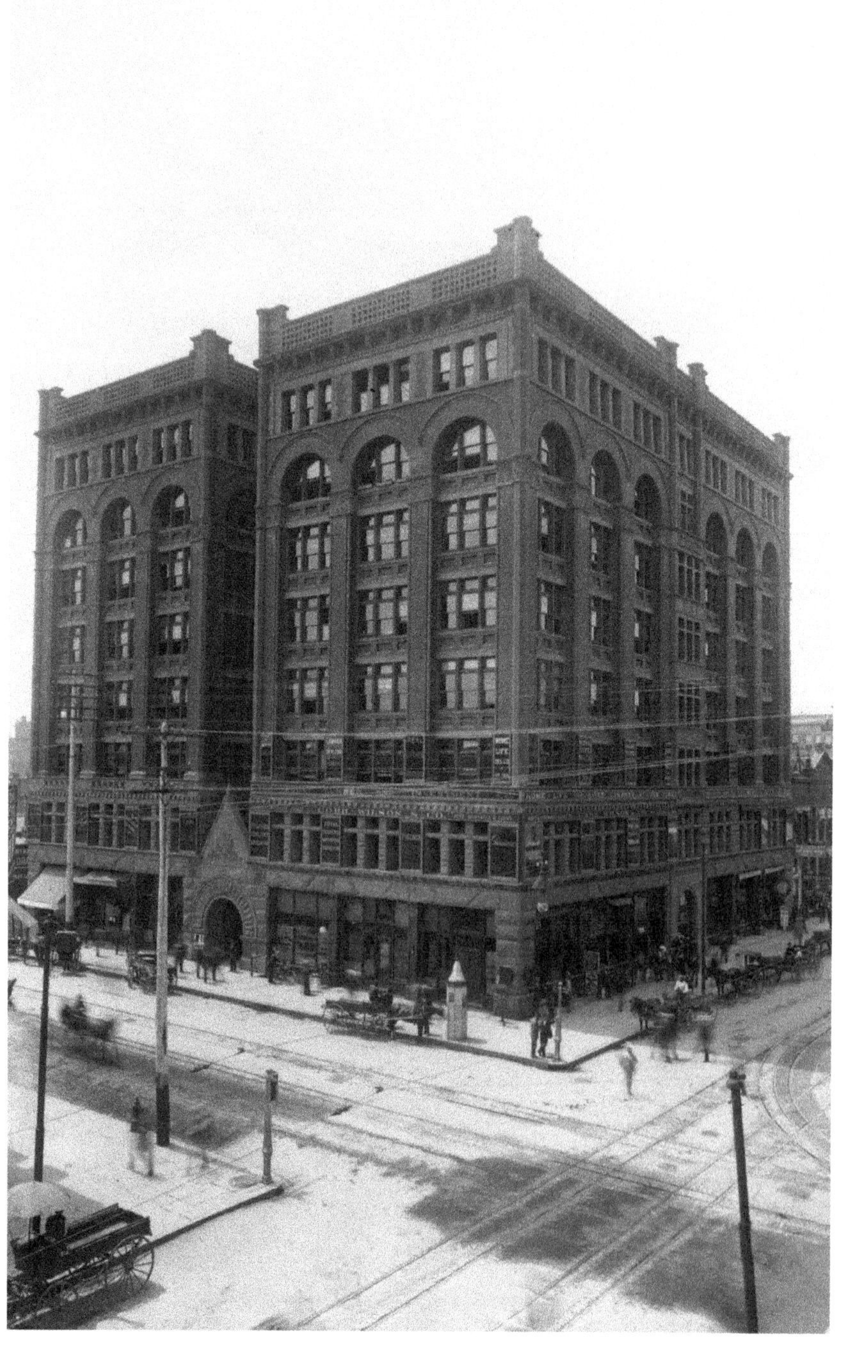

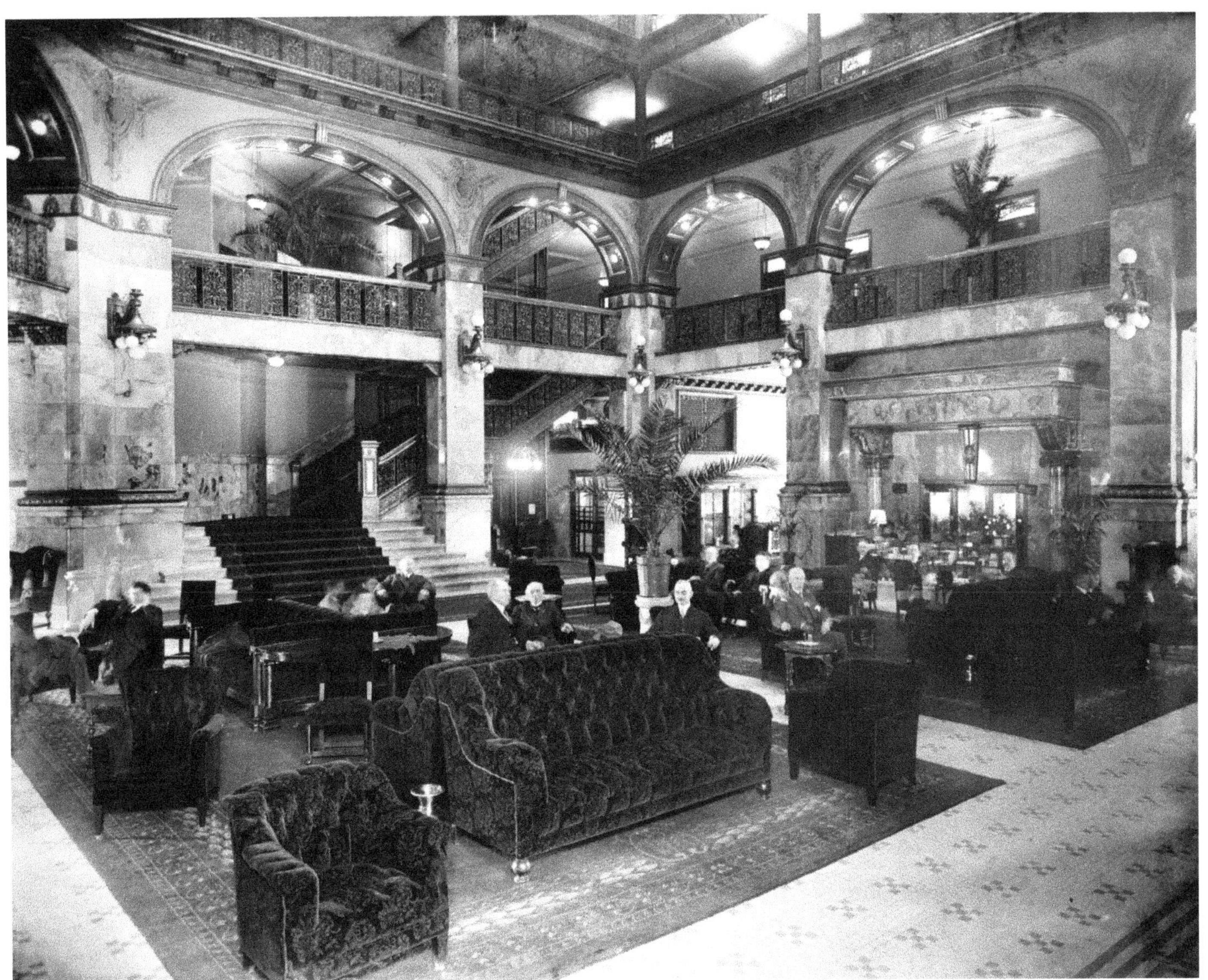

Gentlemen rest in the lobby of the Brown Palace Hotel, lavishly appointed with velvet upholstered furniture with brass ball feet. The eight-story atrium has pillars, elaborate pierced brass railings, and wainscoting of pale golden onyx. Discreetly placed spittoons are scattered about the room.

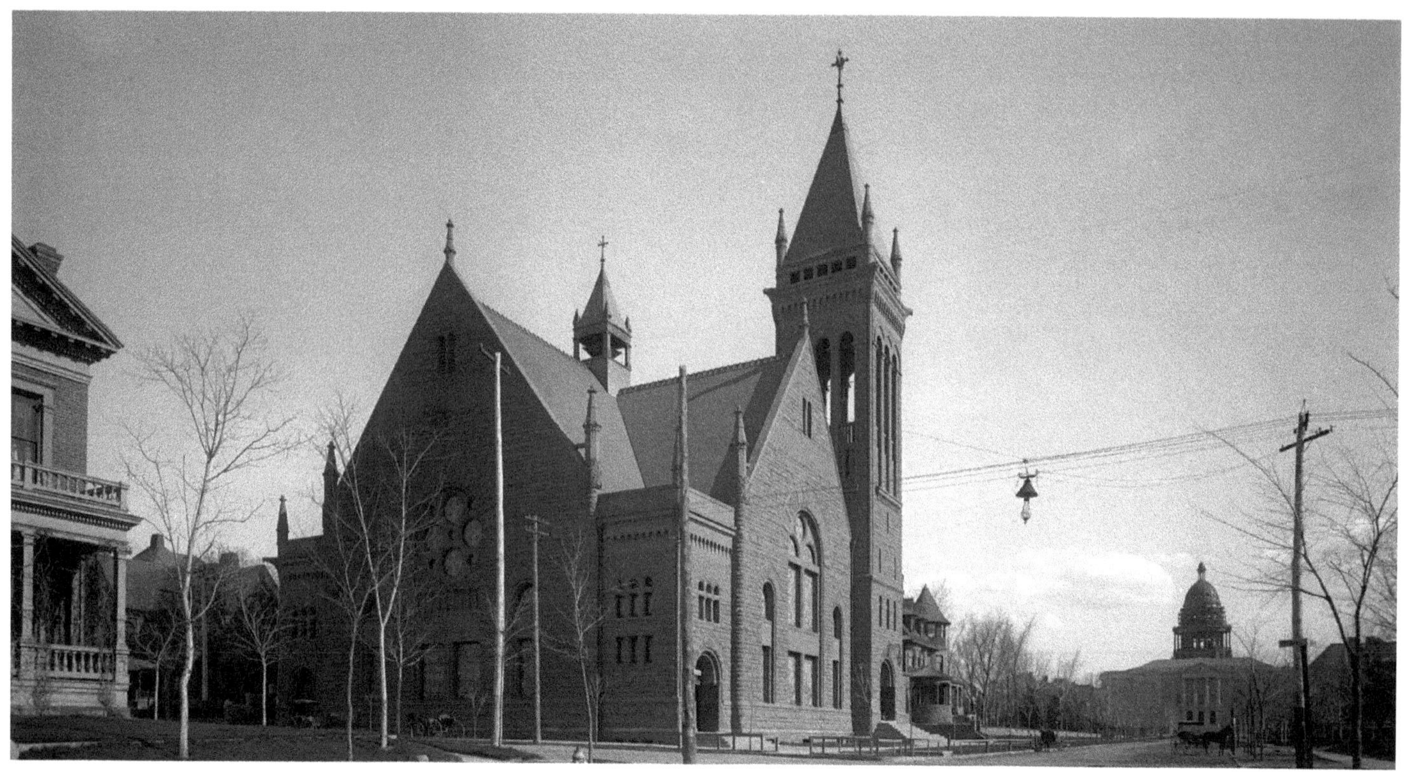

This 1892 Romanesque Revival–style church was designed by Denver architects Frank Edbrooke and Willis Marean. It is located on the corner of 17th and Sherman streets. The Colorado state capitol is visible in the distance.

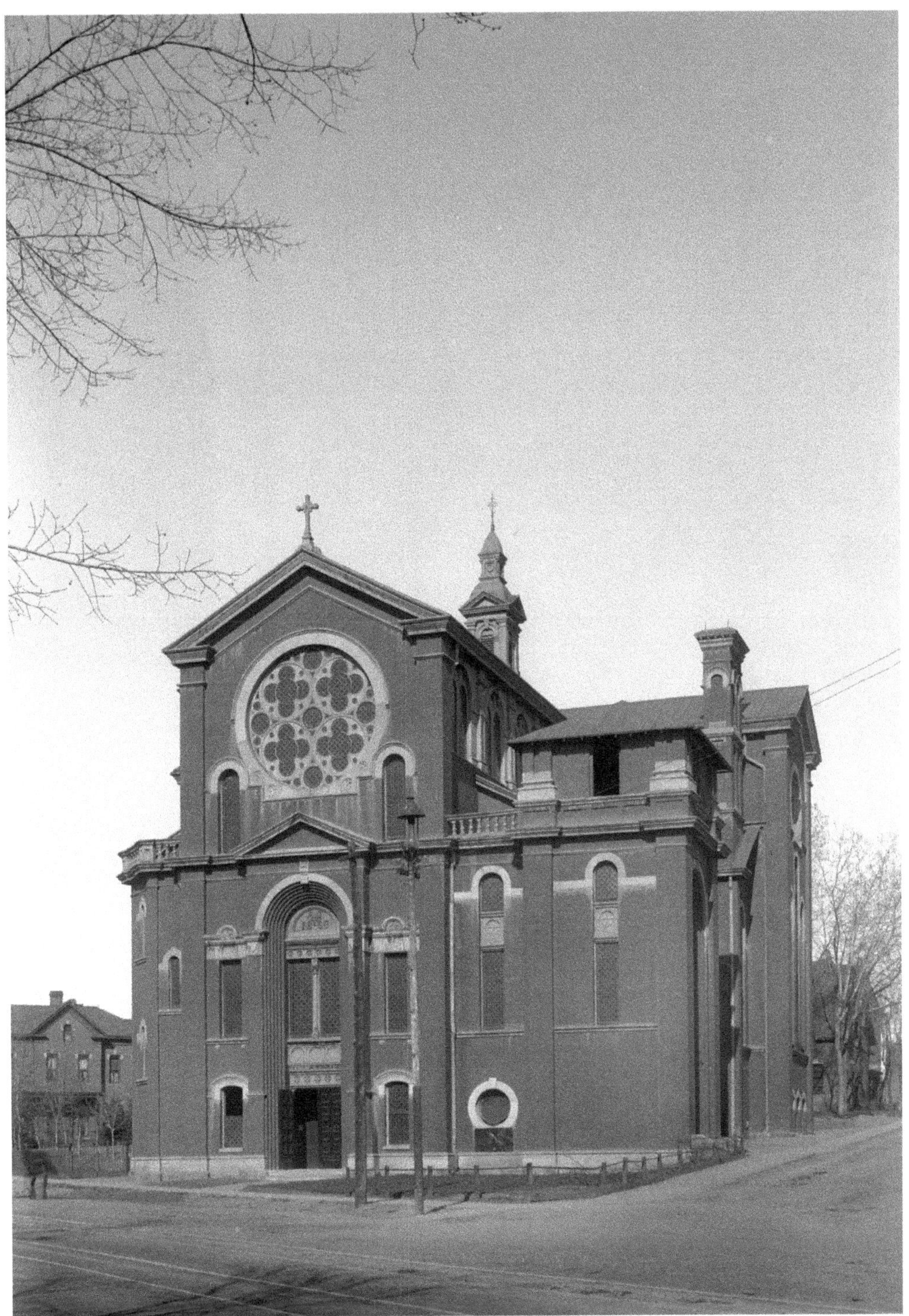

The Cathedral of Saint John the Evangelist was the first Episcopal cathedral in Colorado. Located on the corner of 20th and Welton streets, it opened in 1881 and was destroyed by fire in 1903.

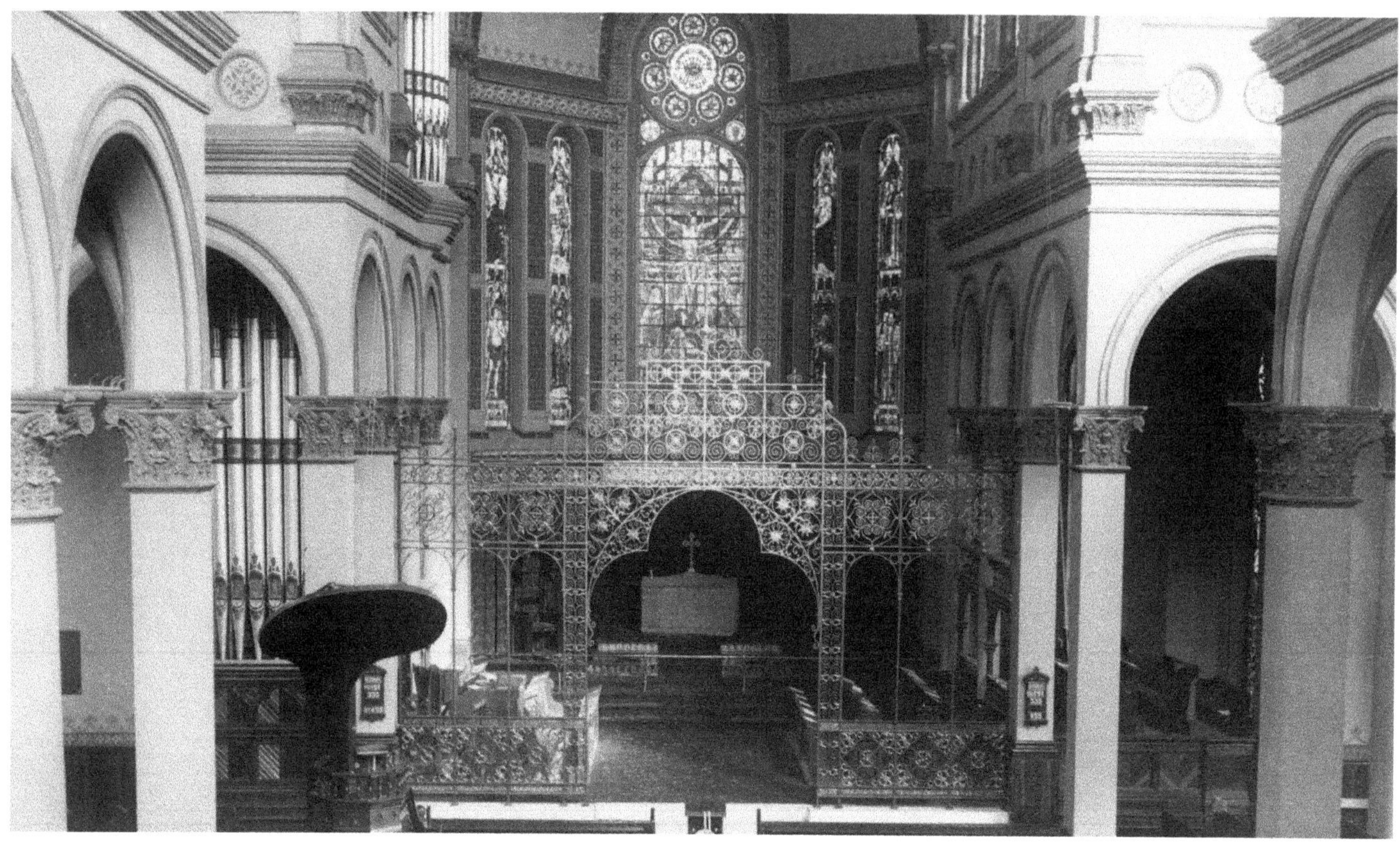

This interior view of the Episcopal cathedral of Saint John the Evangelist shows an ornate filigree rood screen, a stained-glass window of the crucifixion, the altar, and a covered wooden pulpit.

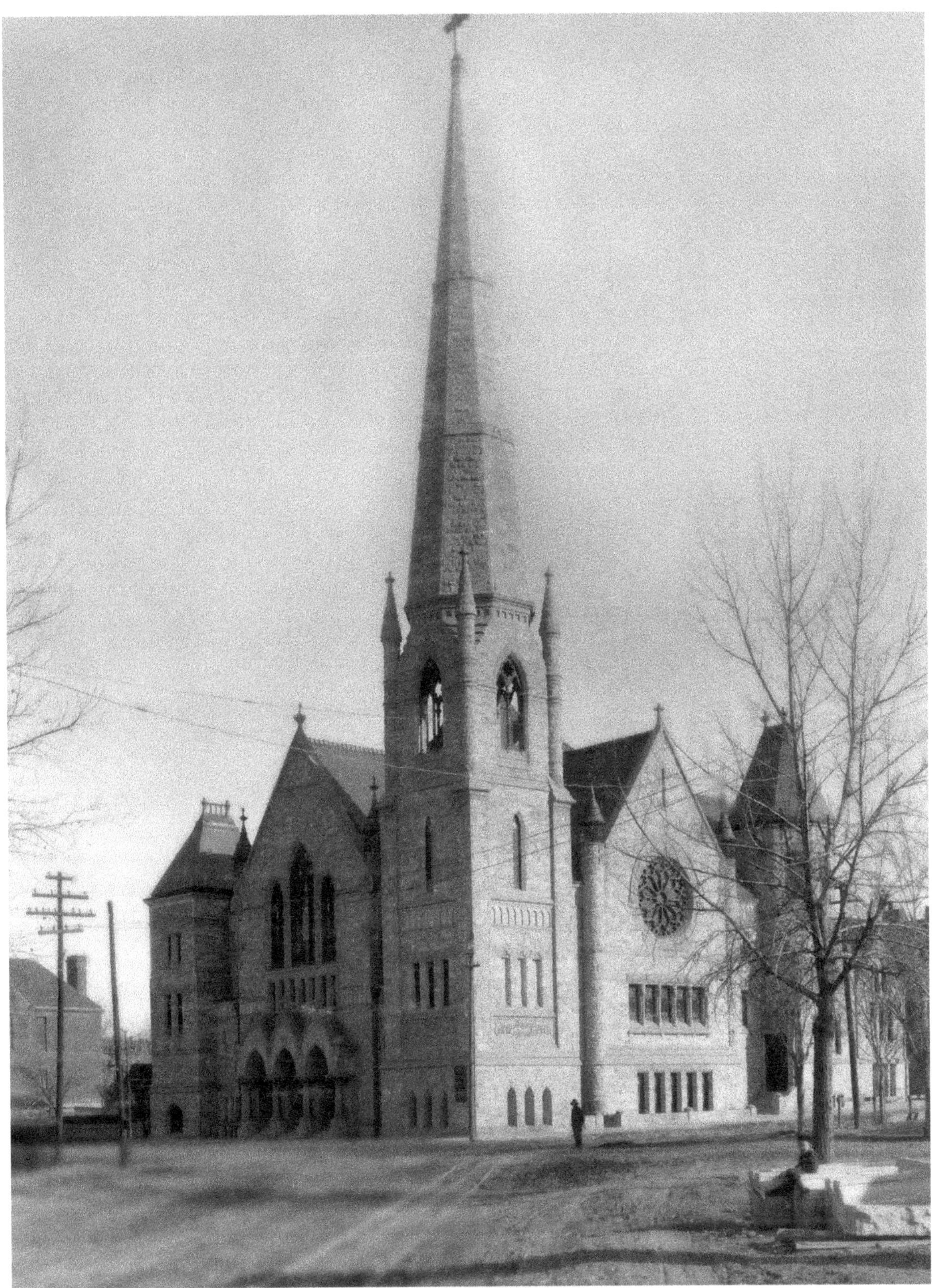

This photograph of Trinity Methodist Episcopal Church, designed by Robert S. Roeschlaub, was taken in the mid 1890s. The church opened in 1888 at the corner of 18th Avenue and Broadway and features an 81-foot hexagonal stone steeple.

People gather in front of the 1896 Spanish Revival–style City Park pavilion to listen to a band concert on the shore of Lake Ferril. Band members sit in the bandstand located in the manmade lake.

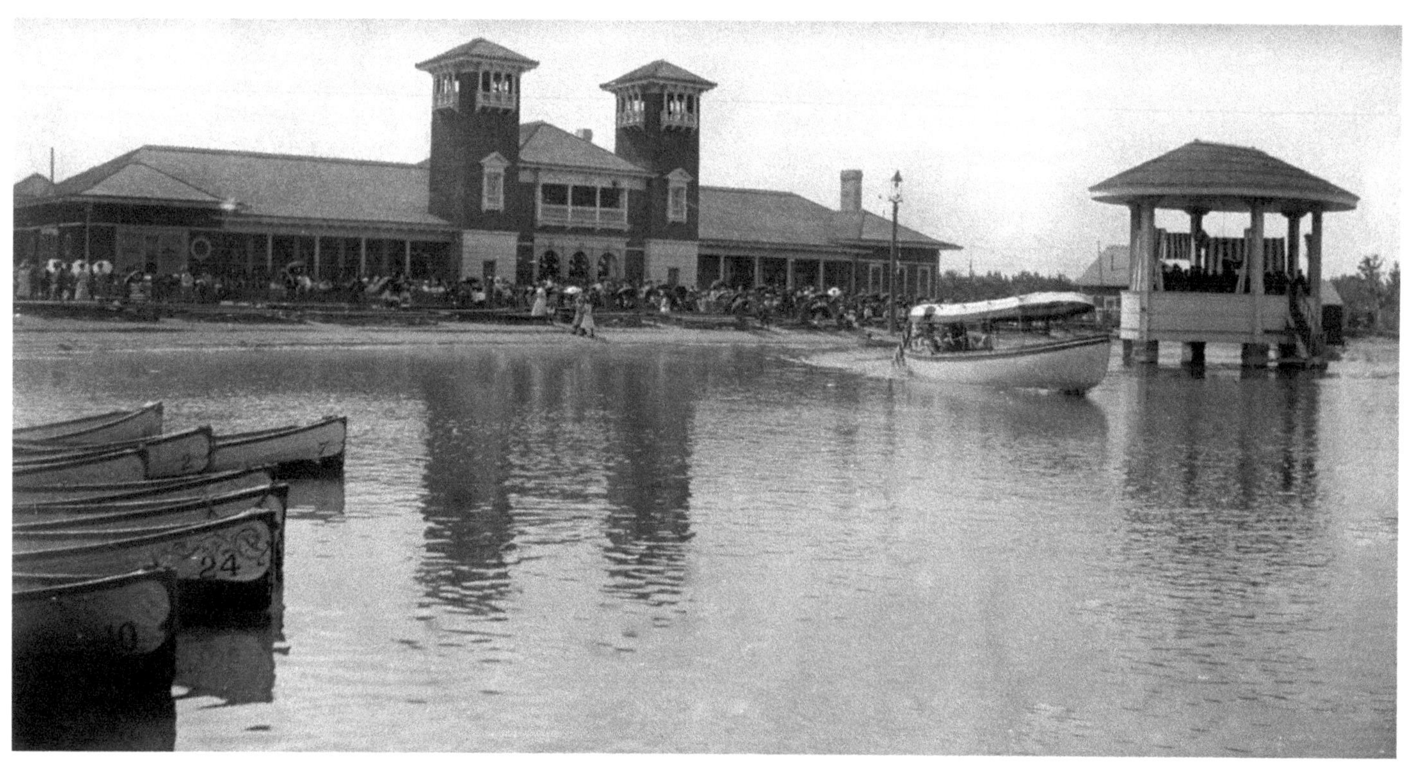

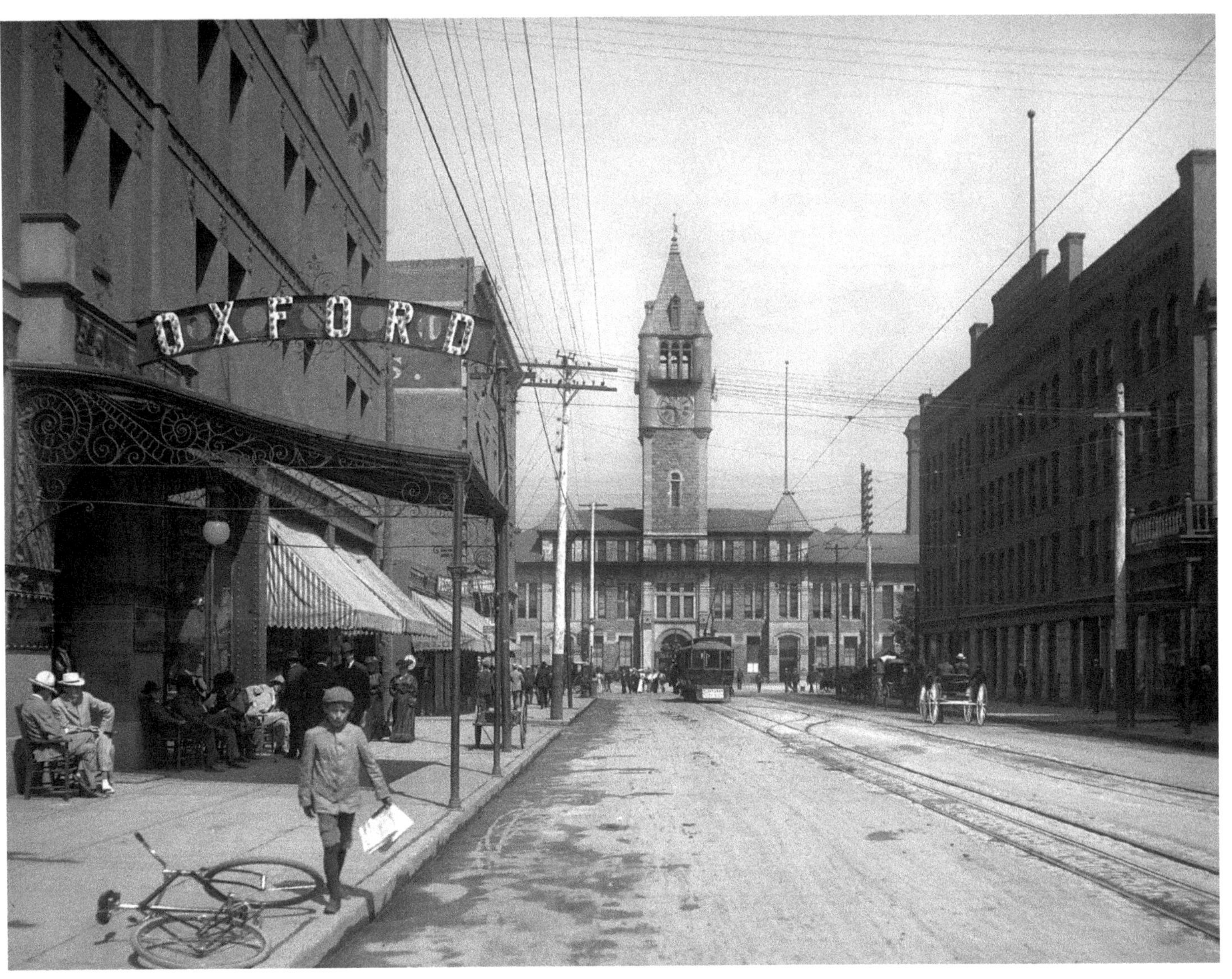

In this view of Union Station, rebuilt after the 1894 fire, a trolley takes on passengers near the Oxford Hotel built in 1891 by Frank Edbrooke. Union Station was rebuilt again in 1912 with the central section becoming today's Union Station.

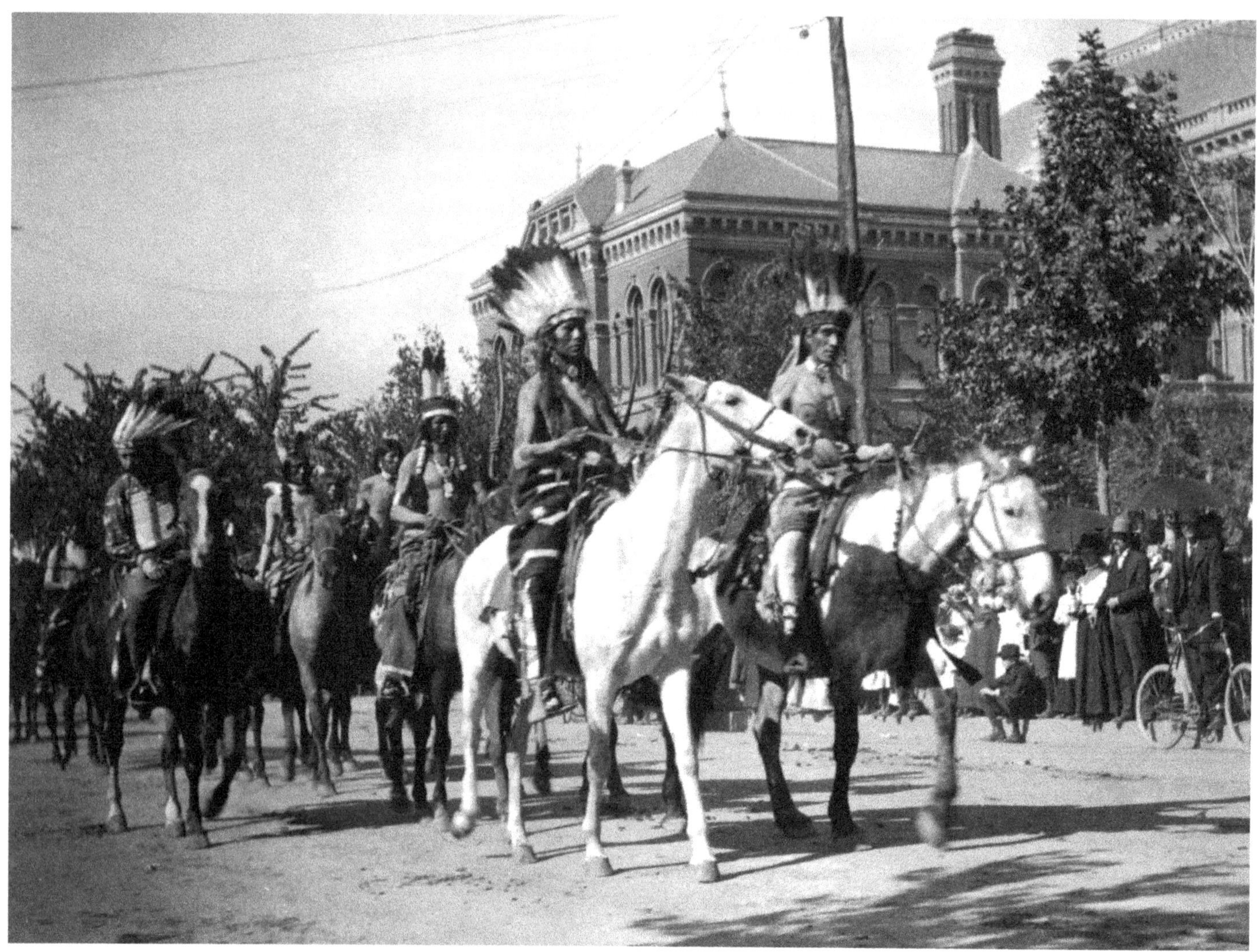

Ute Indians in headdress and headbands ride their horses past the old Denver High School in a Festival of Mountain and Plain parade. The festival was created by the Denver Chamber of Commerce to boost the Denver economy and promote civic pride following the silver panic of 1893. The festival was repeated annually through 1902.

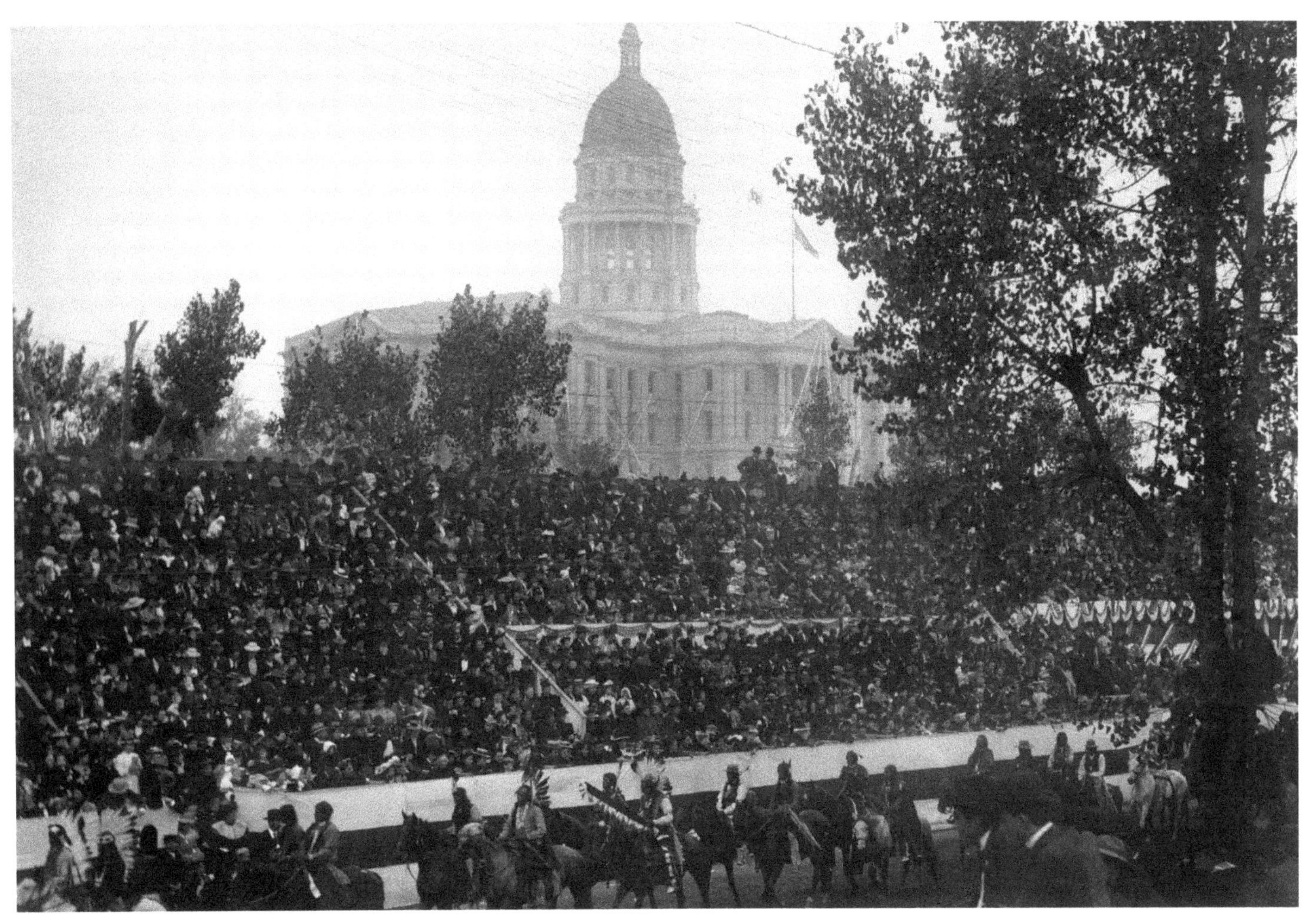

Spectators crowd bleachers set up in front of the Colorado state capitol to watch a parade at the Festival of Mountain and Plain. Ute Indians ride their horses past the grandstands.

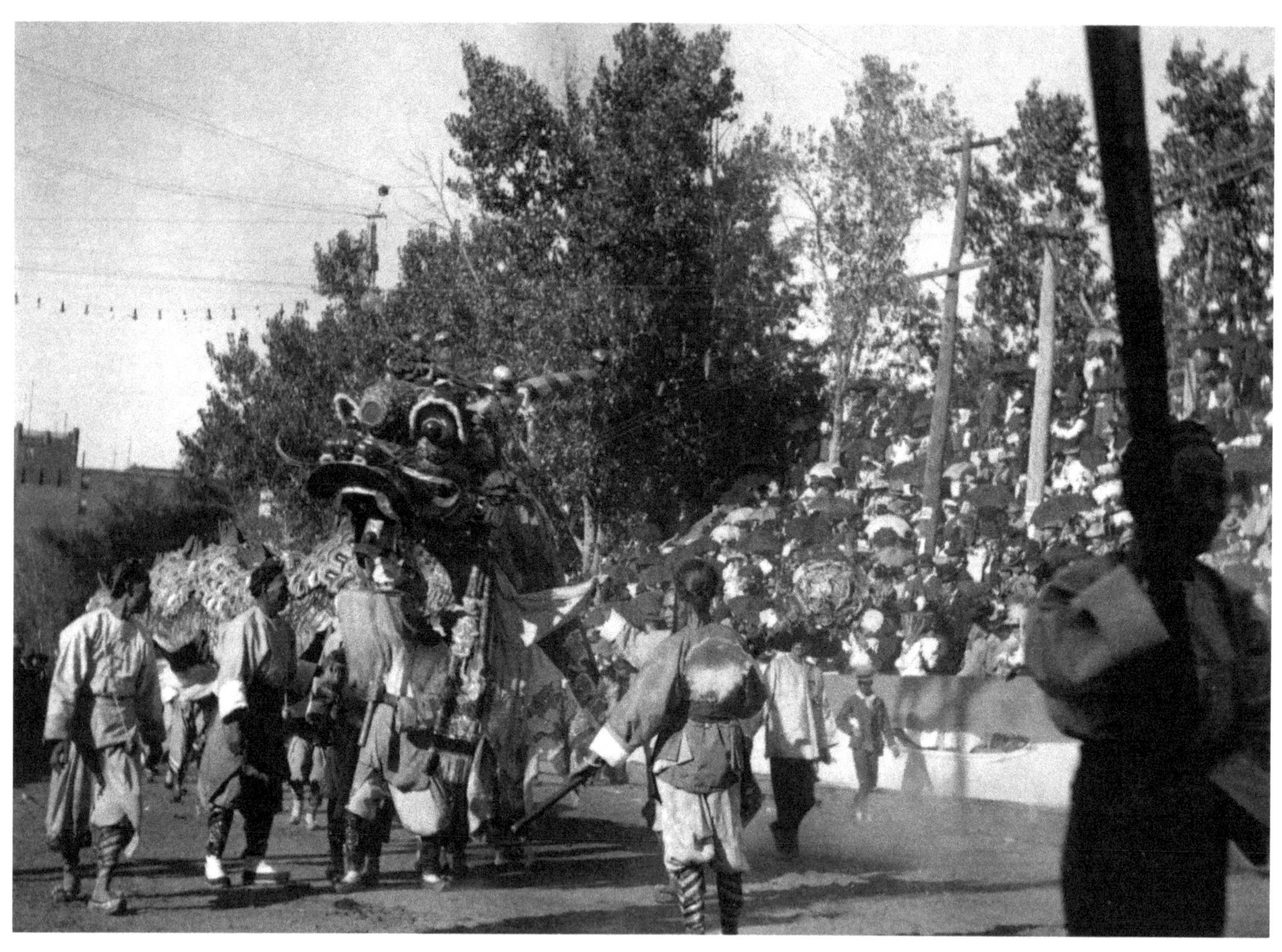

Members of the Denver Chinese community surround a Chinese dragon as it dances through the street during the Festival of Mountain and Plain.

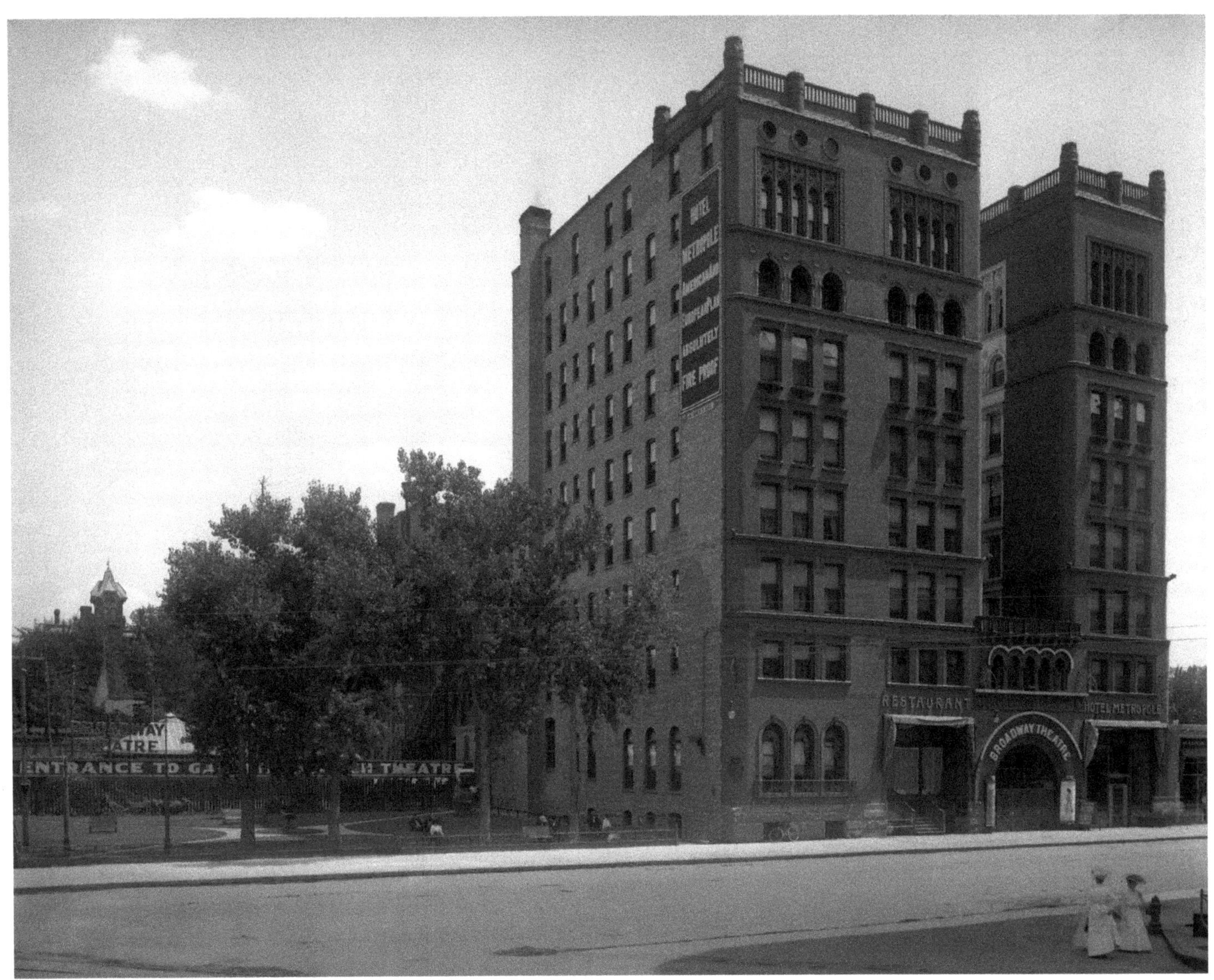

The Hotel Metropole opened in 1891, located at 18th Avenue and Broadway. The building housed the well-known Broadway Theatre. In 1926 the building was combined with, and incorporated into, the Cosmopolitan Hotel.

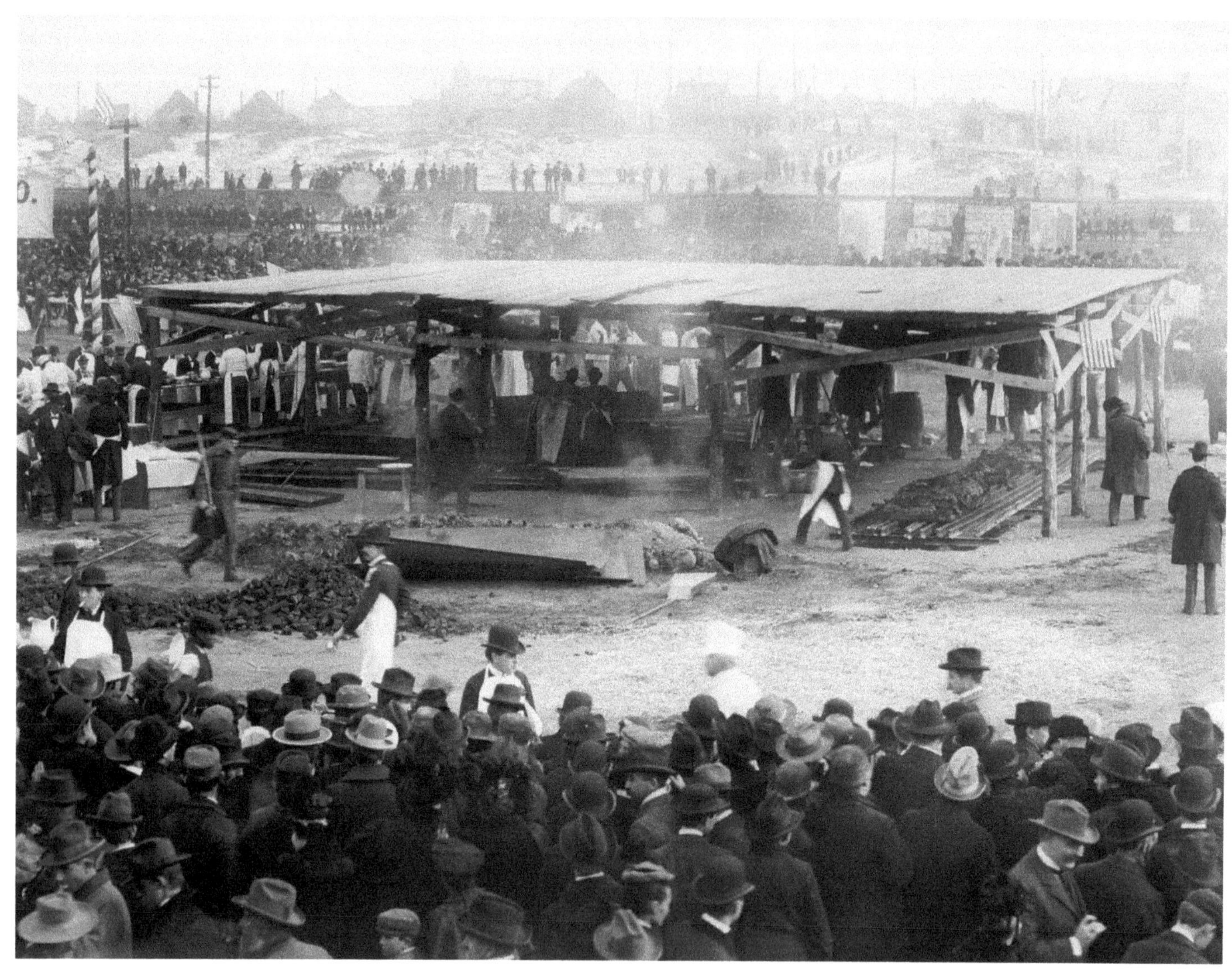

This barbecue at the Denver Union Stock Yards was probably held as a promotional event for the play "Shall We Forgive Her" by Frank Harvey. Women prepare slabs of meat for the well-dressed crowd. Posters in the Distance read "Shall We Forgive Her."

Constructed by the Youngstown Bridge Company at a cost of $367,068, the 14th Street Viaduct was a joint project of the cities of Denver and Highlands (later incorporated into Denver). The bridge had 63 spans and totaled 1,467 feet. It was built to carry wagons, streetcars, and pedestrians across the South Platte River.

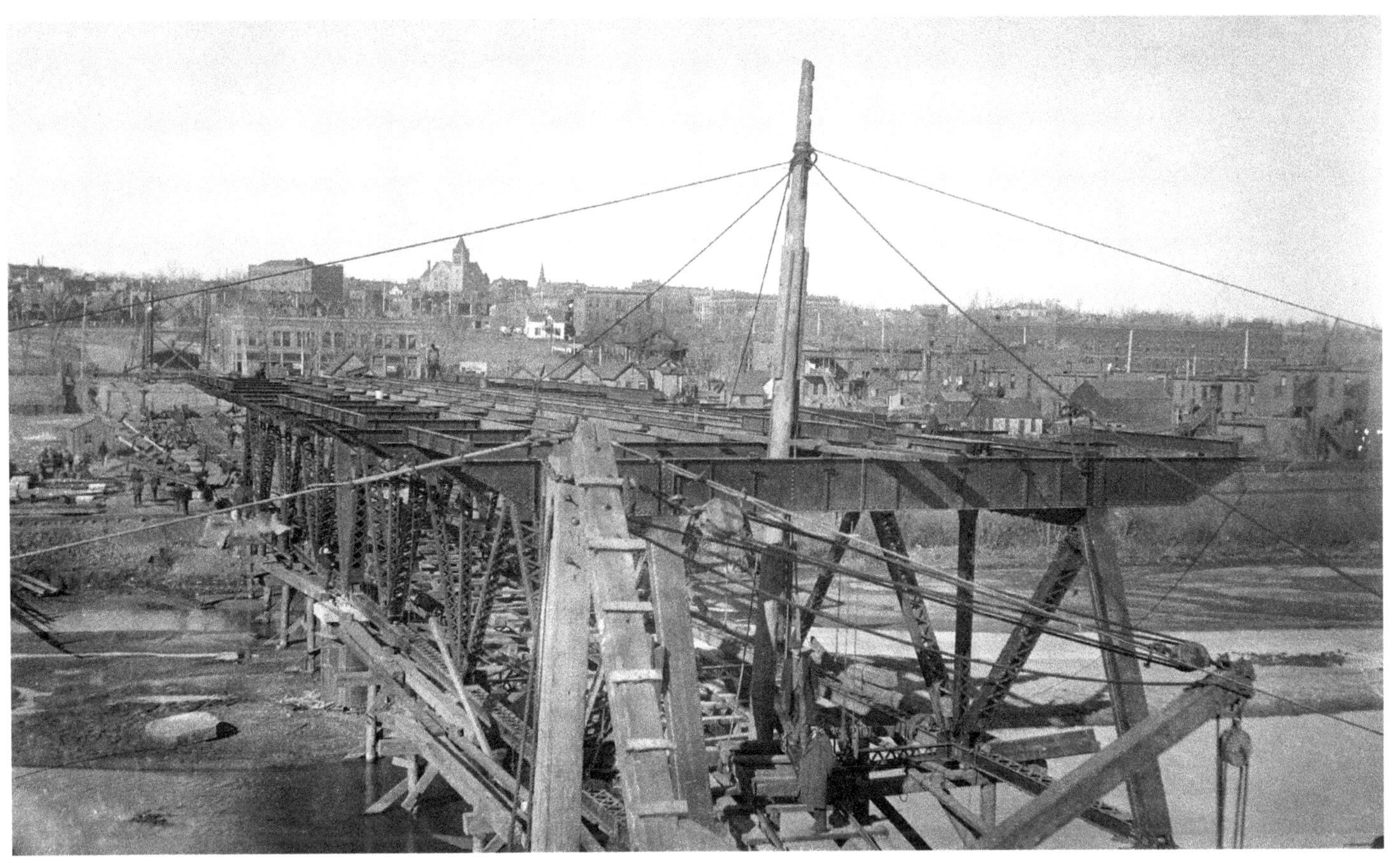

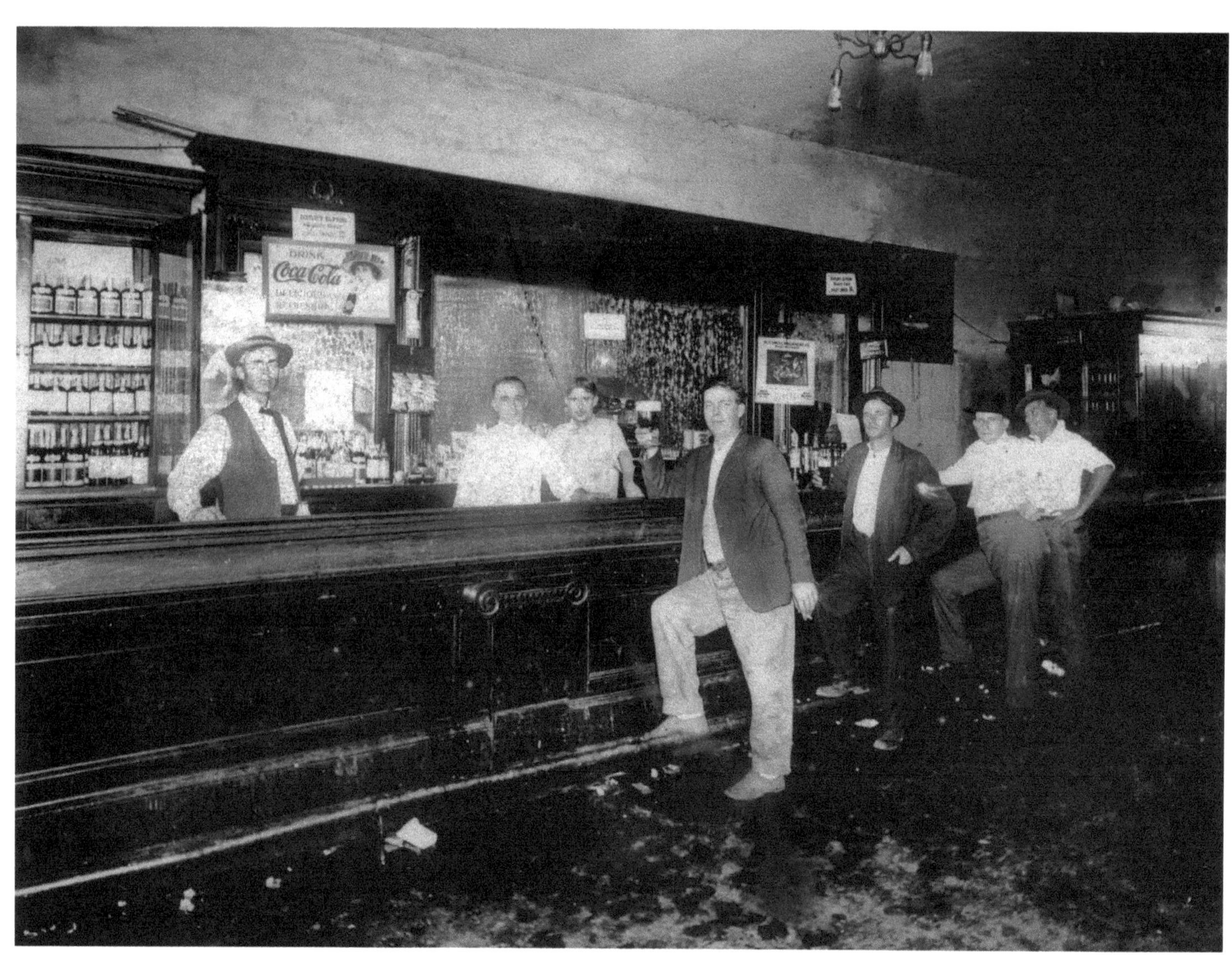

In this image, a bartender, waiters, and customers pose in an unidentified bar in Denver.

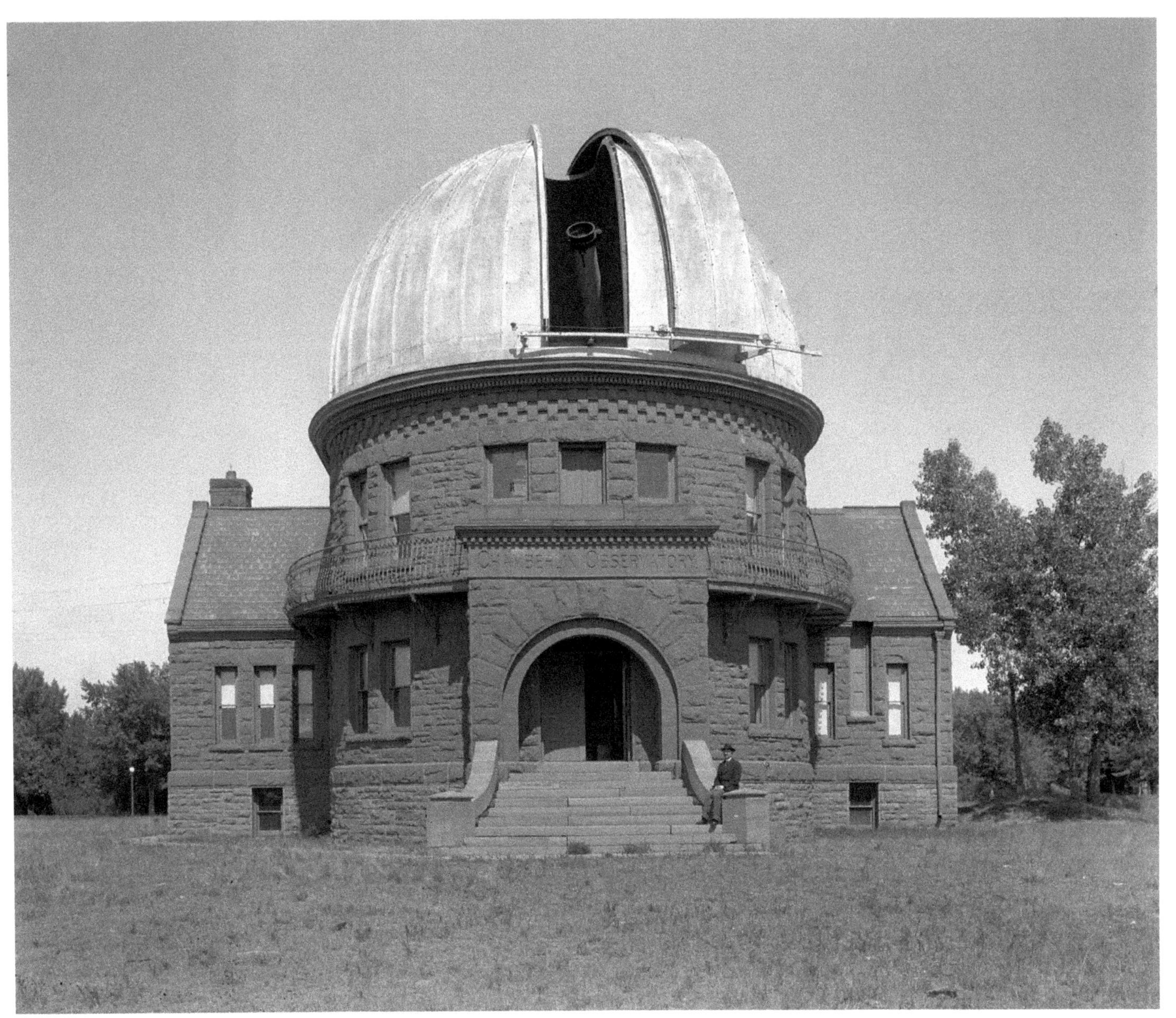

The Chamberlin Observatory at the University of Denver was designed by Robert S. Roeschlaub and built in 1890. It houses the famous 20-inch Alvan Clark-Saegmuller refractor telescope still in use today.

The Iliff School of Theology opened as a department of the University of Denver in 1892. It closed temporarily in the early twentieth century before reopening as an independent institution in 1910.

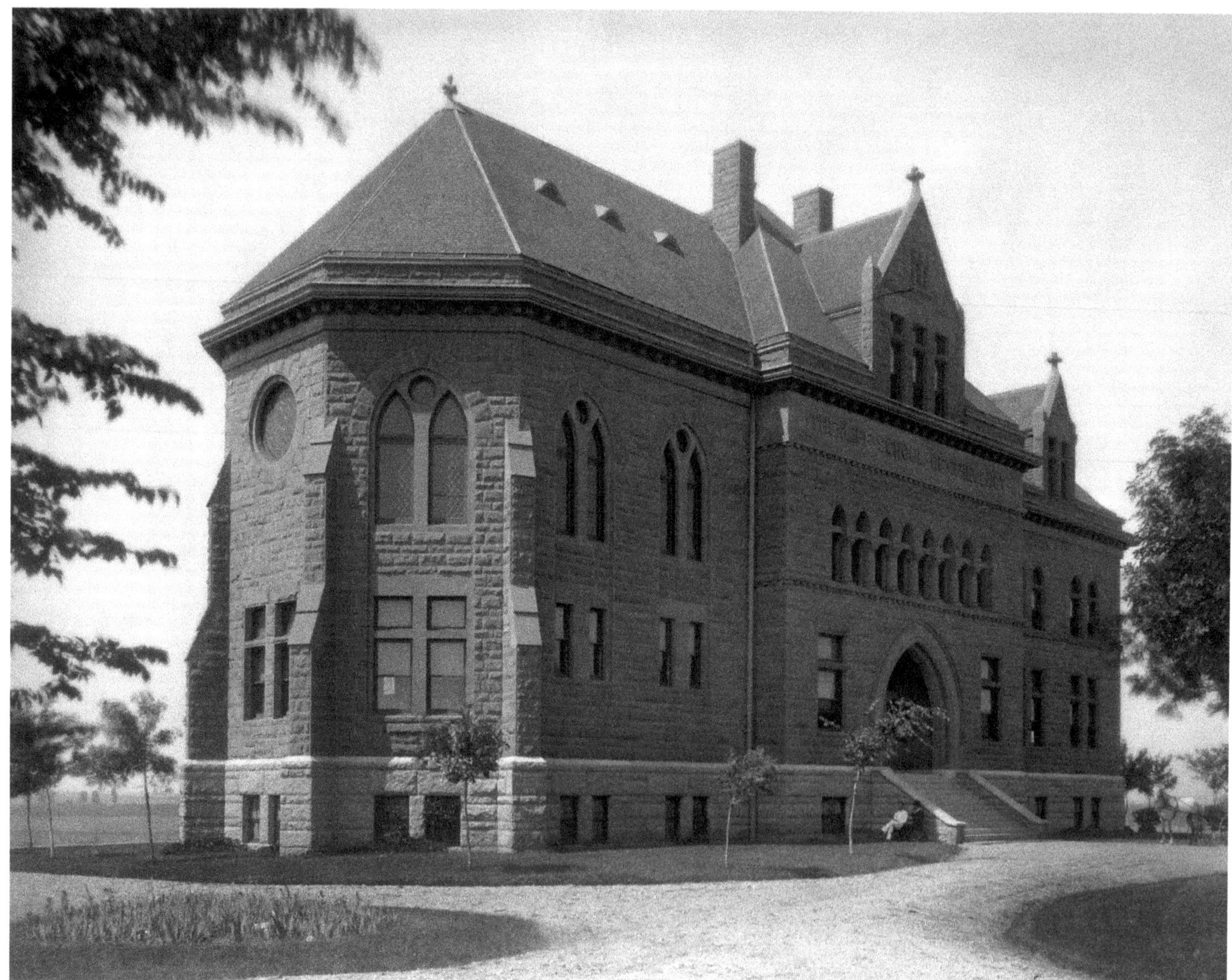

The Birth of the City Beautiful

1900–1919

Early in the twentieth century, farming and ranching began to dominate the Colorado economy and would soon overtake the declining mining industry. Denver with its many railroads was a hub for transportation and tourism as well as a supply center for the mining industry. During this period the city also became a regional center for meat, grain, and sugar beet processing and distribution.

In 1902, voters approved a constitutional amendment creating the City and County of Denver, previously a part of Arapahoe County. The amendment also permitted Denver to annex several small towns resulting in a city and county of 58.7 square miles. The first mayor elected under this amendment was Robert Speer, in 1904. Speer was to become Denver's most powerful mayor. Immediately after his election he pushed through a new city charter that established a strong mayoral form of city government and created an arts commission. These would provide the framework for his vision of a "Paris on the Platte."

During the administrations of Mayor Speer, Denver was transformed from a dusty, polluted city to a city of beautiful parks, wide landscaped boulevards, and impressive civic architecture. In 1912 voters approved a city charter amendment that allowed Denver to acquire land for mountain parks. Eventually the Mountain Parks System would include 14,000 acres scattered over 380 square miles with thirty-one named parks and city-owned bison and elk herds.

The Denver Chamber of Commerce worked to attract many significant conventions to Denver during this period. In 1908, the National Democratic Convention came to Denver with the new City Auditorium as its venue. Delegates flocked to the city from all over the country allowing Denver to promote both the city and the state. In 1913 the 32nd Triennial Conclave of the Knights Templar came to Denver and a gigantic statue of a knight was constructed straddling Champa Street near the post office.

Significant buildings constructed between 1900 and 1919 include the Colorado Telephone Building (1903), the Denver Dry Goods Company (1905), the U.S. Mint (1906), the Gas and Electric Building (1910), City Auditorium (1908), Saint John's Cathedral (1911), the Daniels and Fisher Tower (1912), and Immaculate Conception Cathedral (1912).

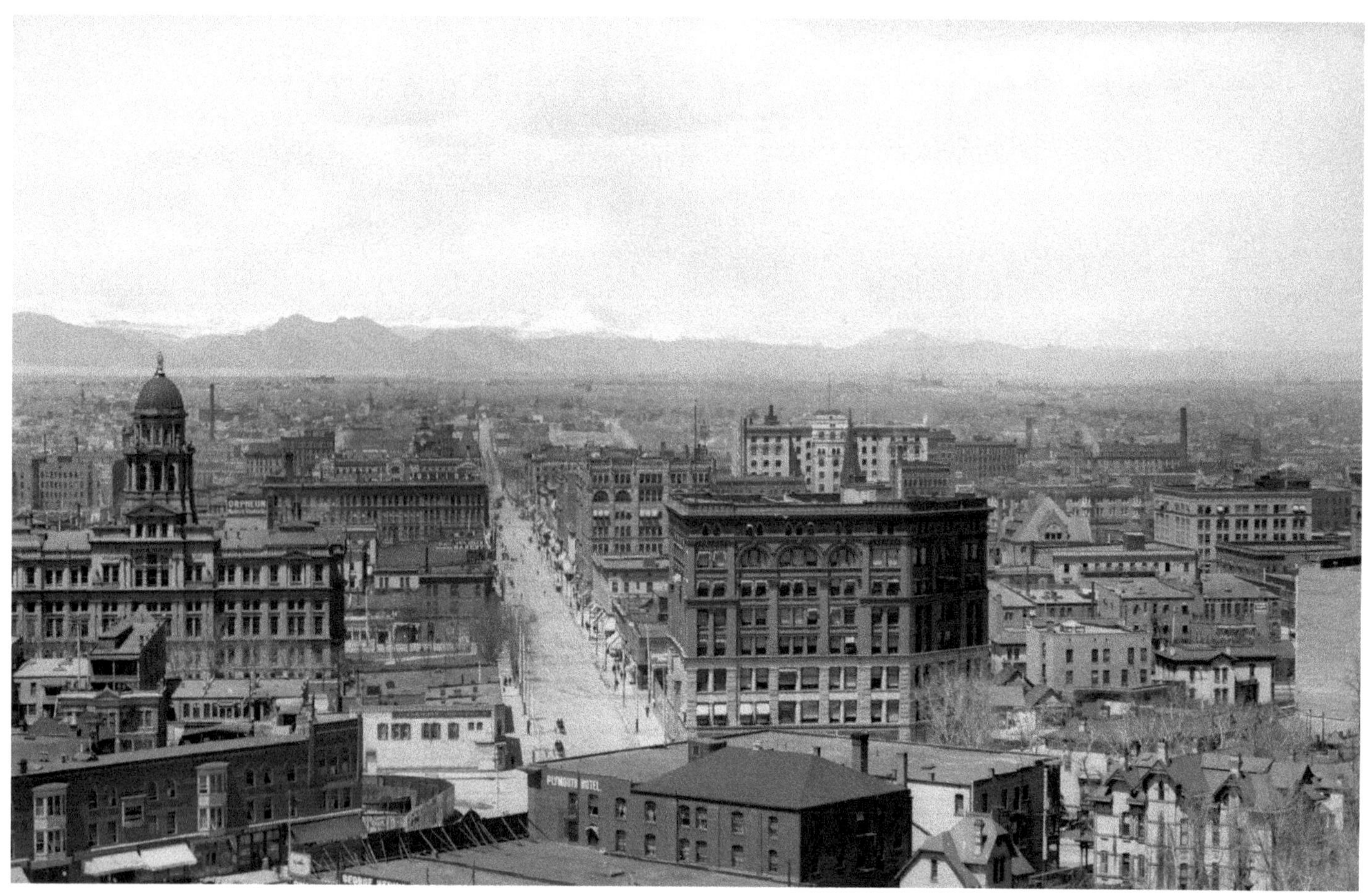

In this view of Denver, 16th Street is in the center of the picture. On the left is the Arapahoe County Courthouse and on the right is the Majestic Building. Behind that is the Kittredge Building. Visible in the distance is the front range of the Rockies.

The Gano Clothing Company, one of Denver's finest men's stores, did business in the Steele Building located at the corner of 16th and Stout streets.

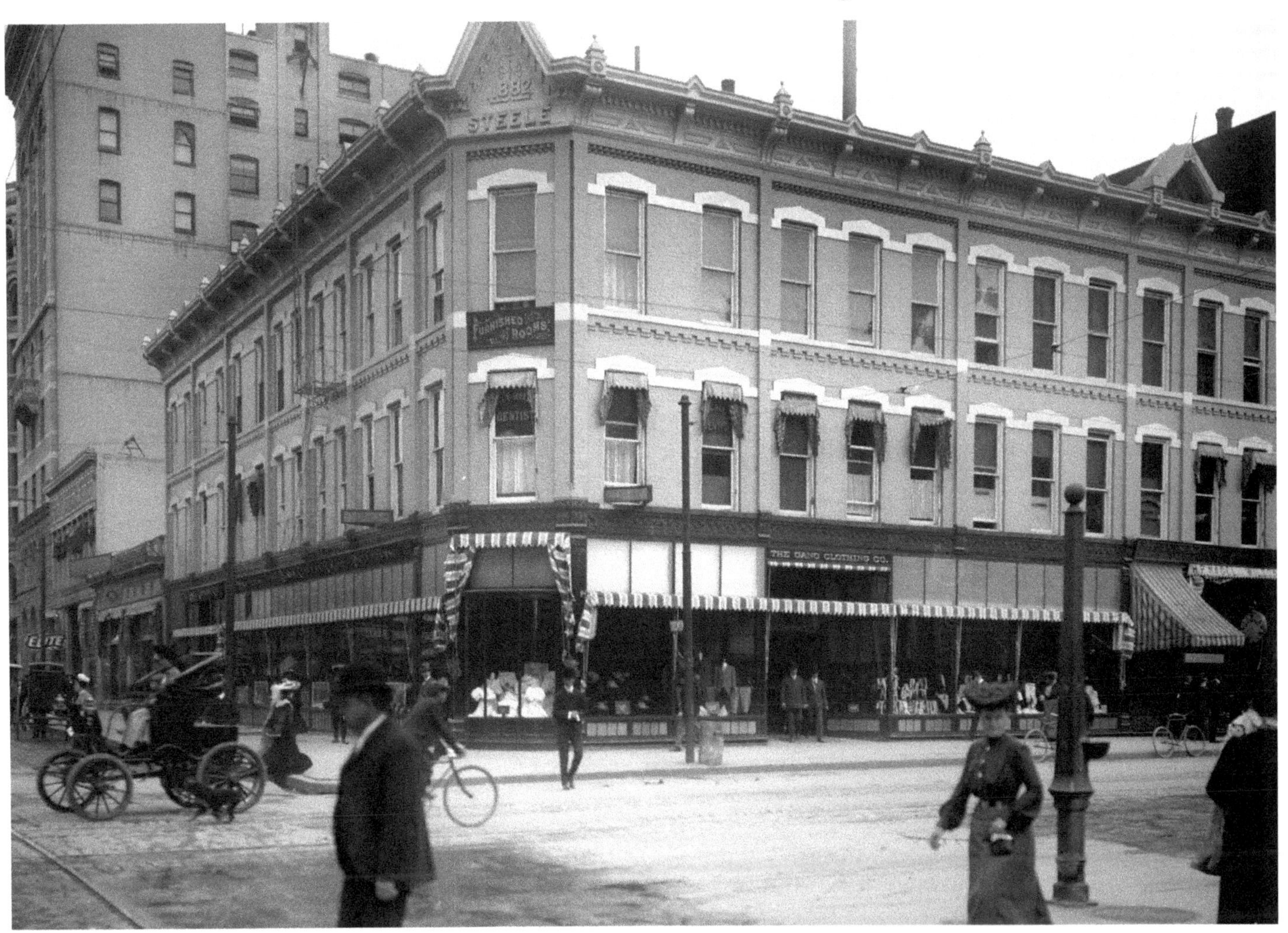

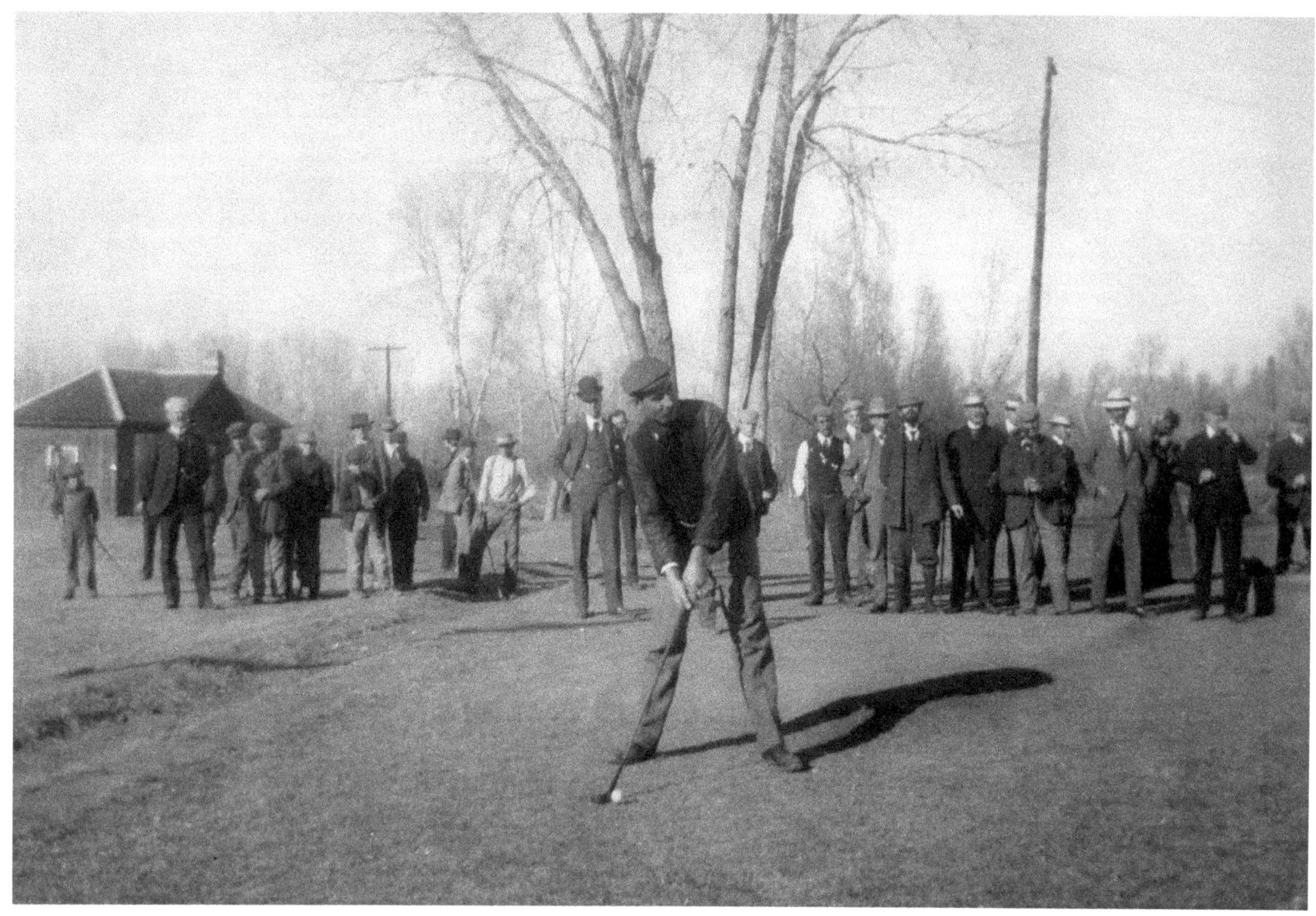

British golfer Harry Vardon was one of golf's first international superstars. He is shown here at the Overland Country Club golf course in December 1900 during an exhibition tour.

The cornerstone for the Denver City Auditorium was laid in September 1907 and the building was dedicated June 1, 1908. Mayor Speer and the Denver Chamber of Commerce raised $100,000 to celebrate both the opening of the new building and the Democratic National Convention, Denver's only national political convention.

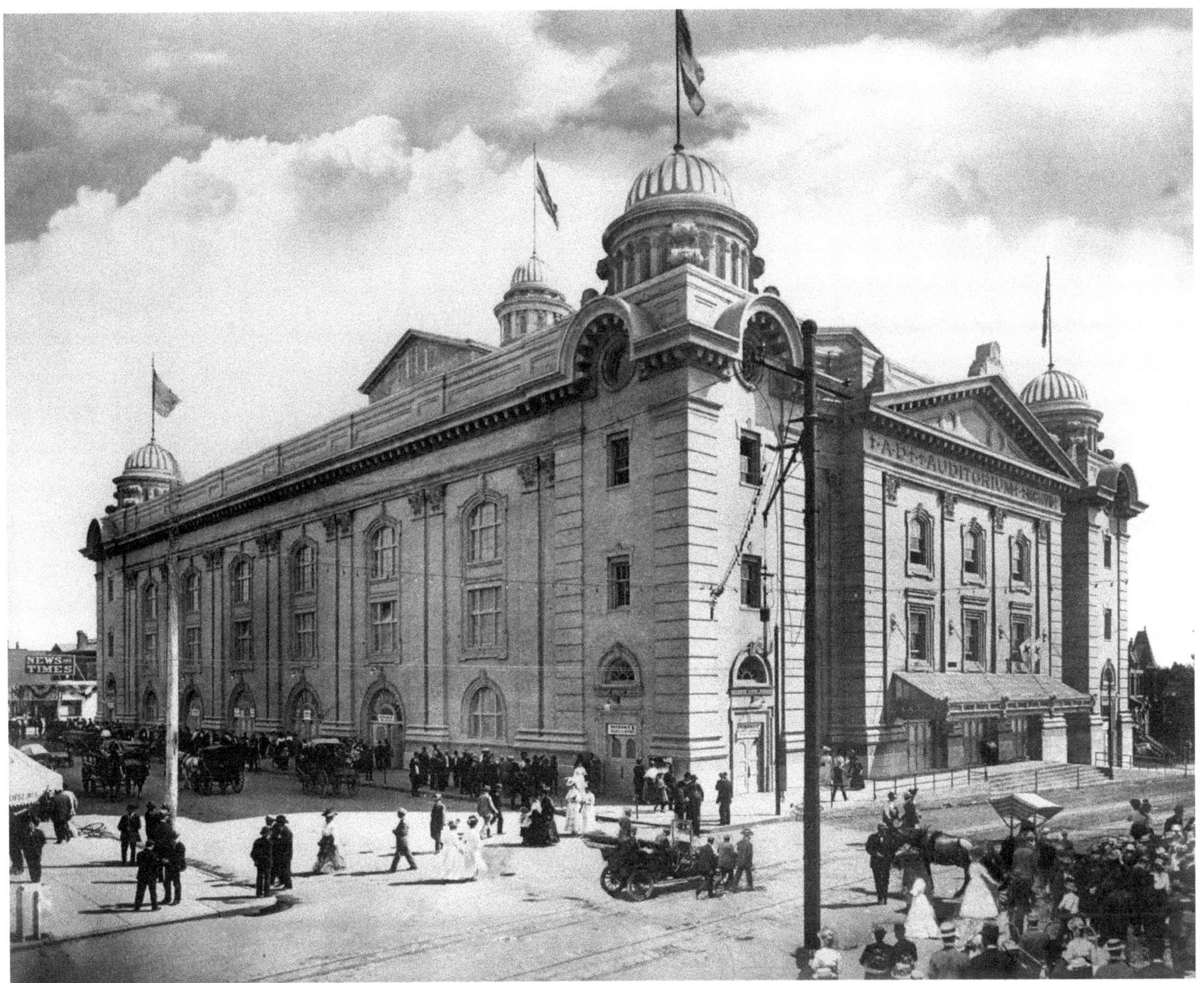

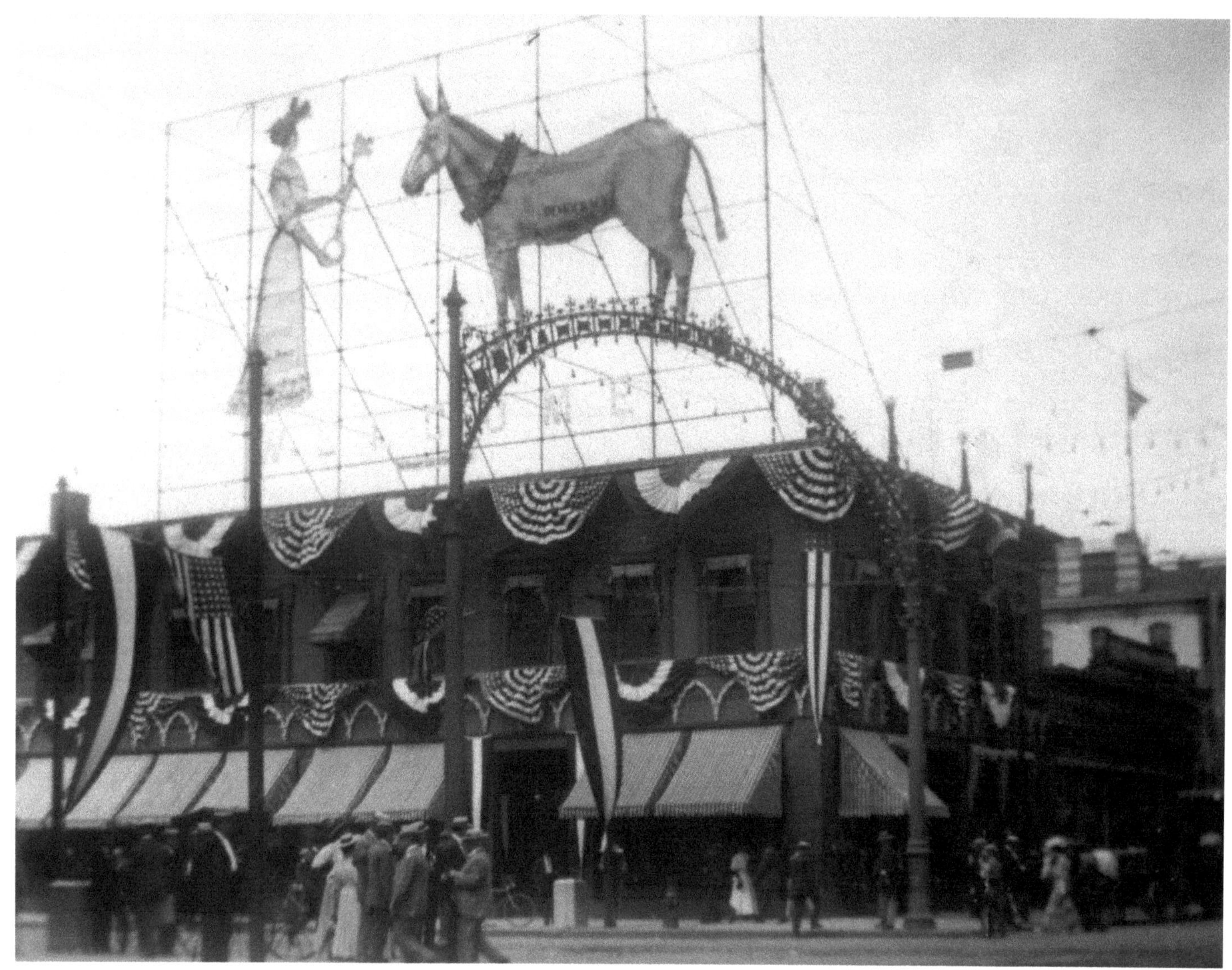

This arch was erected for the 1908 Democratic Convention held at the Denver City Auditorium. The sign shows a woman offering the key to the city to a "Democratic" donkey. William Jennings Bryan became the Democratic nominee for president during the convention.

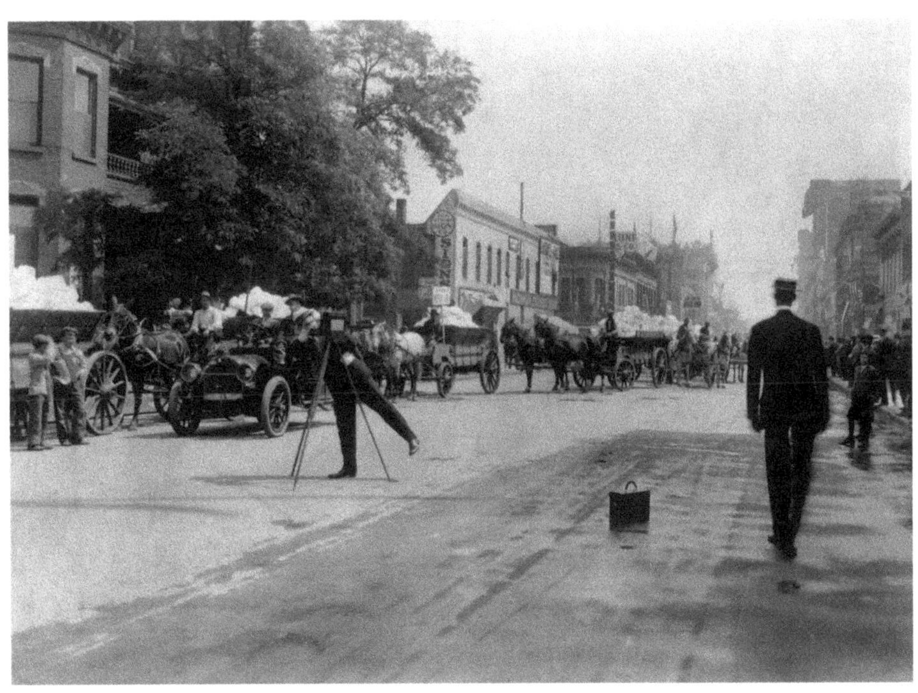

Wagons filled with snow from Rollins Pass are on display on 15th Street probably during the 1908 Democratic Convention. The snow came from the Denver, Northwestern, and Pacific Railway's Moffat Road, the highest railroad line ever built in the United States.

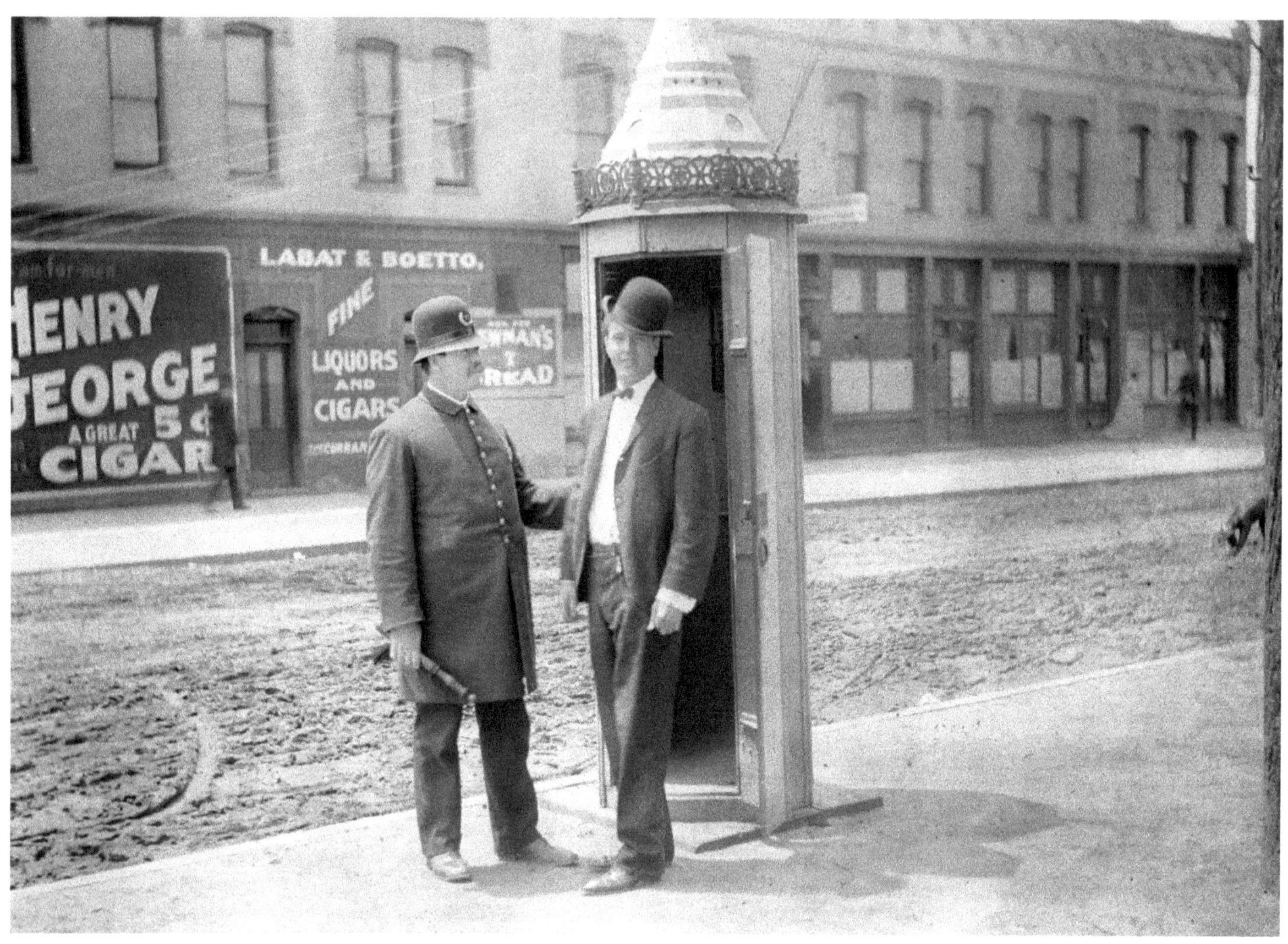

A Denver policeman detains an intoxicated man in front of a "drunk tank" on Larimer Street in 1905.

The Daniels and Fisher Department Store was one of the city's finest retail establishments for many years. In this photograph men on horseback ride down 16th Street past the department store, which has an enormous United States flag draped across its facade.

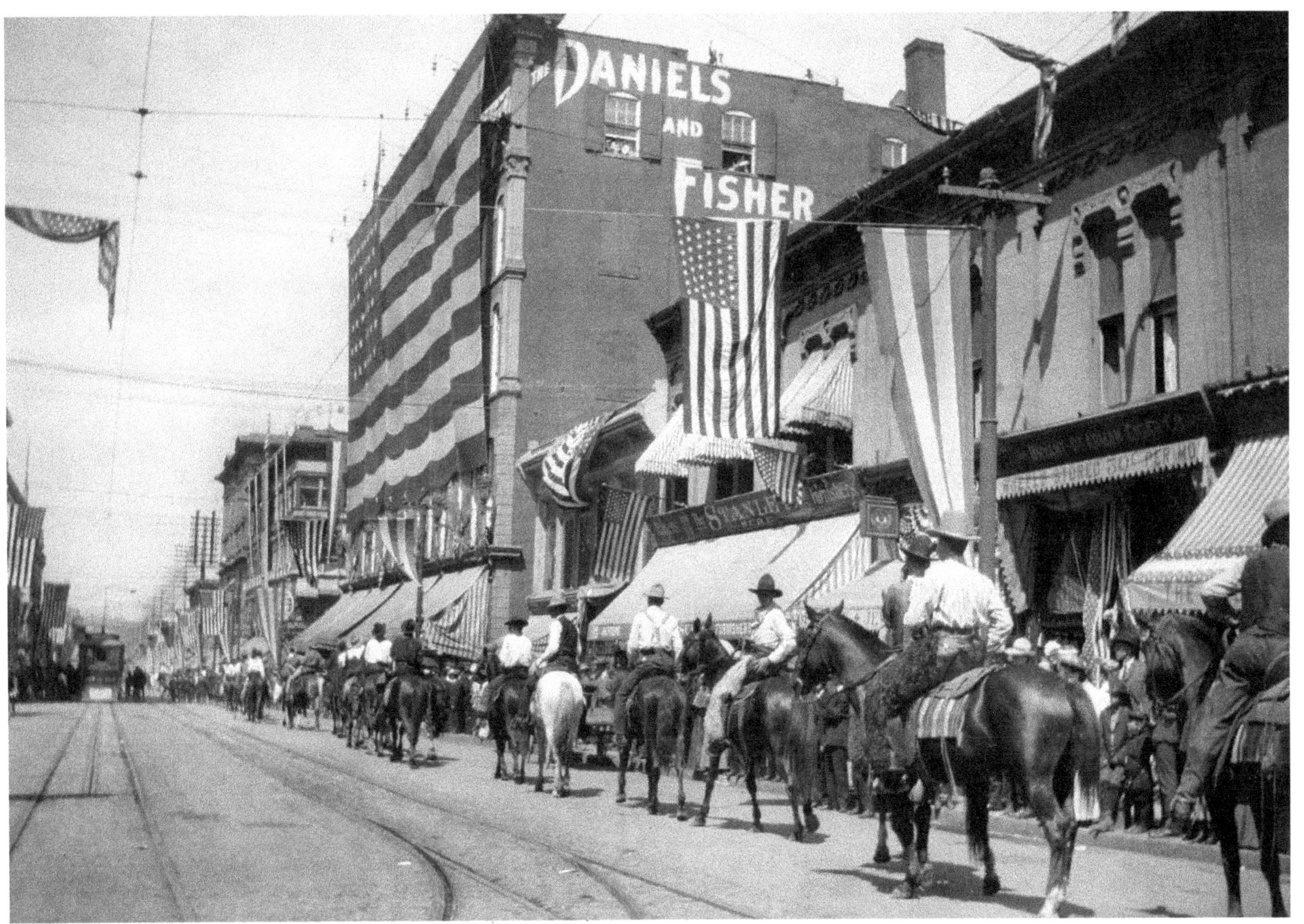

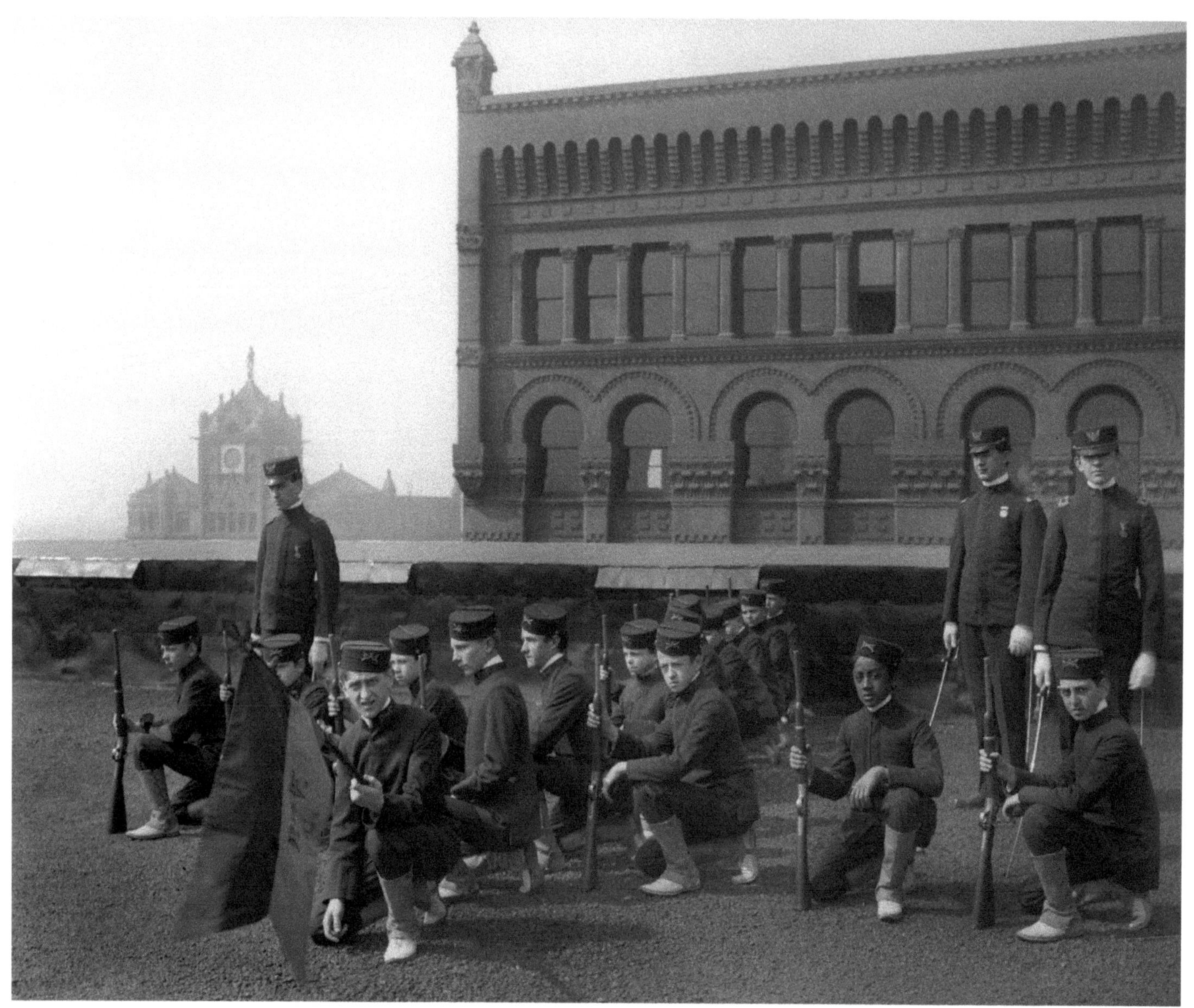

In this photograph, members of the Daniels and Fisher cadets, composed of "cash boys," train on the roof of the store. Cash boys carried a customer's merchandise and cash to an "inspector" and returned with the wrapped merchandise and the customer's change.

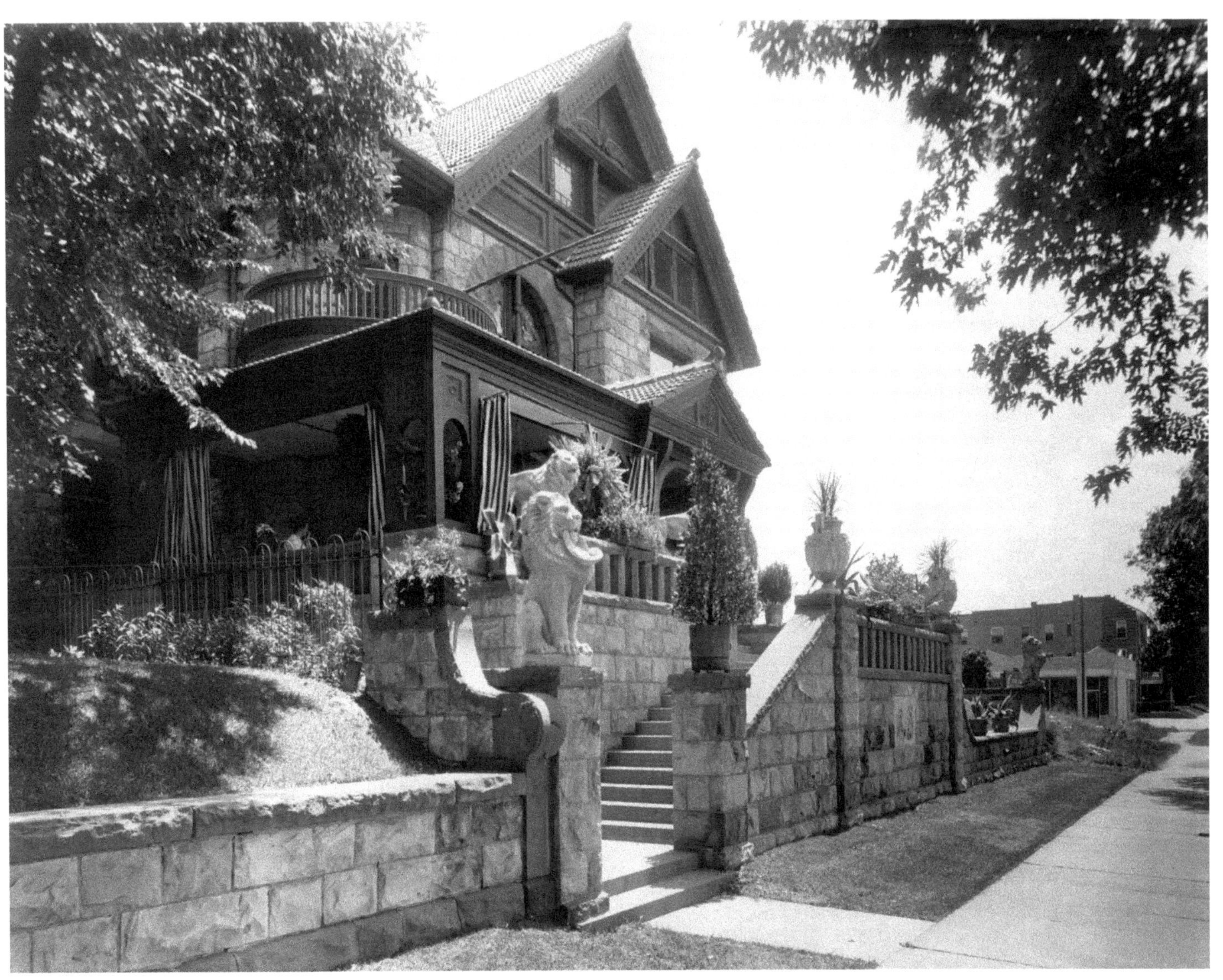

This house at 1340 Pennsylvania Street was the home of James J. and Margaret (Molly) Tobin Brown. J. J. Brown bought the house, designed by William Lang, in 1894. A social activist, Margaret Brown was an advocate for a juvenile justice system that would radically change the way juvenile criminals were treated. Scorned by the Denver elite, the "Unsinkable" Molly Brown would later become a national hero during the sinking of the *Titanic.*

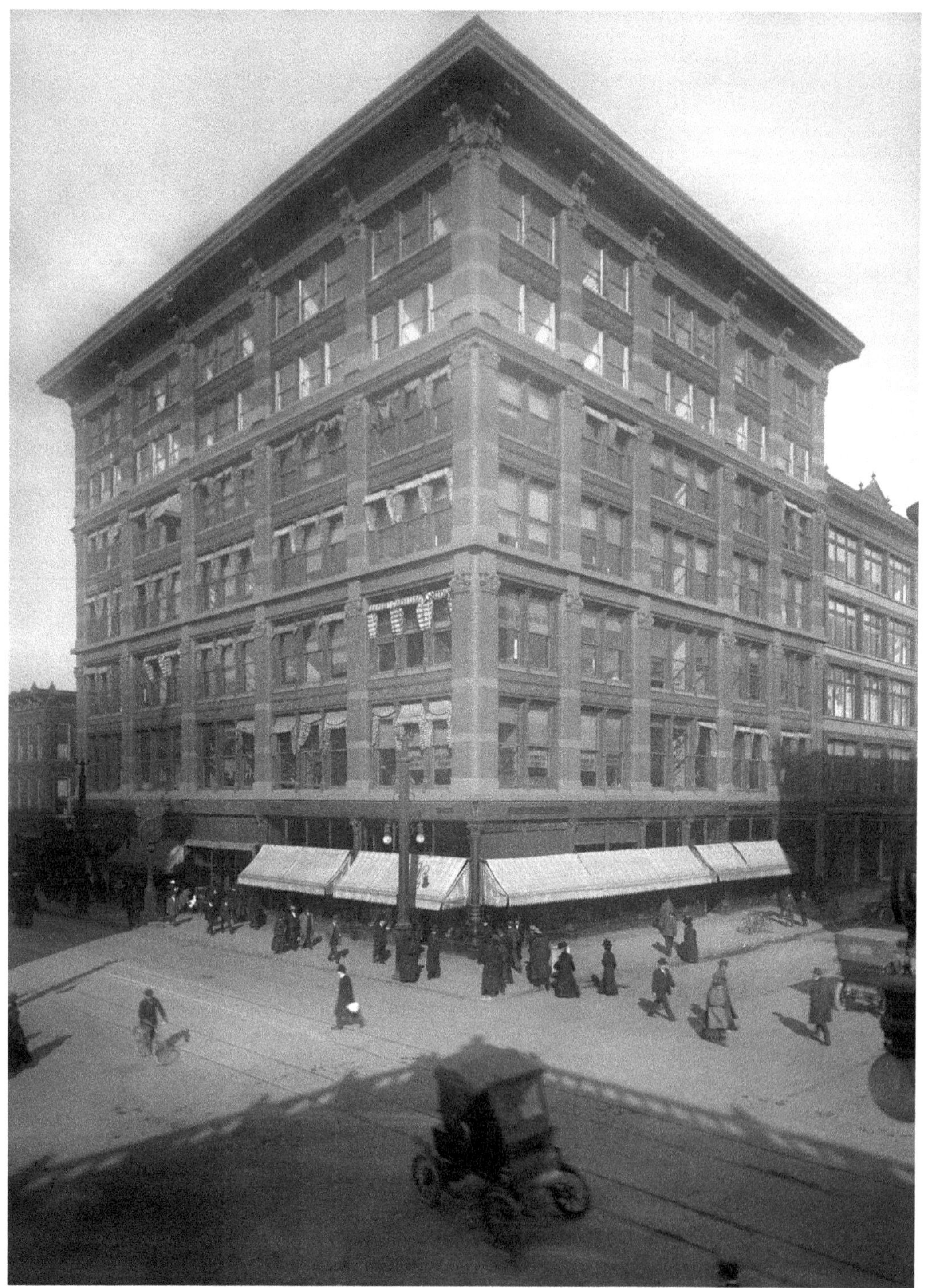

The Hayden, Dickinson, & Feldhauser building was built in 1891 as a retail building and then expanded in 1909 when several more floors were added. It was later renamed the Colorado Building and in 1937 it was given an art deco facade.

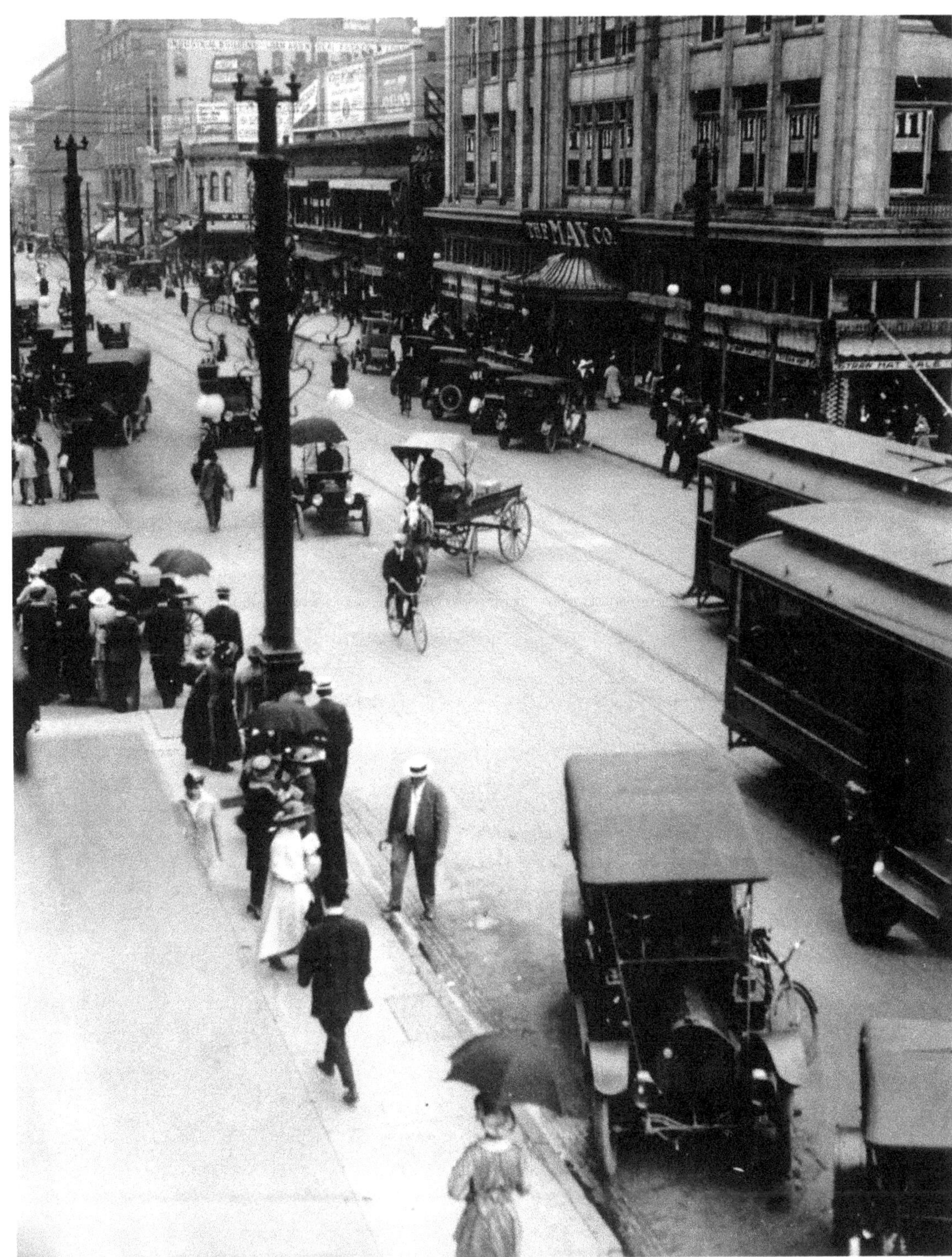

This early 1900s view of 16th Street in the Central Business District shows the transition in the city from horse-drawn vehicles to automobiles and electric trolley cars.

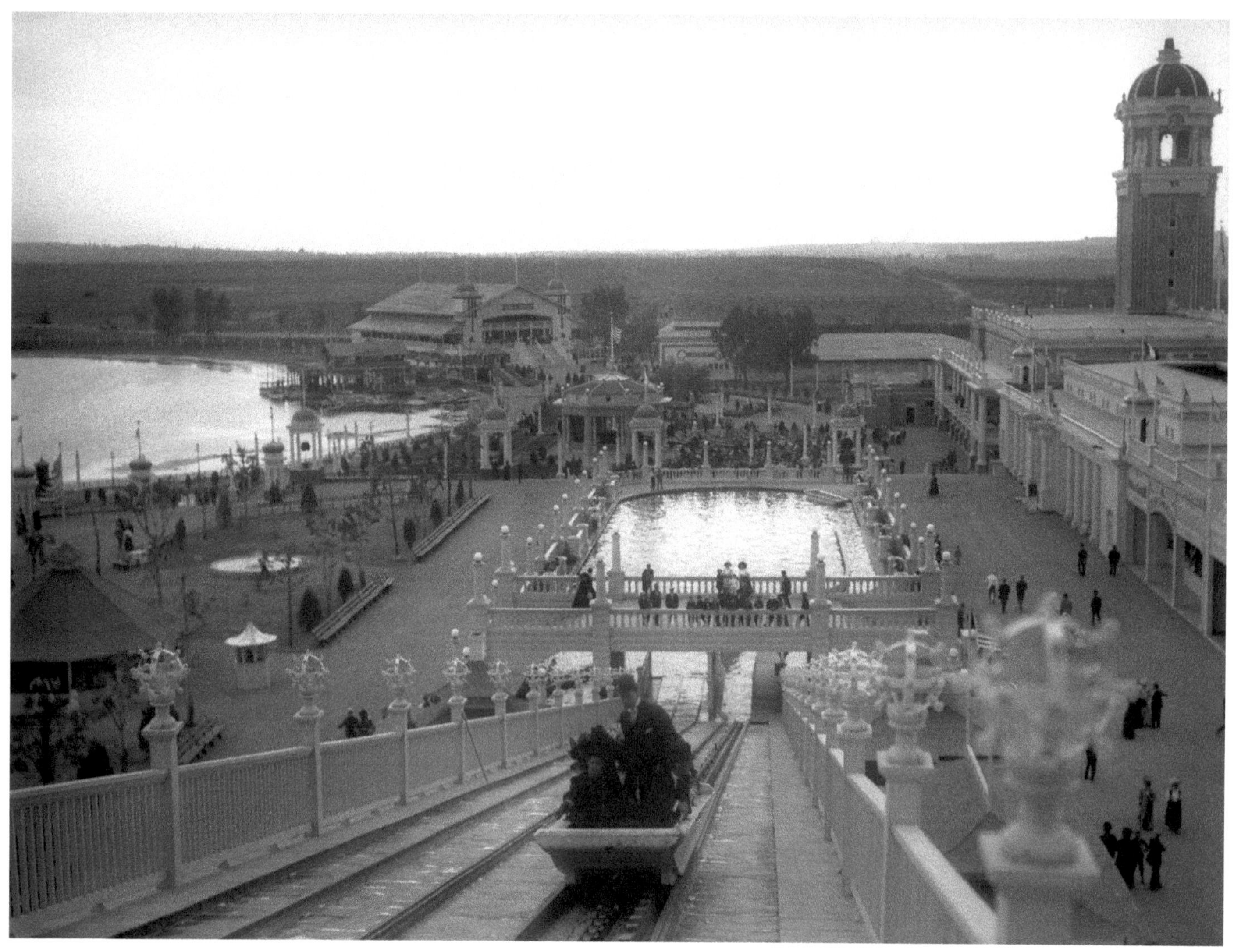

The White City, an amusement park, was inaugurated by Mayor Robert Speer in 1908. This view is from atop the "Big Splash." The park, located right outside the city limits, was a favorite of Denver residents. It was later renamed Lakeside Amusement Park and is still in operation today.

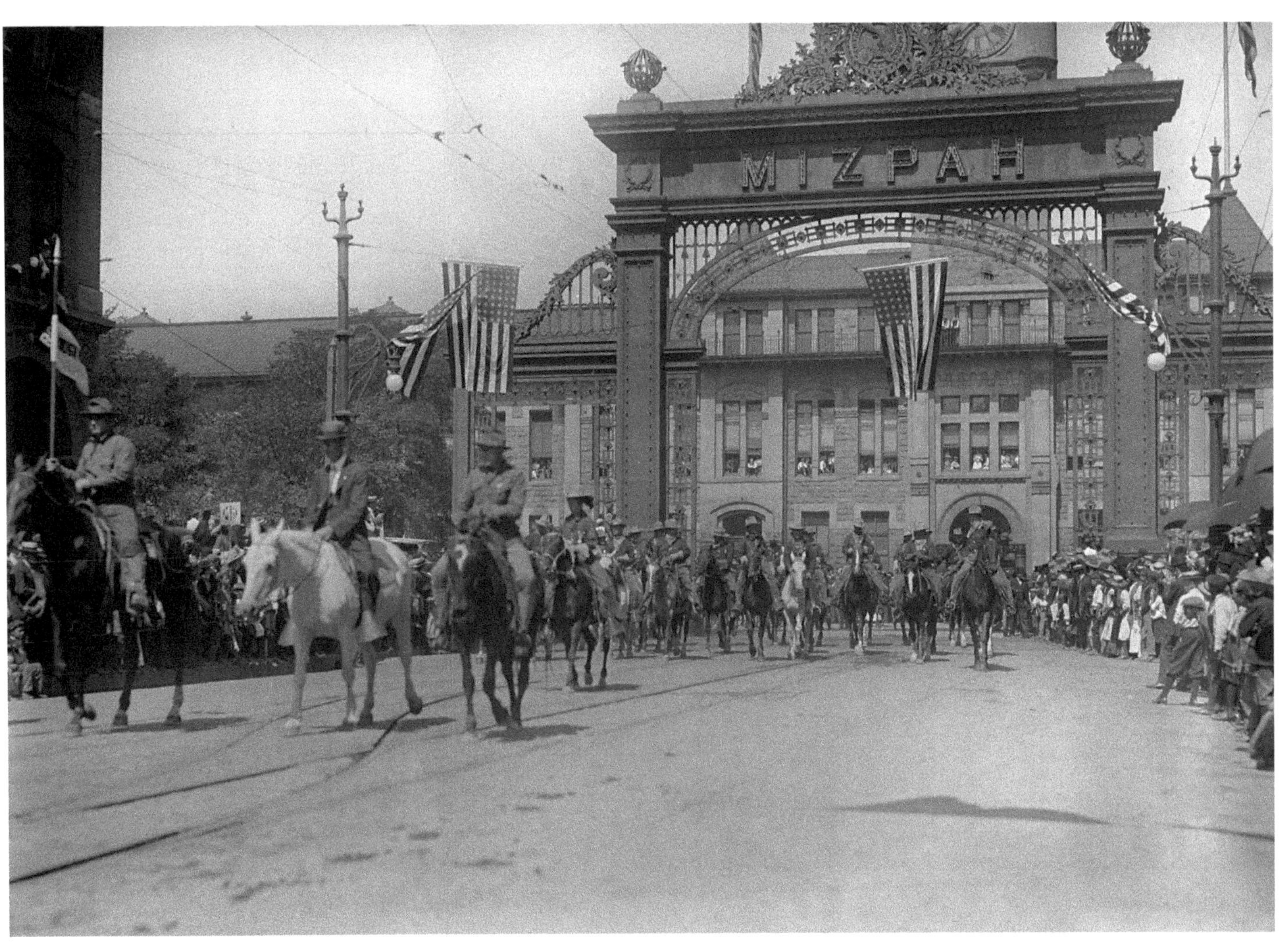

In this photograph taken in 1912 or later, veteran members of the Rough Riders, the 1st U.S. Volunteer Cavalry Regiment during the Spanish American War, ride through the Welcome Arch in front of Union Station. The Welcome or Mizpah Arch was dedicated July 4, 1906. Illuminated with 1,600 light bulbs, it weighed more than 70 tons. The arch was removed in 1931 because it was considered a traffic hazard.

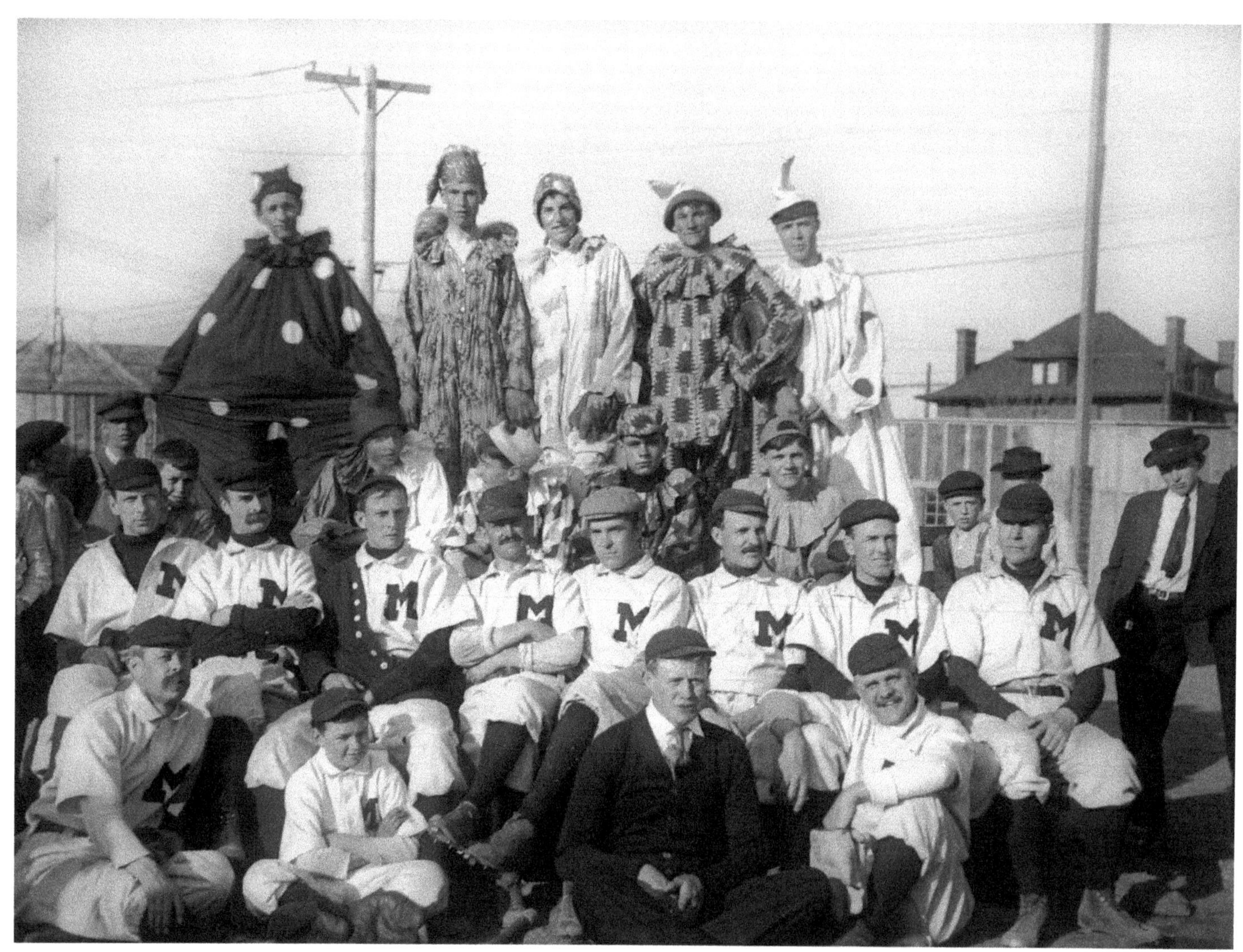

With students dressed as clowns, the teacher's baseball team poses for the camera at Manual Training High School located at 27th and Franklin streets.

In this evening view, 16th Street is decorated for the holiday season. The Daniels and Fisher Tower, illuminated and decorated with lights, was commissioned by William Cooke Daniels and completed in 1909. Built in the style of the campanile of St. Mark's Cathedral in Venice, it was the tallest building west of the Mississippi at the time.

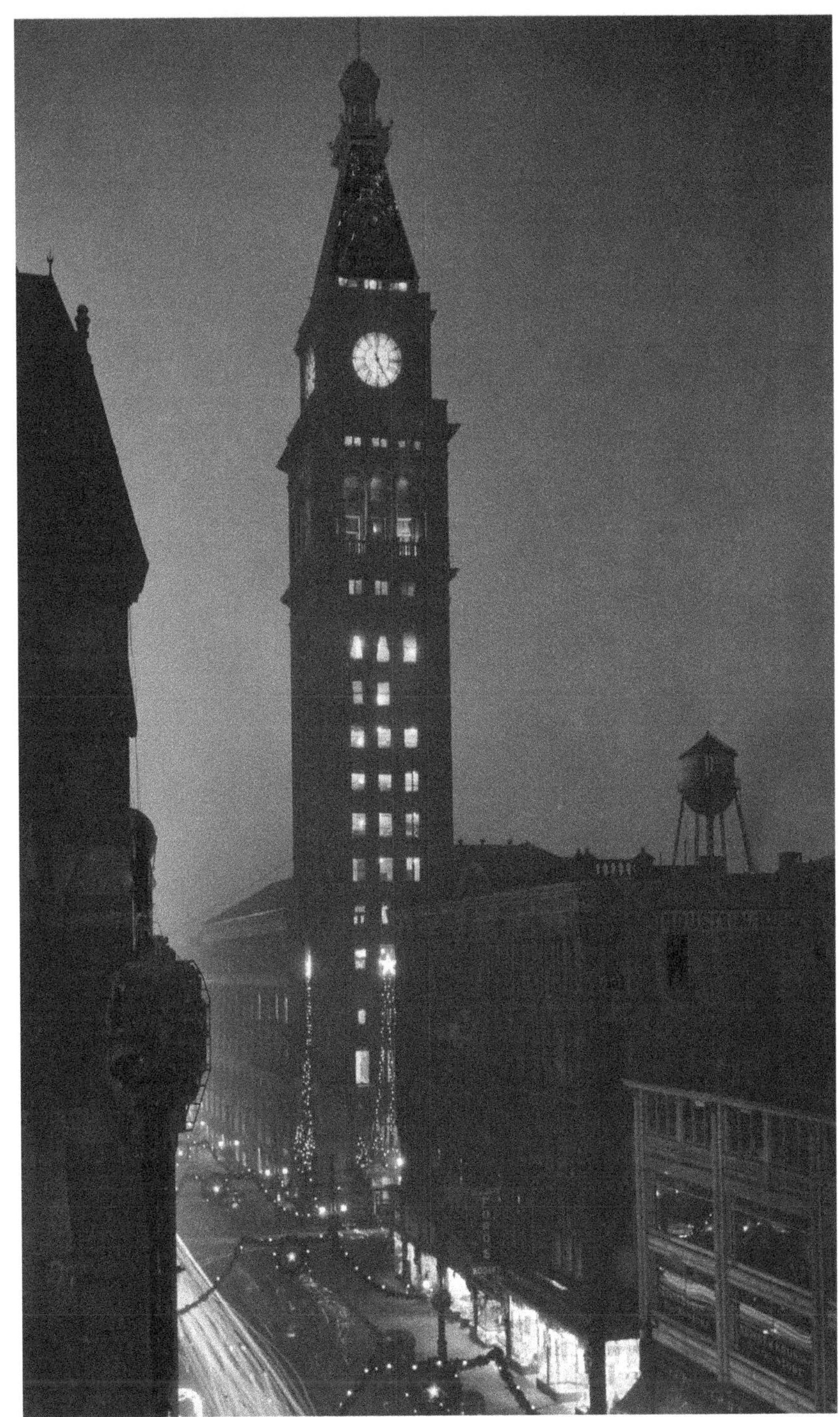

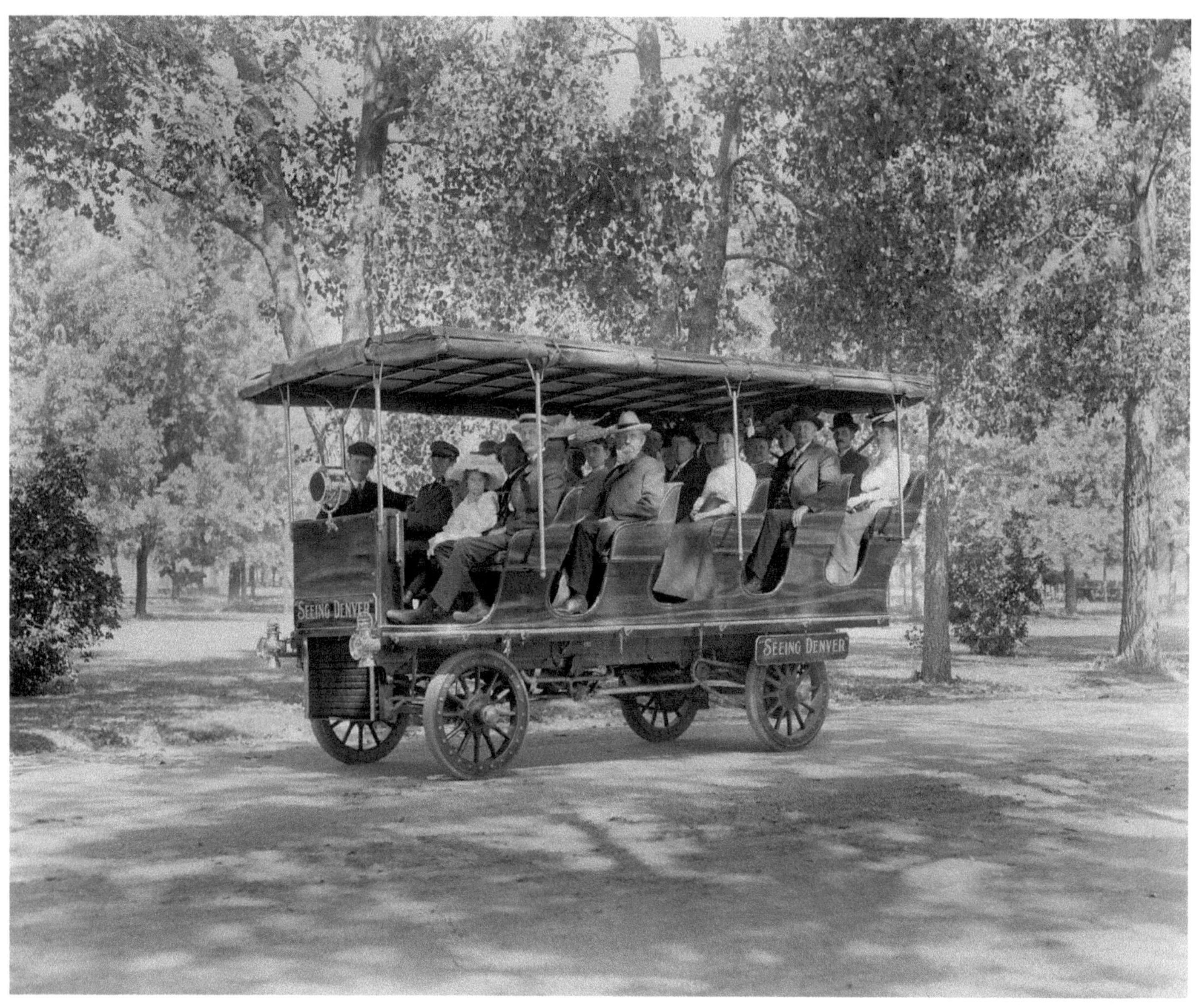

Well-dressed men and women sit in an open tour bus in City Park.

President Theodore Roosevelt rides down 17th Street in an open car during his visit to Denver. A secret service agent is kneeling on the running board of the automobile. During this visit the president delivered a speech to the Colorado Stock Association titled "Conservation." Union Station is visible in the distance.

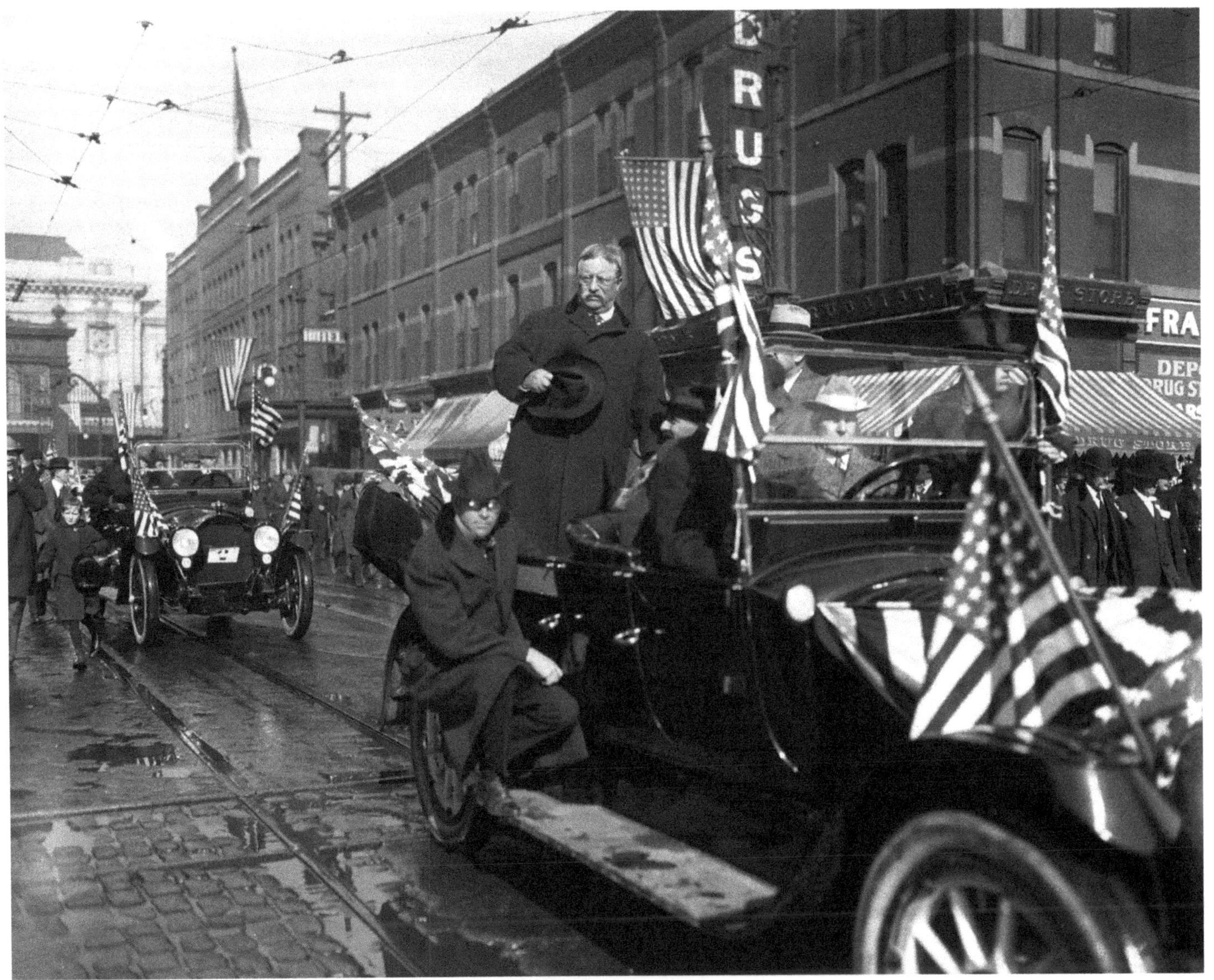

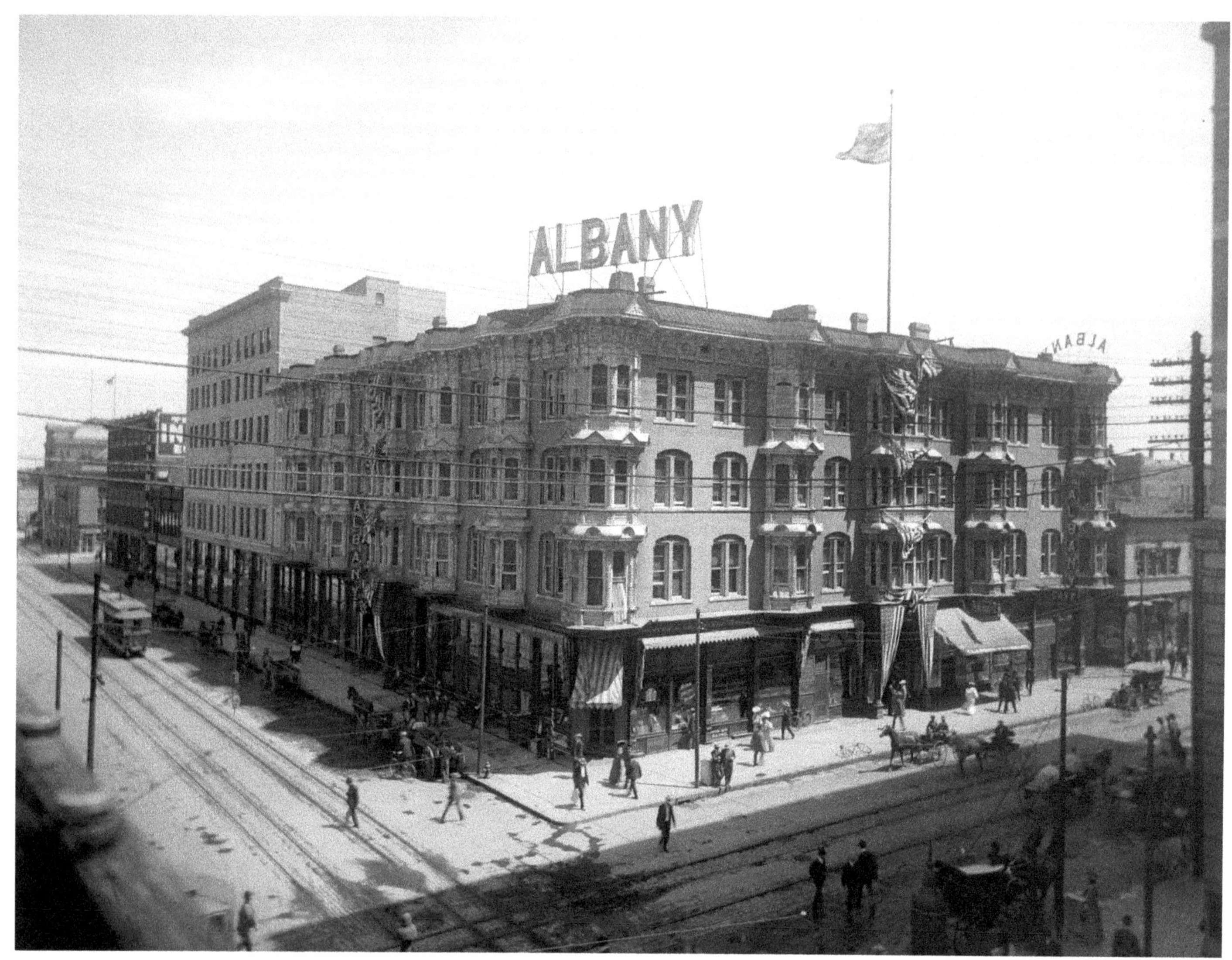

Located at the corner of 17th and Stout streets, the Italianate Albany Hotel opened in 1885. After several sweeping renovations and a catastrophic fire, it was finally demolished in 1977.

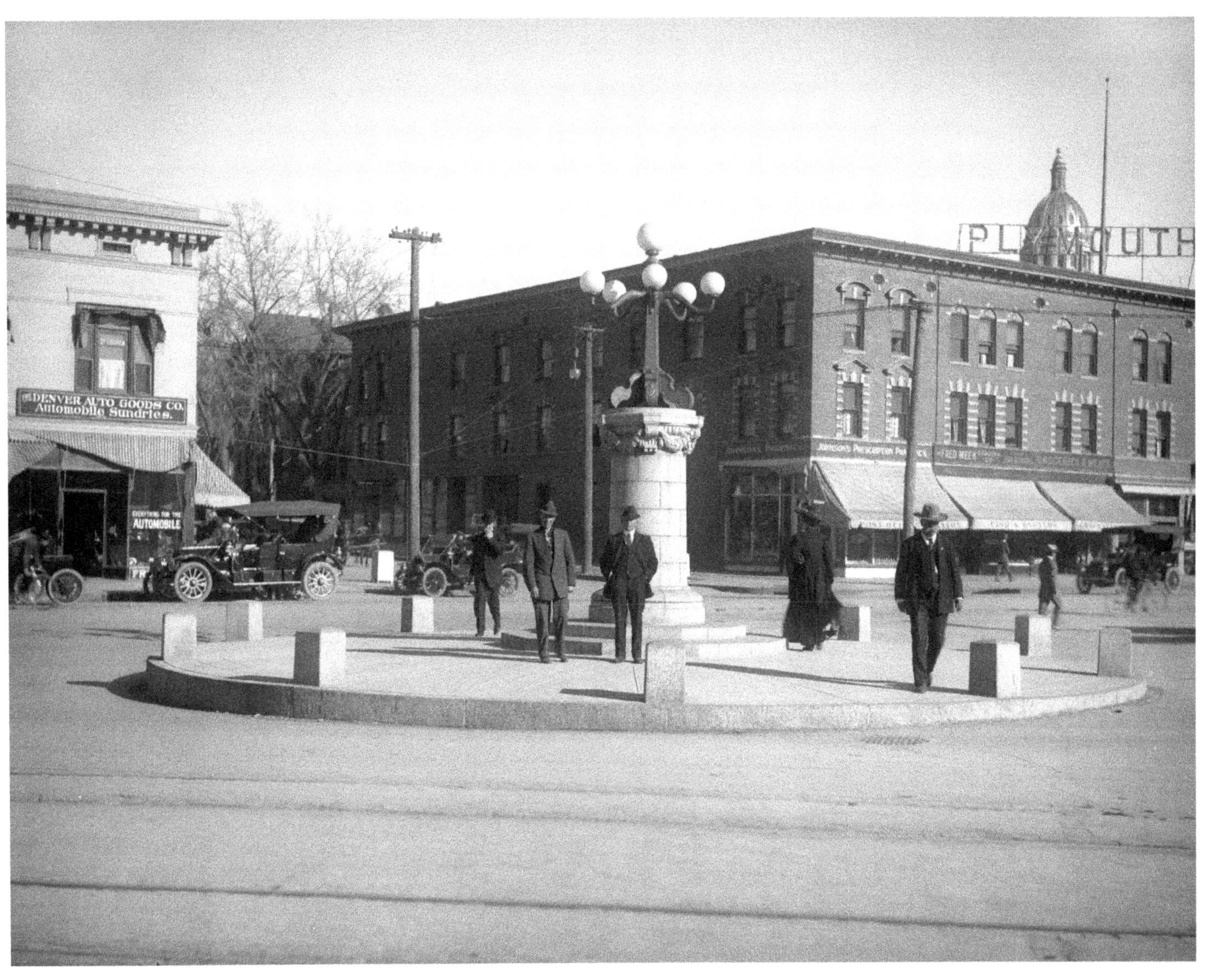

This round-about was located at the intersection of 16th Street and Broadway in the Central Business District. In the distance, the state capitol dome rises behind the Plymouth Hotel.

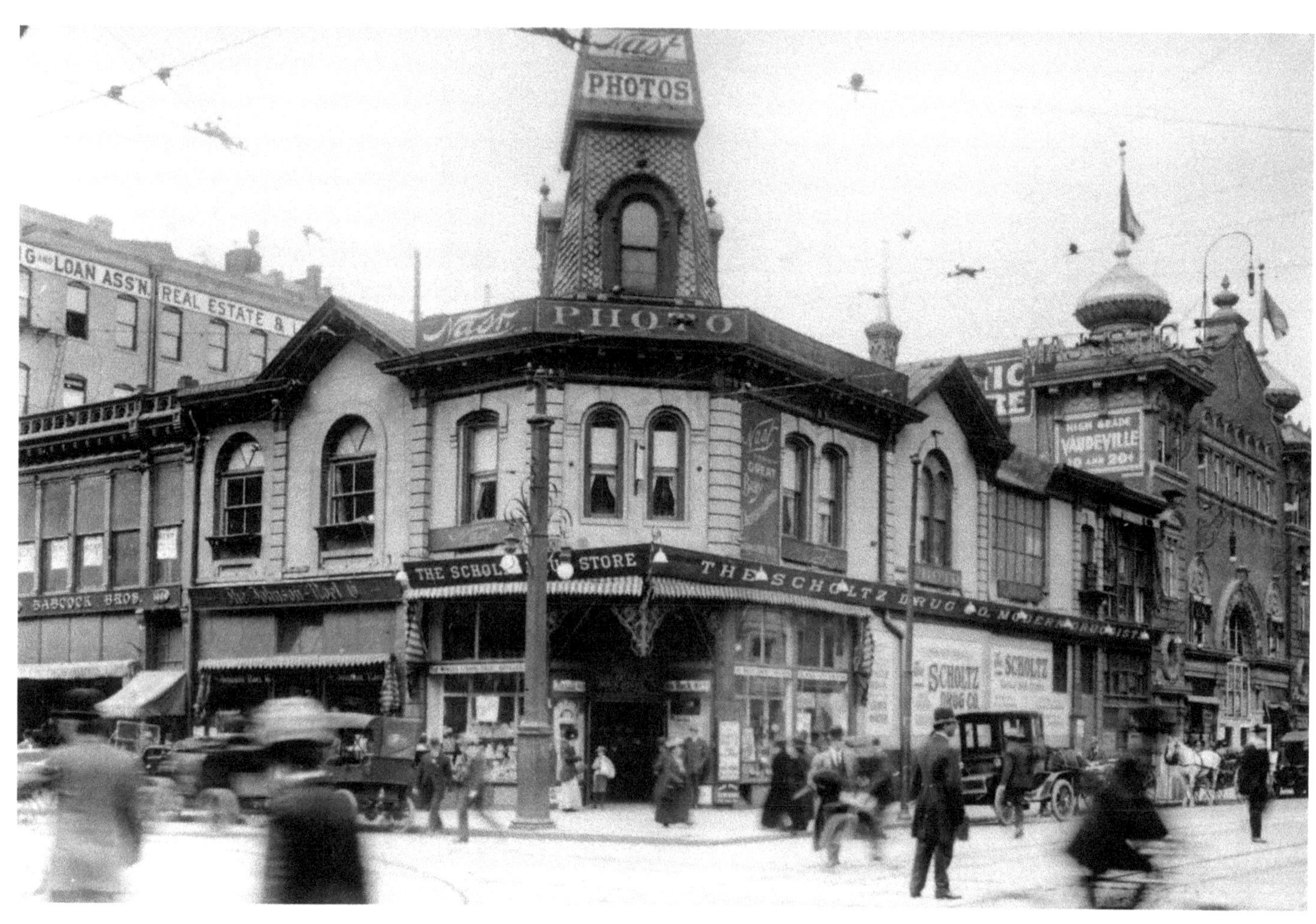

The Nast Photo studio was located on the corner of 11th and Curtis streets. Nast was one of Denver's pioneer photographers. Arriving in Denver in 1875, he worked as a reporter for the *Denver Tribune*, and was active as a photographer from 1880 to 1901. The Scholtz Drug Company was located below the Nast Studio and the Majestic Theater.

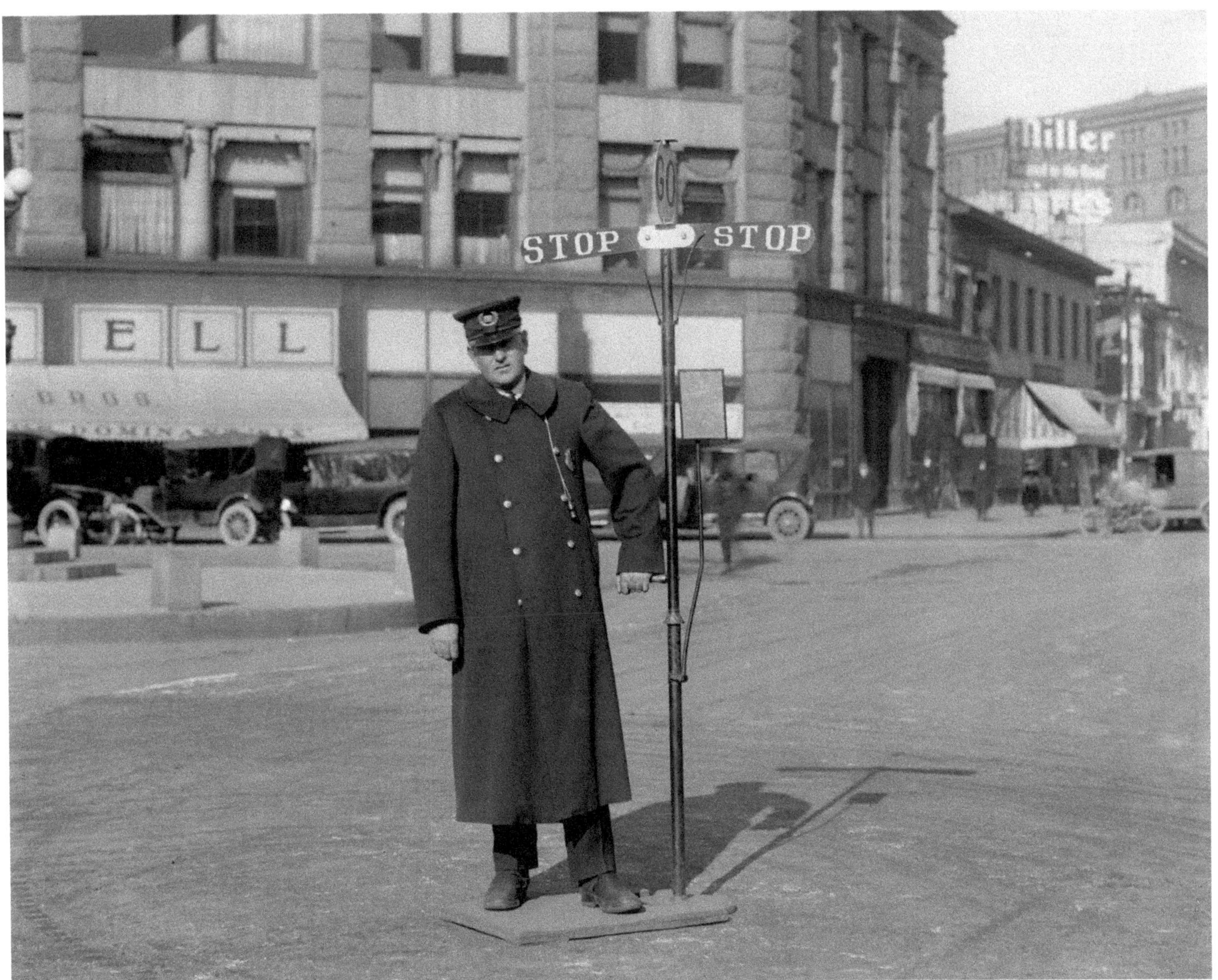

Here a Denver police officer operates a portable traffic signal at an intersection in the Central Business District.

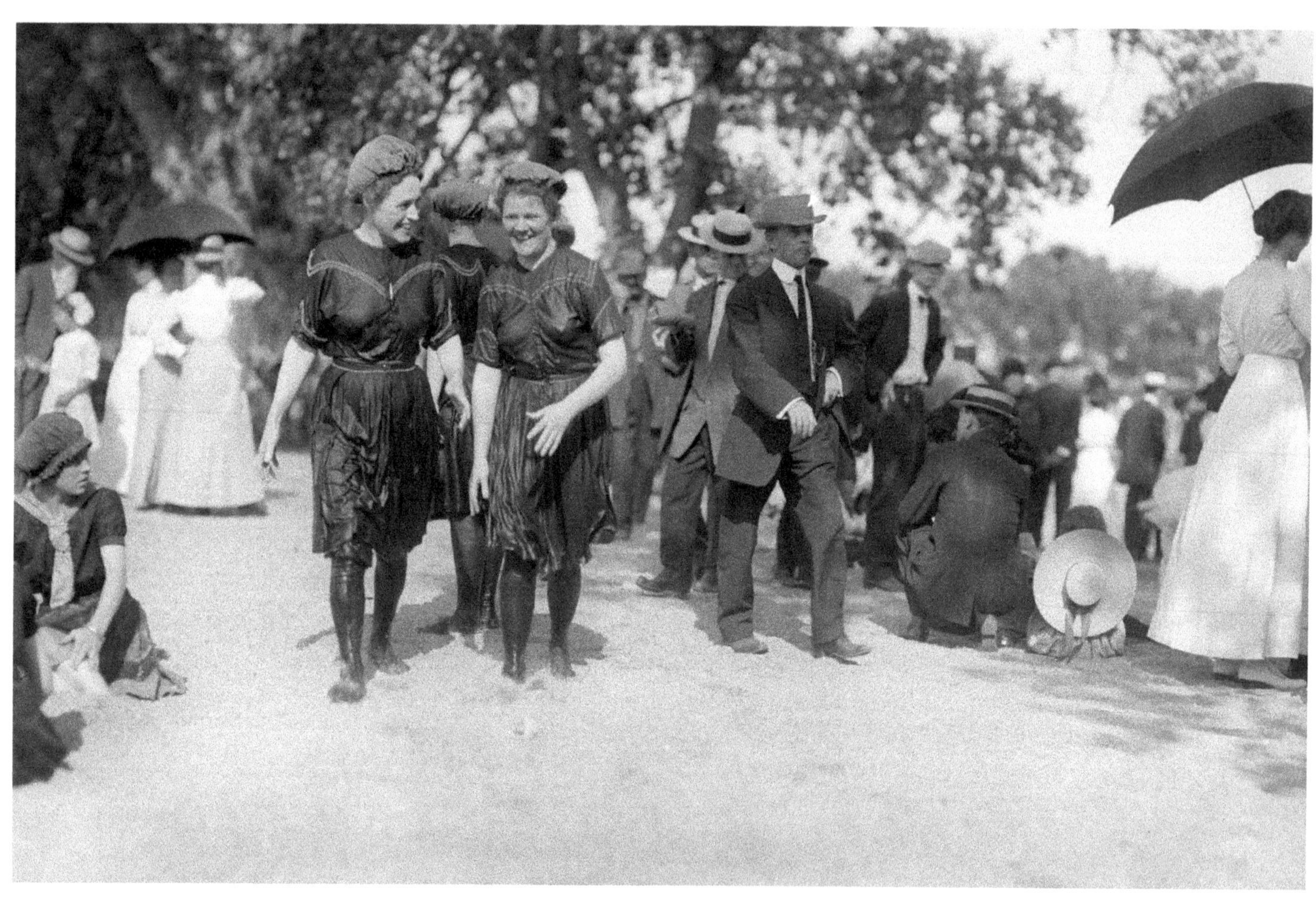

Two women in wet bathing suits and caps walk along the edge of Smith Lake in Washington Park. Many of the women spectators hold umbrellas to shield themselves from the sun.

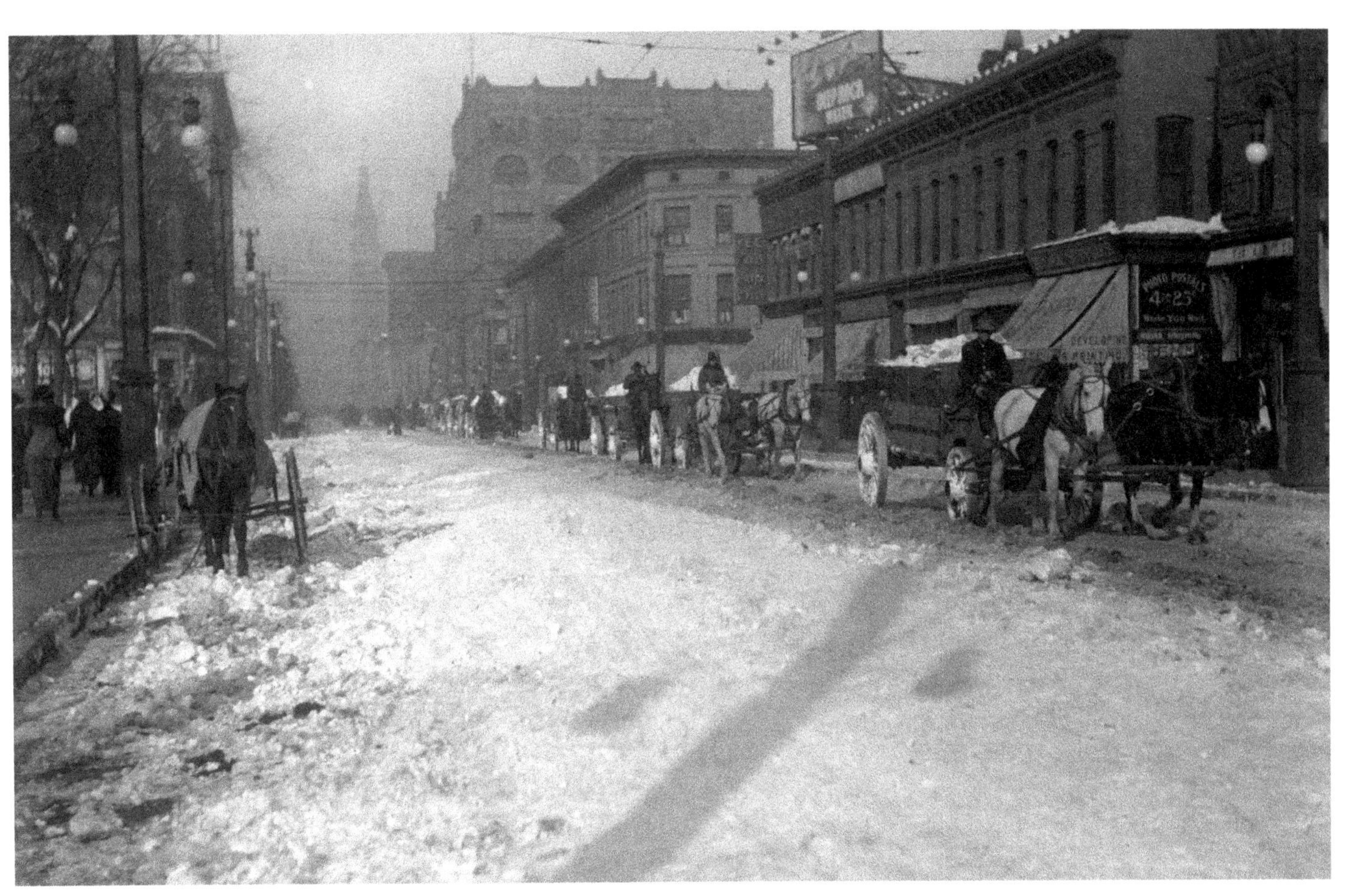

Horse-drawn wagons filled with snow line 16th Street after the great blizzard of 1913, in which thirty-six inches of snow brought the city to a standstill. The snow was carted to Civic Center where it was piled in front of the state capitol building.

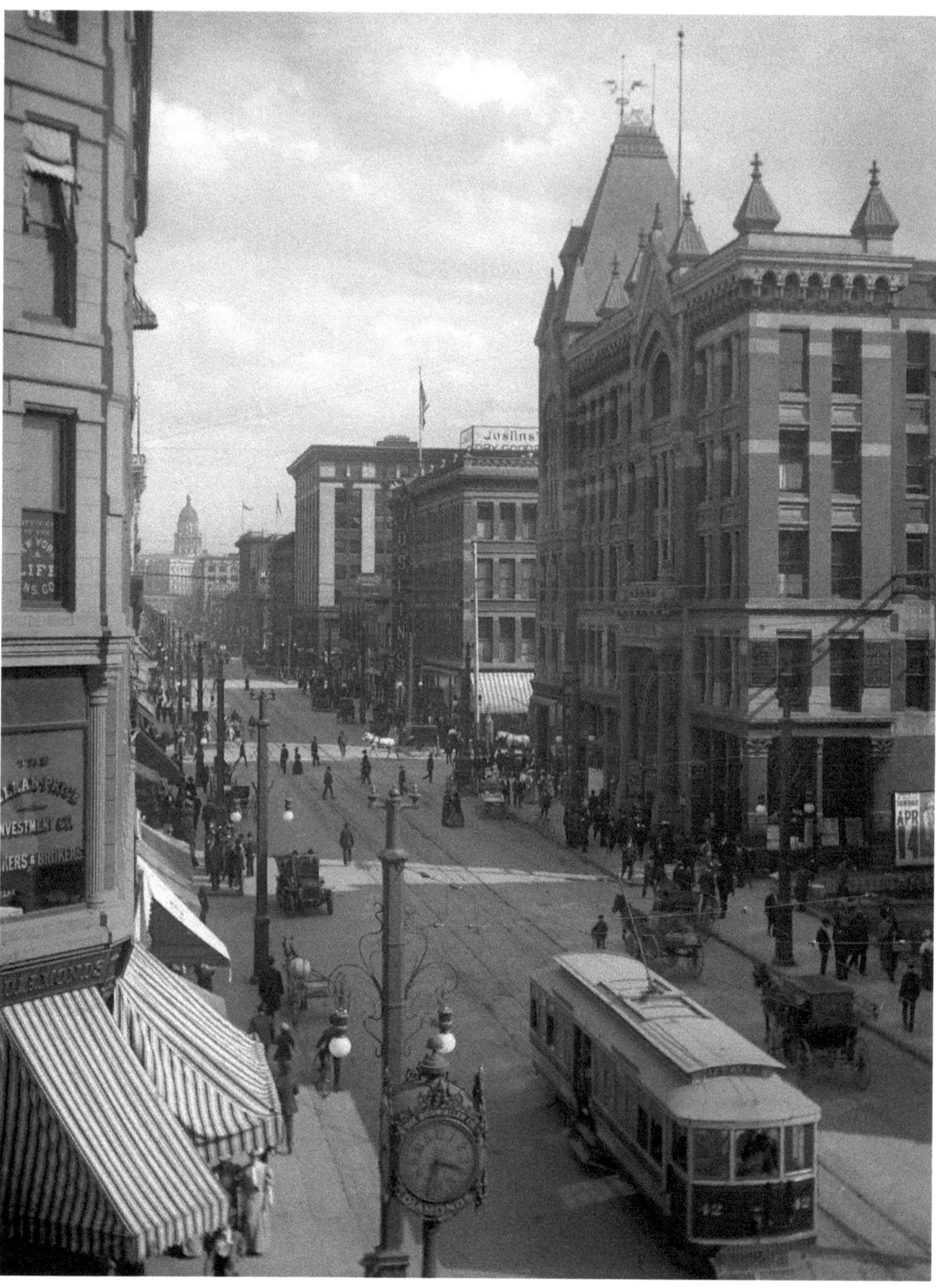

This view shows turn-of-the-century 16th Street filled with pedestrians, horse-drawn wagons and carriages, automobiles, and an electric streetcar. The capitol building is visible in the distance.

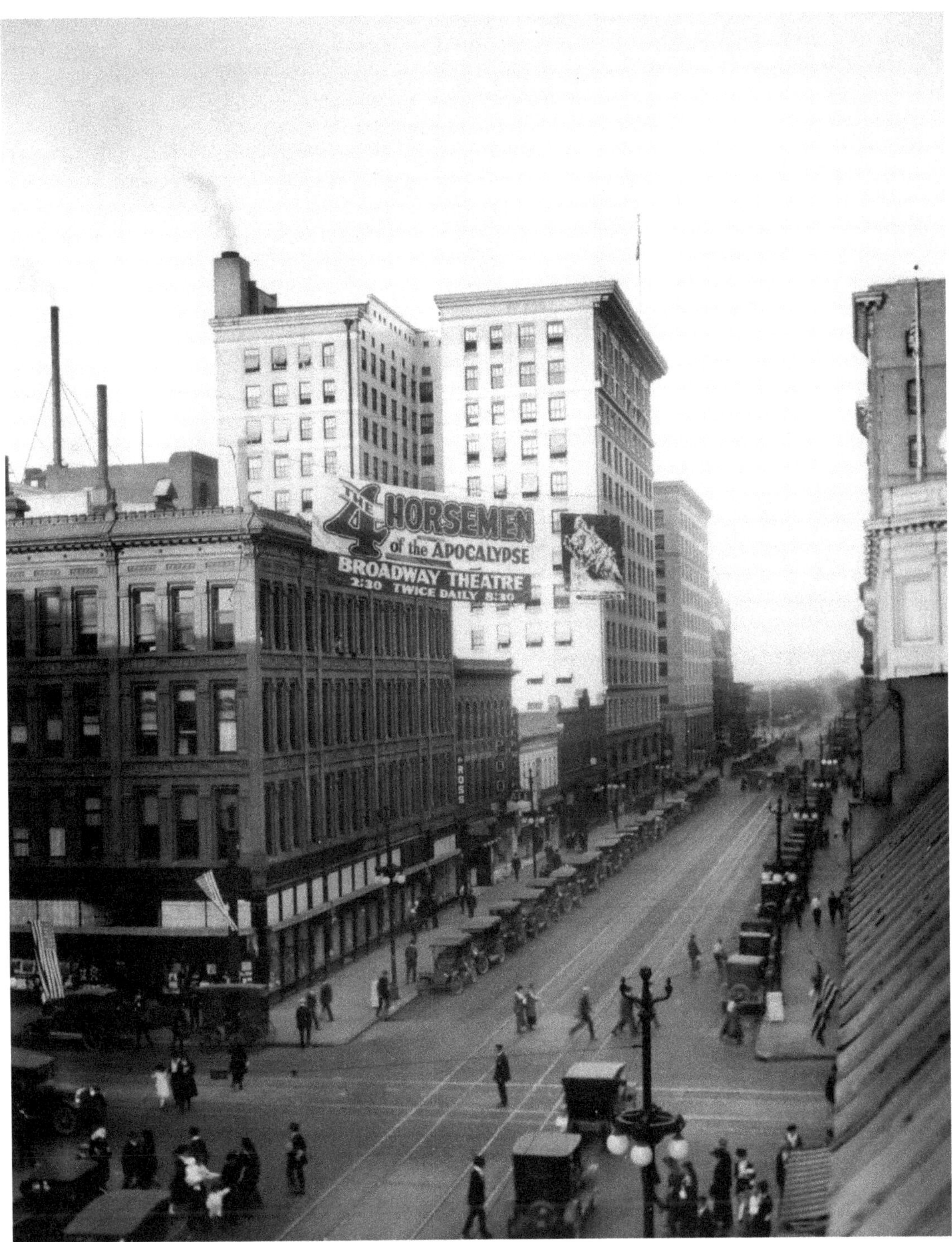

Parked cars line 16th Street in this view of the Central Business District. A banner over the street advertises the movie *Four Horsemen of the Apocalypse.*

Plainclothes policemen escort a handcuffed prisoner out of Union Station.

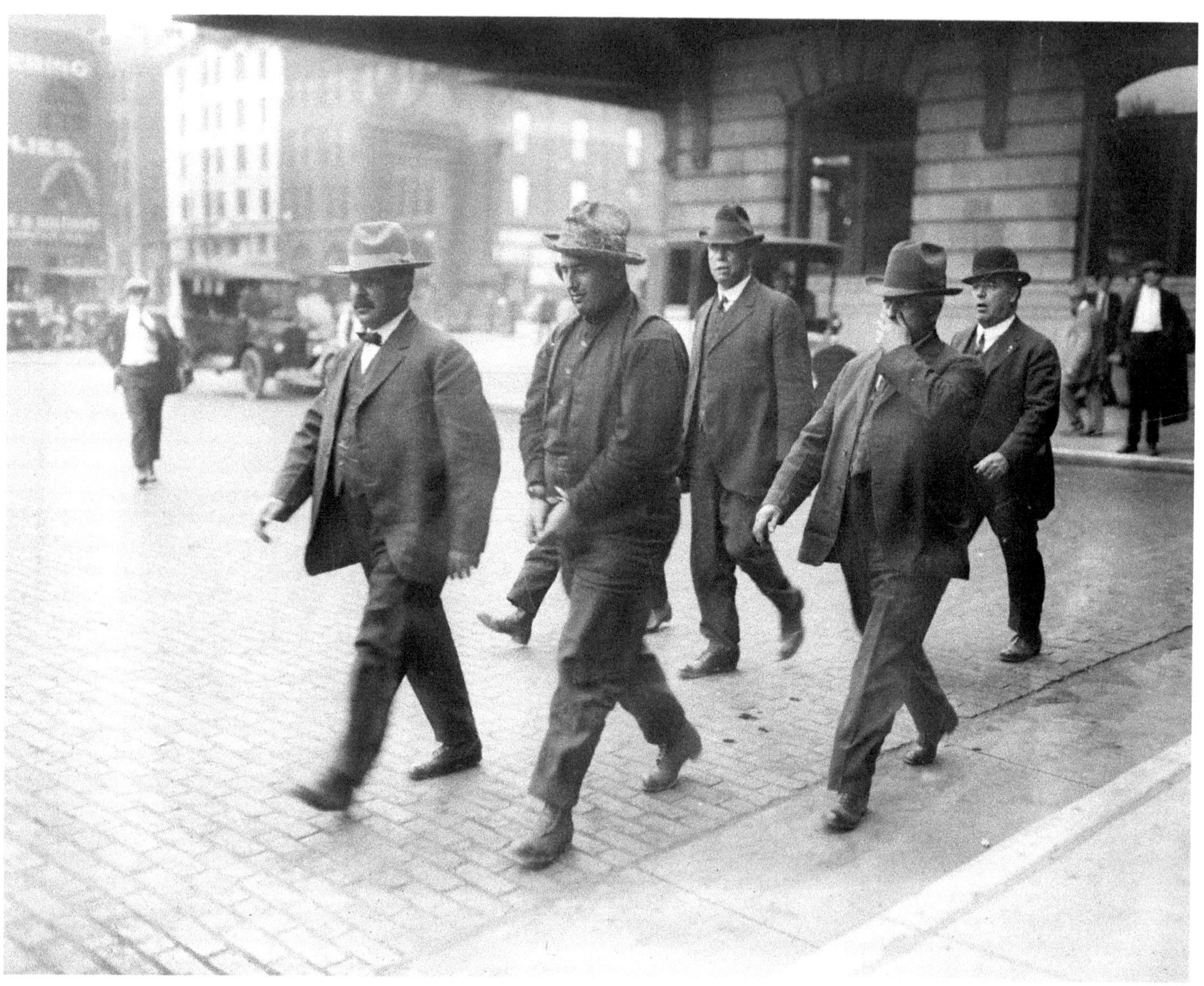

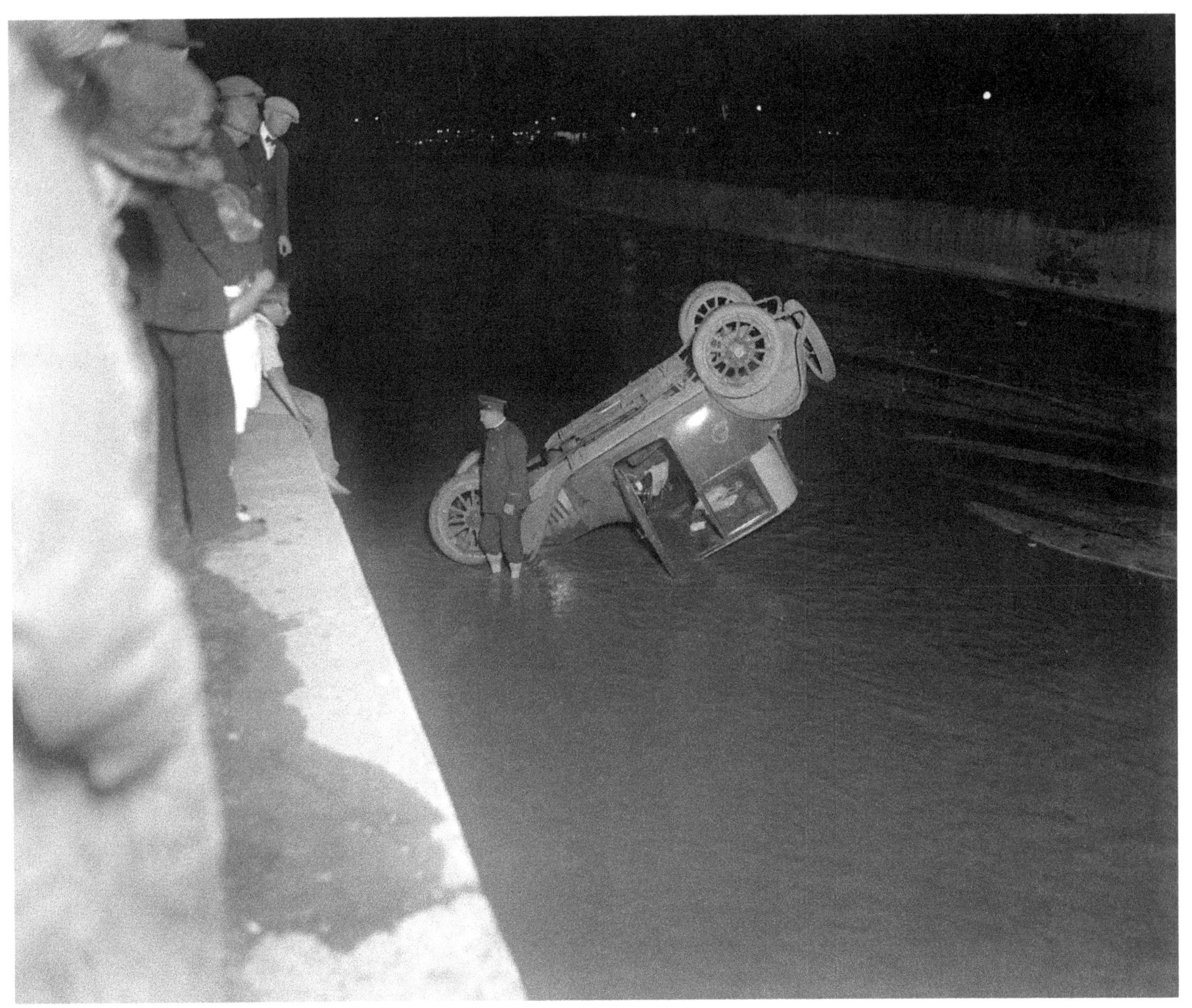

A policeman stands near an overturned car in Cherry Creek near Speer Boulevard.

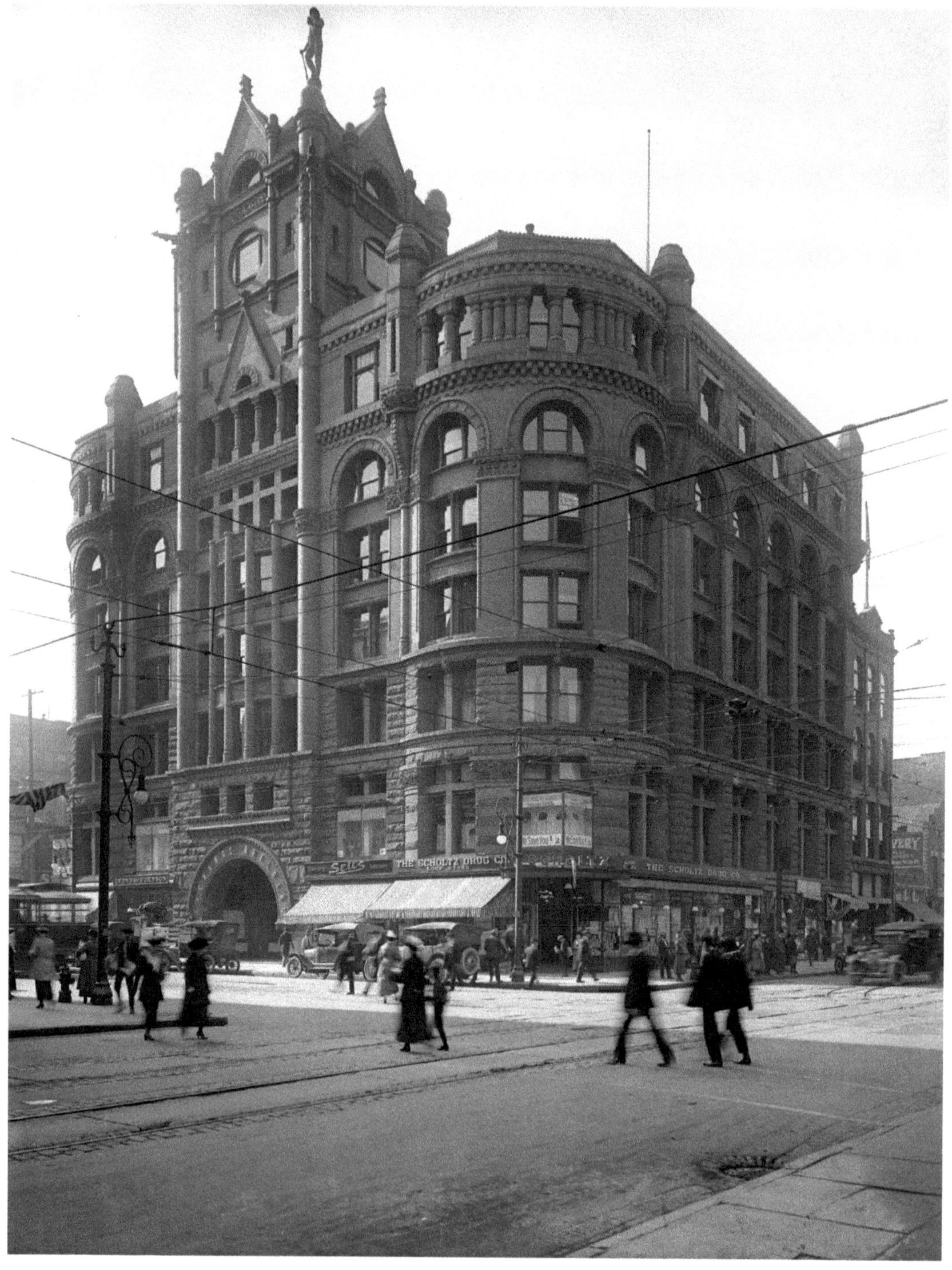

The Mining Exchange Building located on the corner of 15th and Arapahoe streets opened in 1891 to become the financial center for the mining industry in the Rocky Mountain West. In 1963 the structure was razed to make way for a modern office building. The *Old Prospector,* the statue mounted on top of the building, was saved and is now on display in front of Brooks Towers on 15th Street between Curtis and Arapahoe.

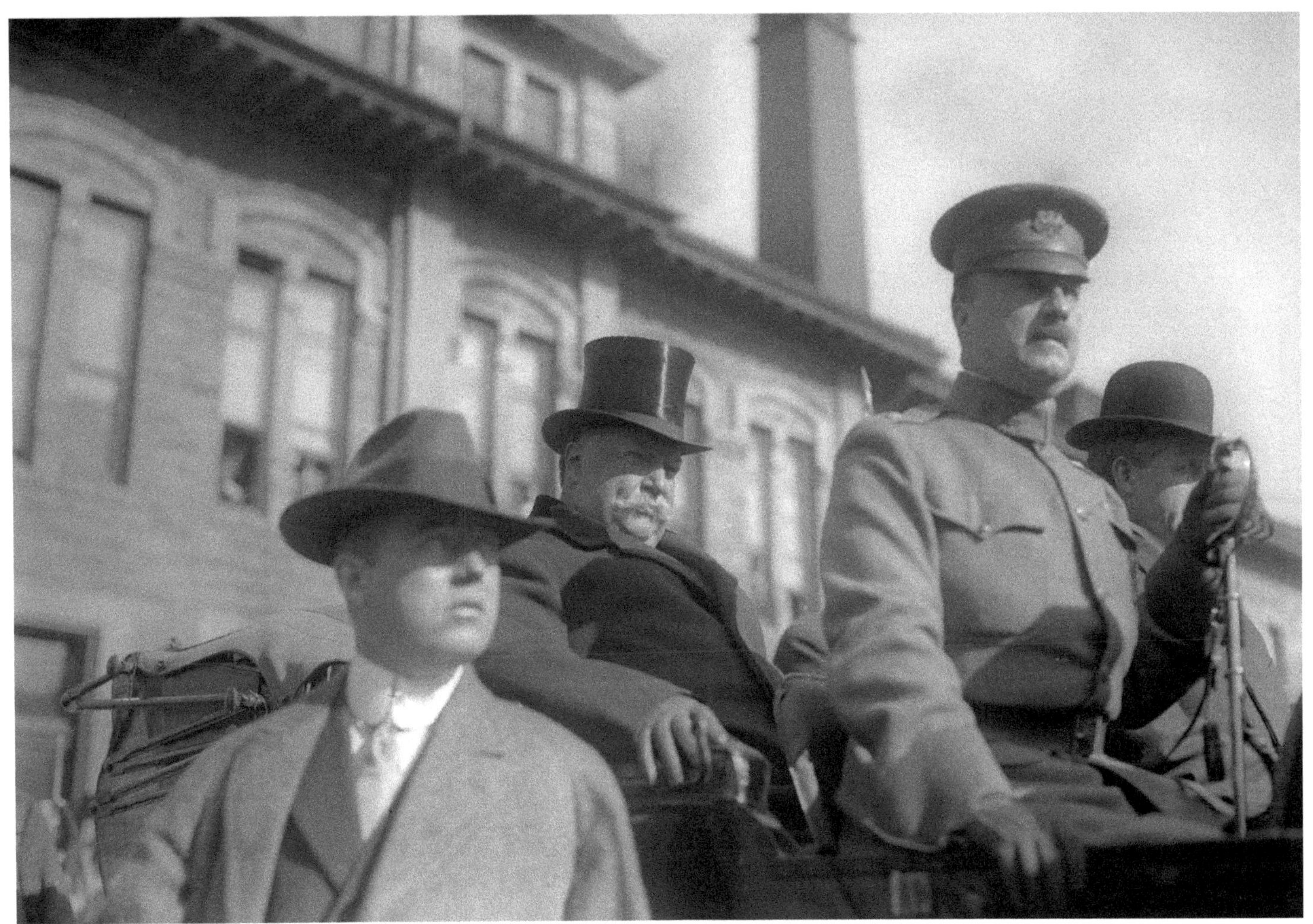

President William Howard Taft visited Denver on October 3, 1911. The president came to the city to address the Public Lands Convention.

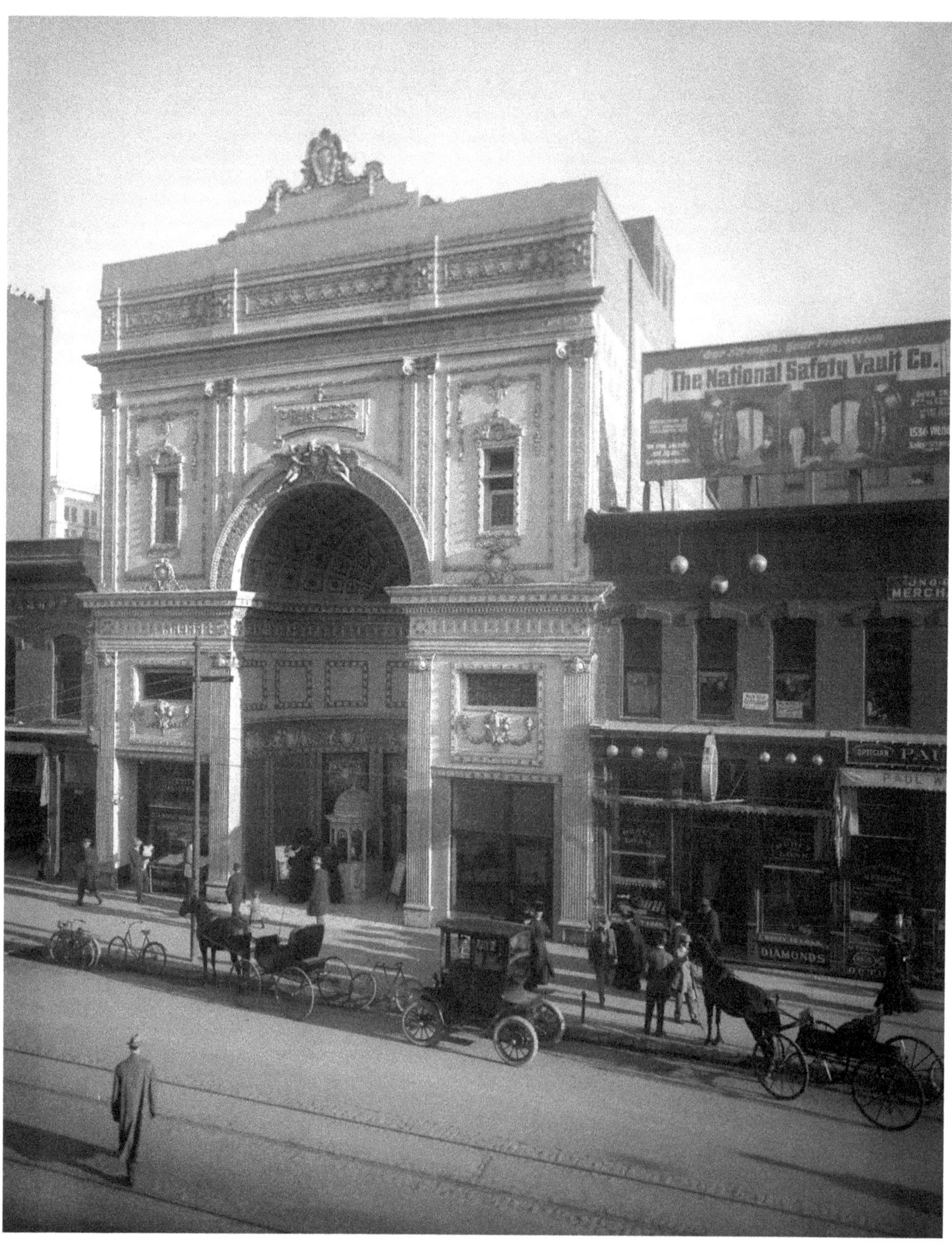

The Princess Theatre in view here was located at 1620 Curtis Street.

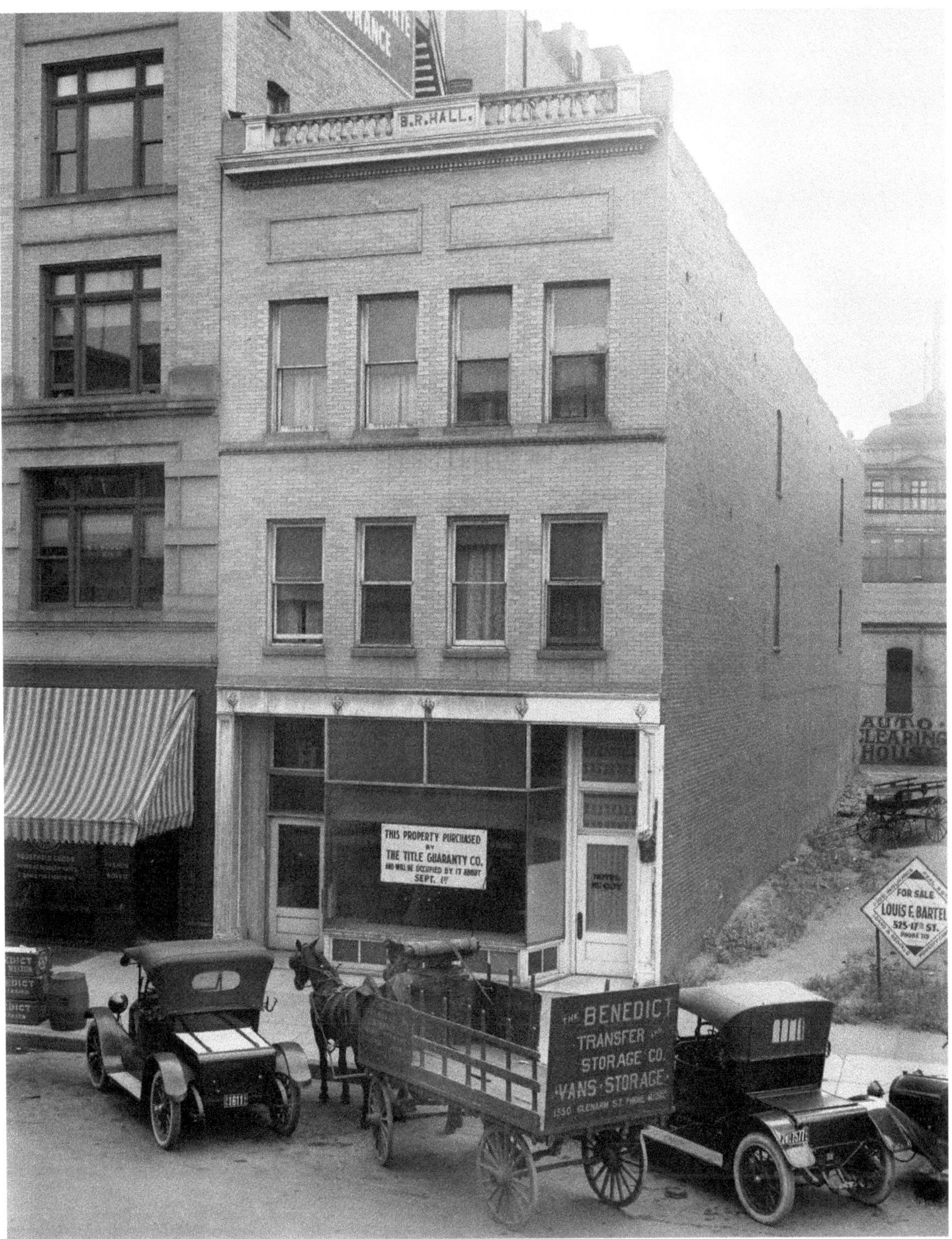

A Benedict Transfer and Storage Company horse-drawn wagon is parked near the company's office in the 1500 block of Glenarm Place.

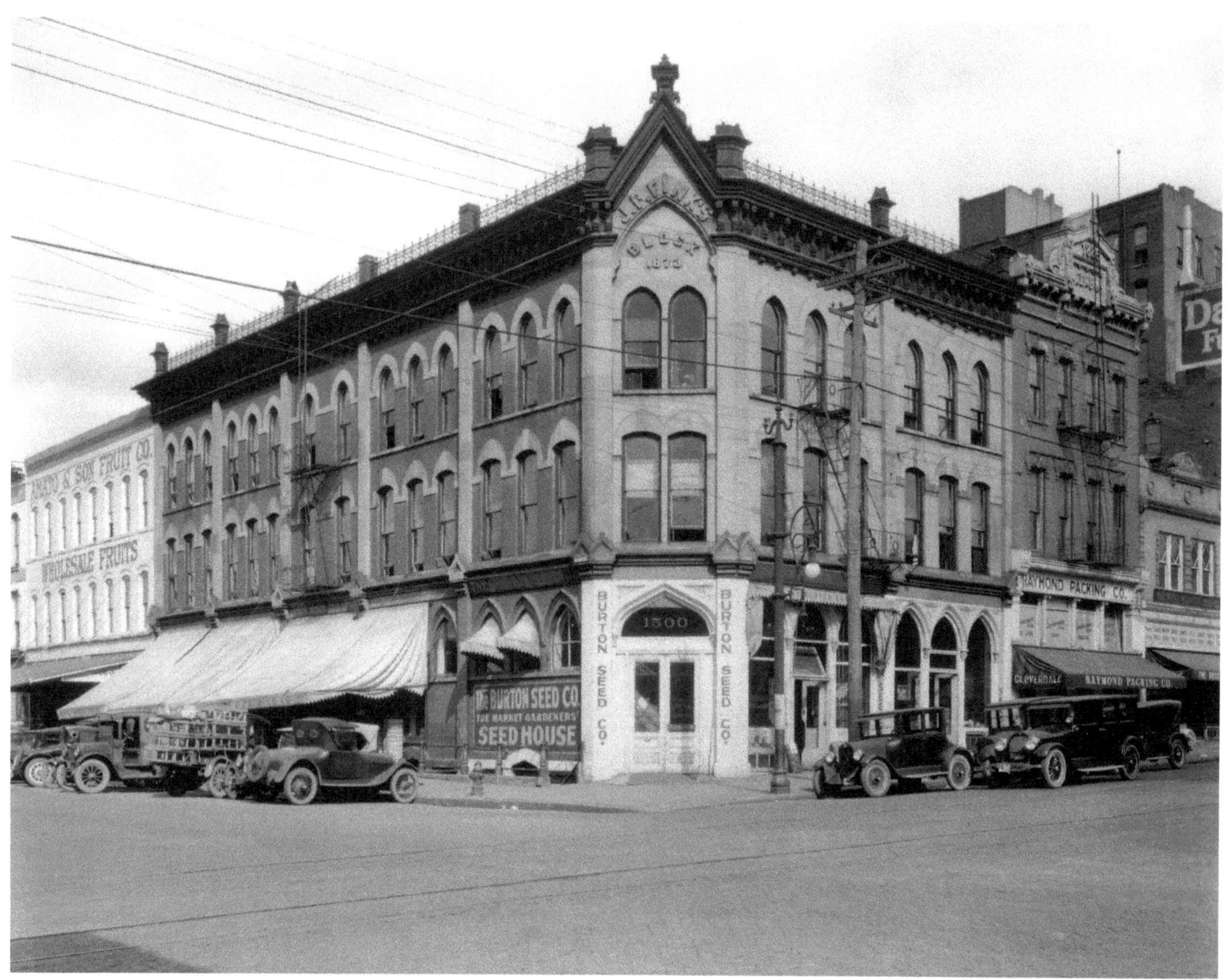

The J. P. Fink's Block was located on the corner of 15th and Market streets. When it was erected in 1873 it was considered one of the city's finest buildings.

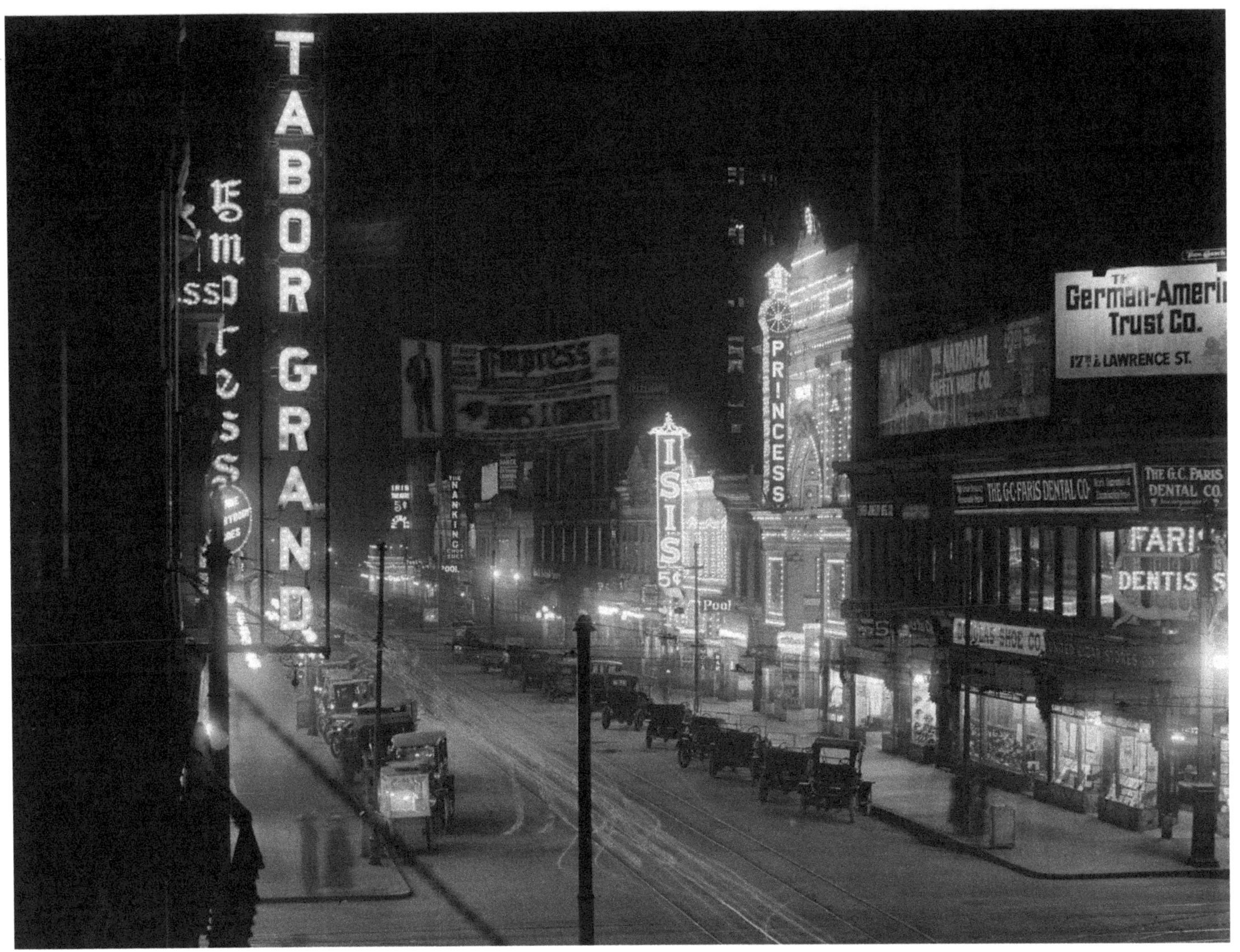

Curtis Street, known as Theater Row, was home to many of Denver's most illustrious movie theaters. This 1913 view shows the Iris, Isis, Princess, Empress, and Tabor Grand theaters.

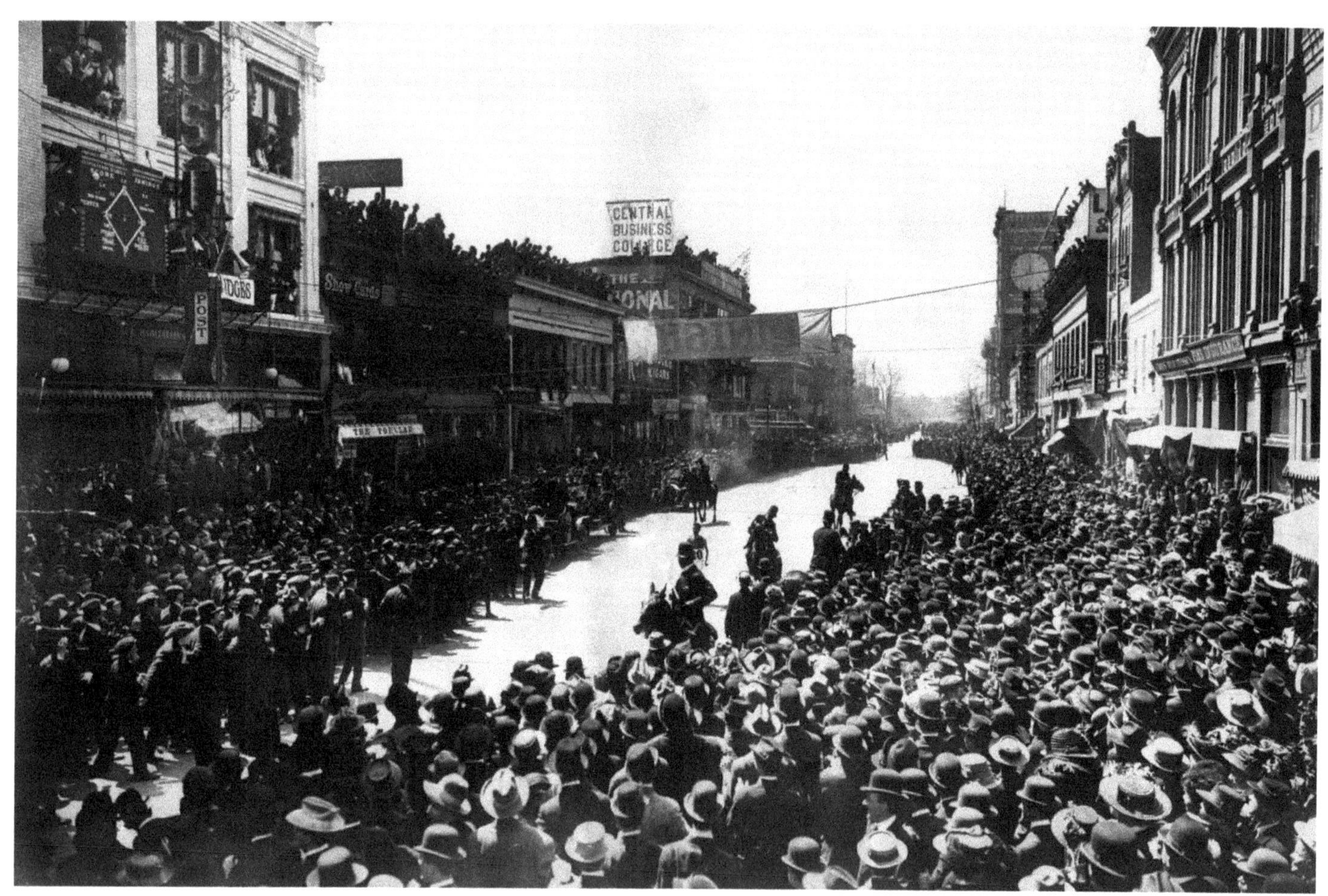

Policemen on horseback hold back a throng of spectators at a foot race on Champa Street. The Denver Post building is on the left; a close look reveals an electric baseball scoreboard over the front door.

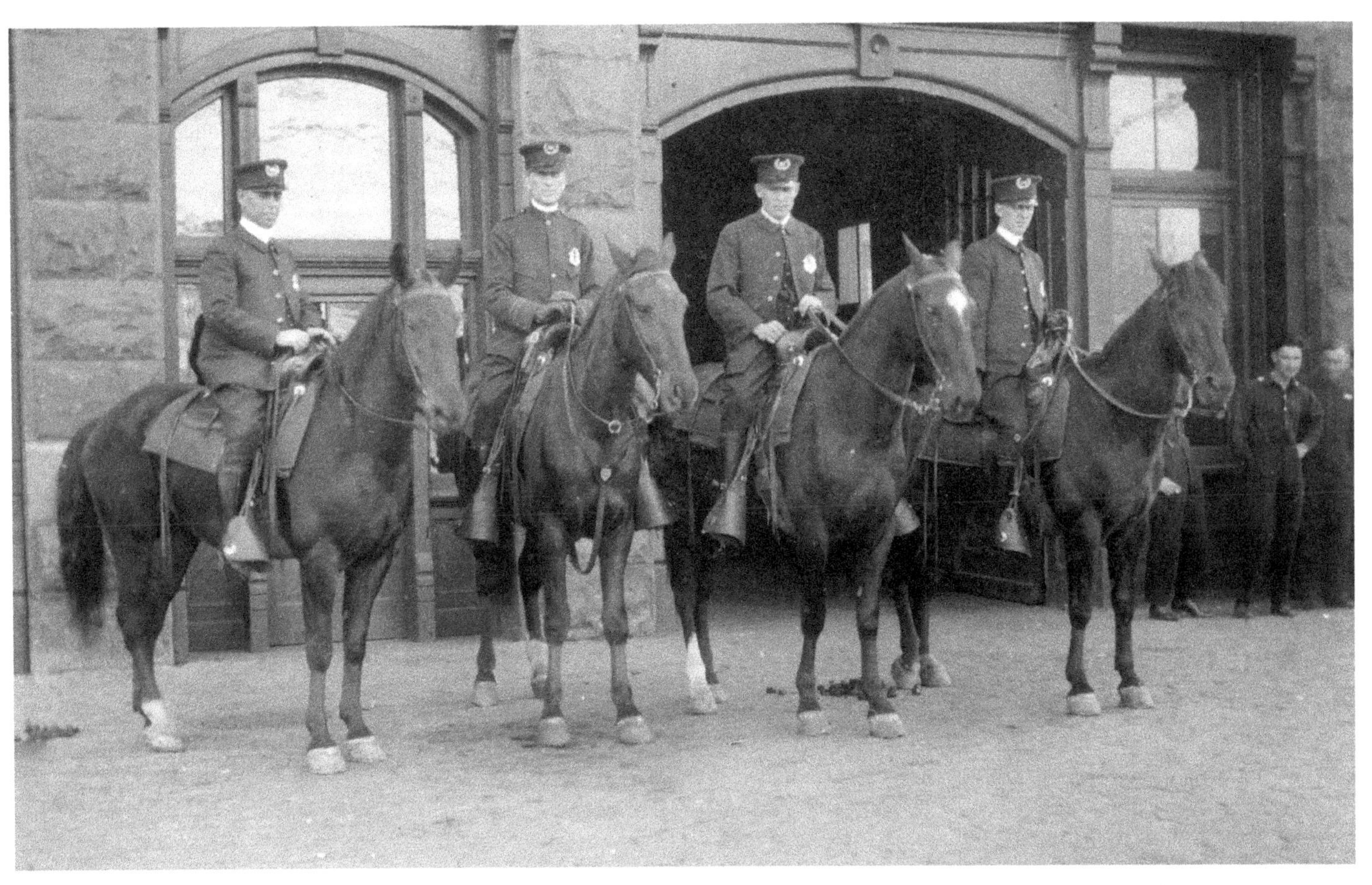

Members of the Denver police department mounted patrol pose on horseback in front of the Denver County jail, located at Colfax and Santa Fe avenues.

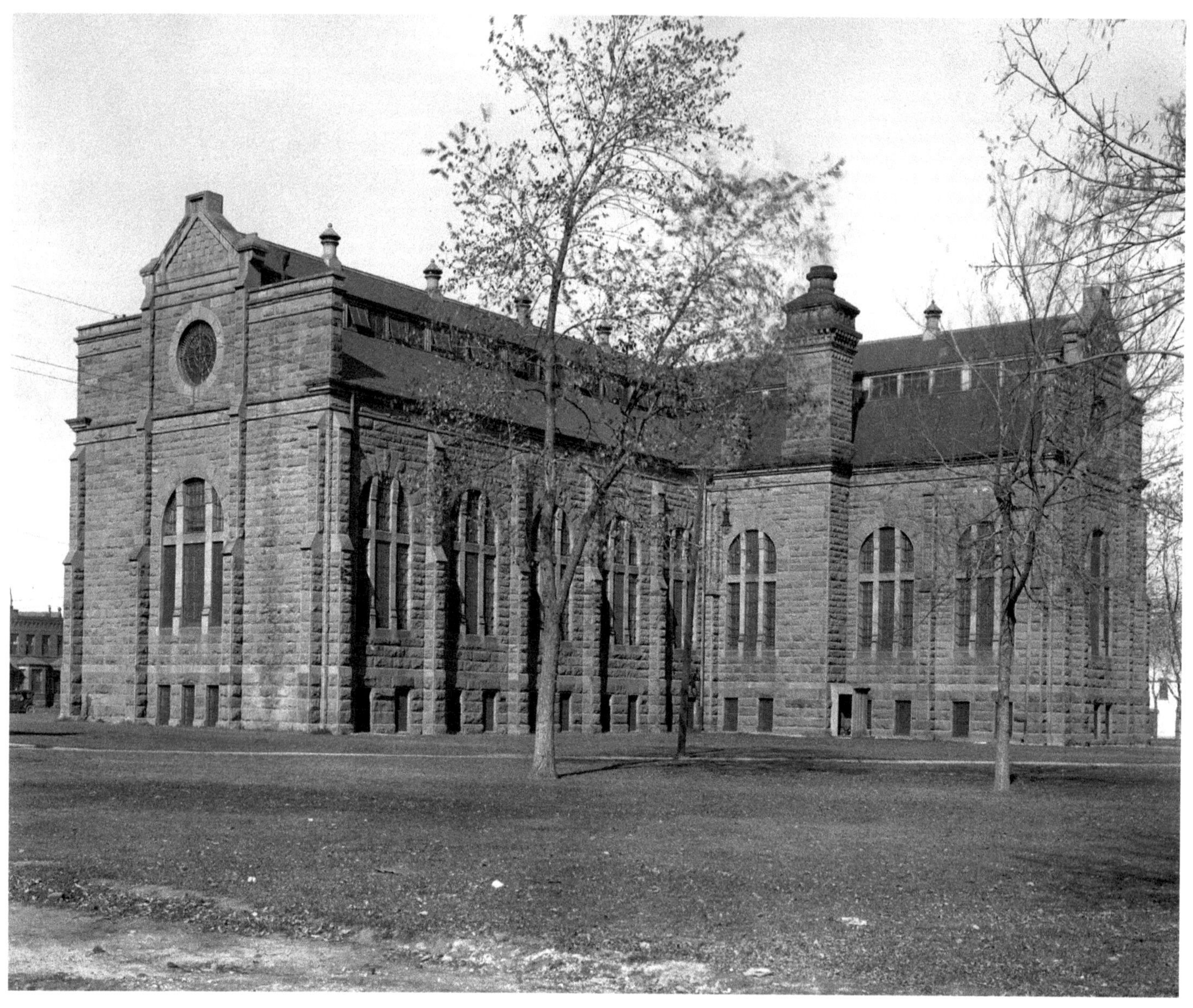

The Denver County jail, originally the Arapahoe County jail, was located at West Colfax and Santa Fe avenues. It was built in 1891 and remained in use until 1956.

This man in dirty overalls and a hat poses next to a touring car in City Park. An elderly woman in the backseat has on a touring hat and goggles.

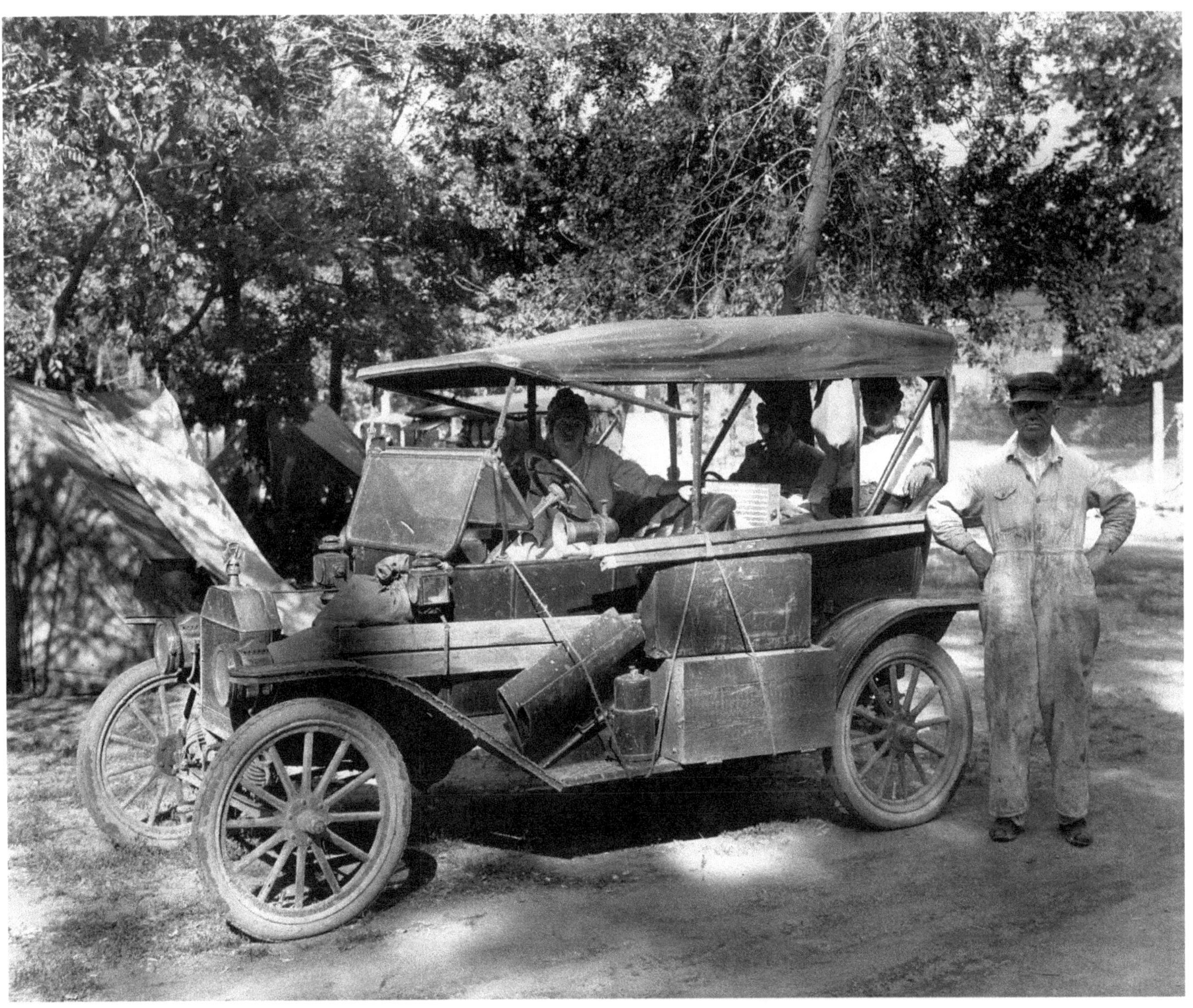

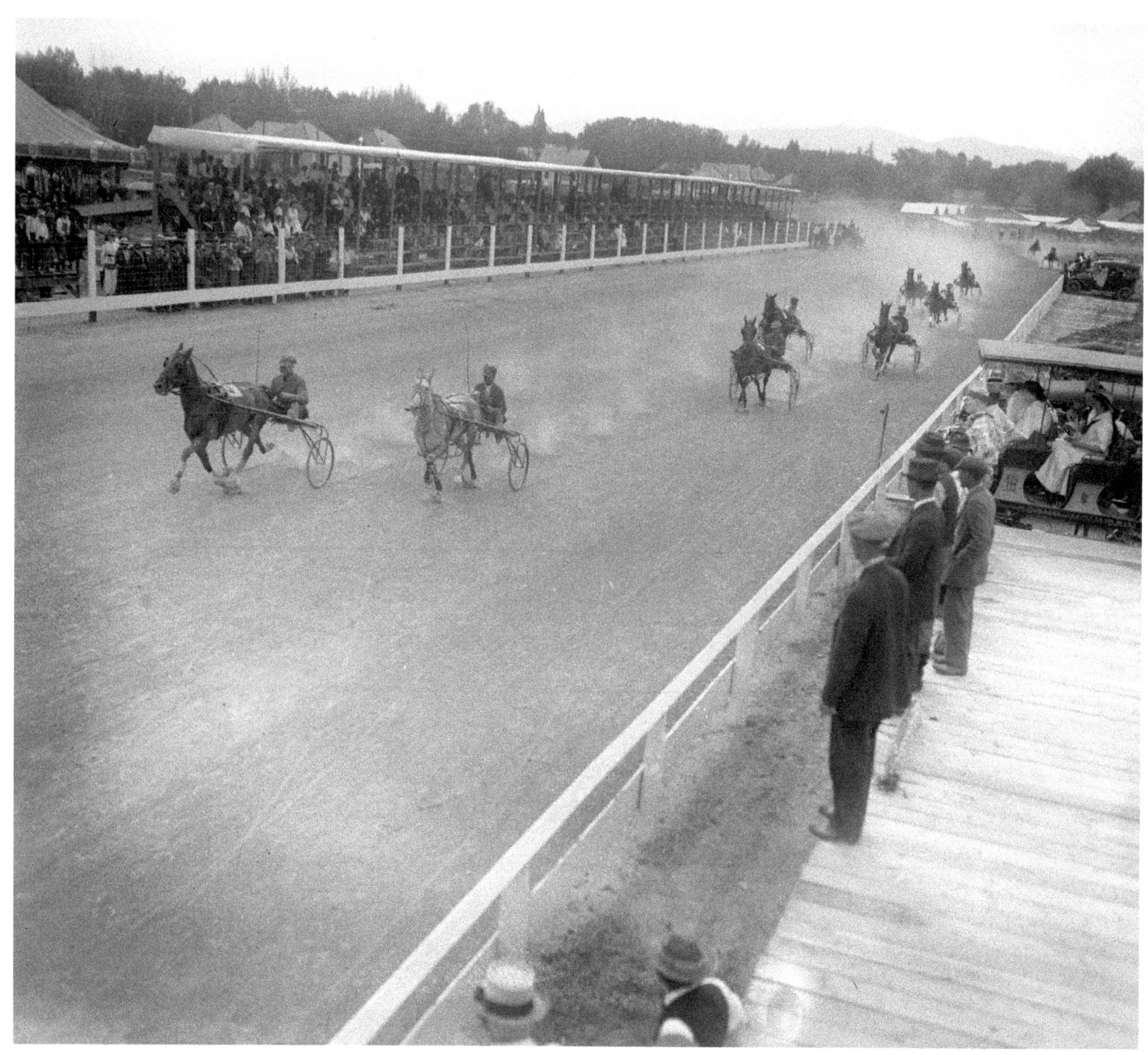

In this harness race at City Park, sulkies pass the covered grandstand and spectators watch from a tour bus parked beside the track. The racetrack was built in 1898 and was finally razed in 1950.

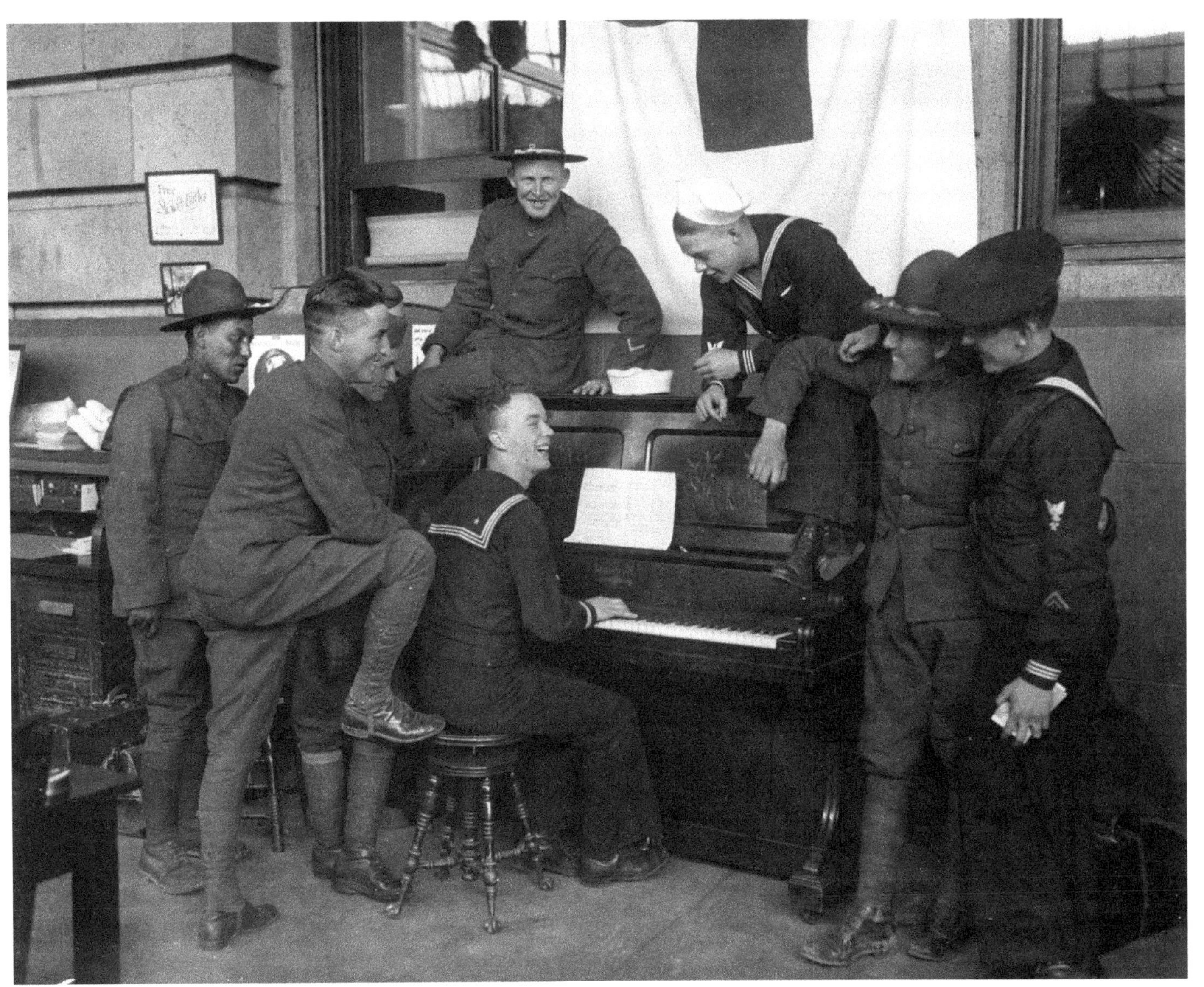

Sailors and soldiers gather around a piano at a Red Cross canteen.

In 1917 recruits for World War I ride in a parade in Denver. Men on a car carry a sign that reads "The Kaiser has"; a dead duck hangs from the sign. Another sign reads "Their jobs are waiting."

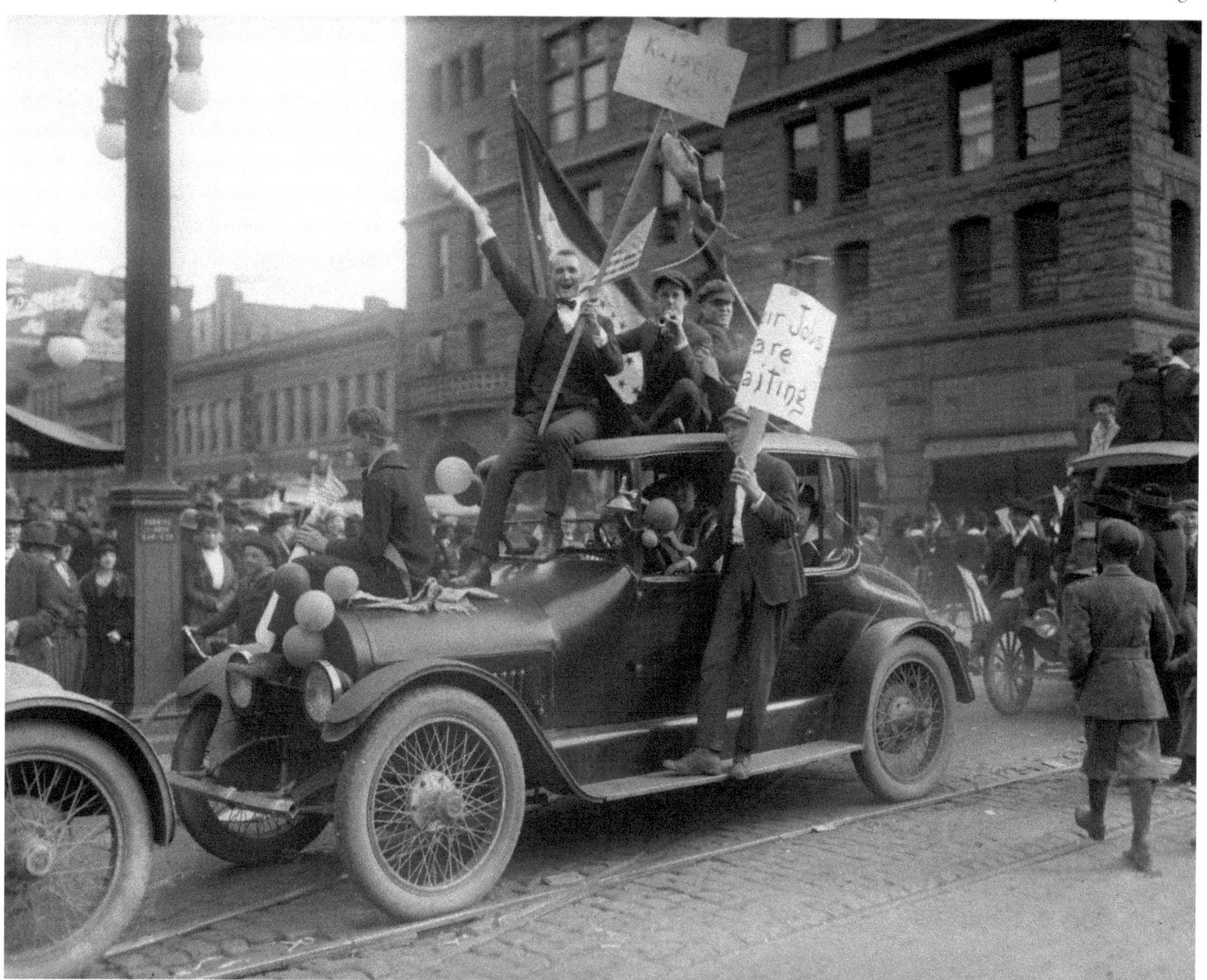

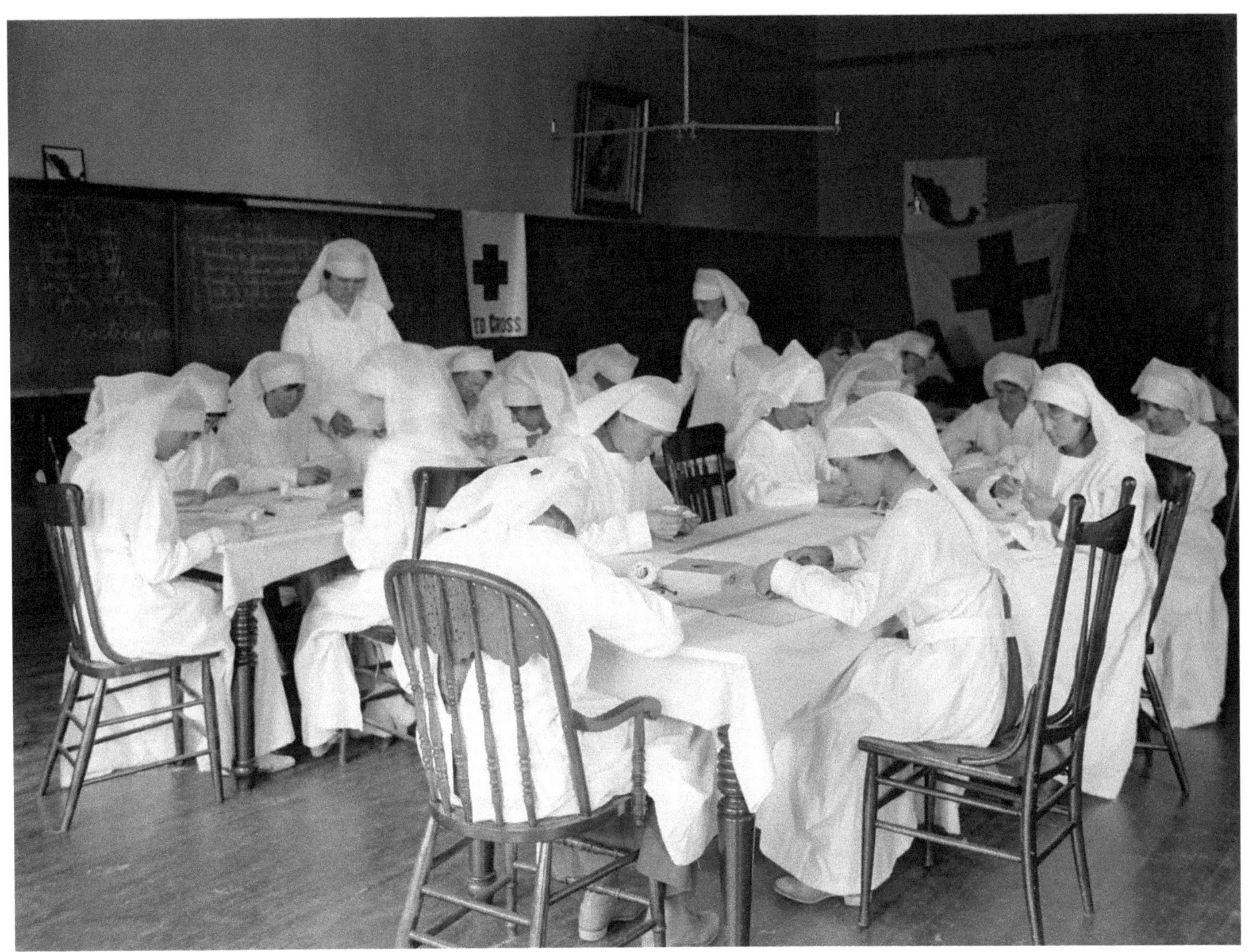

Red Cross nurses at Loretto Heights College teach first aid trainees how to roll bandages for the World War I war effort.

Recruits depart from Fort Logan, a military training camp in Denver. The troops wait to board Denver and Rio Grande Western Railroad cars.

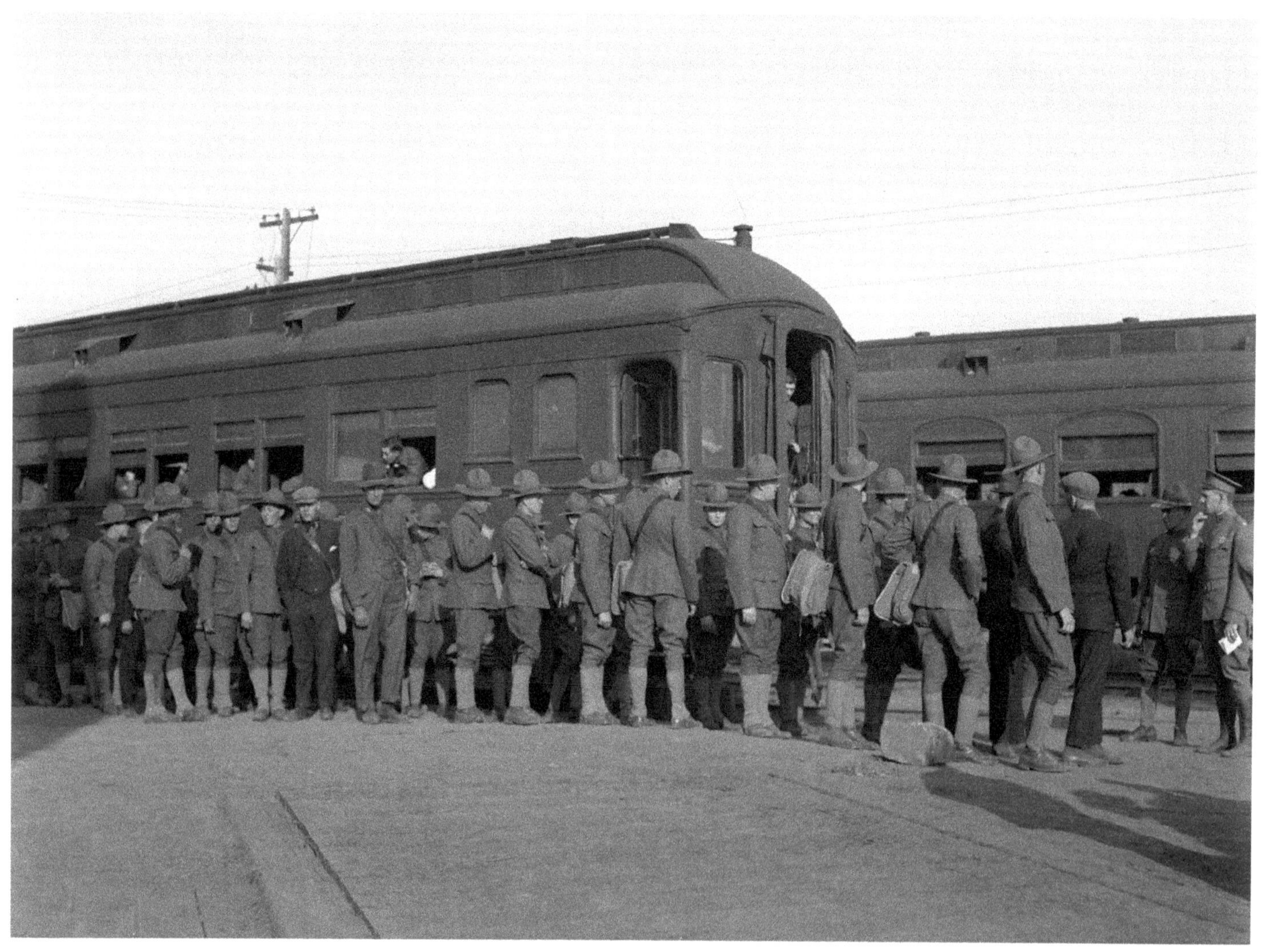

Ushers for the Broadway Theater pose in front of the entrance at 1756 Broadway. The theater was part of the Metropole Hotel and was for years one of Denver's finest movie houses. One of the ushers wears an Army uniform.

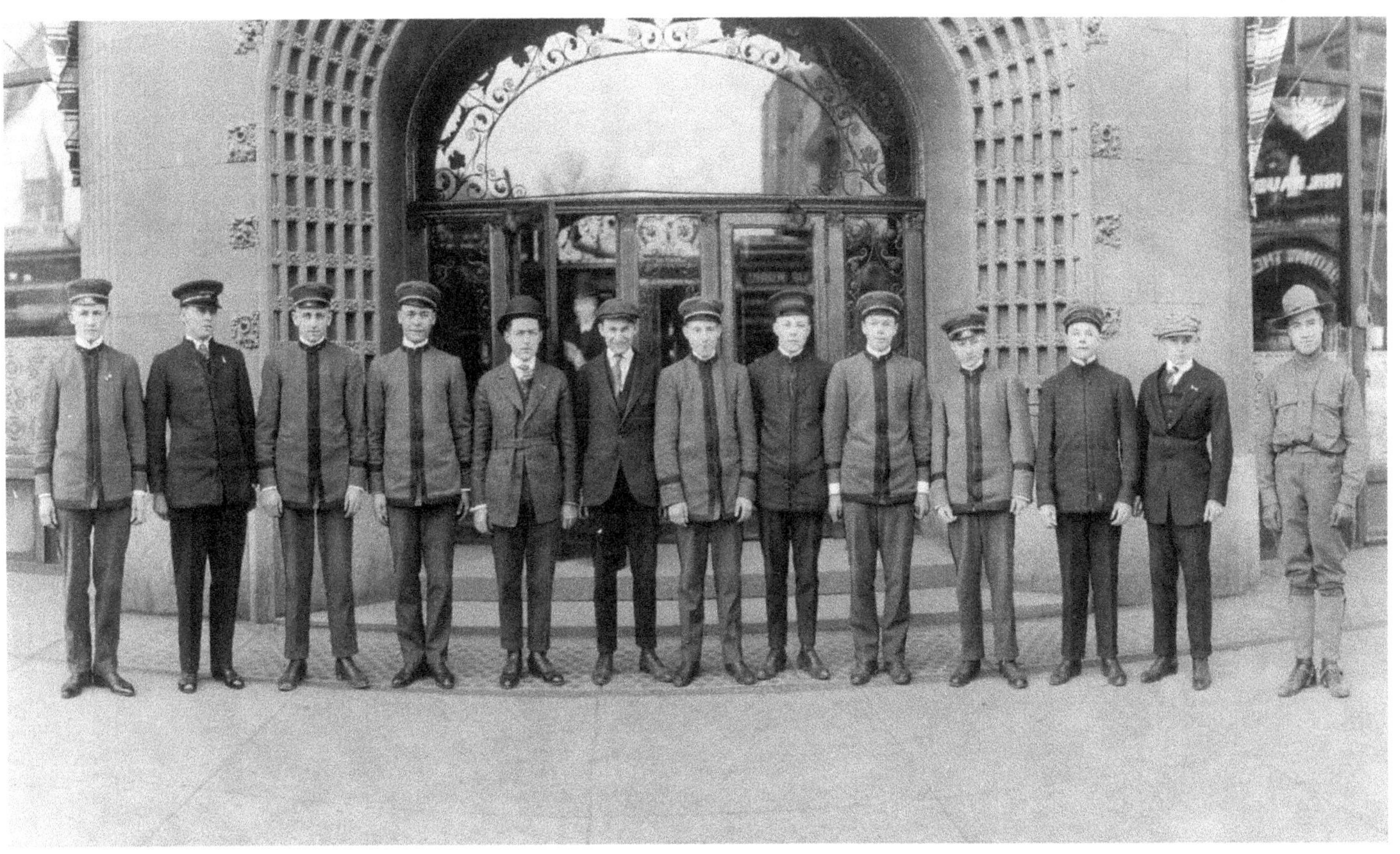

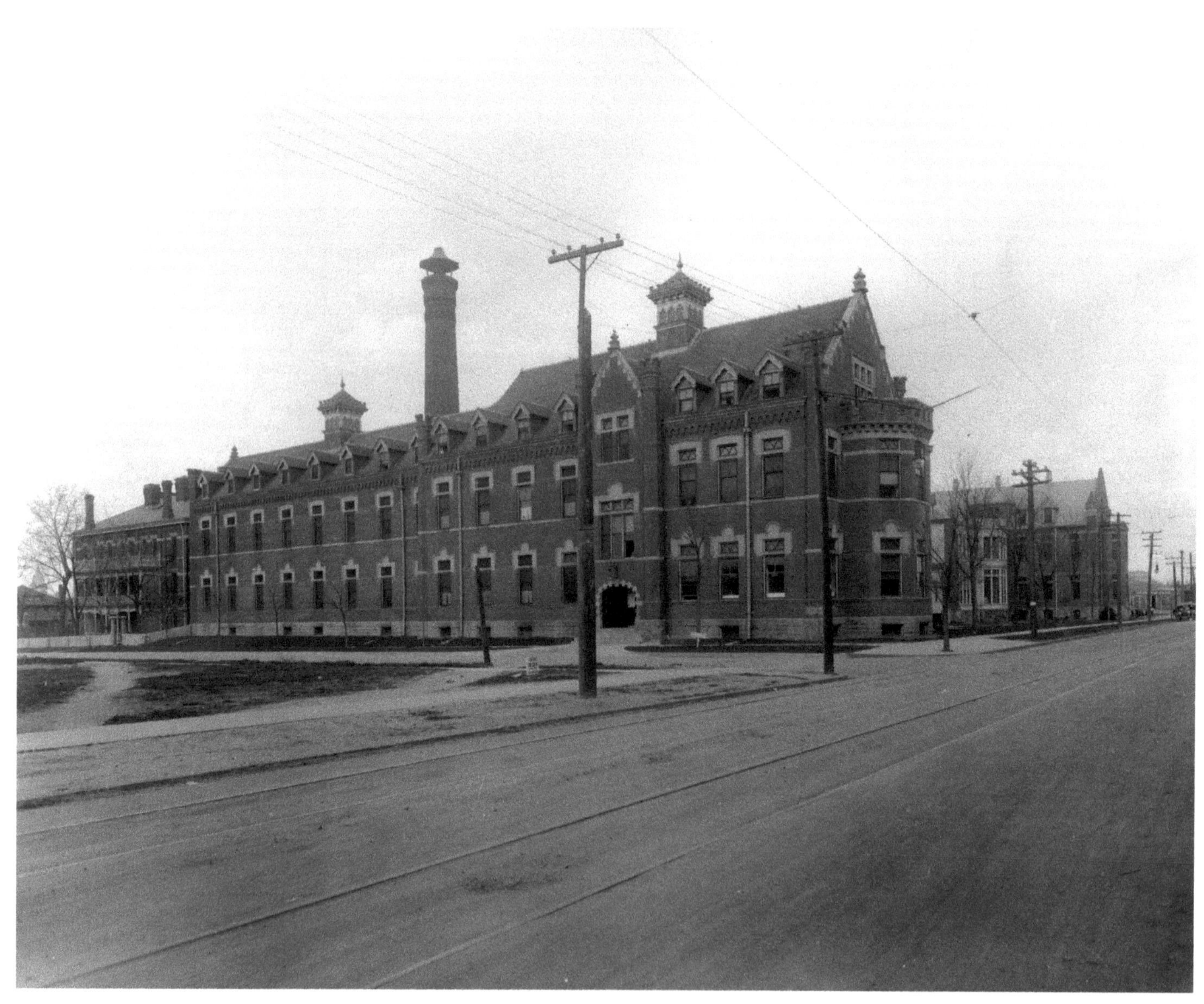

Tracing its history back to 1860, Denver General Hospital is located at West 6th Avenue and Cherokee. These buildings were built in 1889, 1892, and 1900. The hospital, but not the buildings, is still at this location.

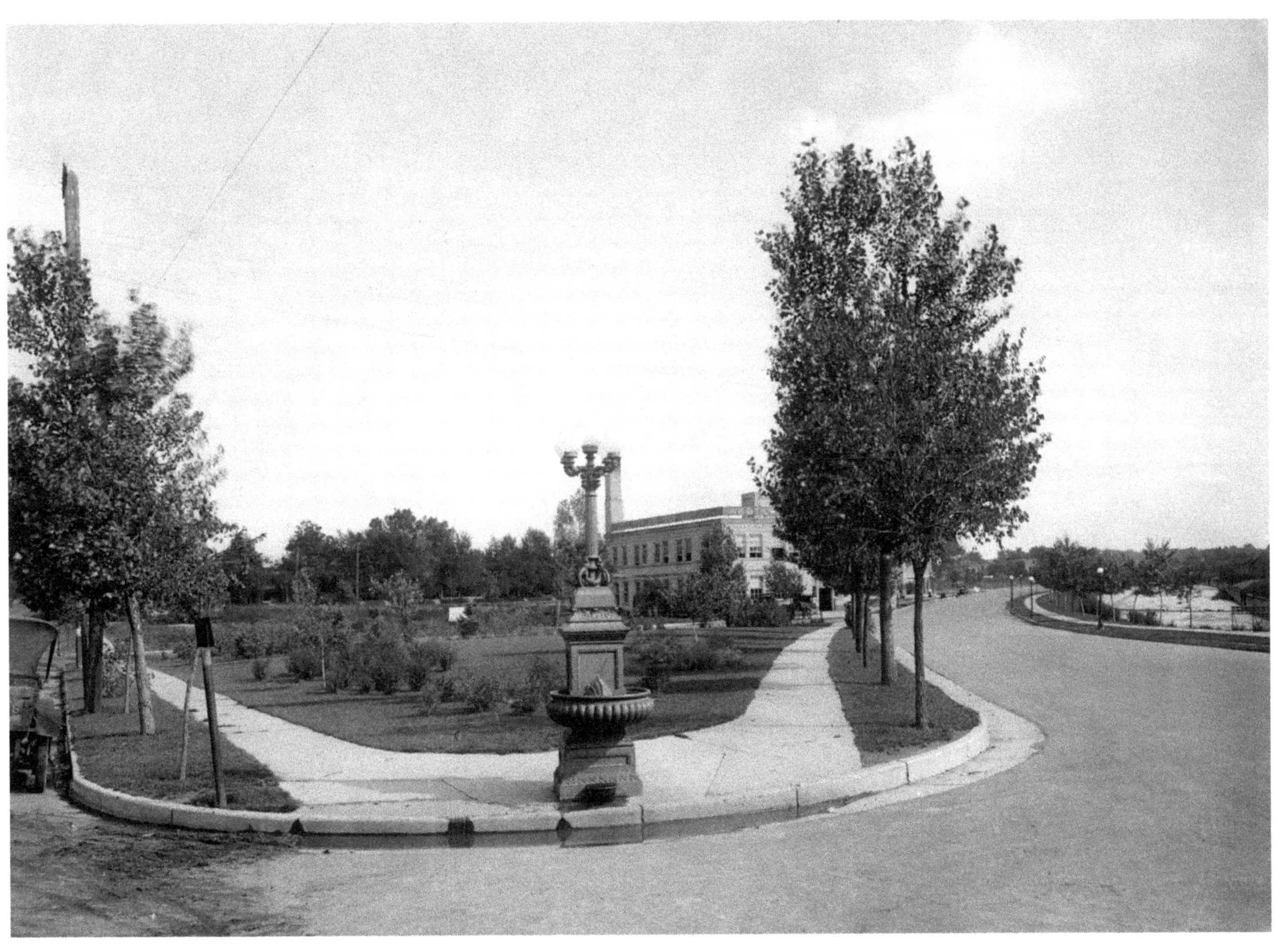

One of Mayor Speer's first projects was to contain Cherry Creek, adding landscaping and making the road beside it into one of Denver's most beautiful boulevards. In 1910 the boulevard was named Speer Boulevard to honor the mayor.

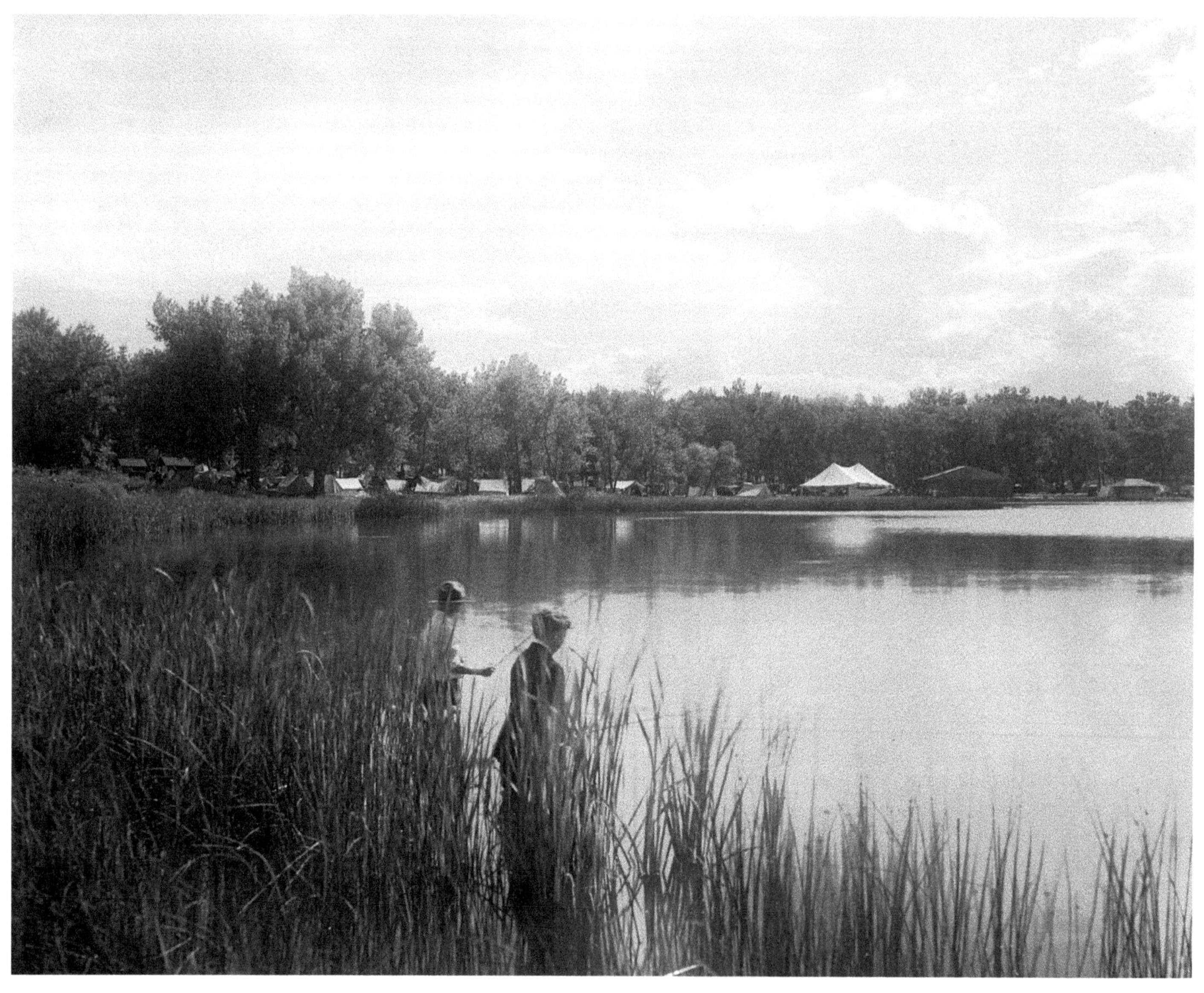

Rocky Mountain Park was another of the parks created during the Speer administration. Located in the Berkeley neighborhood, it was established in 1906.

Progress, Depression, and New Deal

1920–1939

In the 1920s Denver was rife with corruption and residents were looking for a new direction. So when William Joseph Simmons, Imperial Wizard of the Knights of the Ku Klux Klan, came to Denver, many residents eagerly embraced his message of family values and "racial purity." In 1923 the city elected Klan member Benjamin F. Stapleton as mayor, although his affiliation with the group was not widely known. Mayor Stapleton was a savvy politician who continued the progressive path of Mayor Speer, making numerous civic improvements and implementing projects begun by his predecessor.

During Mayor Speer's first administration the city planned the Denver City and County Building and opened the Denver Municipal Airport.

With the Great Depression, Denver, like most urban areas, experienced increasing unemployment. The city's population surged as falling farm prices and a severe drought drove people into the cities. By the mid 1930s, more than 25 percent of Colorado's citizens were unemployed.

Under the New Deal, Denver and Colorado slowly began to recover economically. The city benefited from New Deal programs that ranged from the construction of schools, community centers, and street improvements, to public art projects and aid programs.

The Denver Mountain Parks system expanded and was made more accessible with the construction of new roads and trails. One of the most significant Mountain Parks' projects was the Red Rocks Amphitheatre. The project, which began in the late 1930s, was completed in 1941. Built in sandstone rock formations, the theater was designed by prominent Denver architect Burnham Hoyt and built with Civilian Conservation Corps labor.

Another important mountain park created during this period was the Winter Park ski area. Located in Grand County west of Denver, this Denver Mountain Park was built on leased Forest Service land, built with WPA and city funds, and constructed with Civilian Conservation Corps and volunteer labor.

It wasn't until the onset of the Second World War that Denver once again began to experience rapid economic and population growth.

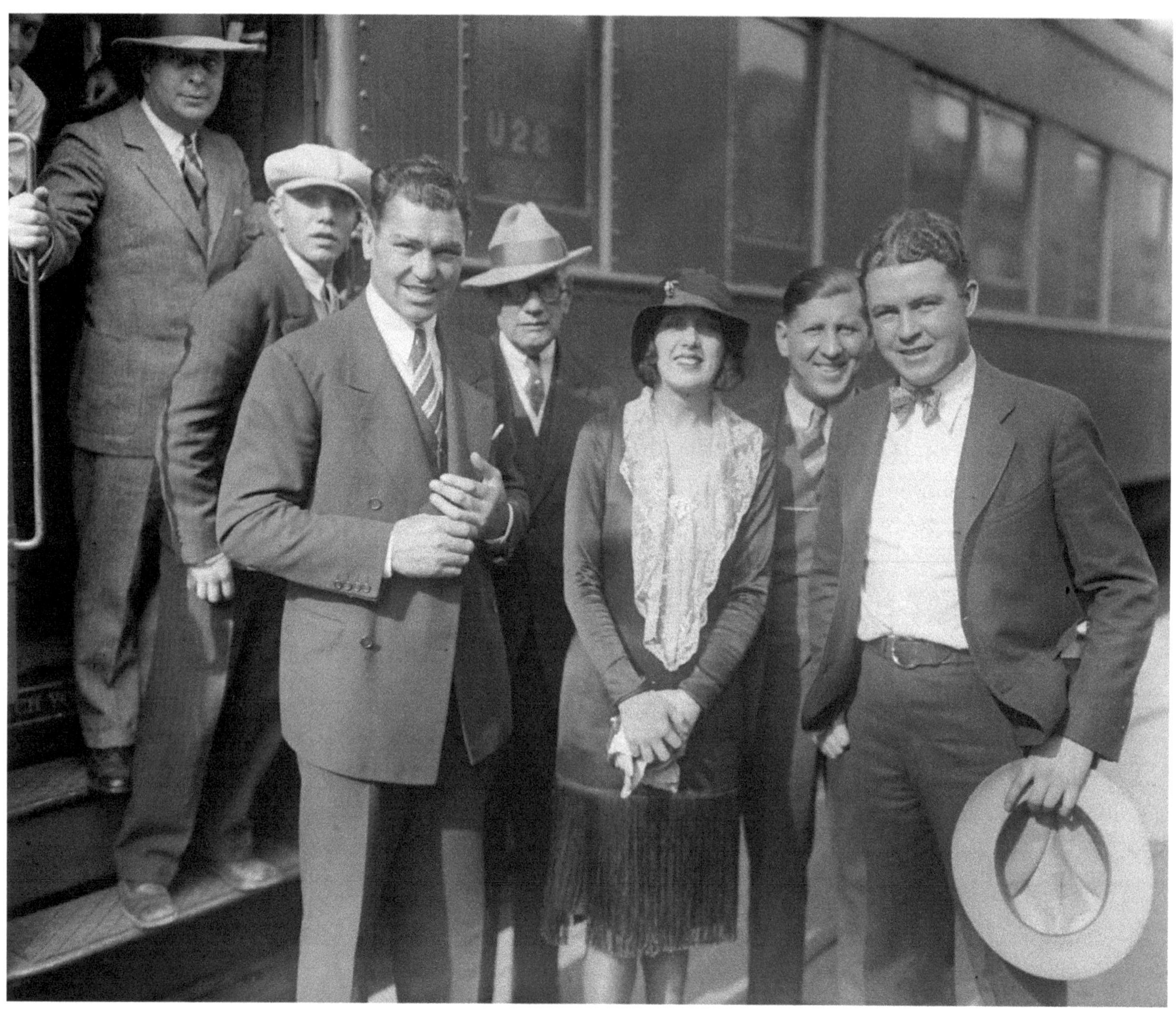

Boxer Jack Dempsey and his wife, actress Estelle Taylor, pose in front of their train at Union Station.

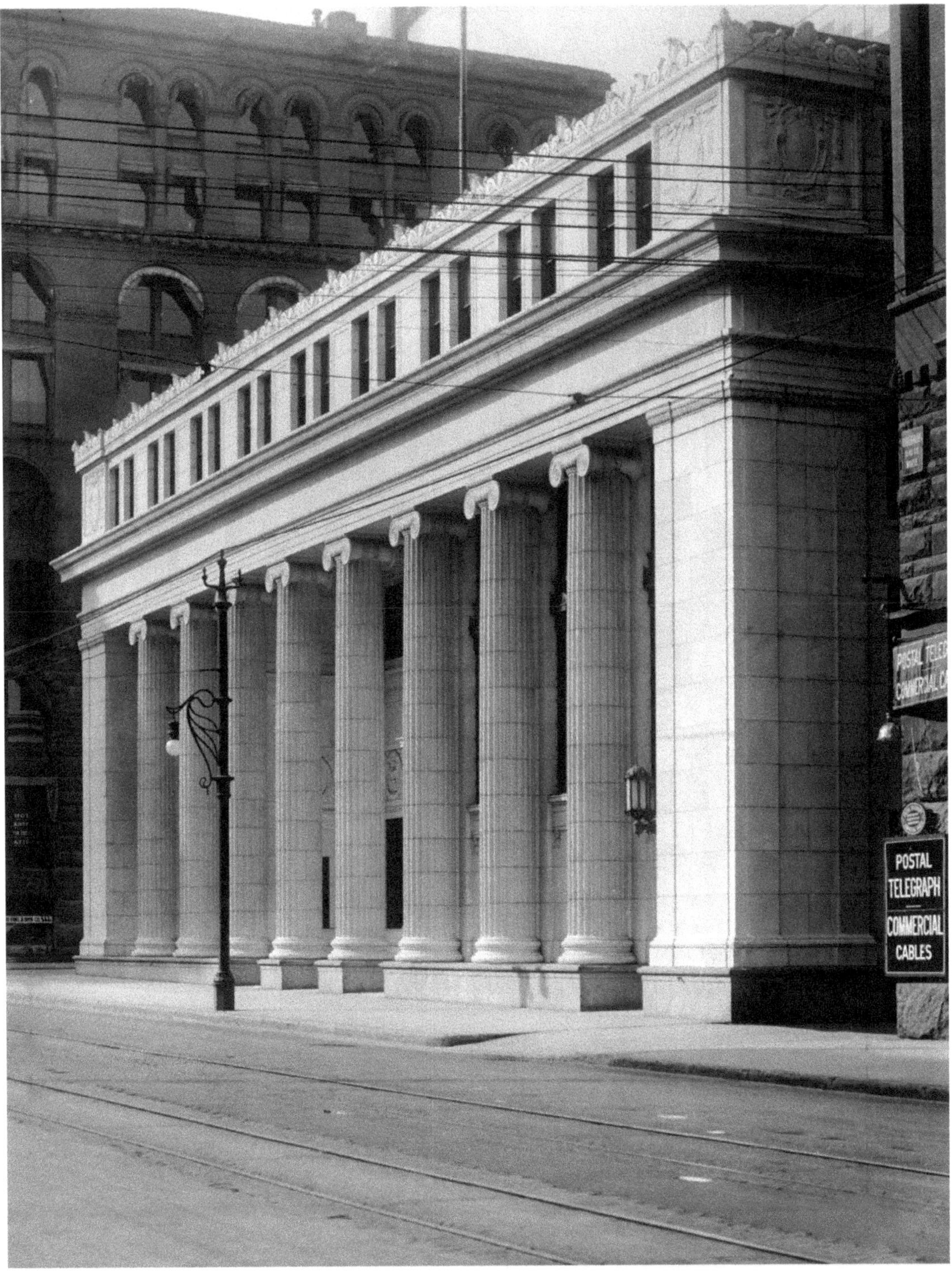

The Colorado National Bank building located at 17th and Champa streets opened in 1915. It was designed in the neoclassical style by the firm of Fisher and Fisher. The building is constructed of Colorado yule marble.

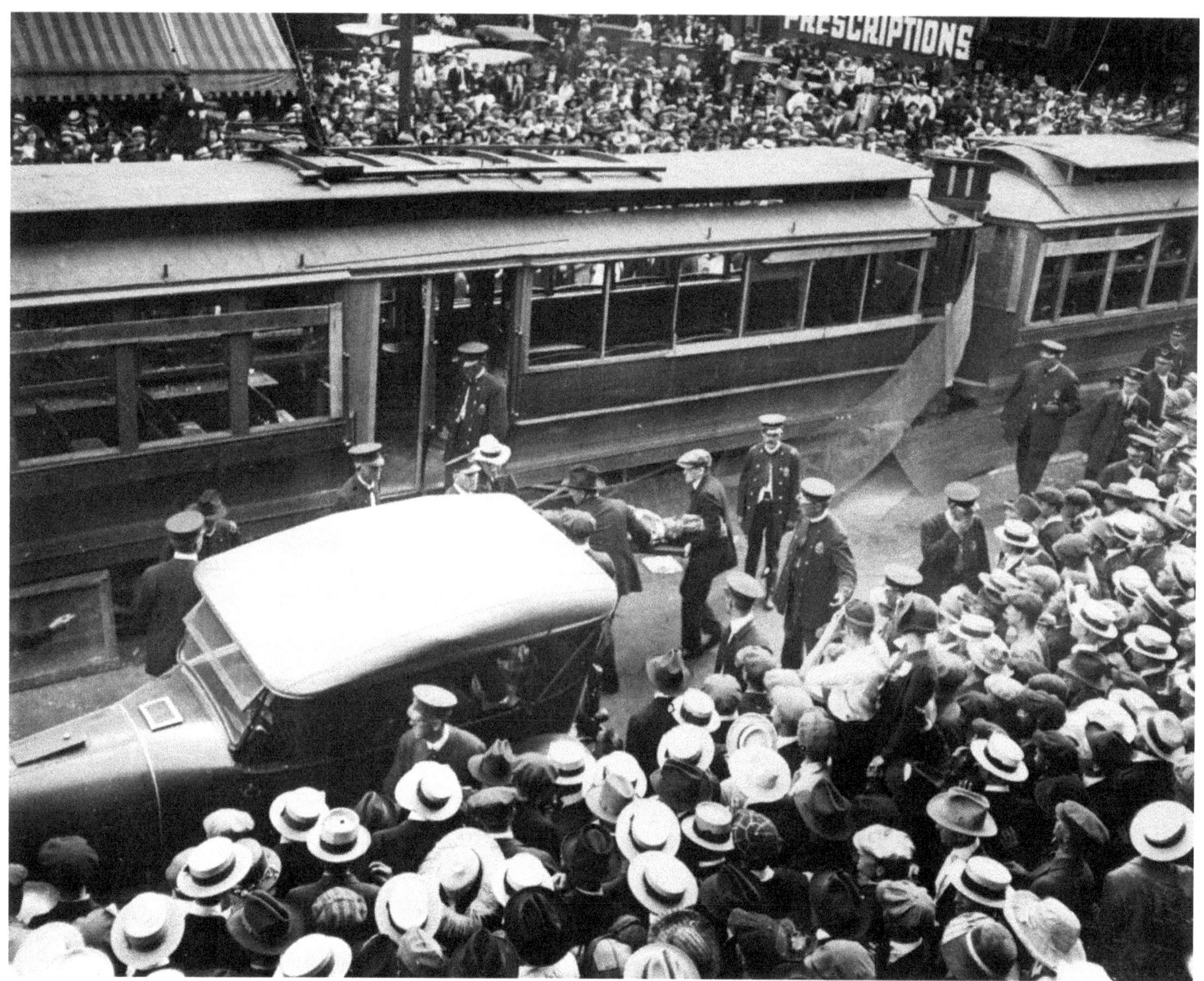

On the first of August 1920, the Denver Tramway employees union declared a strike over wages. The company hired a professional strikebreaker, John C. "Black Jack" Jerome, to attempt to restart streetcar service. Several violent clashes occurred between the strikers and the strikebreakers. Days later the strike culminated in a riot, streetcars were damaged and overturned, and streetcar barns were burned. Eventually federal troops from Fort Logan and Camp Funston, Kansas, were brought in to quell the strike, but not before six people had been killed.

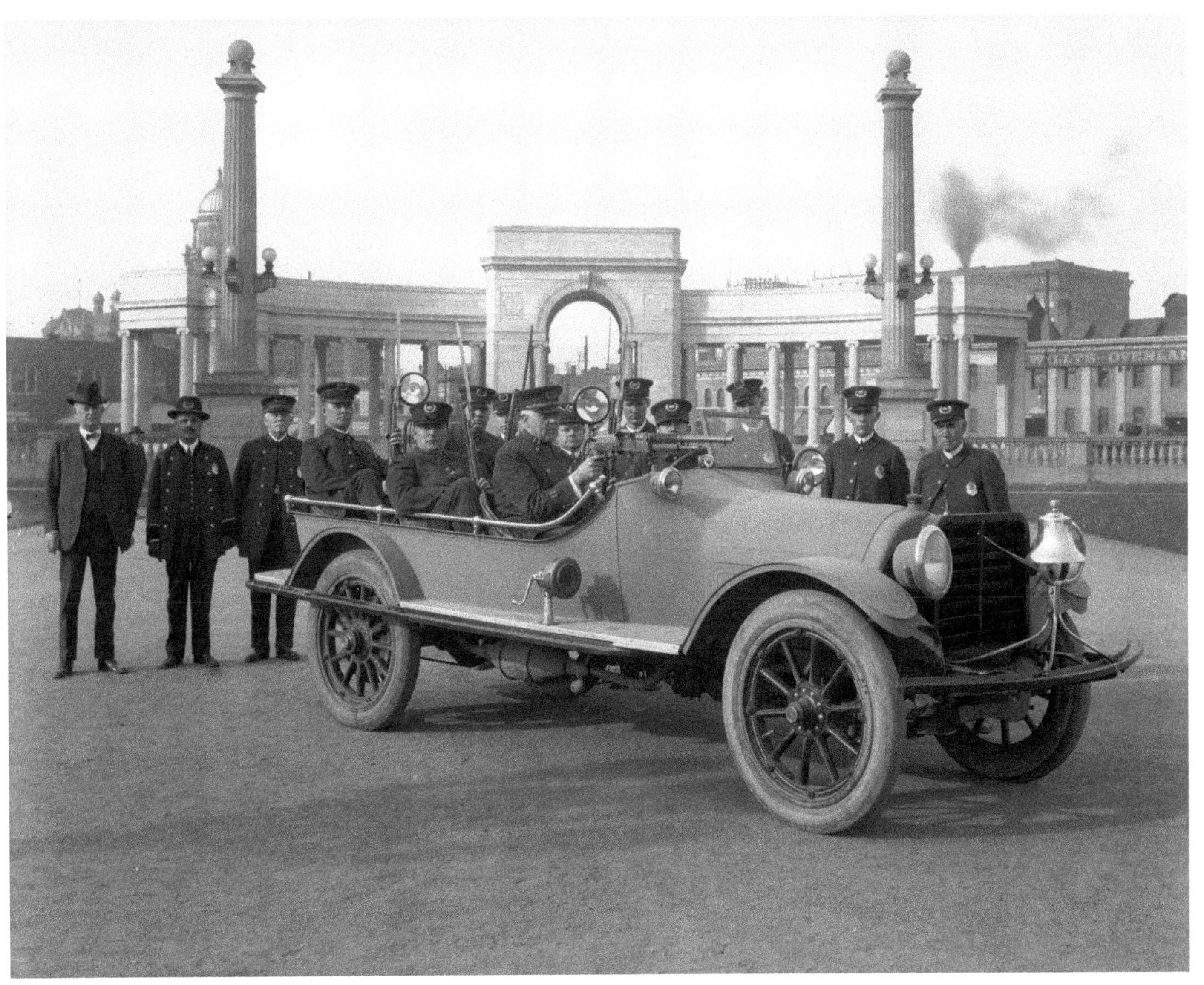

Denver's "Auto Bandit Chaser" was designed by the Denver police department. The specially equipped vehicle was armor-plated and had a mounted machine gun, siren, and bell. The vehicle was in service for a very short time in 1921 before it overturned in an accident. The "Bandit Chaser" was never repaired.

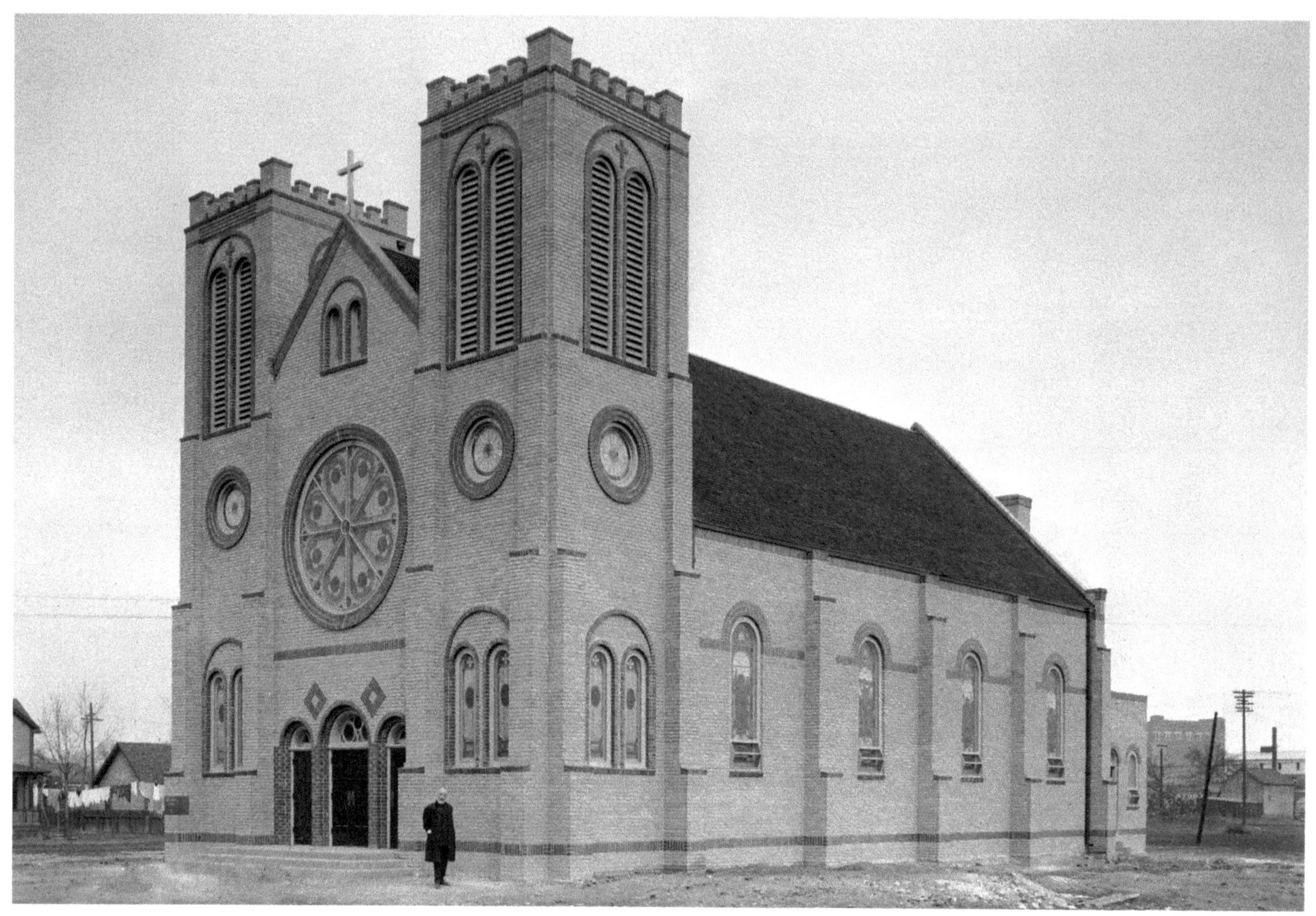

The Romanesque Revival Holy Rosary Church, designed by Denver architect L. A. Desjardins, is located at 4695 Pearl Street in the Globeville neighborhood. The church played an important role in the lives of the Slovenian and Croatian members of the parish.

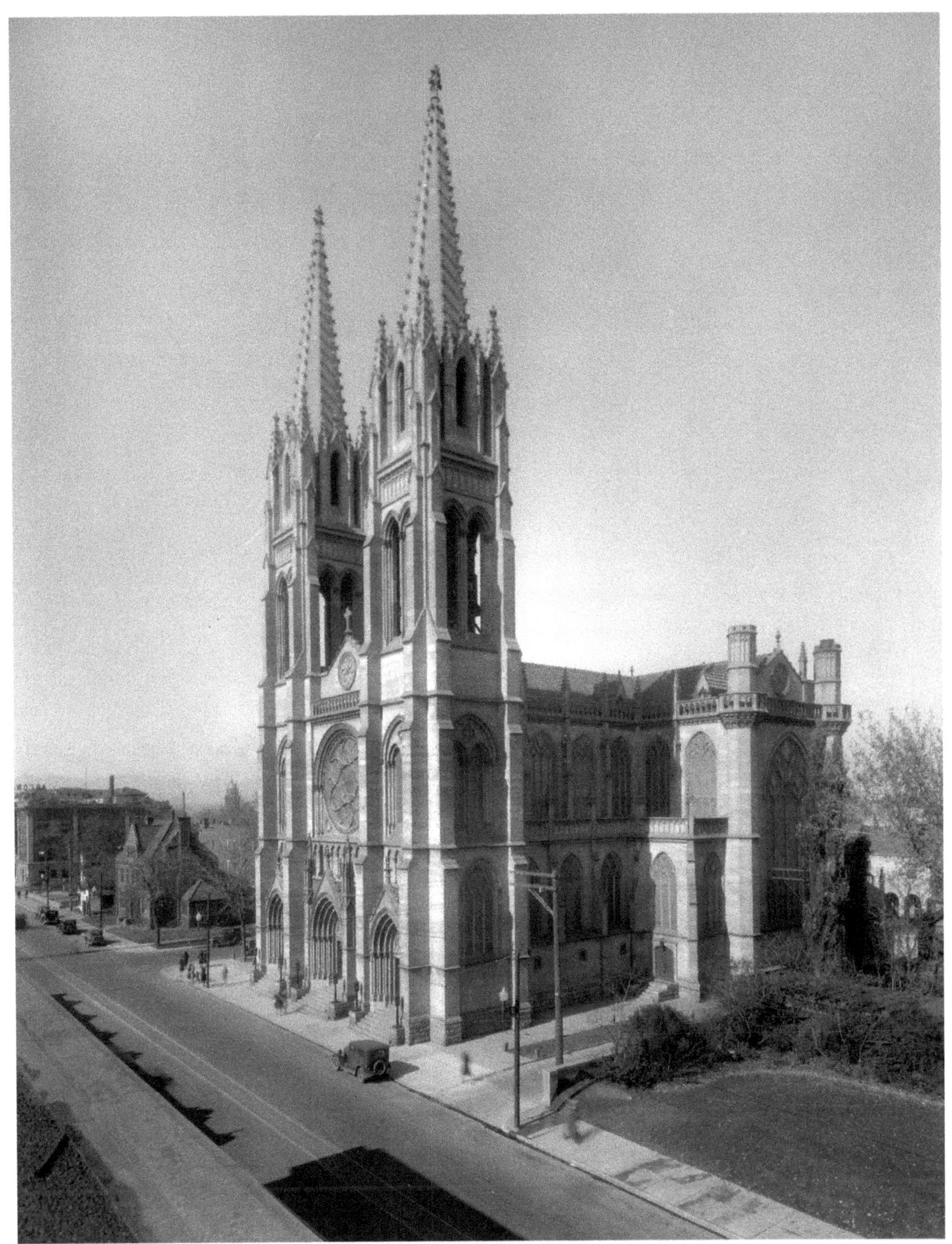

The Cathedral of the Immaculate Conception, is a French Gothic Revival–style building, with 75 stained-glass windows. The building was designed by Leon Coquard of Detroit and construction was supervised by Denver architects Aaron and Thomas Gove. The opening celebration on October 27, 1912, included a parade of more than 20,000 people.

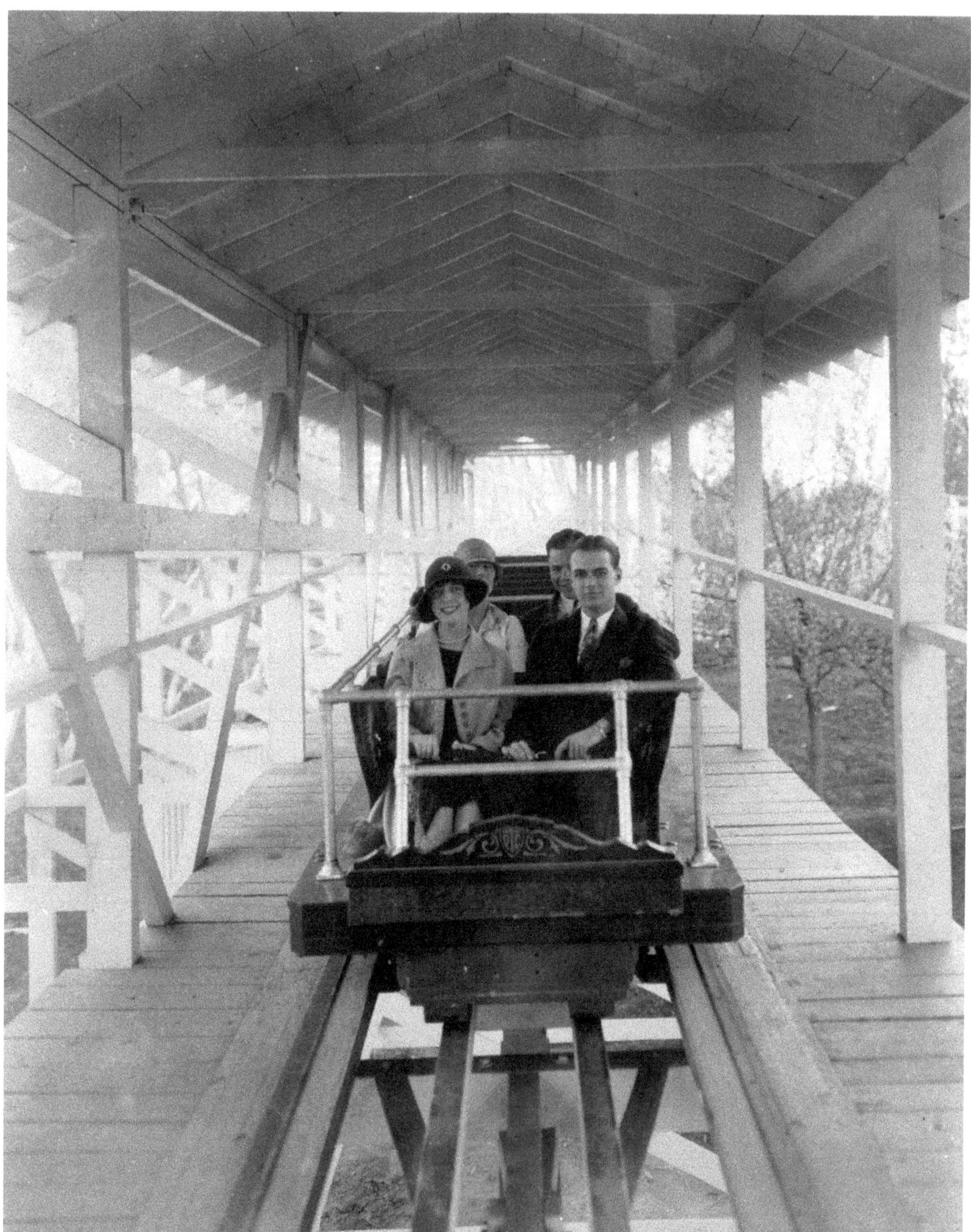

Two couples sit in the "Wildcat," a traditional camelback wooden roller coaster in Elitch Gardens, which was located at 4620 West 38th Avenue. Elitch's, opened by John and Mary Elitch in 1890, was on the site of Chilcott Farm. The park grew to include beautiful gardens, the Trocadero ballroom, a zoo, a summer stock theater, and a wide variety of amusement rides. The park was closed in 1994.

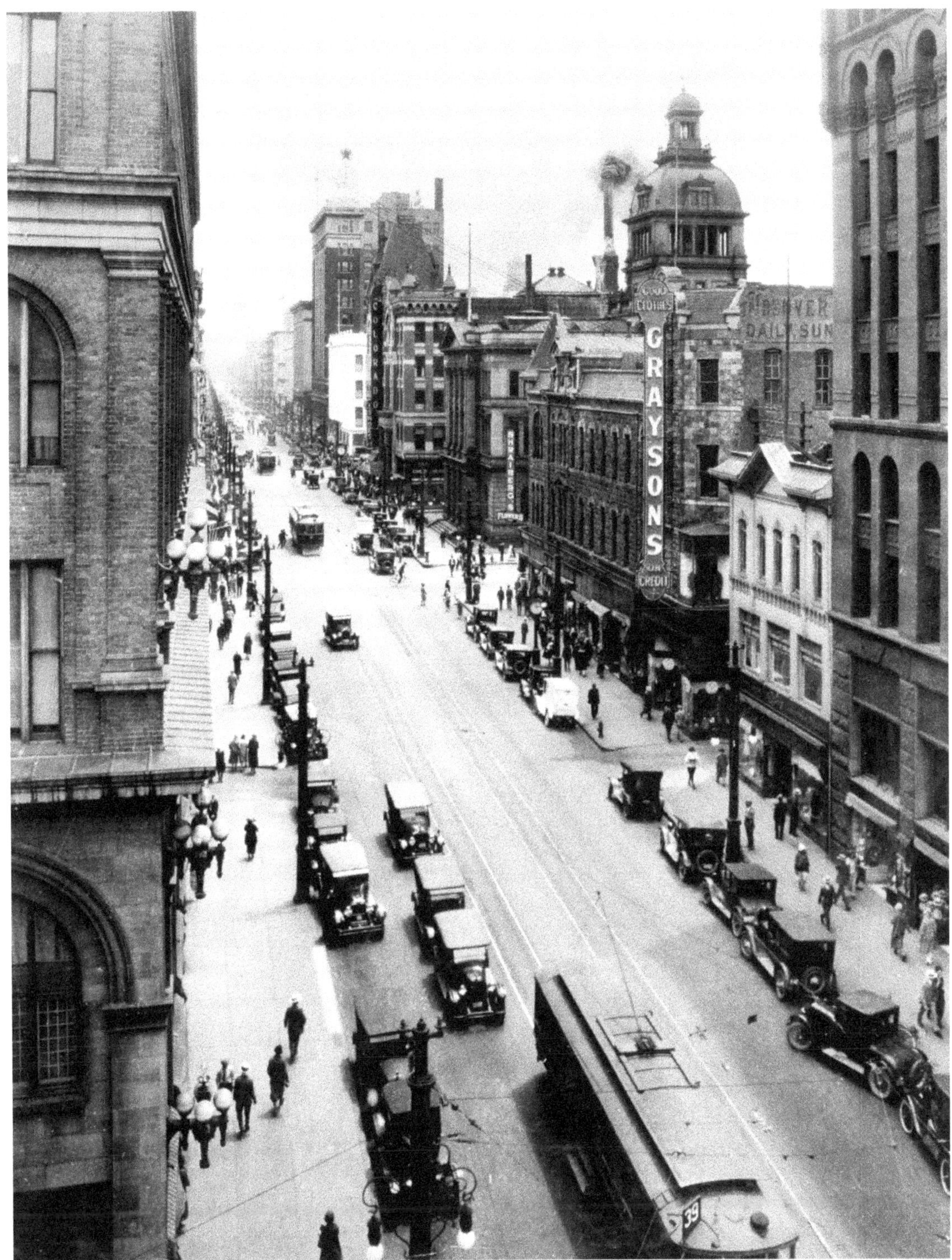

A 1920s view of a busy 16th Street looking toward the State Capitol building. The cupola in view is part of the U.S. Customs House.

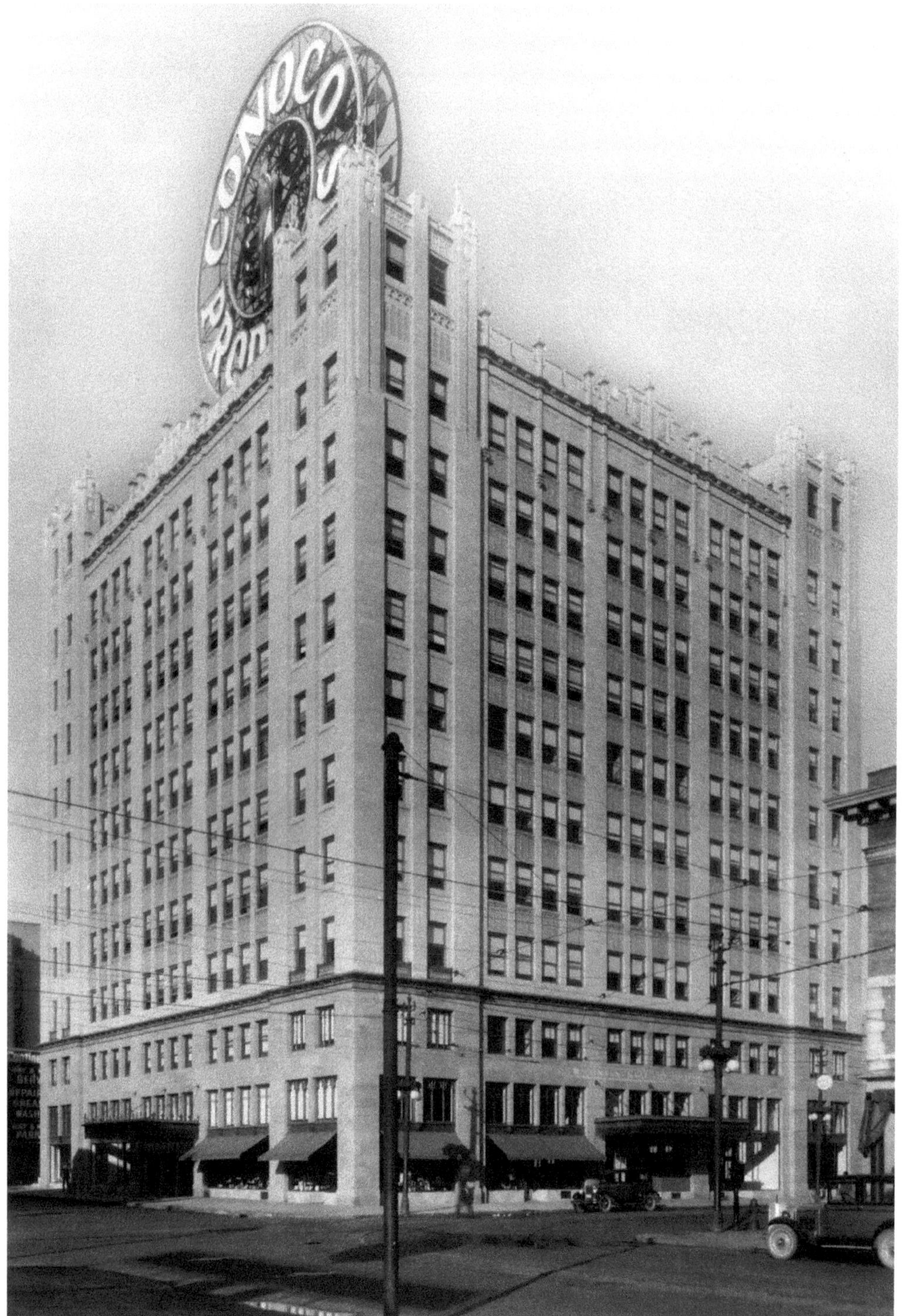

The art deco-style Continental Oil building at 18th Street and Glenarm Place is attributed to William N. Bowman and was built in 1926. The building has been demolished.

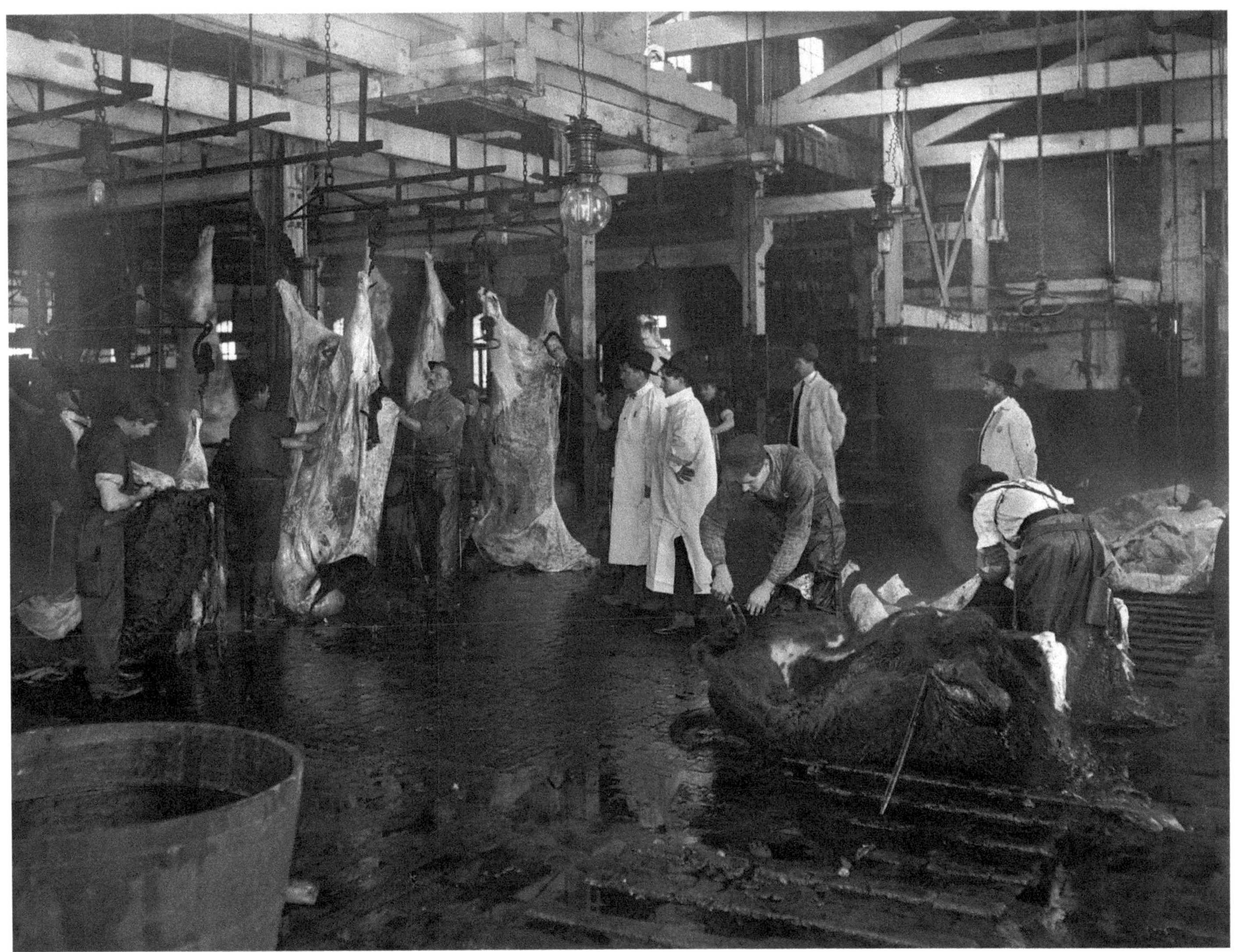

By the 1920s Denver had become the leading live stock market west of the Missouri River. It was home to five leading packing plants and numerous slaughterhouses. This interior shot shows men removing the hides from cattle carcasses.

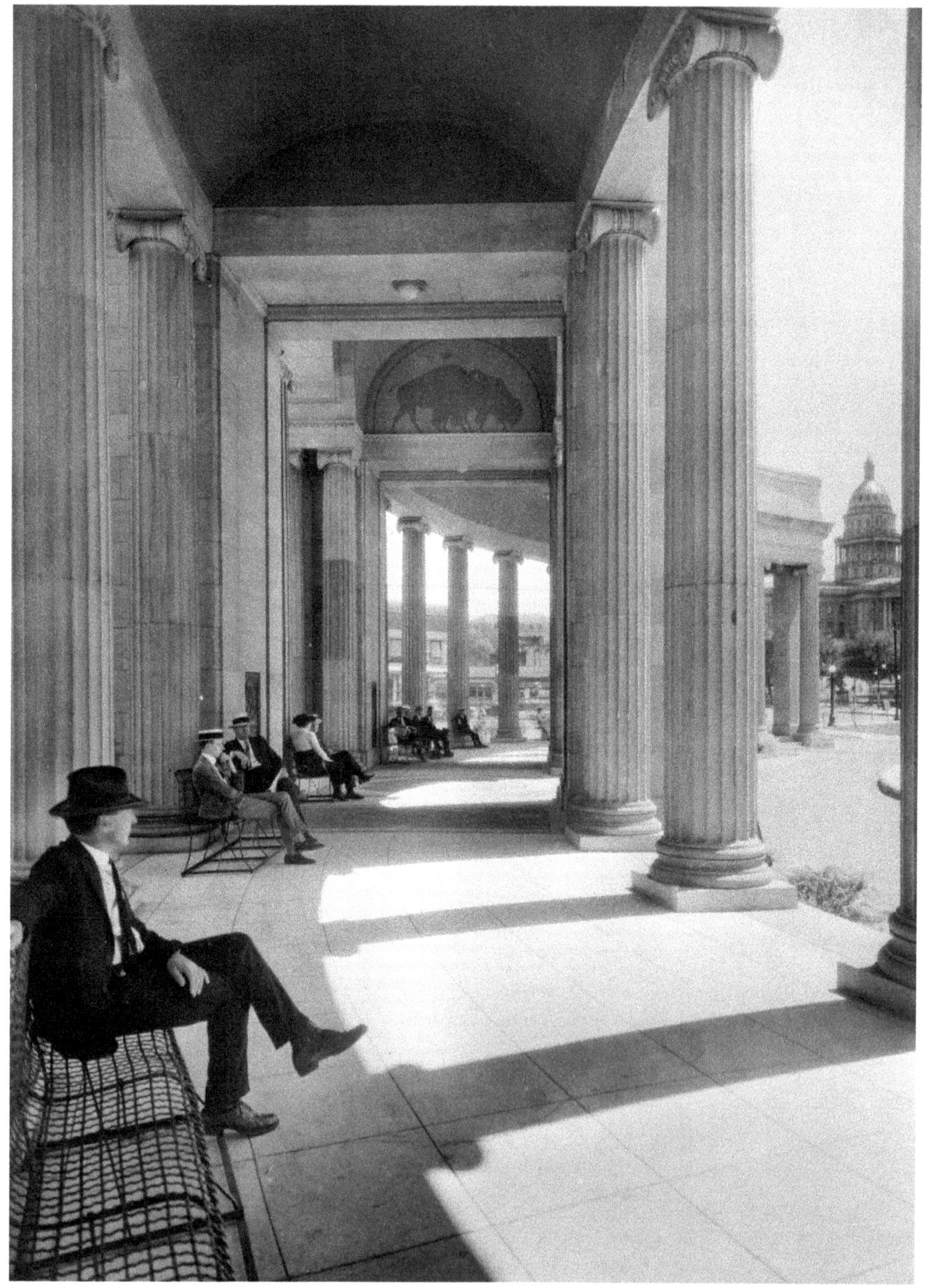

People sit on wire benches in the Voorhies Memorial pergola in Civic Center. The memorial, inspired by the Water Gateway at the 1893 Columbian Exposition, was designed by Fisher and Fisher Architects and completed in 1919. Allen True, a well-known Colorado painter, created silhouette buffaloes and elk in the Greek style for the lunettes of the arches in the memorial. The state capitol is visible in the distance.

Pedestrians crowd the sidewalk on Curtis Street. The Empress Theater, across the street, opened in December of 1907 as the Majestic.

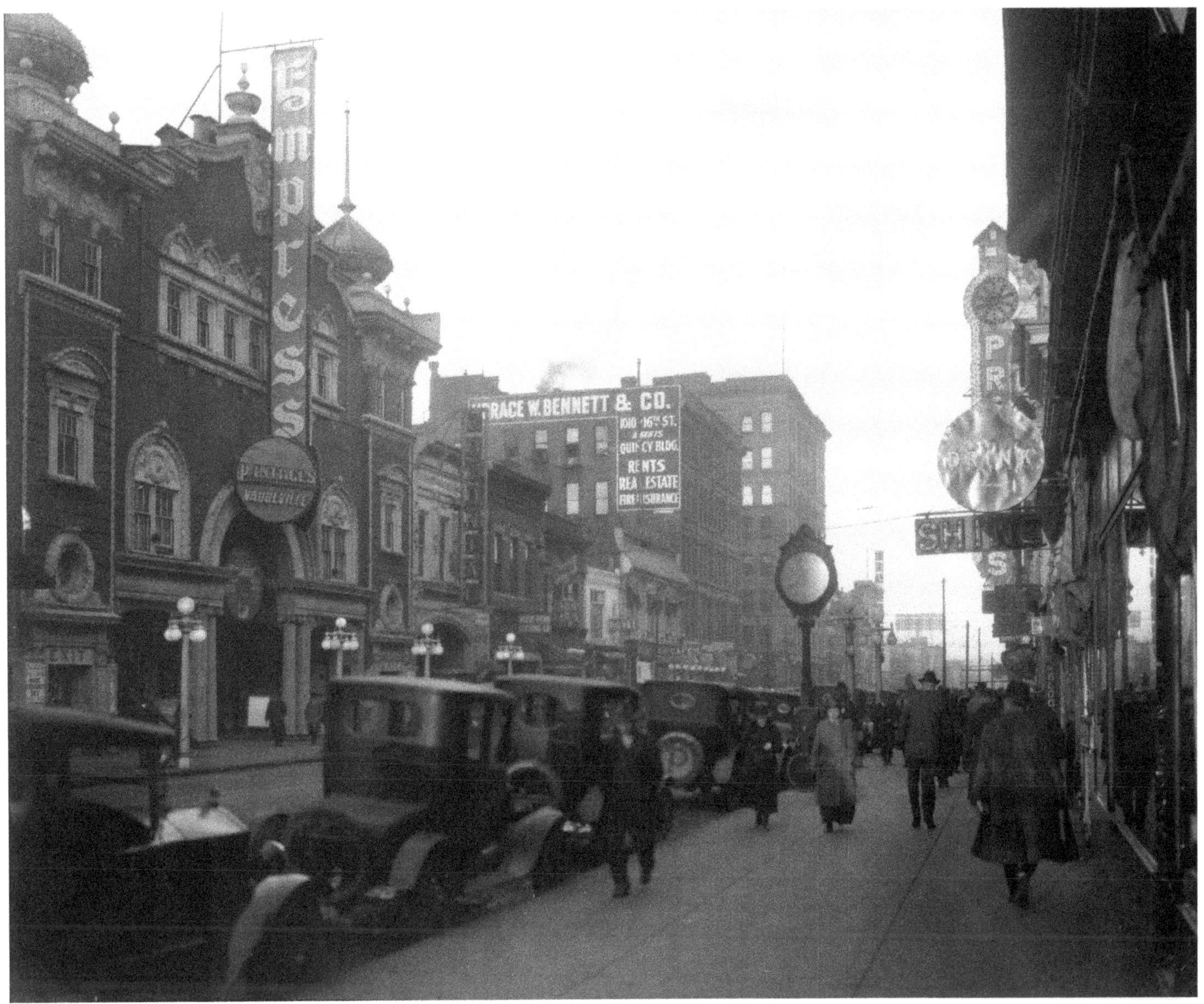

The Federal Building–Post Office is located at 18th and Champa streets. The building was erected between 1910 and 1916 and is considered Denver's finest neoclassical structure. The building was renovated and restored in 1994 and is now known as the Byron White Courthouse.

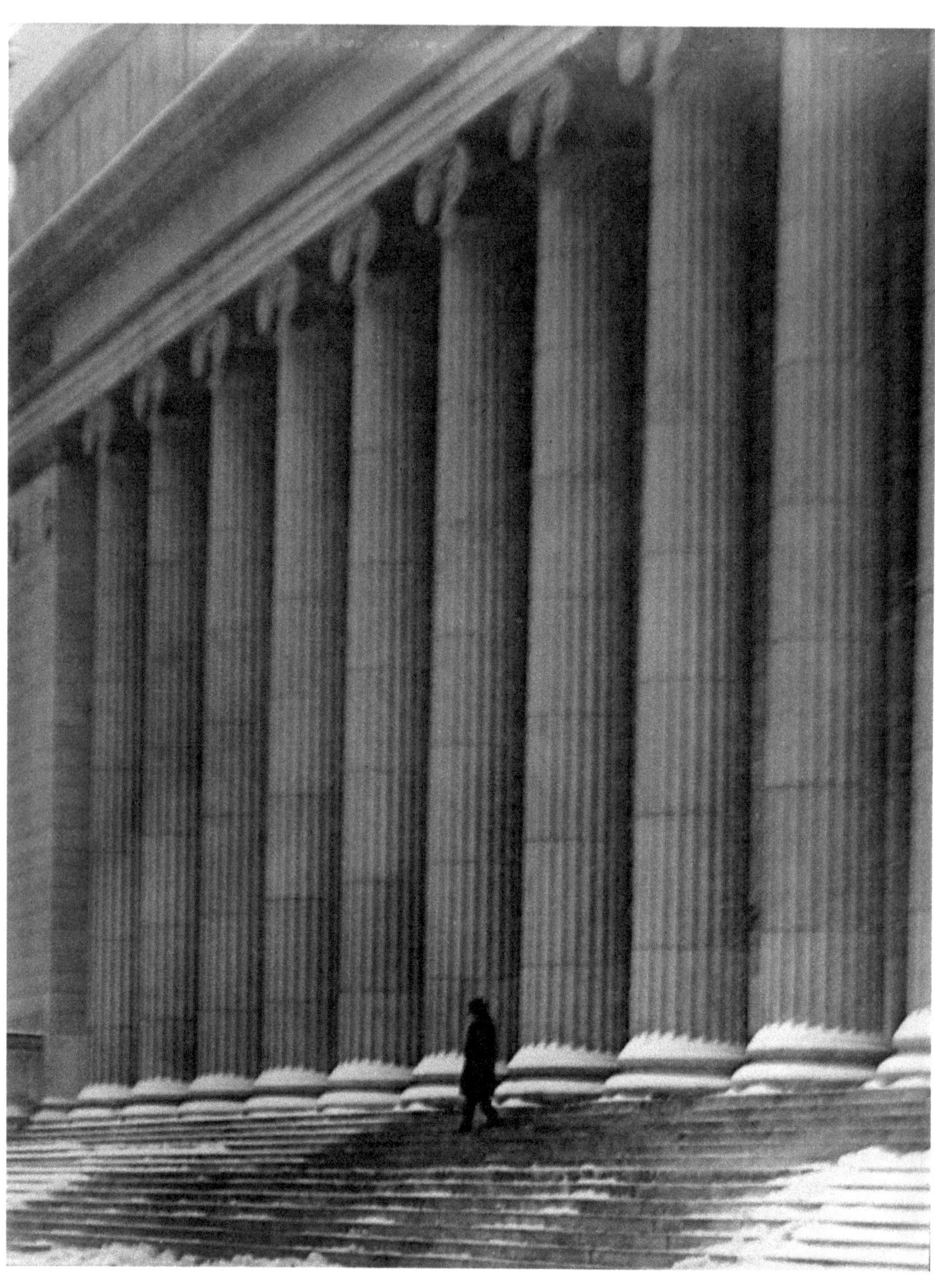

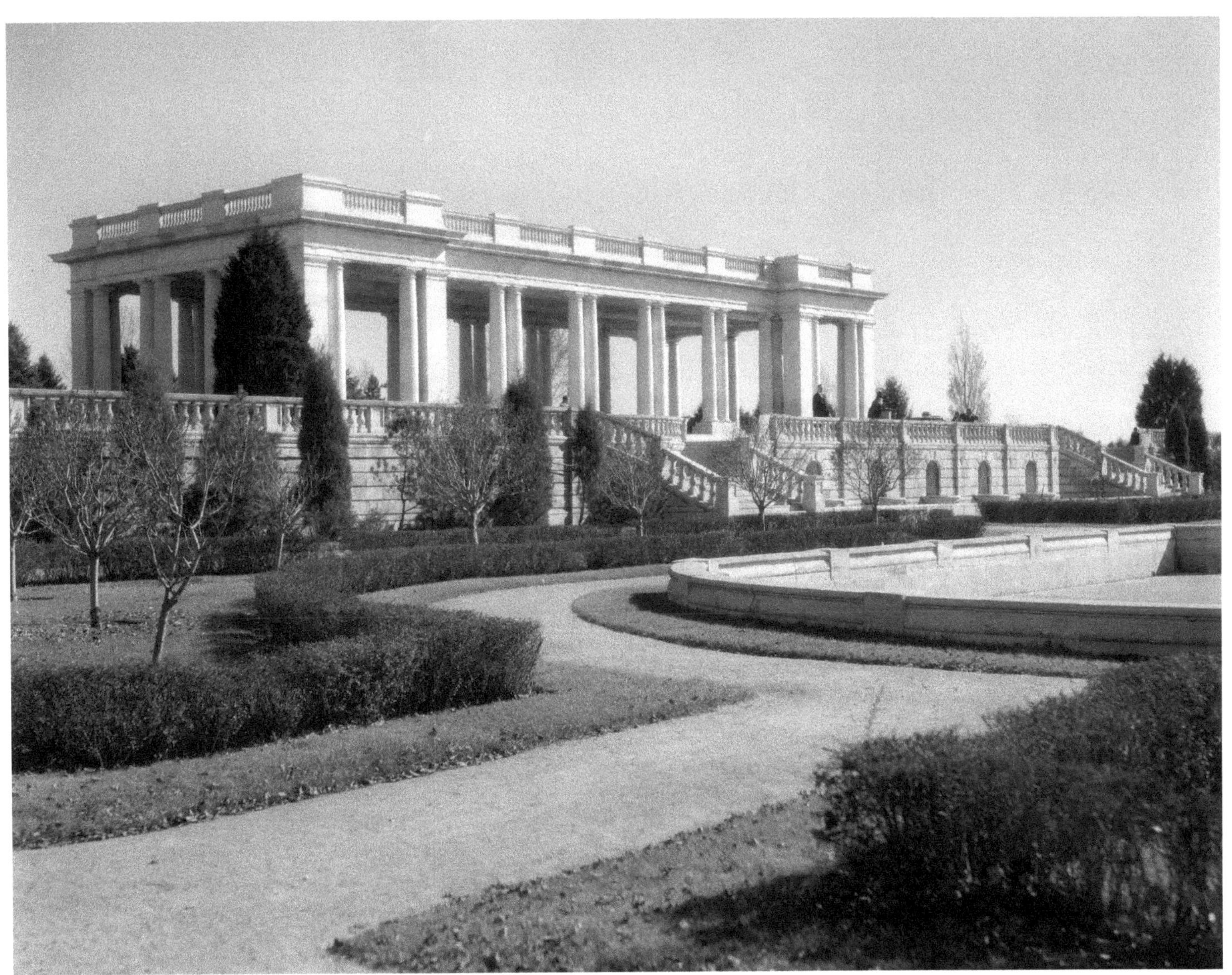

Cheesman Park is located on a hill overlooking the Front Range. Originally Mt. Prospect Cemetery, in 1890 it was discovered that the land had originally been Indian land ceded to the government by treaty. The government then sold the land to Denver, and the cemetery was renamed Denver City Cemetery. The following year the city decided to vacate the cemetery. This resulted in a major scandal. Corrupt officials allowed haphazard removal of bodies, and as a result many still lie buried under what would become Cheesman Park. In 1909, the widow of prominent Denver businessman Walter S. Cheesman donated the neoclassical Cheesman Pavilion.

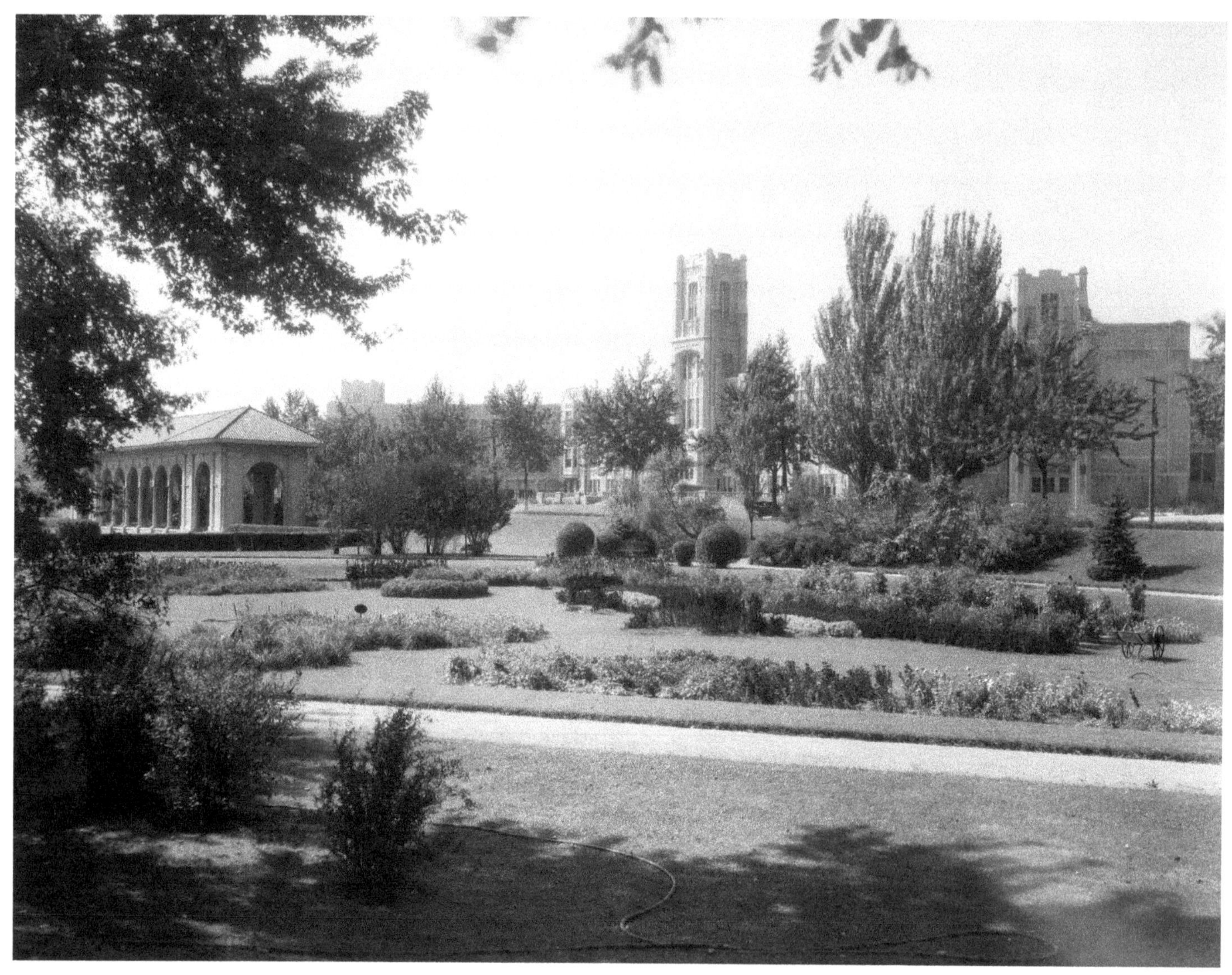

Sunken Garden Park, part of Mayor Speer's City Beautiful initiative, is located at 8th Avenue and Elati Street in front of West High School. The park was completed in 1907 and the school was built in 1925. Both are still in use today.

In this view a light snow covers 17th Street. The neoclassical Colorado National Bank opened in 1915 on the corner of Champa Street.

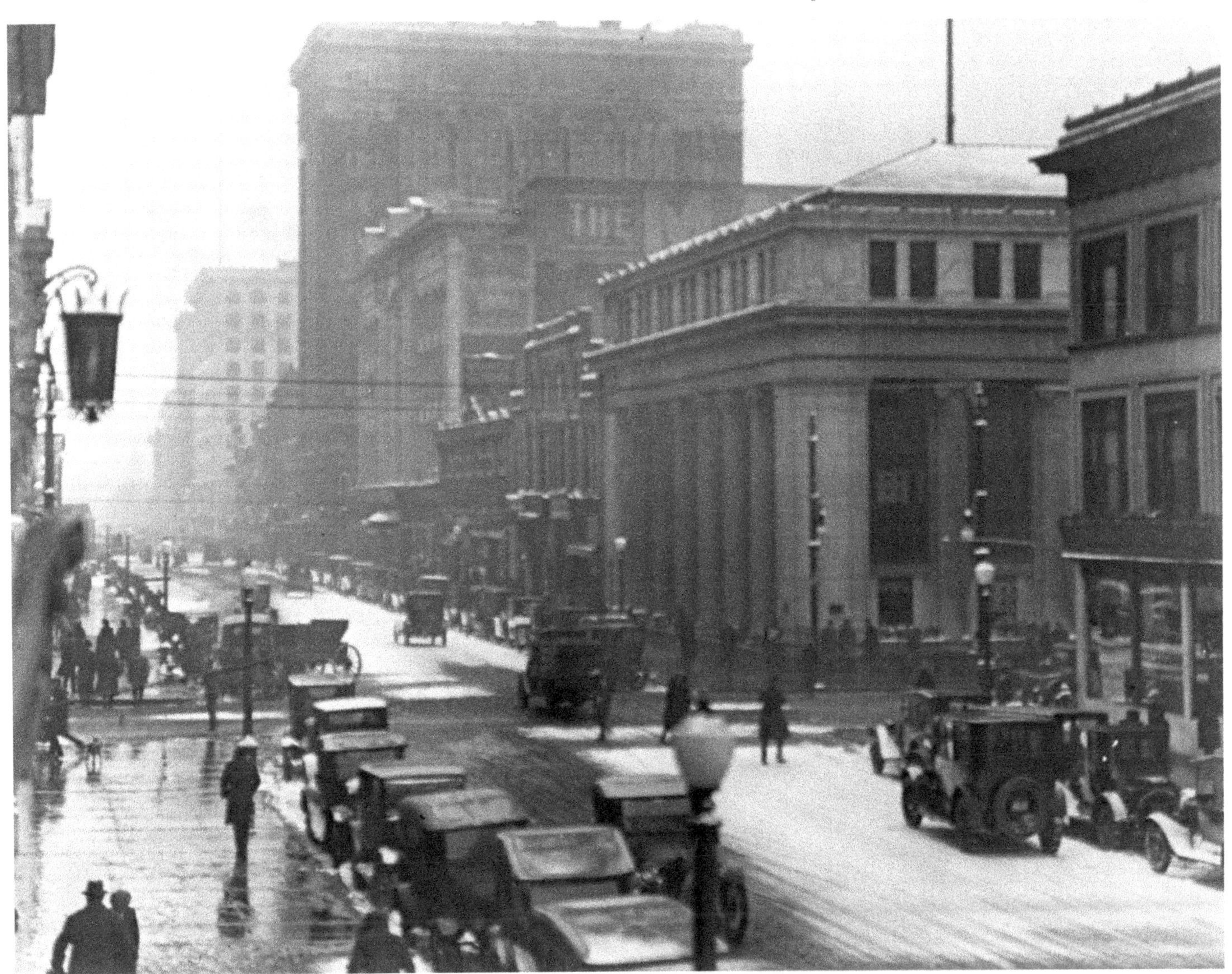

The United States Mint, located at Cherokee Street and Colfax Avenue, was completed and began coinage in 1906. The Colorado State Capitol, in the background, is just a few blocks away.

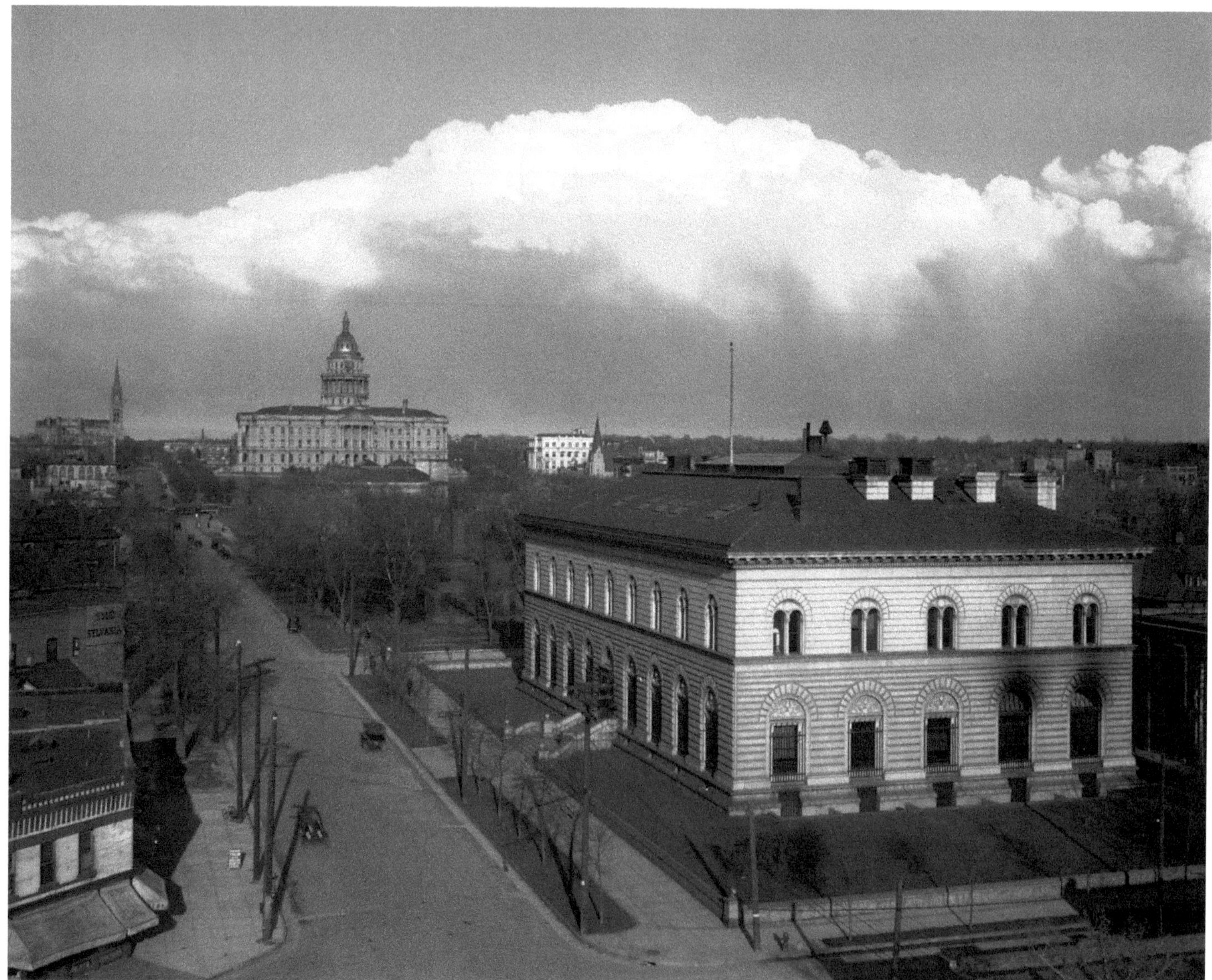

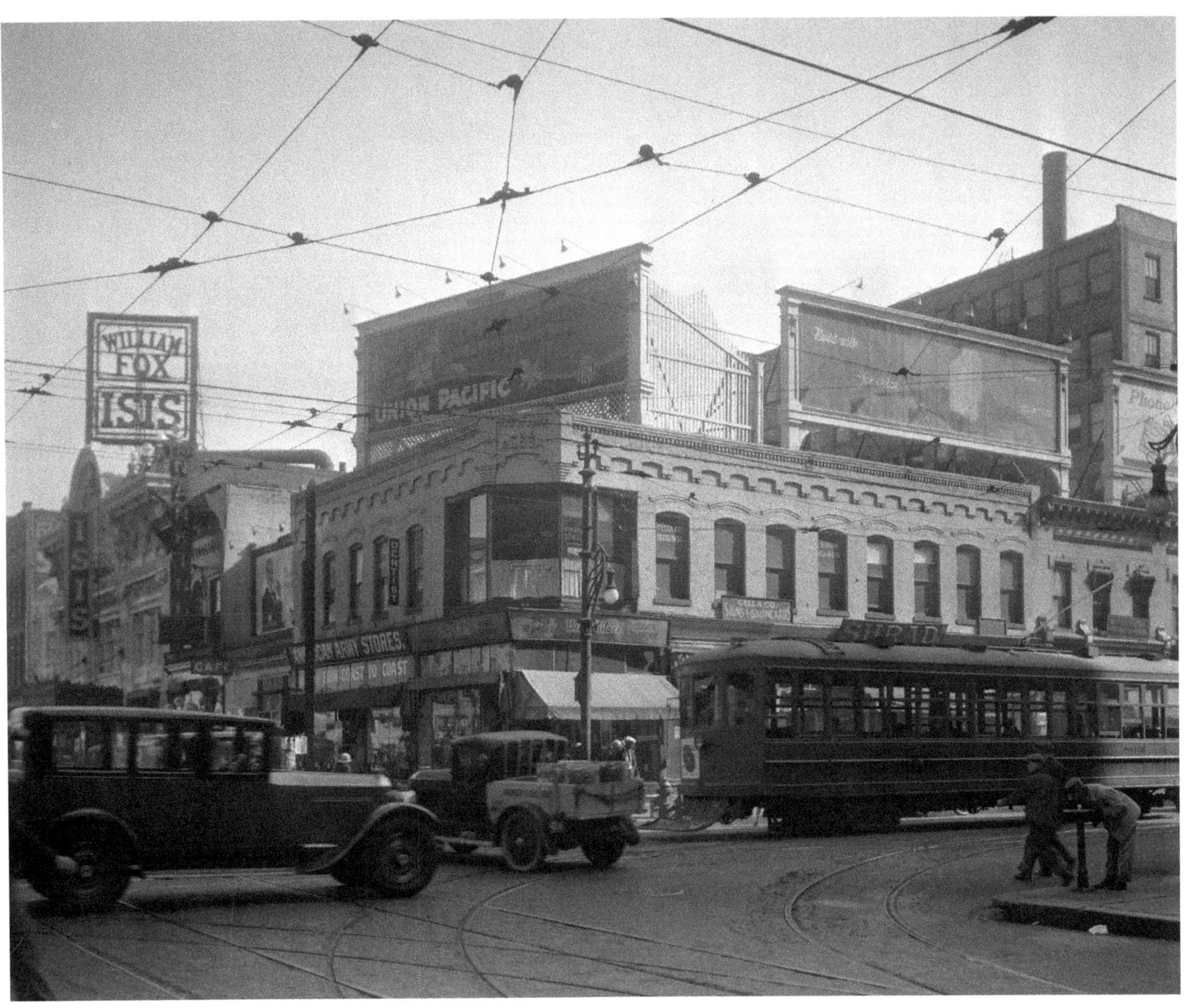

The A & B Block faces the busy intersection of Curtis and 17th streets. The Isis Theater is on Curtis. A man on the right takes a drink from a public drinking fountain.

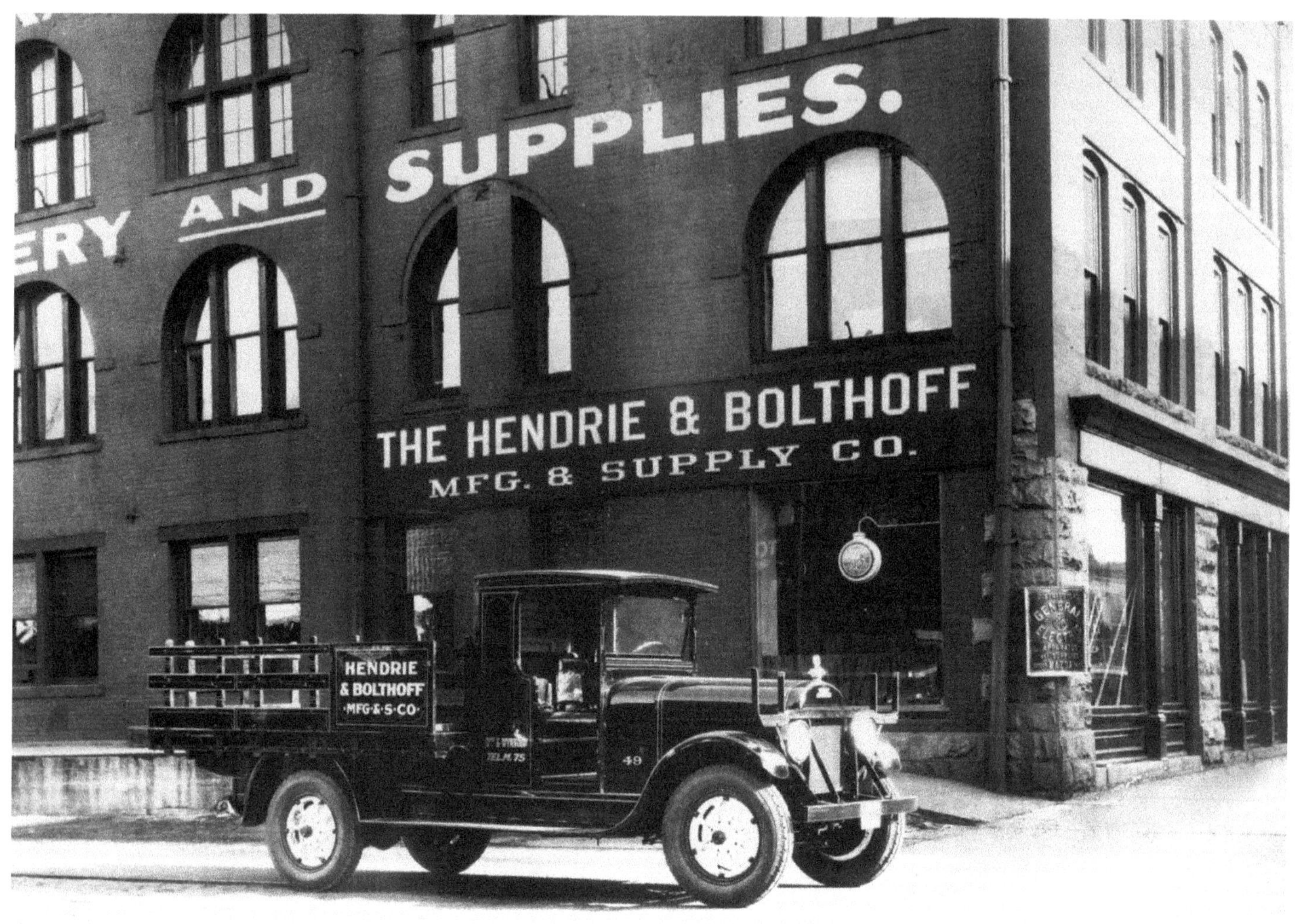

A delivery truck is parked in front of the Hendrie & Bolthoff Manufacturing and Supply Company building at 1743 Wazee Street. The company was the largest manufacturer of mining machinery in the West. The warehouse was designed in 1907 by Frank Edbrooke.

Colorado members of the Ku Klux Klan march down Larimer Street during a 1929 convention. The Klan had a great political influence. Mayor Benjamin F. Stapleton and Governor Clarence J. Morley were both elected with strong Klan support.

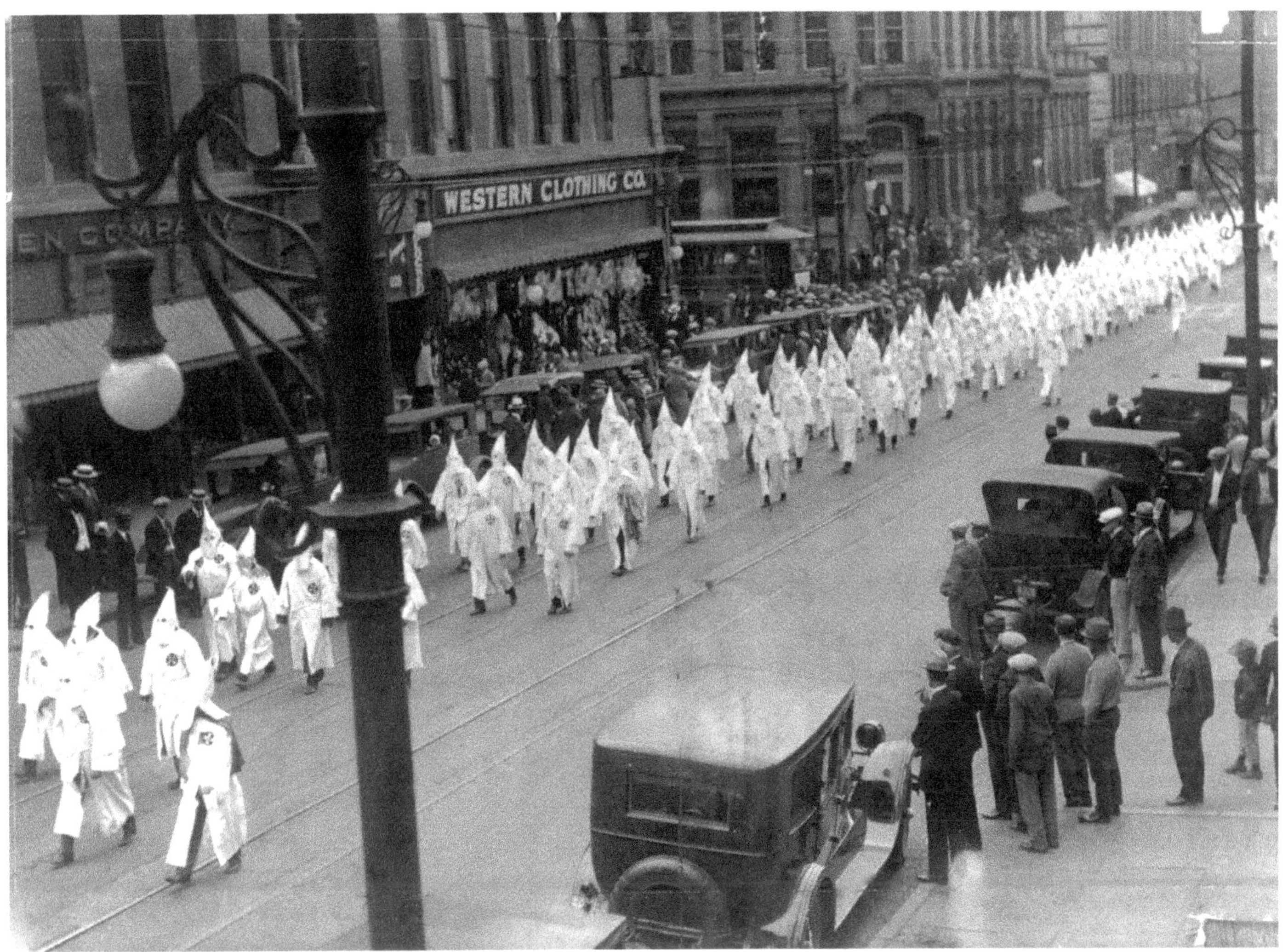

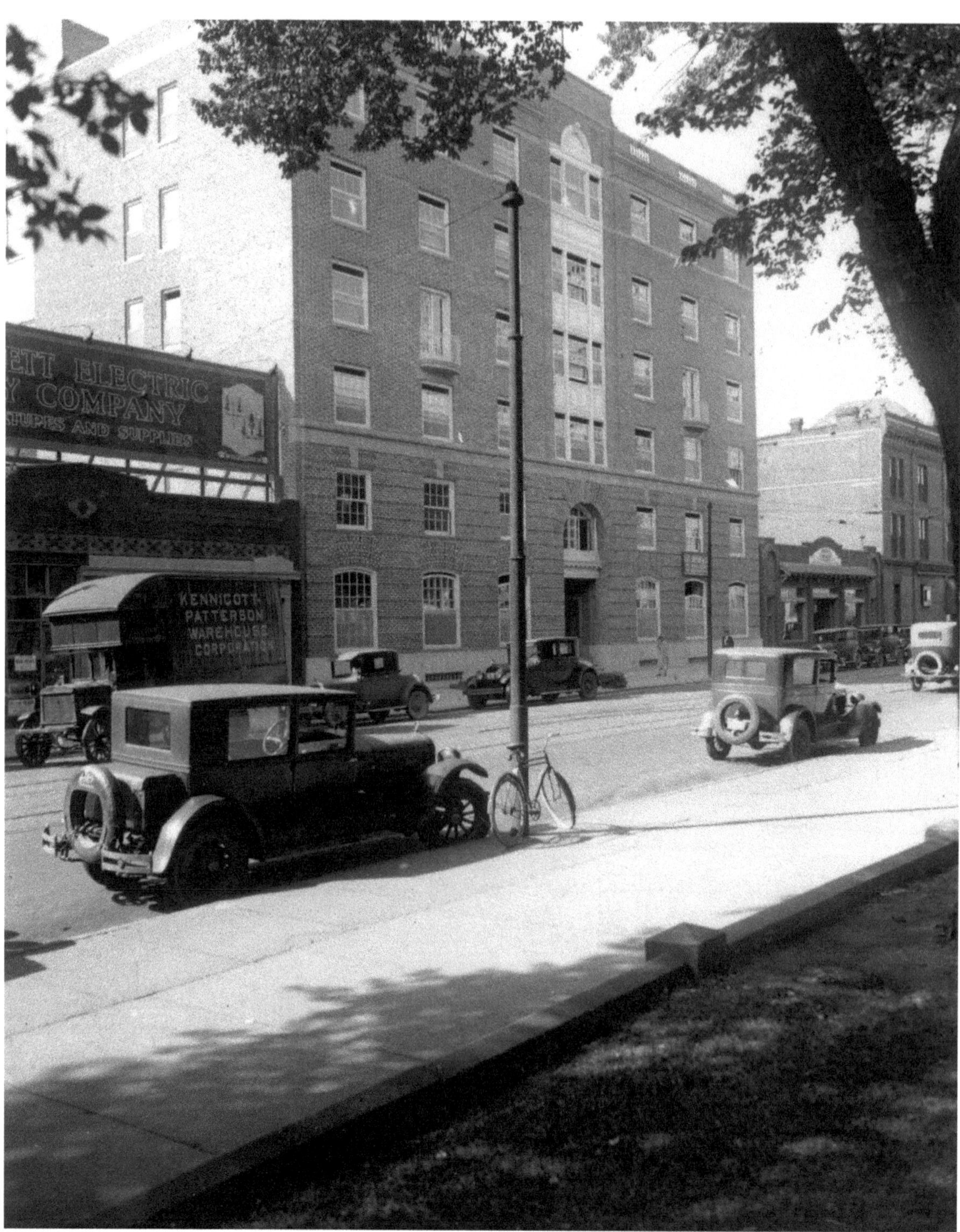

The Young Women's Christian Association building, pictured here, was located at 1545 Glenarm Place.

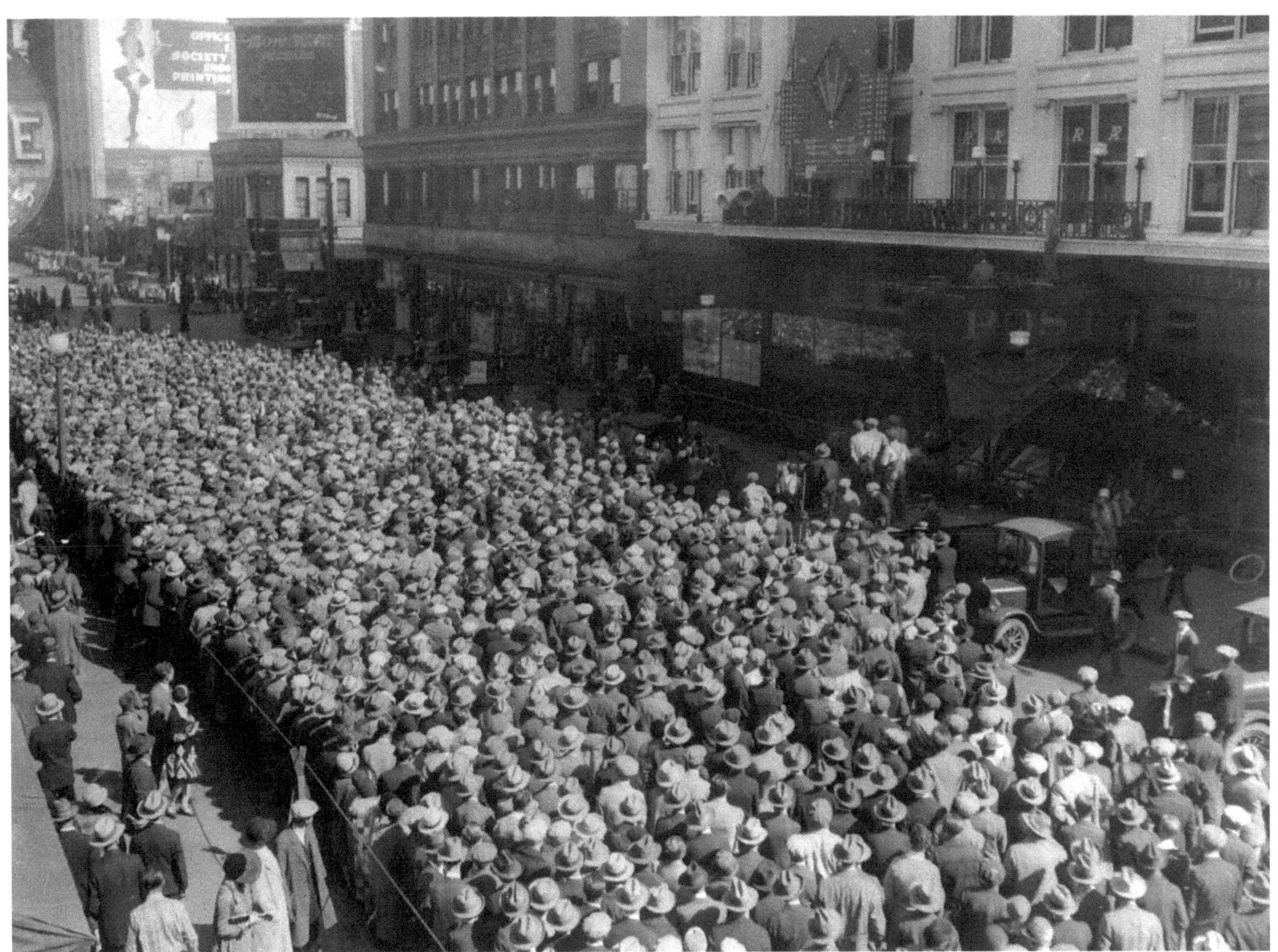

A crowd gathers in front of the Denver Post building located on Champa Street. They are listening to a man give a play-by-play of the 1927 World Series from a balcony on the building. He uses three large megaphones. An electric scoreboard mounted on the wall behind the man posts the score and the game's statistics.

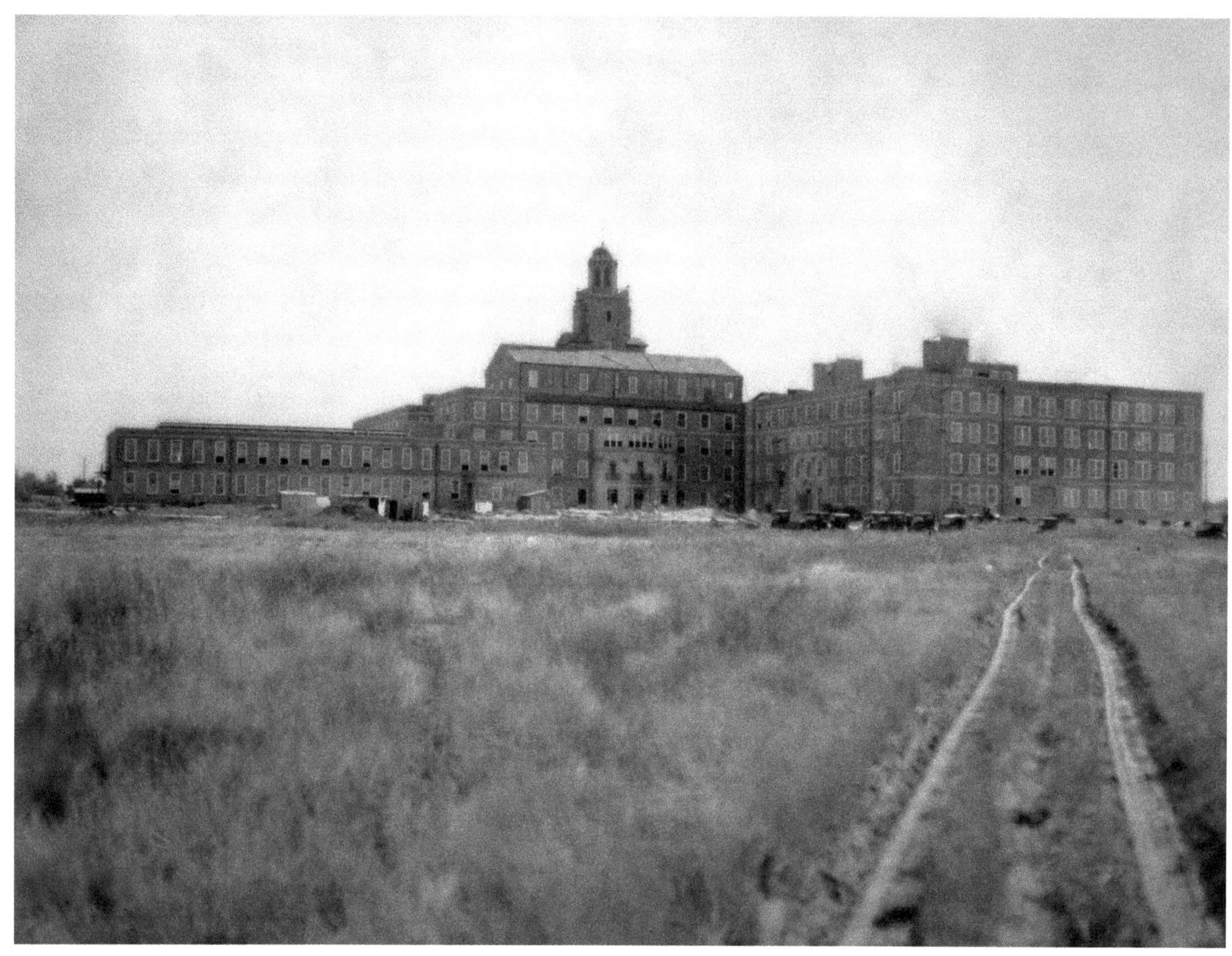

The University of Colorado General Hospital is shown here while under construction at the University of Colorado Medical Center located at 12th Avenue and Colorado Boulevard.

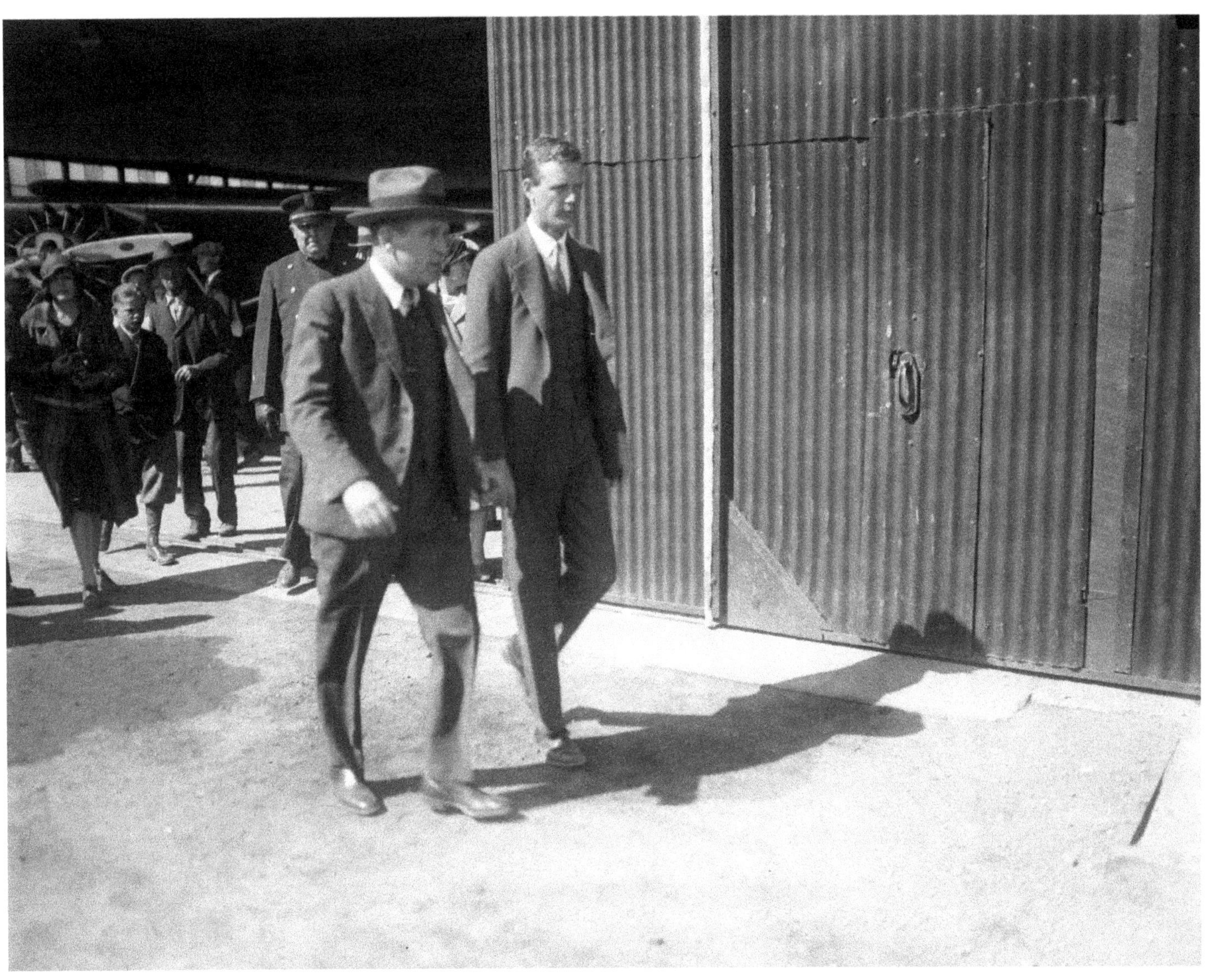

Charles Lindbergh is seen here upon his arrival in Denver on August 31, 1927. Lindbergh was on a three-month nationwide tour of the United States following his historic trans-Atlantic flight. The Daniel Guggenheim Fund sponsored Lindbergh's cross-country tour.

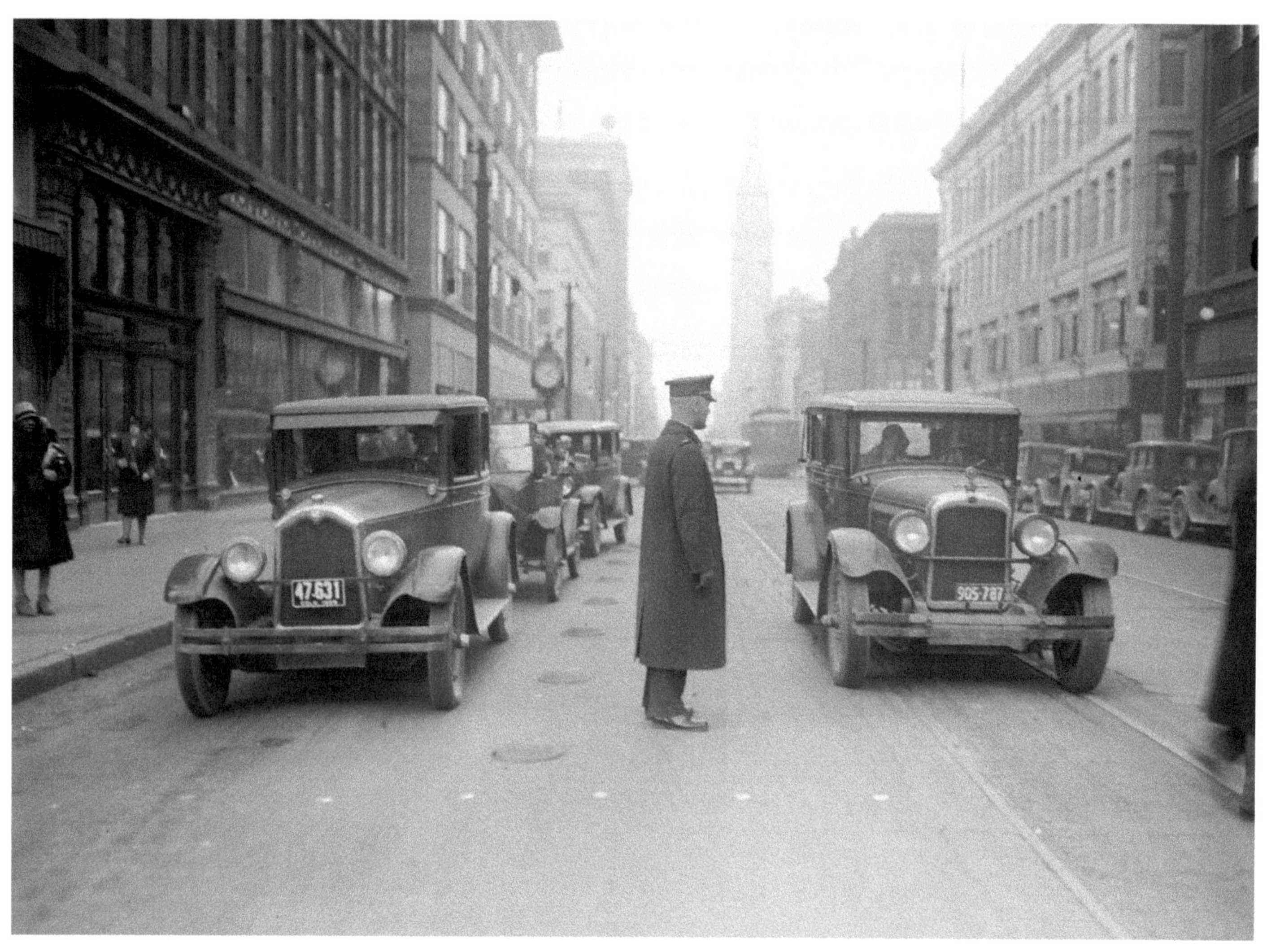

A Denver traffic officer stands in the tramway boarding zone and stops traffic on 16th Street. The Daniels and Fisher Tower is visible in the distance.

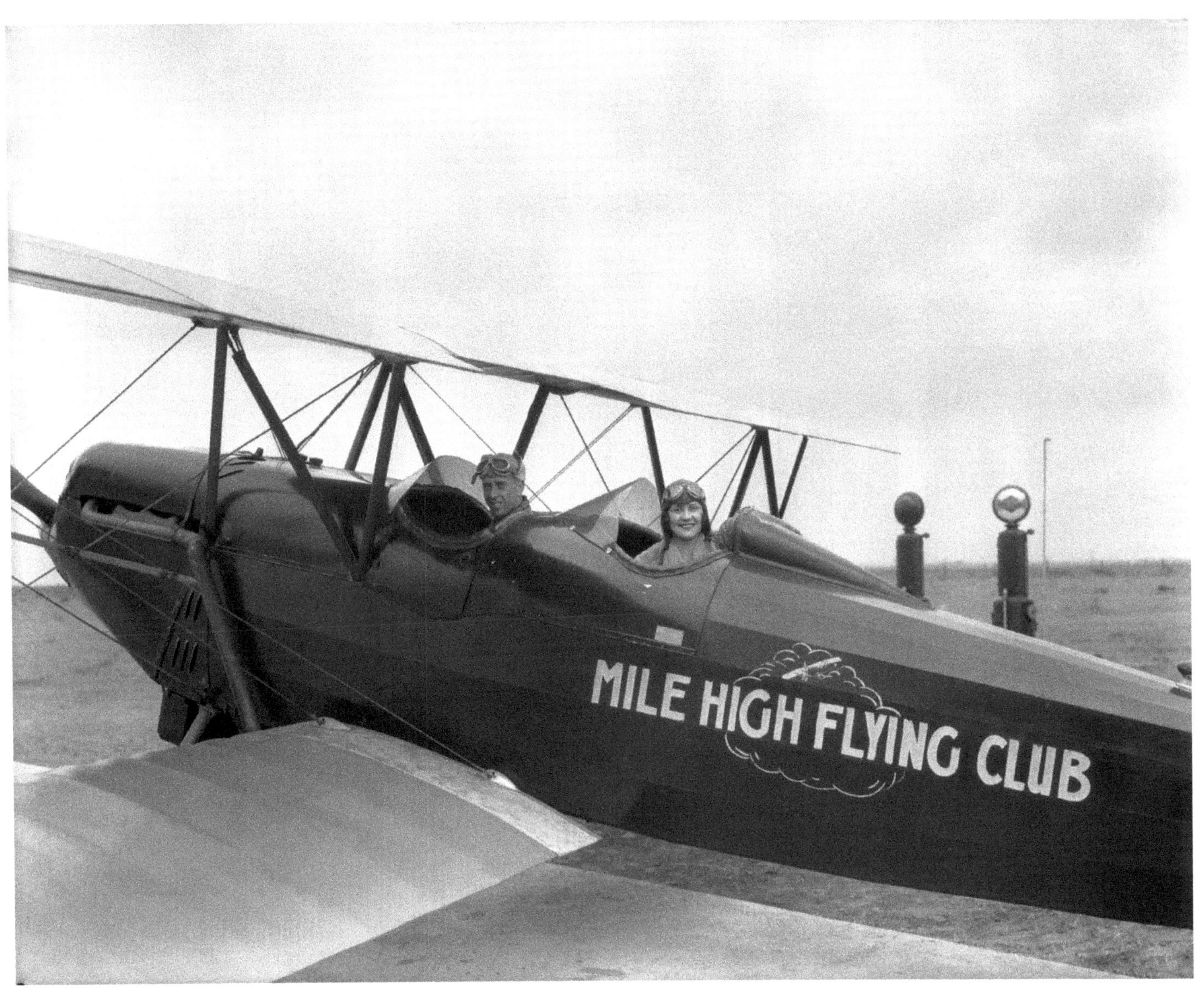

Lita Grey Chaplin, an actress and Charlie Chaplin's second wife, sits in an open two-seater plane at Denver Union Airport.

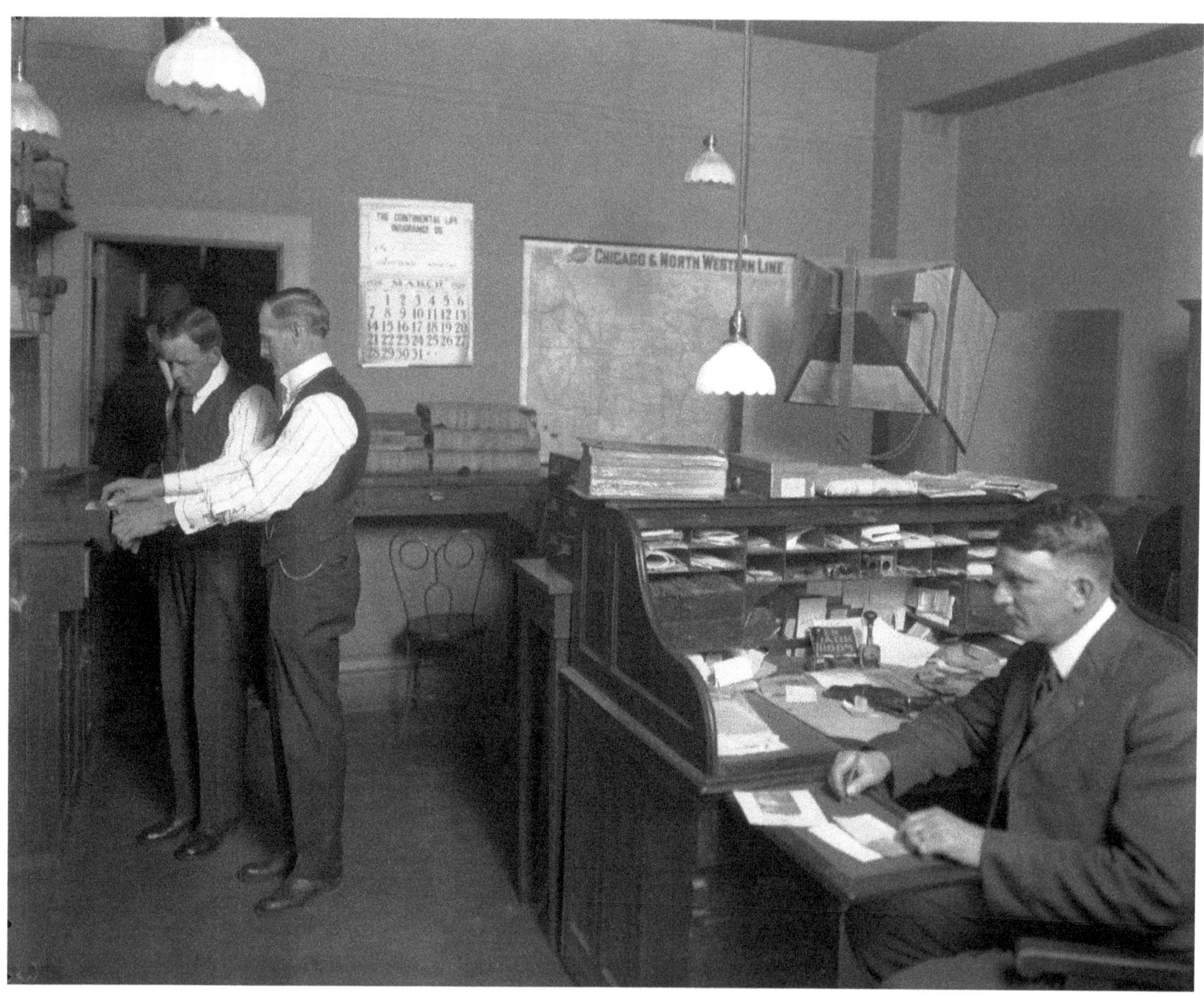

A clerk fingerprints a man in the fingerprint and mug shot room at the Denver police department, which was located at 14th and Larimer streets.

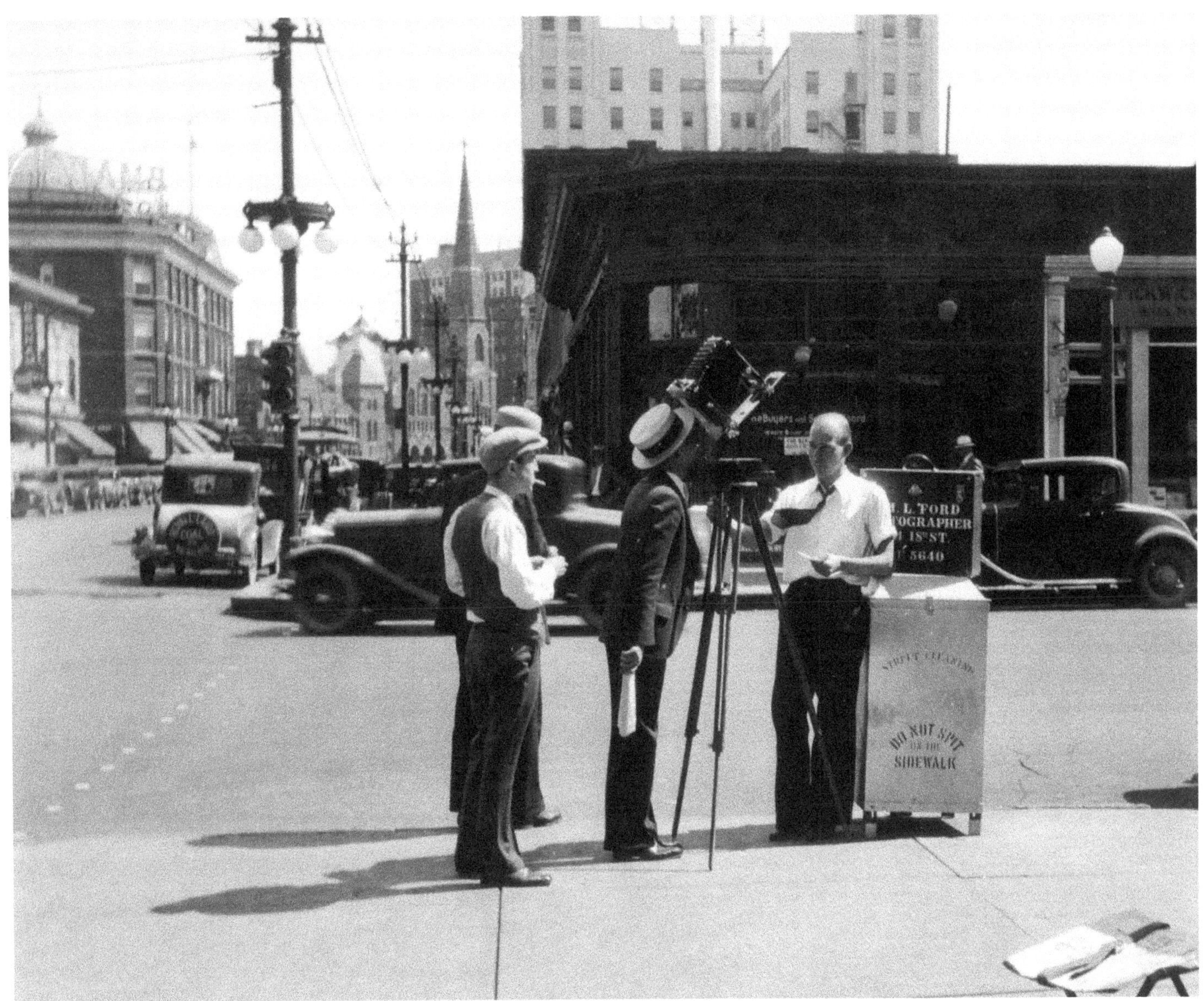

Photographer William L. Ford stands on the corner of 16th Street downtown. A man in a strawboater looks through the viewfinder.

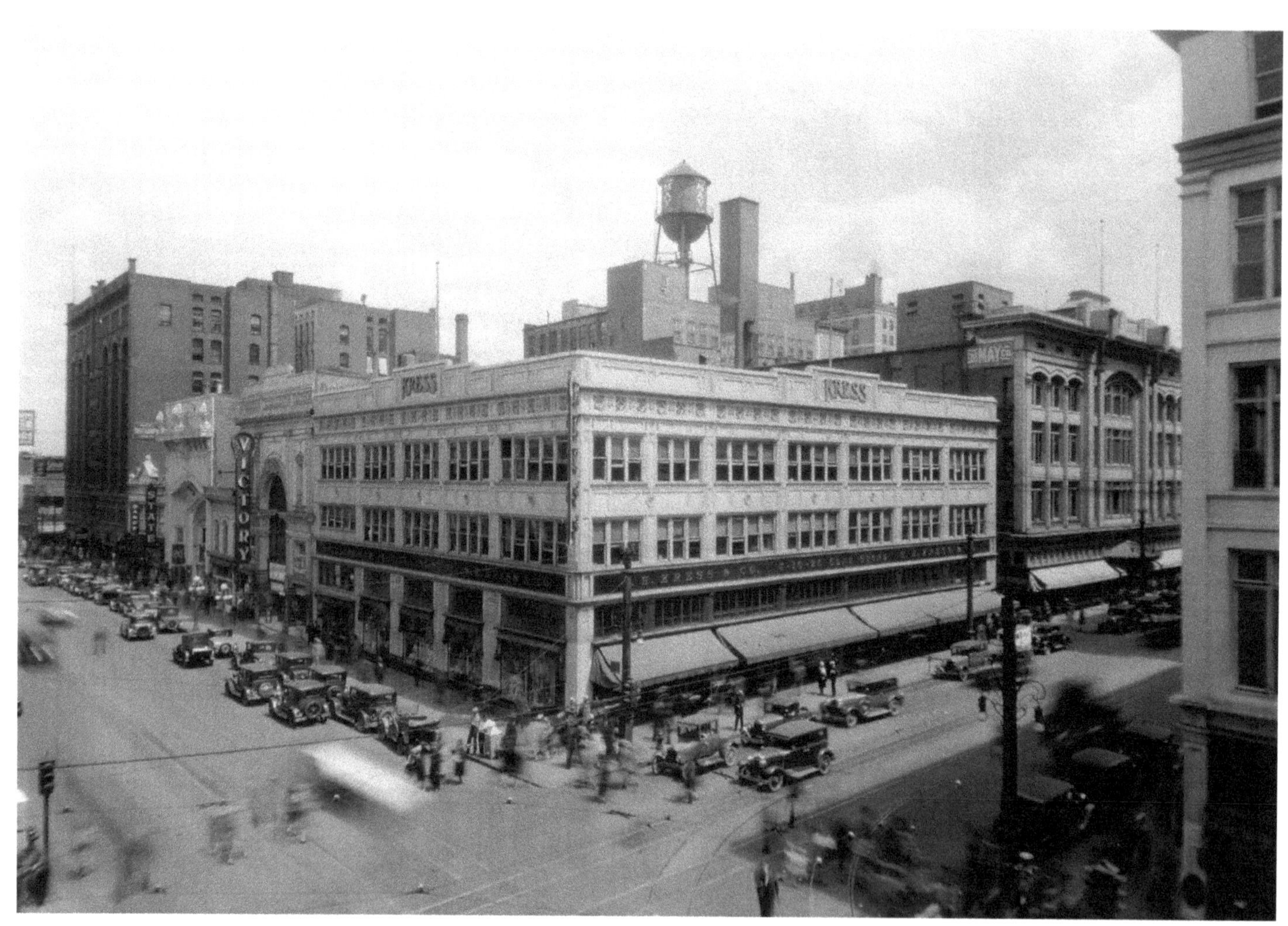

The art deco S. H. Kress & Company 5-10-25-cent Dime Store was located on the corner of 16th Street and Curtis in the Central Business District. The May Company is next door.

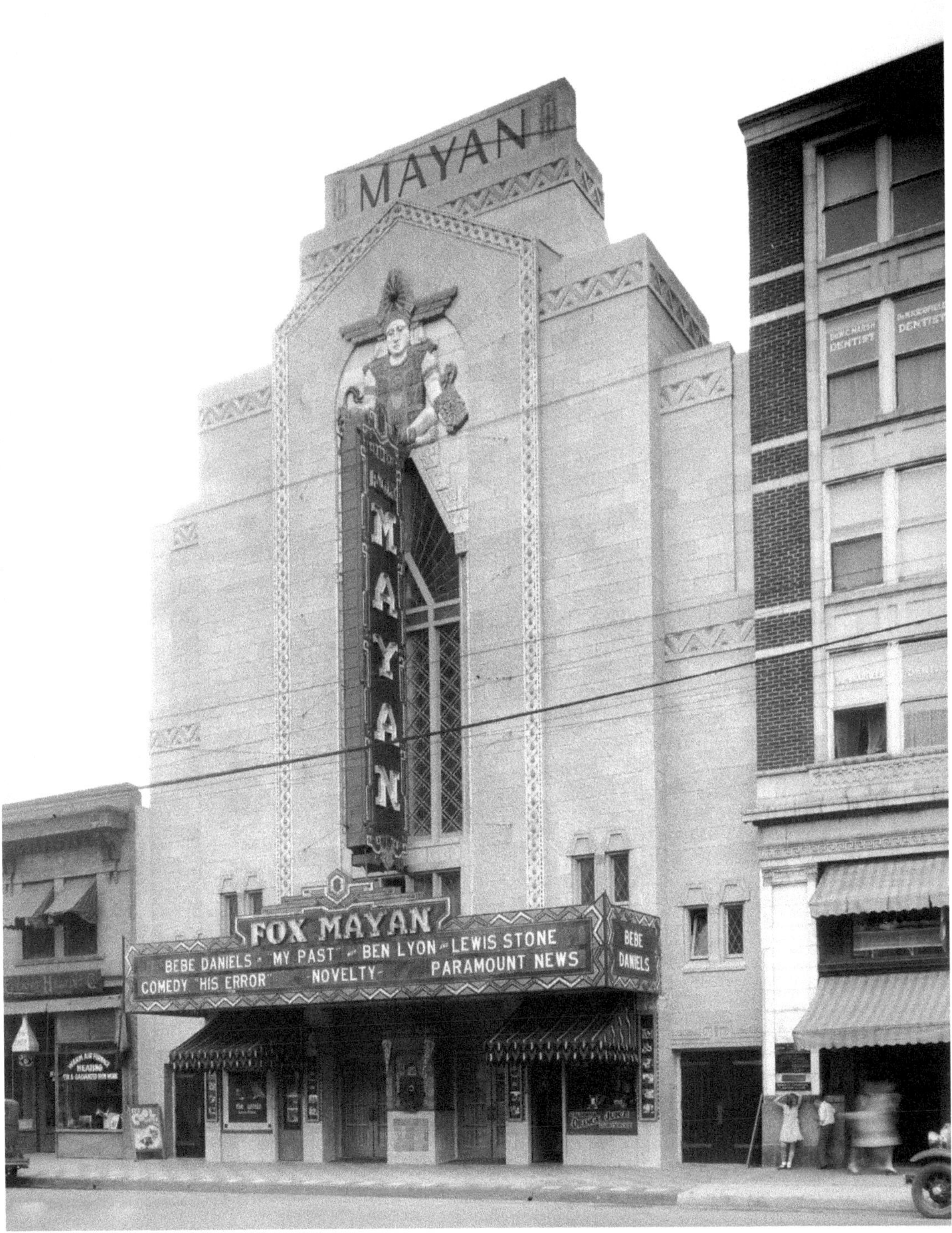

The Mayan Theater was designed in the art deco Mayan Revival style by Montana S. Fallis. The theater opened in 1930 and is located at 110 Broadway in the Speer neighborhood. The terra-cotta figure on the facade of the building was created by Julius P. Ambrusch.

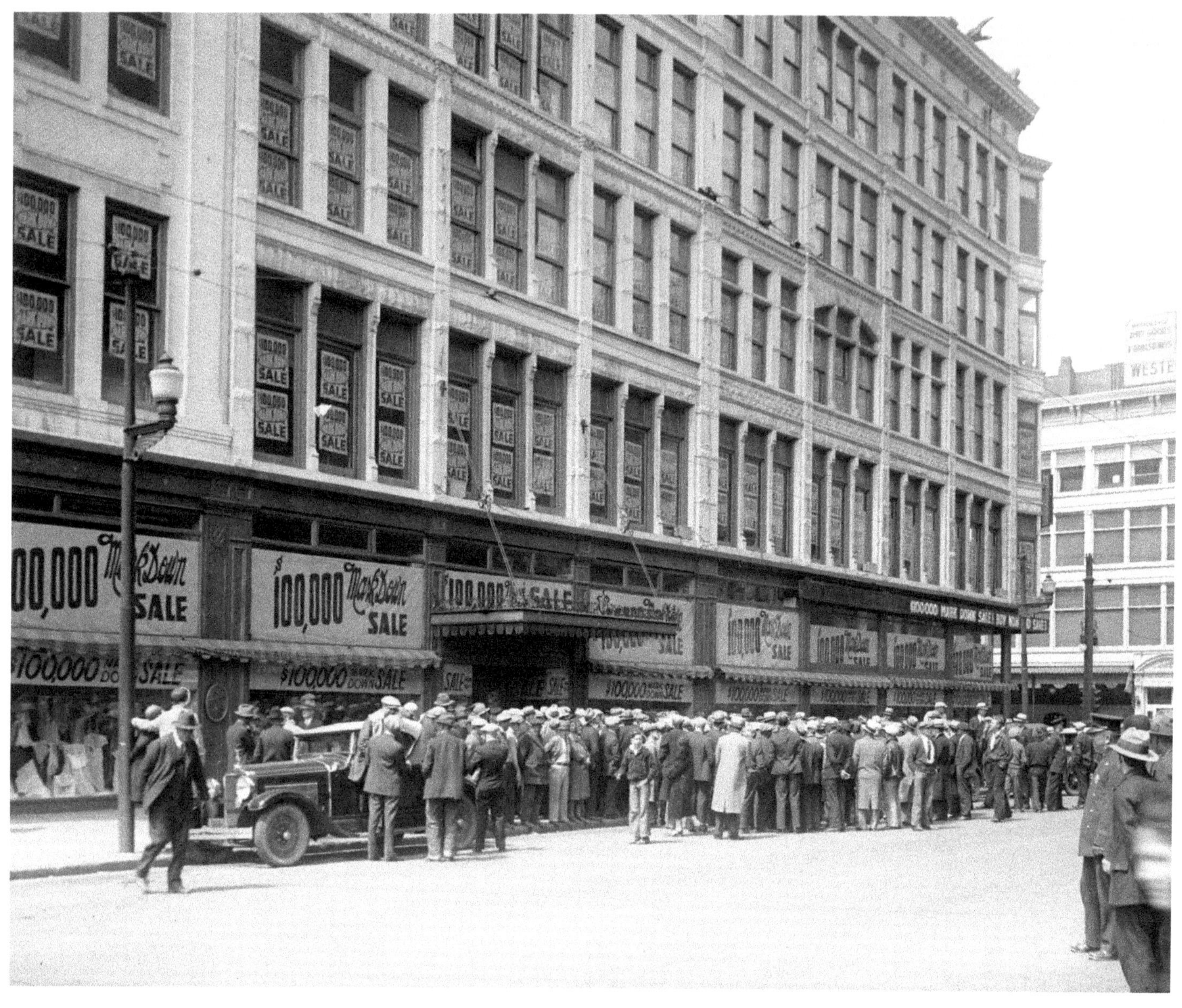

Customers crowd the entrance to the Golden Eagle Dry Goods Company department store, located at 16th and Lawrence streets, following a robbery in May 1931. Signs and banners on the building advertise a $100,000 markdown sale.

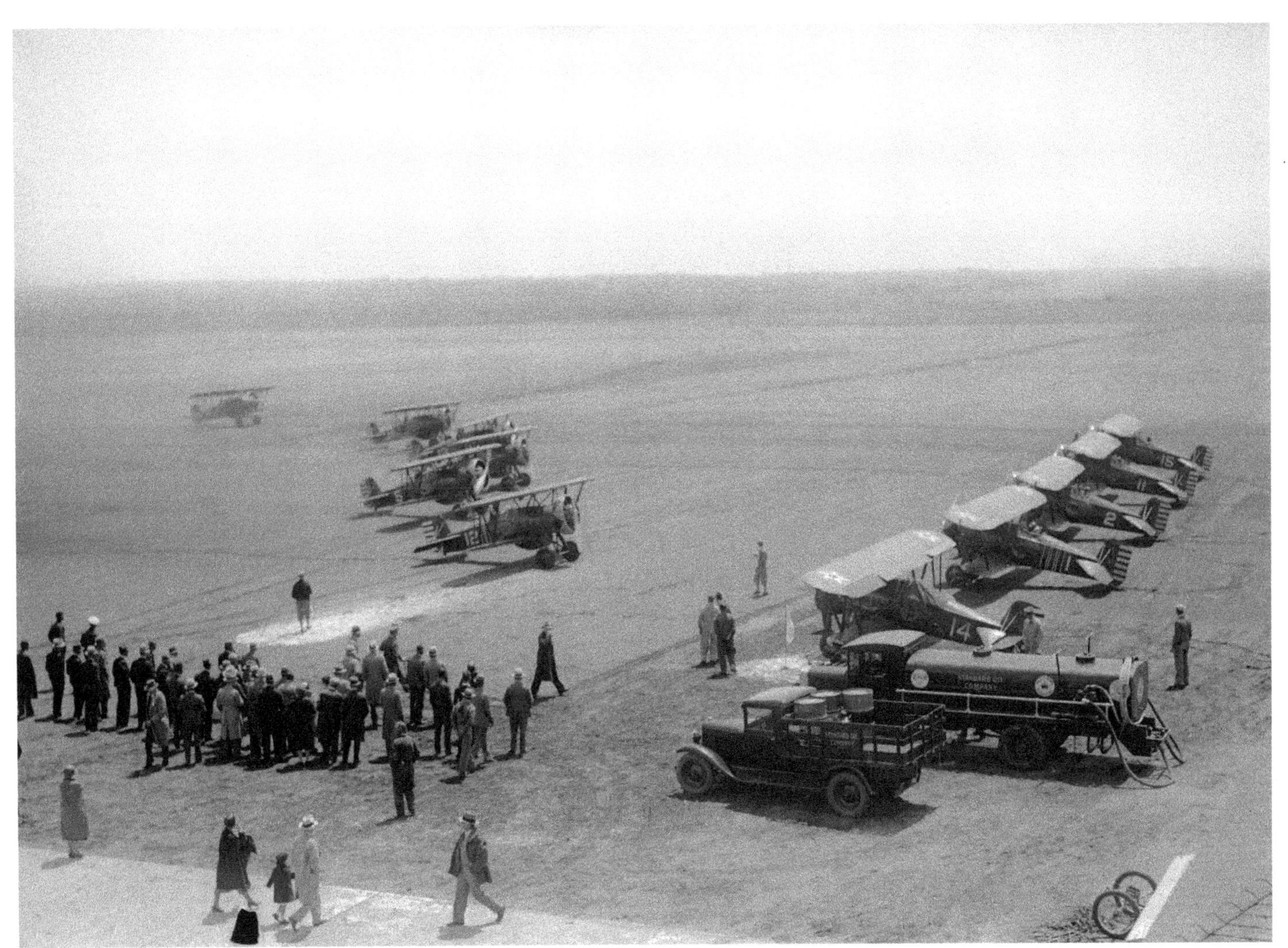

In this image spectators view bi-wing aircraft of the Denver Municipal Squadron of the Colorado National Guard at the Denver municipal airport.

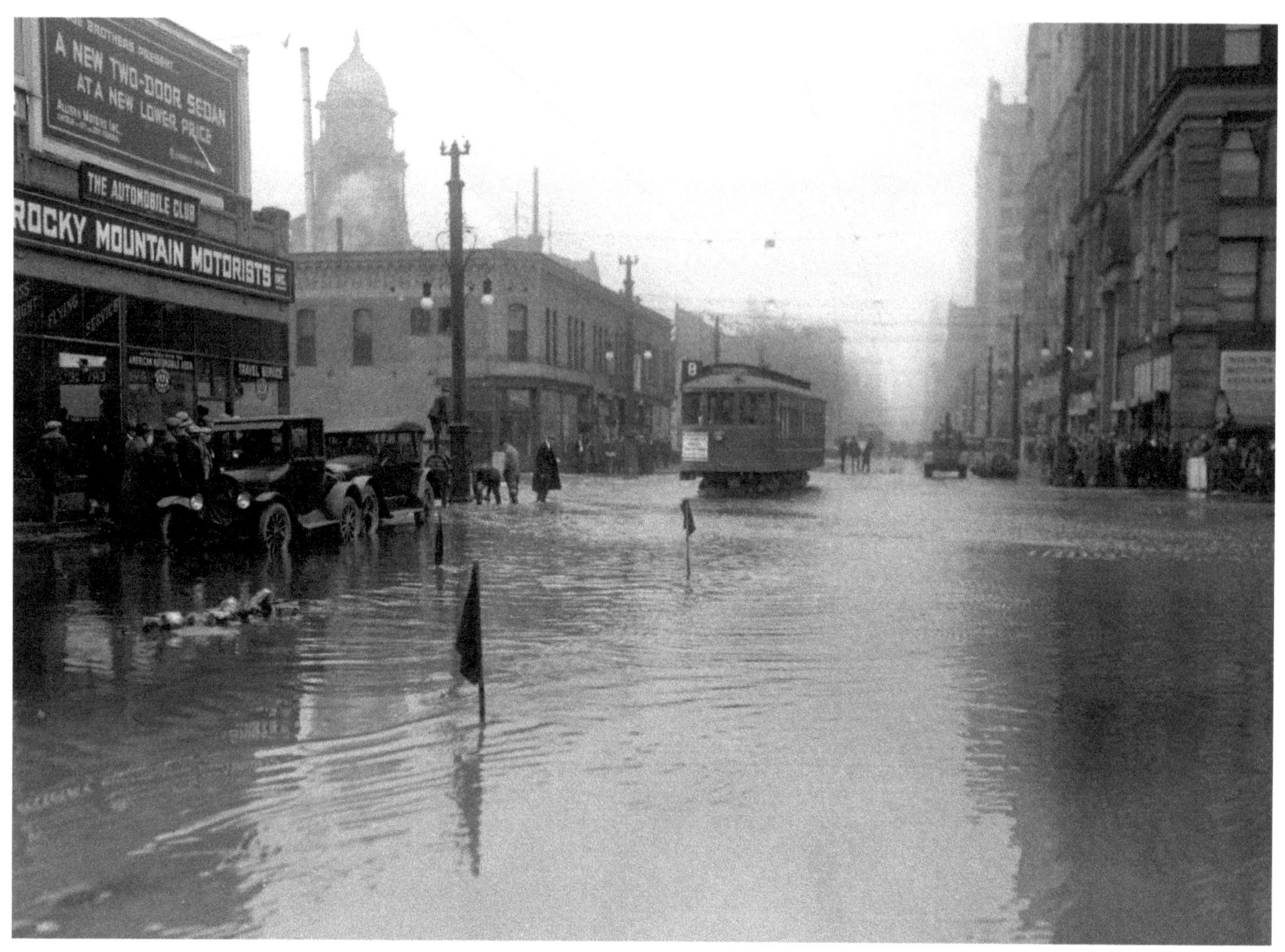

On August 3, 1933, the 1889 Castlewood Dam failed. Cherry Creek flooded and inundated parts of Denver. The flood cost two lives and over $1,000,000 in damages. Here we see a flooded 16th Street in the Central Business District.

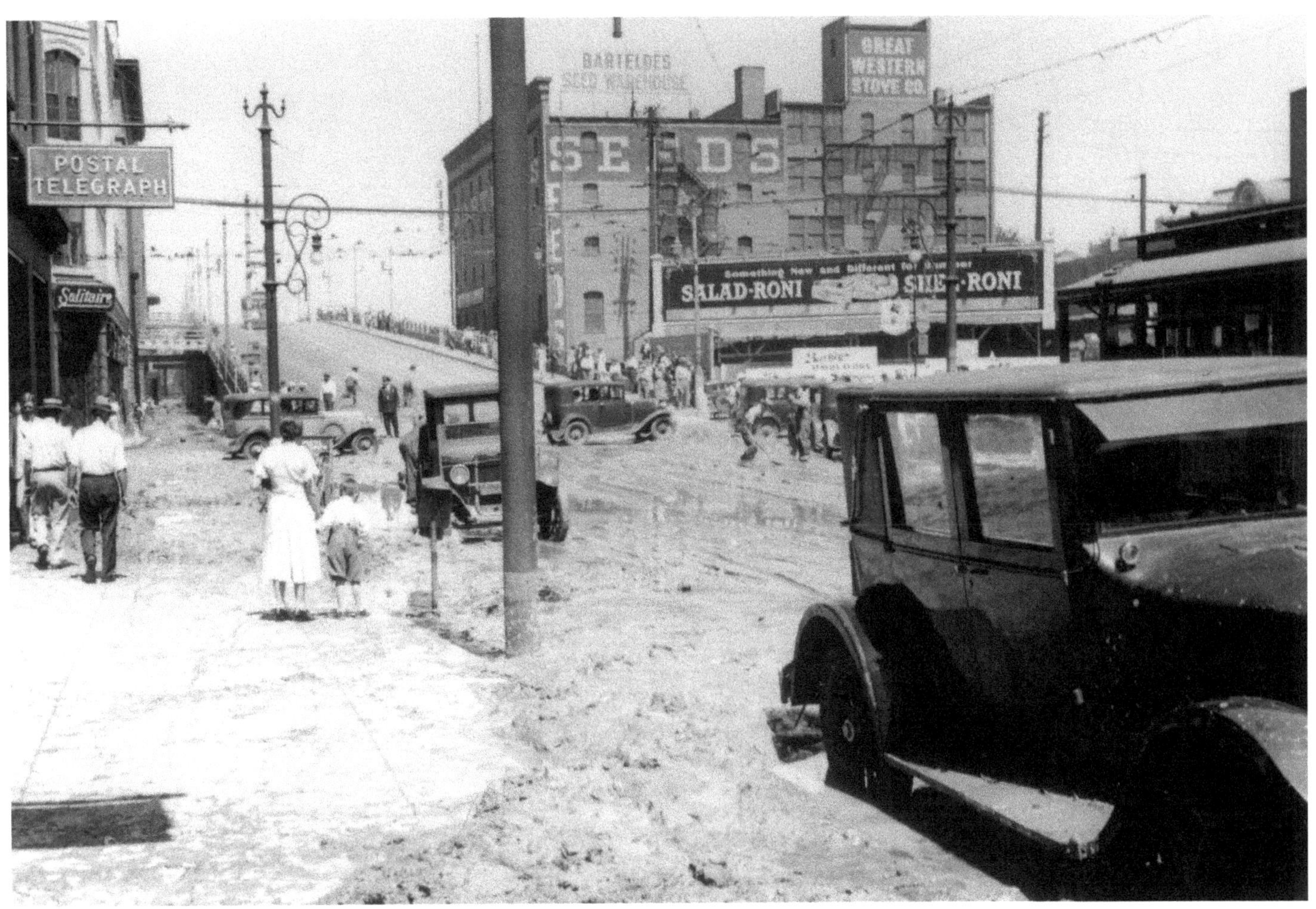

Mud covers 16th Street after the 1933 Cherry Creek flood. Several cars are mired in the muck and a policeman directs traffic in the intersection of Wazee Street. Pedestrians cross the 16th Street Viaduct near the Barteldes Seed Warehouse because most public transportation in the central part of the city has been shut down.

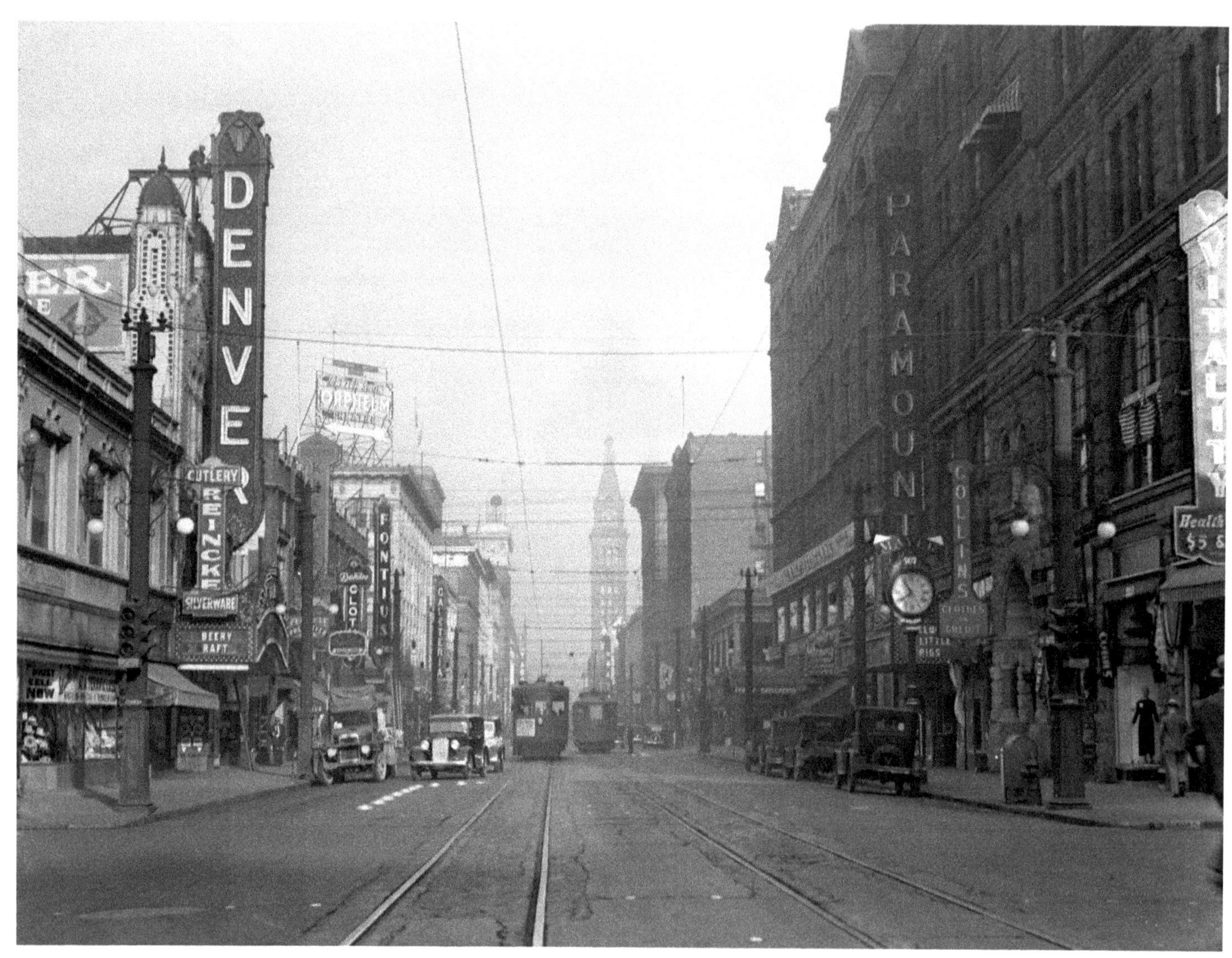

In this view of 16th Street the signs for two of Denver's most famous movie theaters are visible, the Denver and the Paramount.

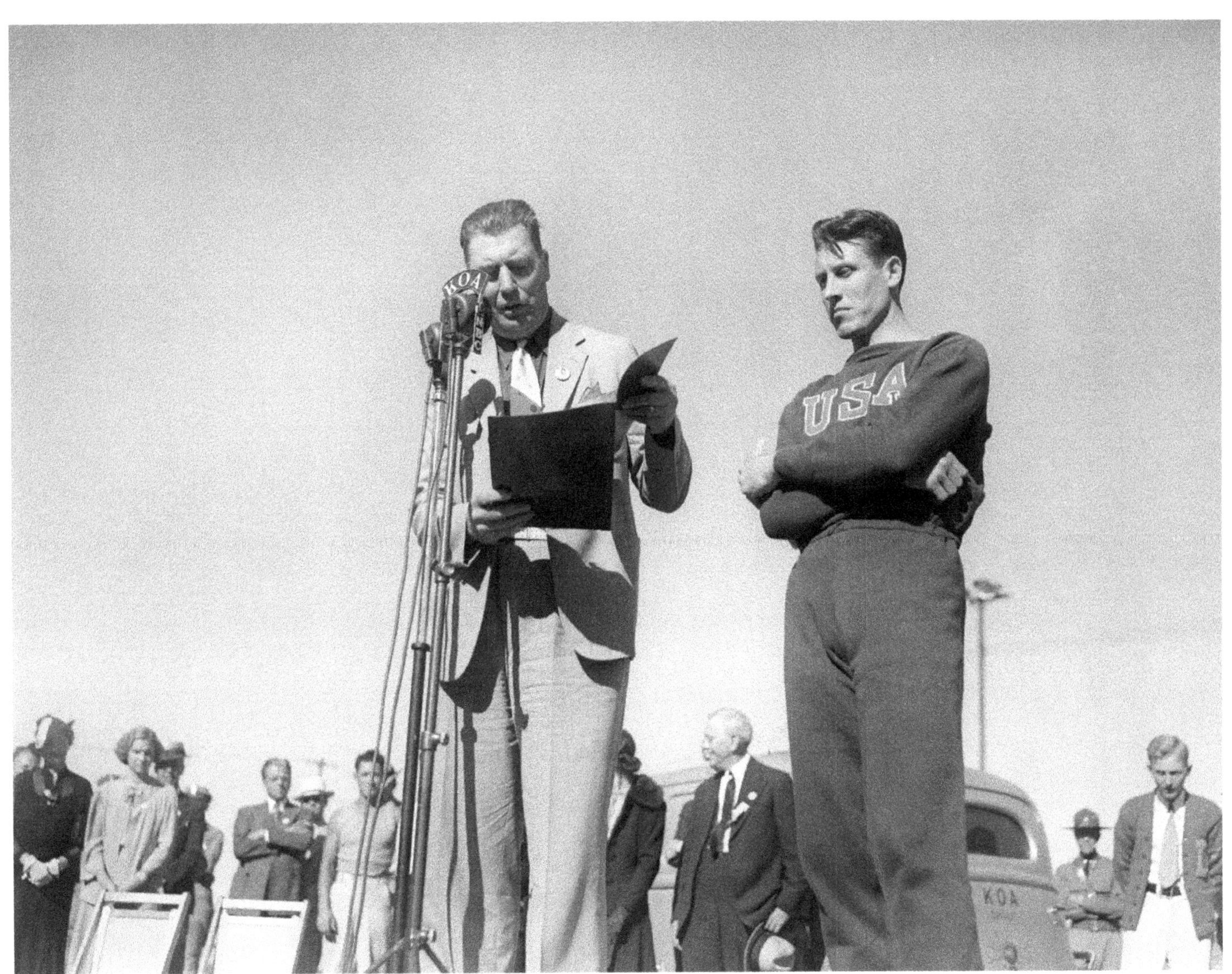

Colorado Governor Edwin C. Johnson stands at a radio microphone with University of Colorado football star Byron "Whizzer" R. White at his side. During his career, Byron R. White was a Rhodes scholar, played professional football for the Pittsburgh Steelers and the Detroit Lions, and served as a United States Supreme Court Justice for 31 years.

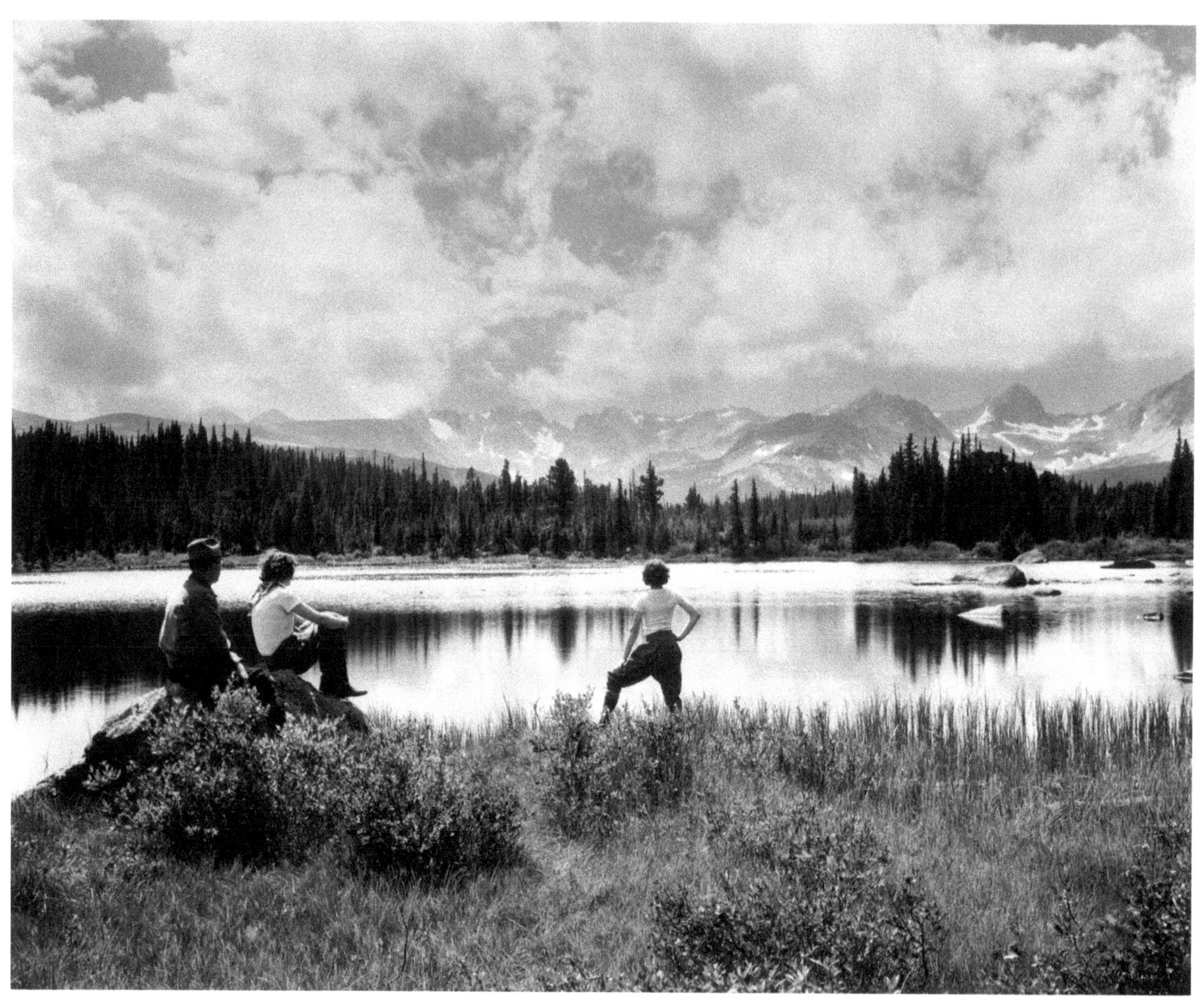

People pose in Echo Lake Park, one of Denver's mountain parks. Mount Evans, one of Colorado's "fourteeners," is visible in the distance.

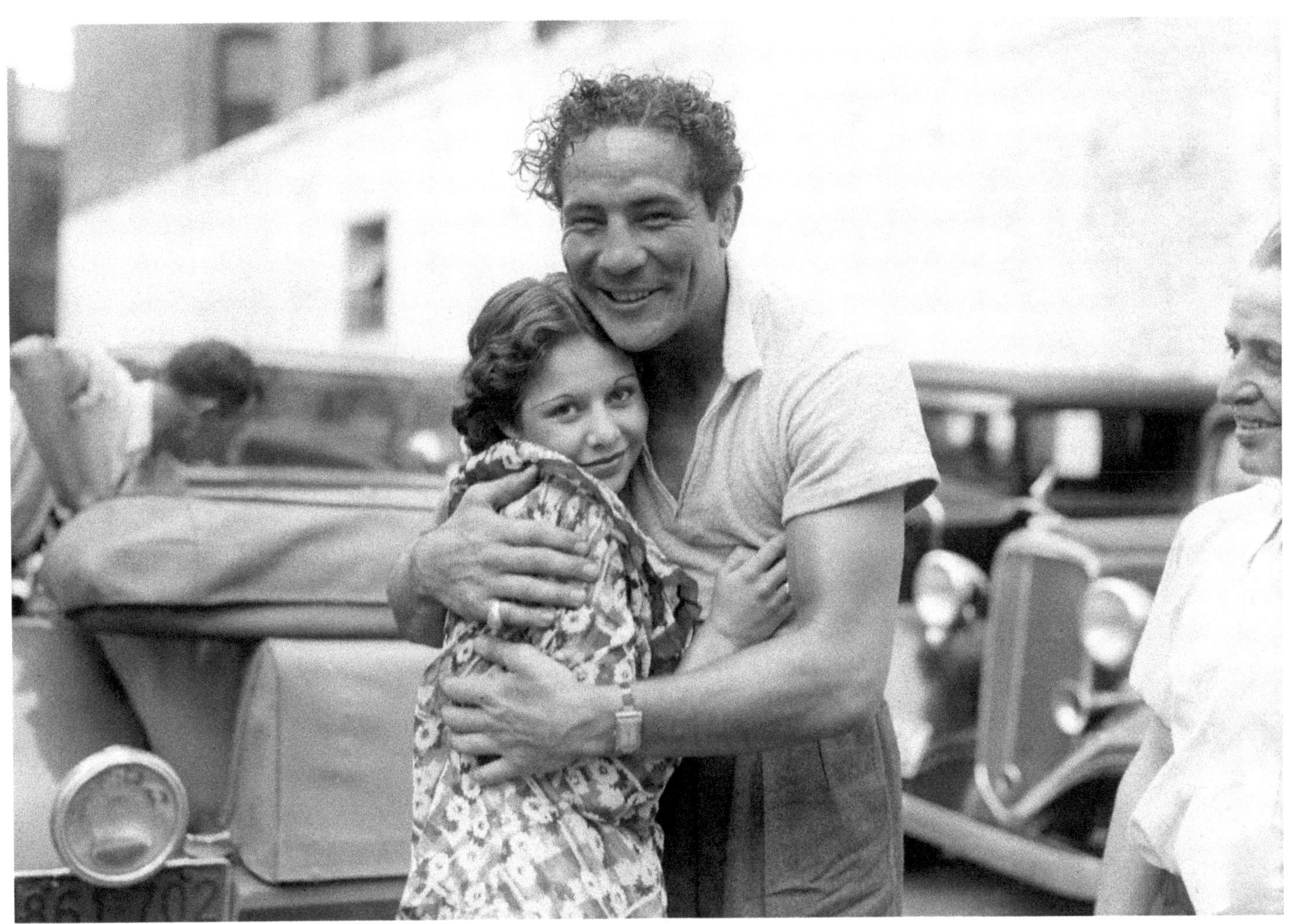

Heavyweight champion boxer Max Baer poses with his cousin Thelma. Baer fought and won two fights in Denver on April 4, 1933. The first was against Sam Greer, and the second against "Wee" Willie Medivitch.

President Franklin D. Roosevelt sits in an open touring car during a campaign visit to Colorado in 1936.

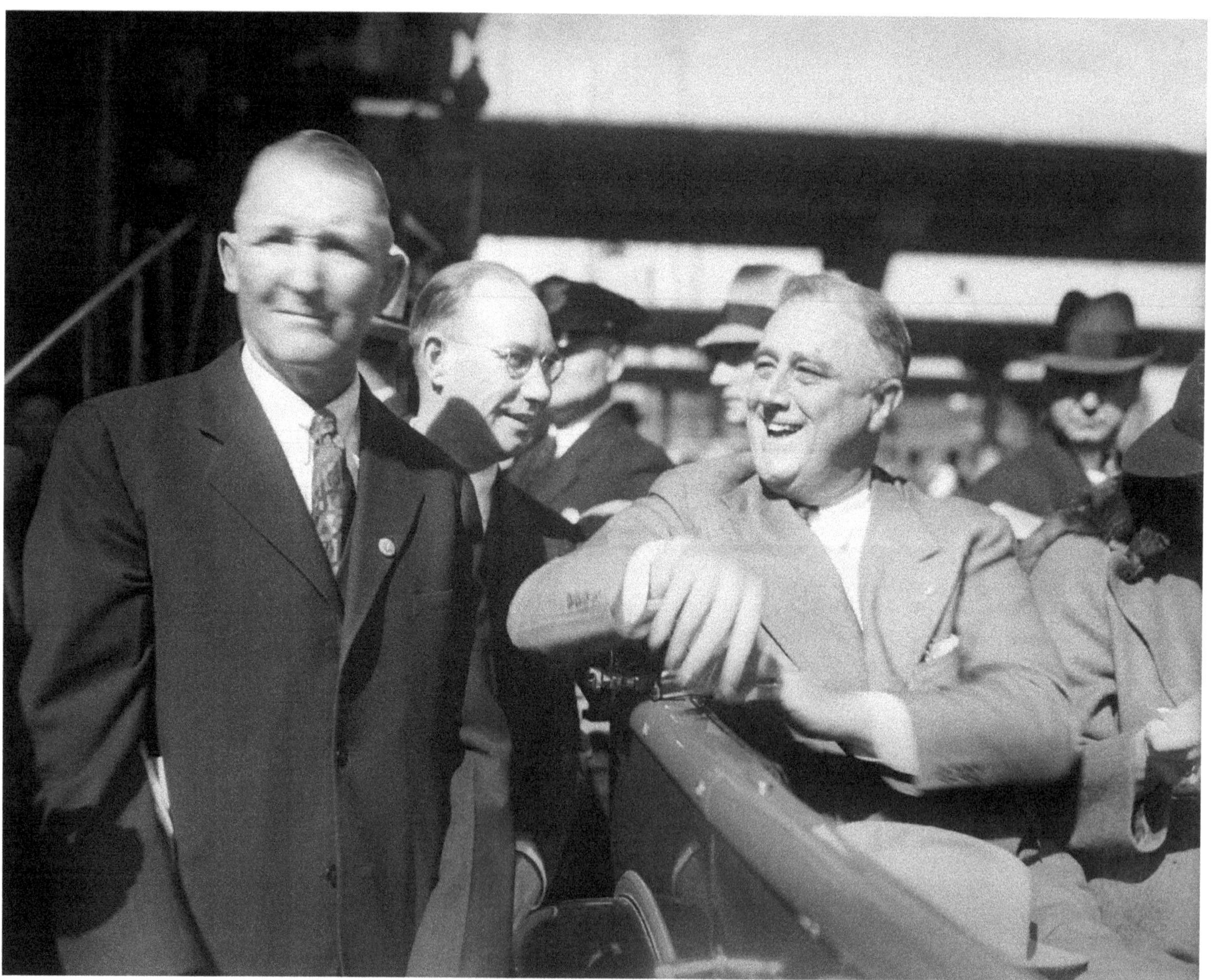

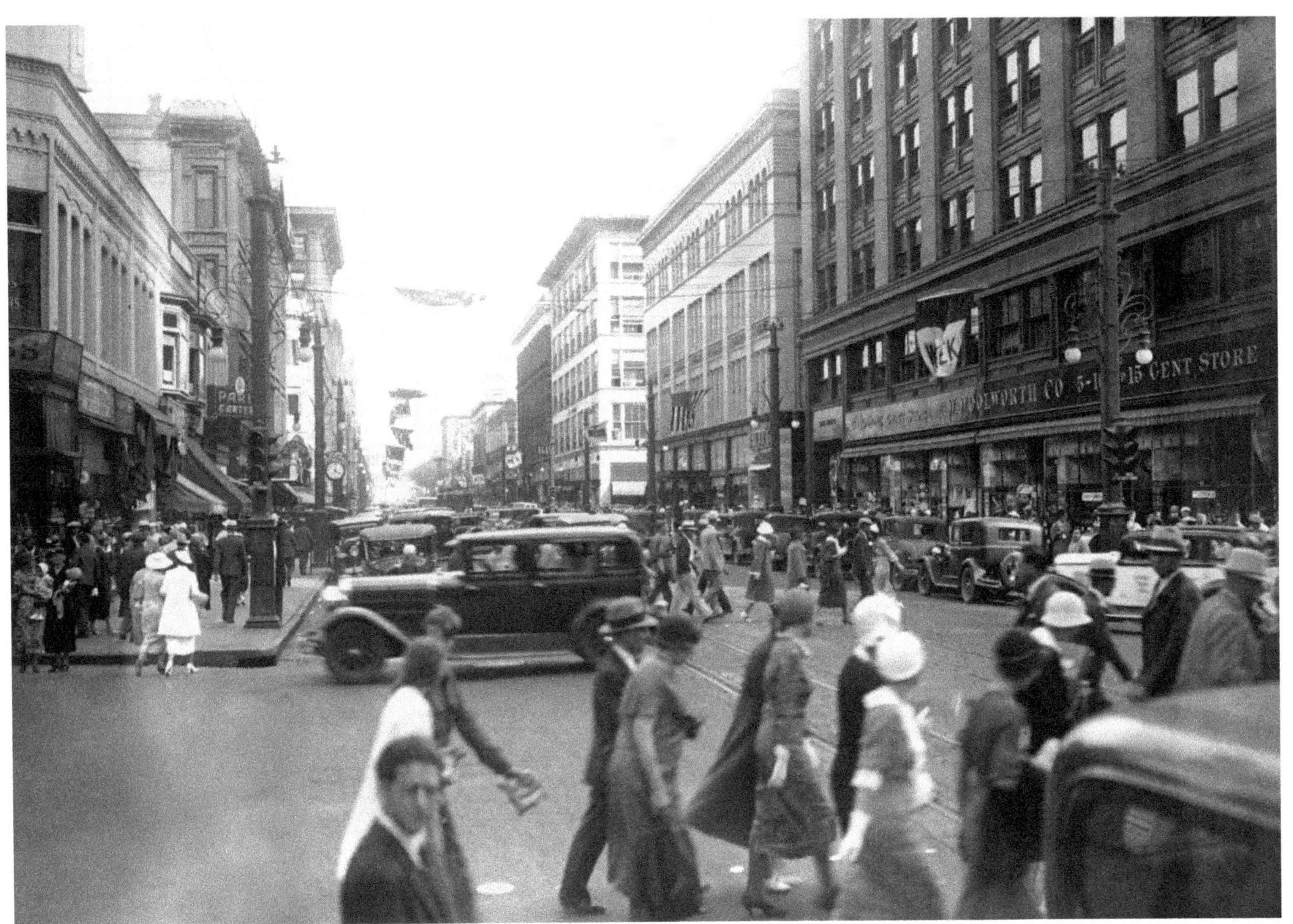

Pedestrians crowd the sidewalks of 16th Street. The F. W. Woolworth Co. 5, 10, and 15 Cent Store is open for business at the corner of 16th and Champa streets. The store is located in the Symes building erected in 1905.

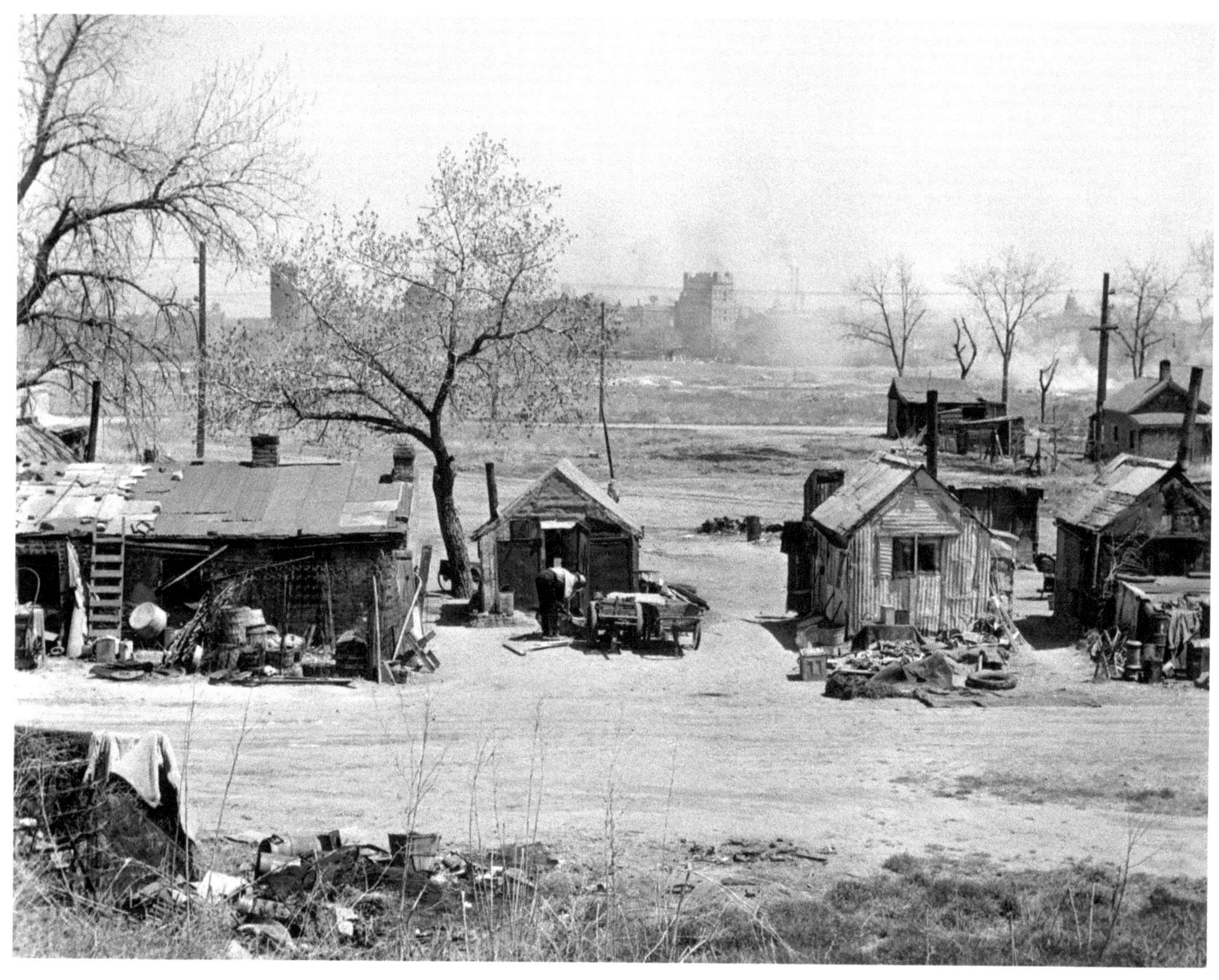

This Depression-era shantytown was located in the floodplain of the South Platte River. The Hungarian Flour Mill and the State Capitol dome are visible in the distance.

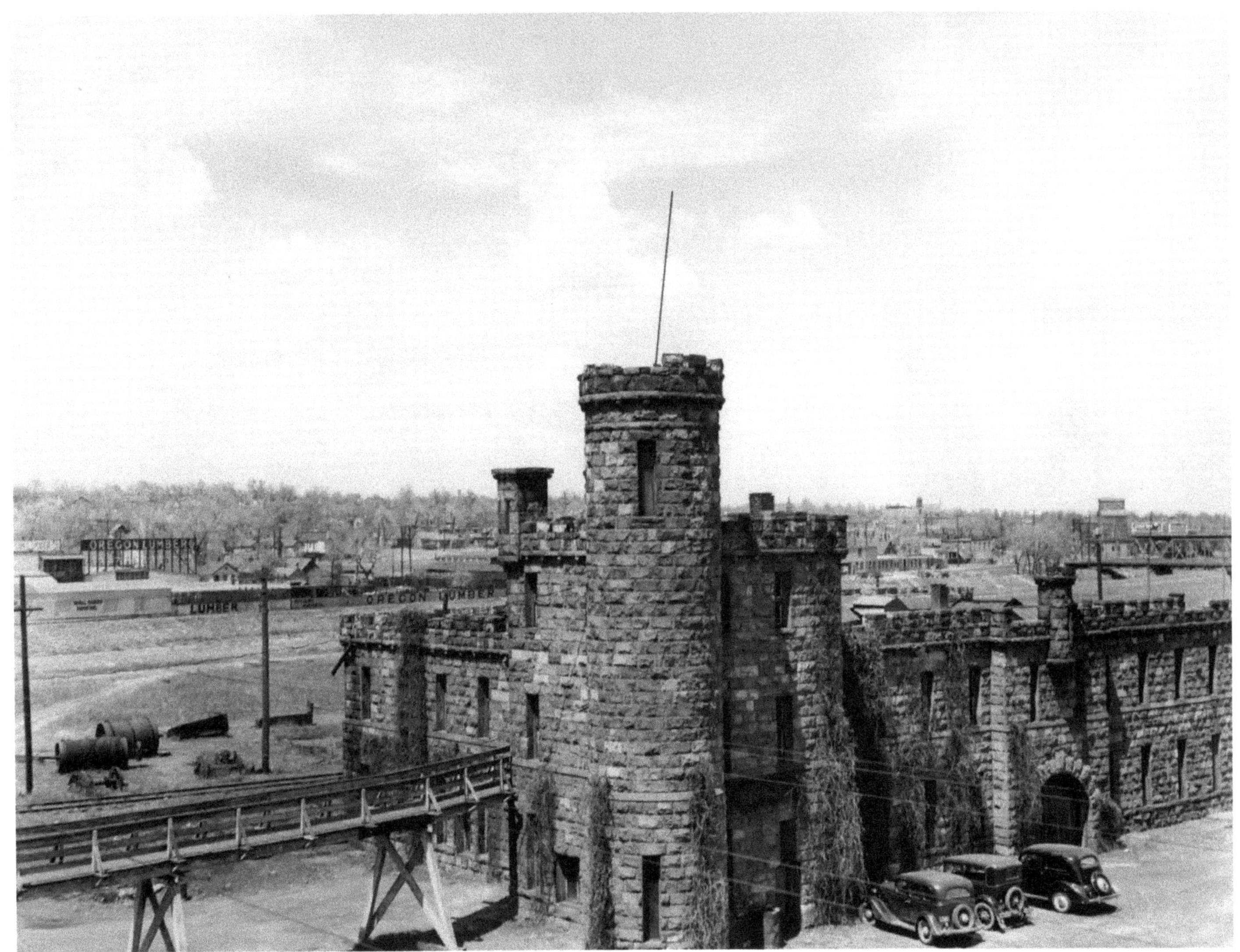

The Walker Castle, built by John Brisben Walker, was located in River Front Park. It was part of a development that included a racecourse and was located on the South Platte River between 16th and 19th streets. The building originally housed exhibits, but by the 1930s the offices of the Denver and Salt Lake Railway had located there.

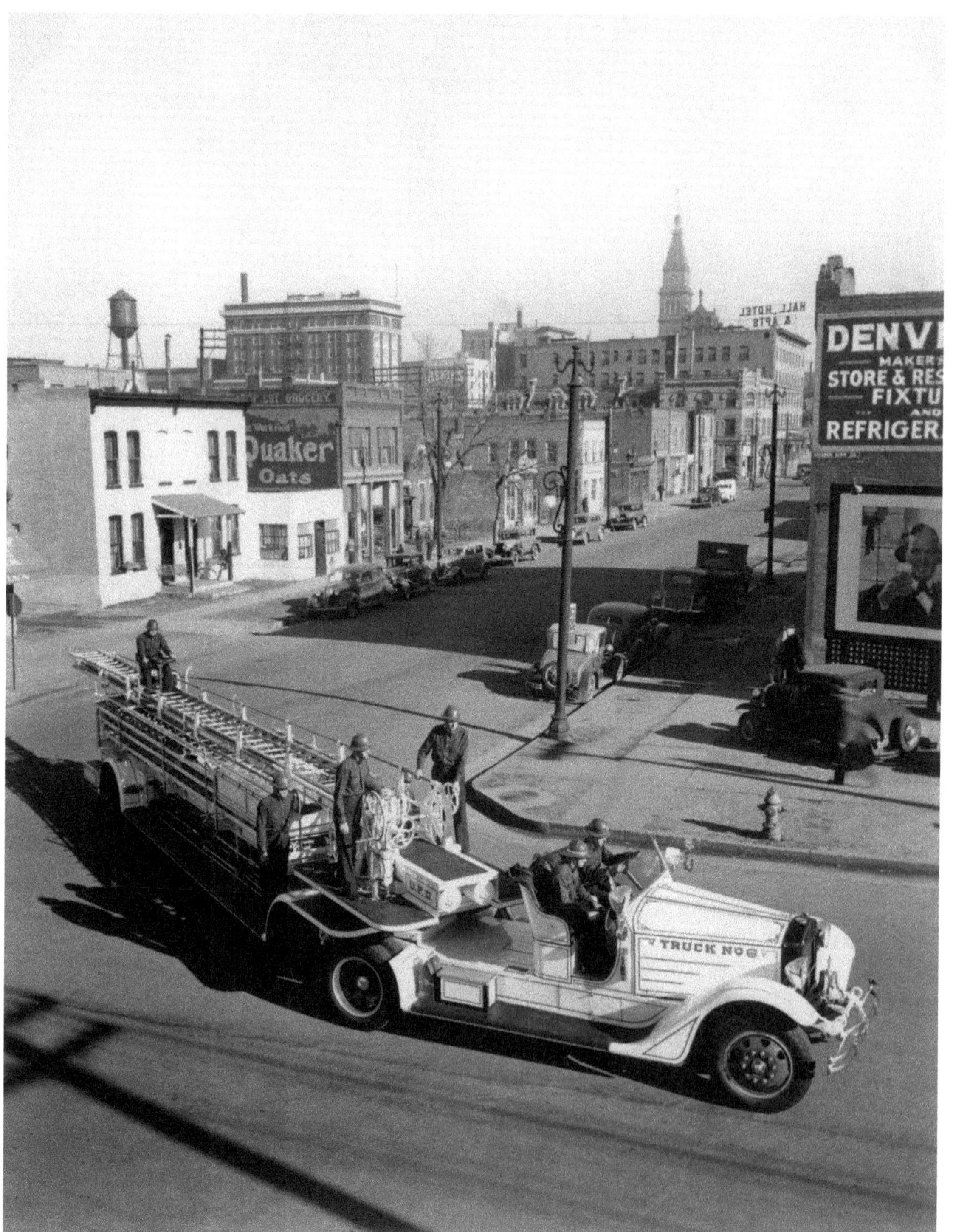

A Denver fire department hook-and-ladder truck turns a corner at 12th and Curtis streets during training in the central business district.

Post World War II and the Growth of Denver

1940–1972

During and following World War II, the military and defense industries greatly spurred Denver's economic and population growth. In 1941 Denver donated land to the Department of the Army for the construction of Buckley Field and the Army Air Corps Technical School. Fitzsimmons Army Hospital was expanded, as was Lowry Air Force Base. The secret Rocky Mountain Arsenal was opened to produce nerve gas and napalm bombs; west of Denver, the Remington Ordnance Plant was built, employing more than 22,000.

With the end of the war, Denver saw continued growth as returning veterans and newcomers flocked to the city creating an unprecedented demand for housing. To deal with the growth in population in the surrounding suburbs, the city built a freeway system that would eventually lead to uncontrolled urban sprawl.

The city experienced many economic ups and downs after the 1950s. In the early 1960s the city's economic growth came to a near standstill, and the city, like the nation at large, began to see demands by ethnic minorities for equal employment, housing, and education. By 1970, as the result of white flight, population had peaked and started to decline.

During the urban renewal frenzy of the sixties and seventies many historic landmarks were destroyed such as the Tabor Theater and the downtown May D & F store (the original Daniels and Fisher store). Much of the old Central Business District and Larimer Street were razed for the city's Skyline Urban Renewal project, and most of the historic Auraria neighborhood was razed for the Auraria Higher Education Center. Denver, it seemed, was nothing more than a series of vacant lots and parking lots.

Buildings of significance were built during this period. Four were designed by I. M. Pei—Mile High Center, the Hilton Hotel, and the May D & F store and hyperbolic paraboloid located at Zeckendorf Plaza. Pei would later design the 16th Street Mall.

The completion of Burnham Hoyt's Cherry Creek Shopping Center in 1955 signaled the decline of the central city as a retail destination. By the 1980s, most of central Denver's historic department stores had relocated or gone out of business. It would not be until the turn of the century that Denver would once again experience an urban renaissance.

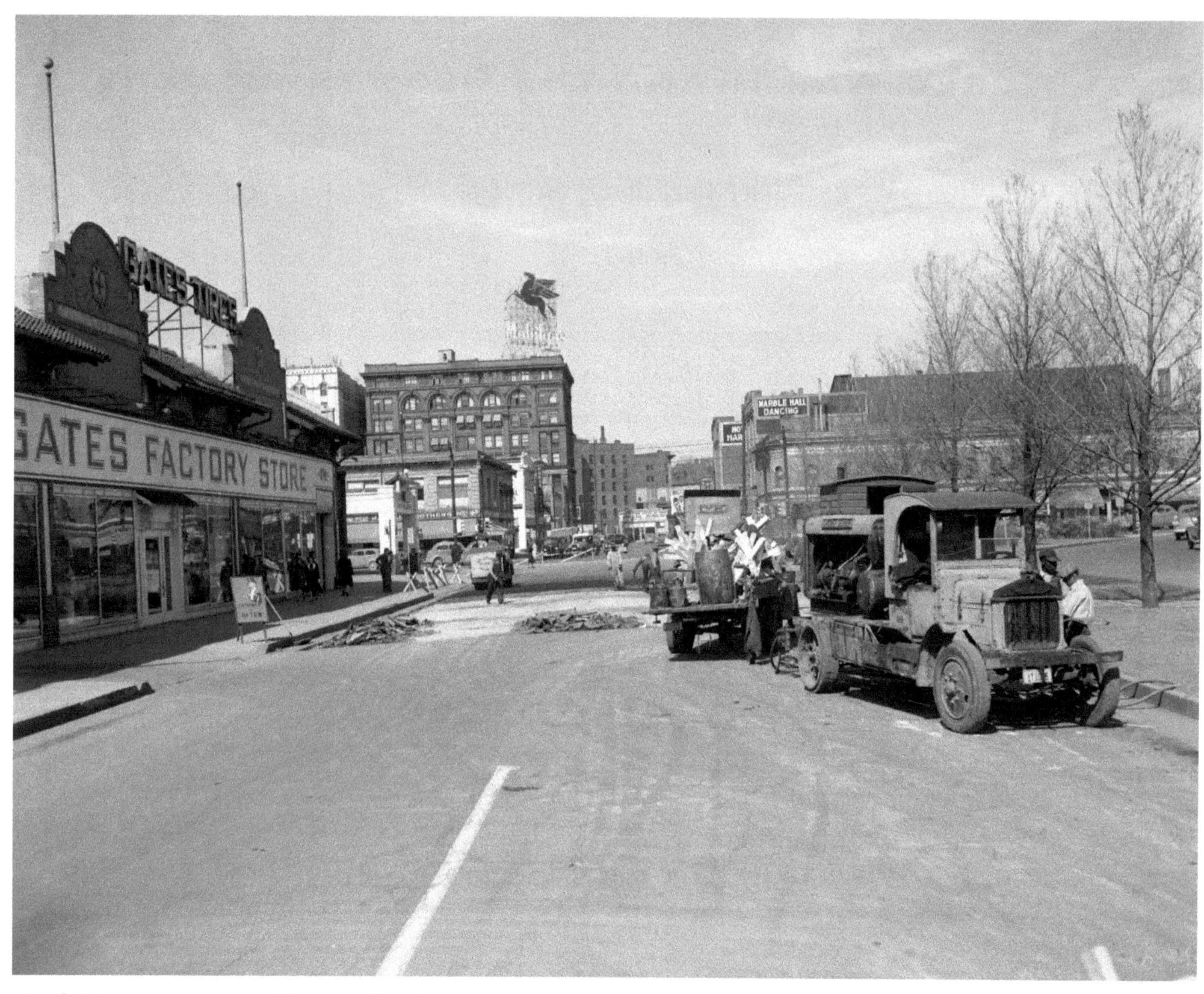

Men finish paving a portion of Cleveland Place in the Central Business District.

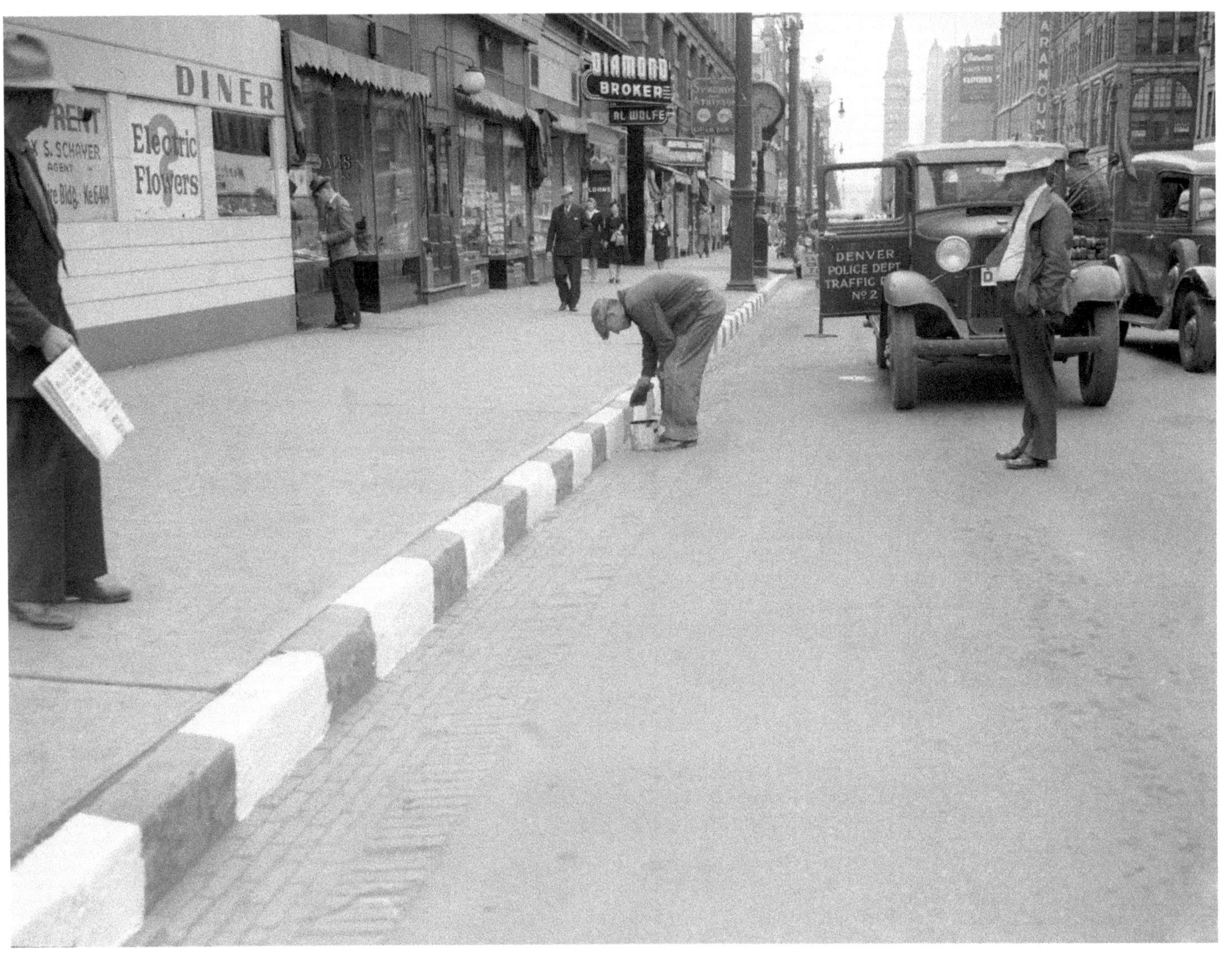

An employee of the Denver Police Department Traffic Division no. 2 paints no-parking stripes on the curb on 16th Street.

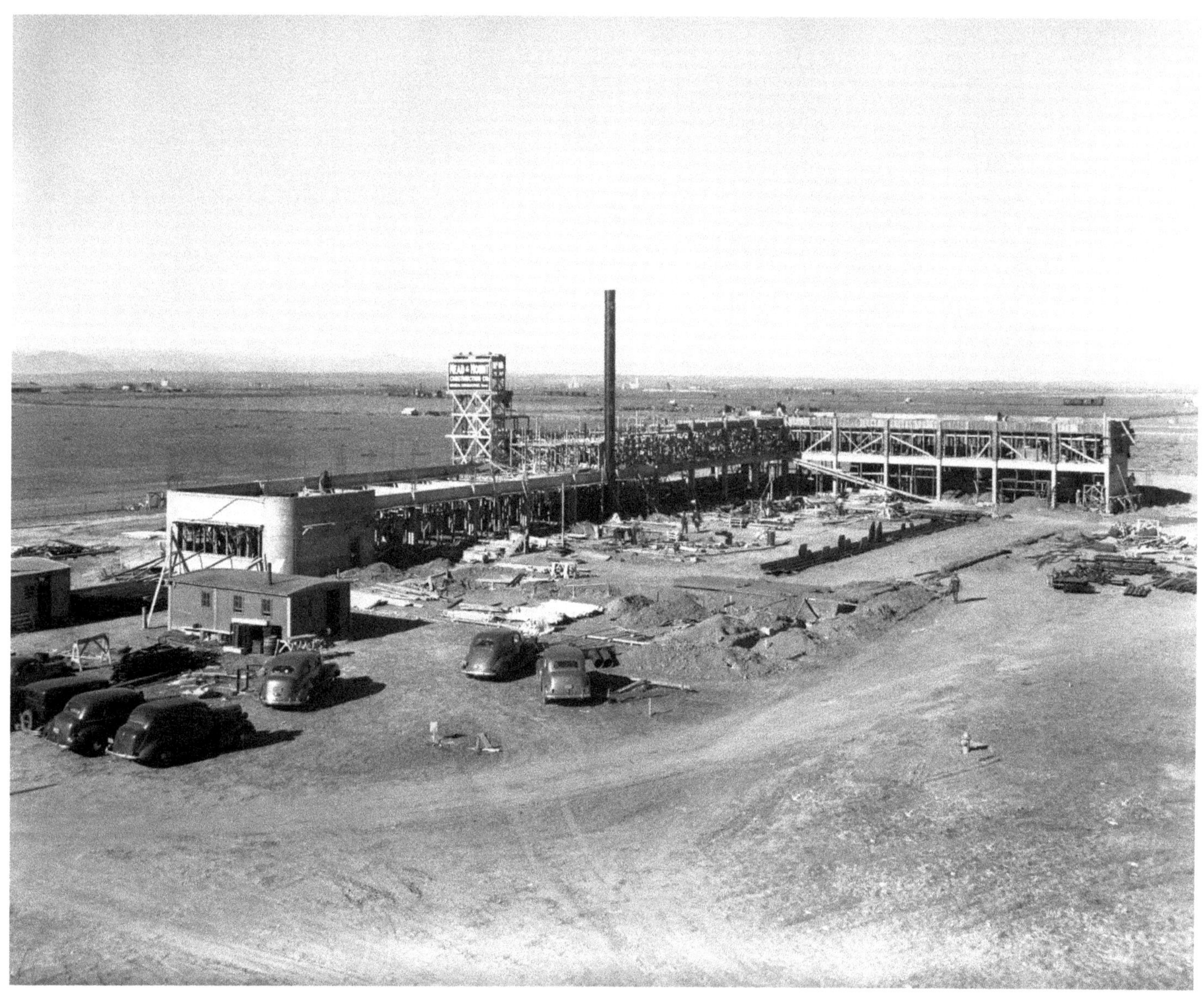

The United-Continental Airlines hangar and office building is under construction at Denver Municipal Airport in this photo taken on December 2, 1940.

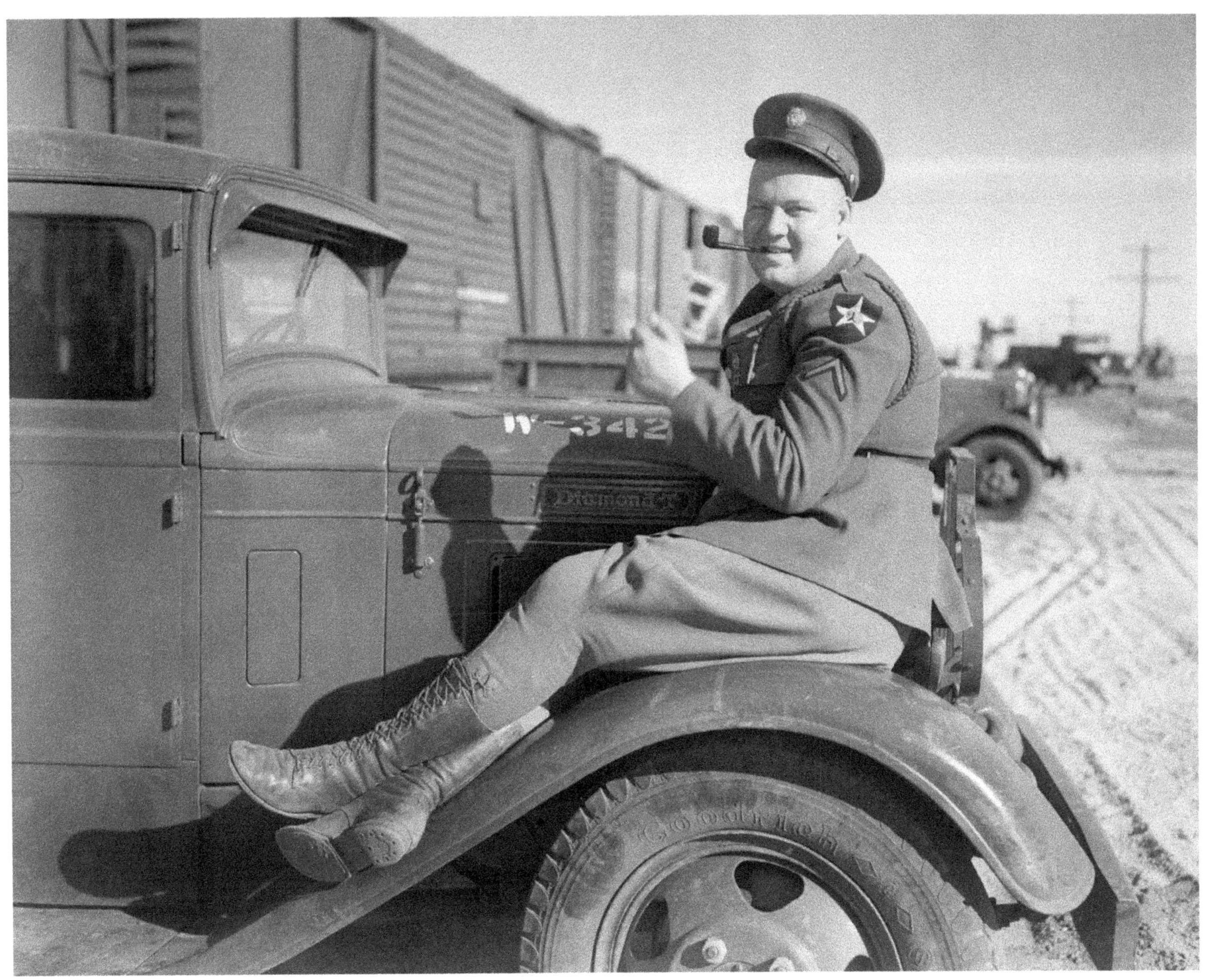

An Army private first-class smokes a pipe on the fender of a truck at Lowry Field during World War II.

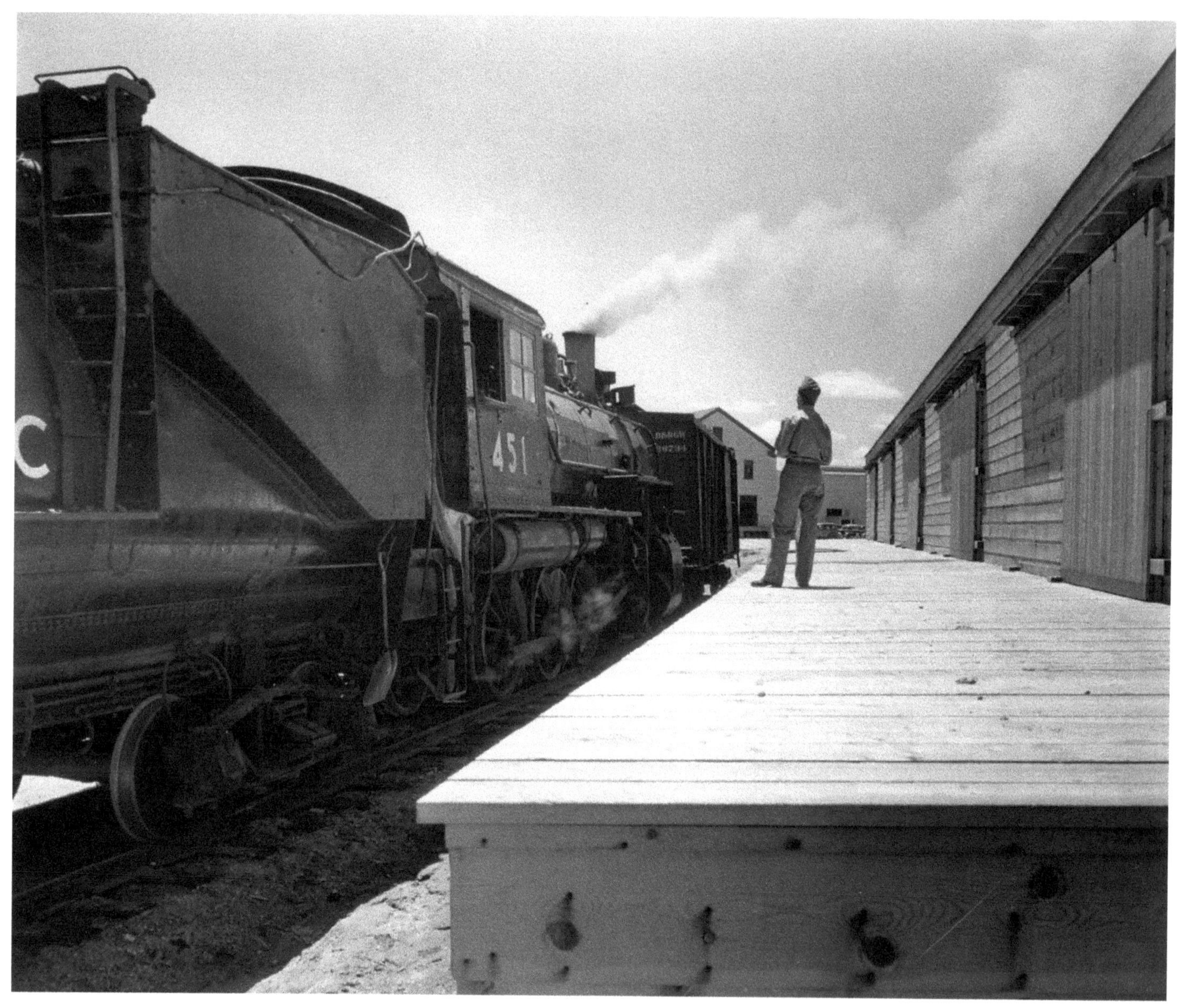

A soldier stands on a railroad platform at Lowry Field. The 4.6-mile standard gauge railroad was built by the Work Projects Administration and connected with the main line of the Union Pacific Railroad.

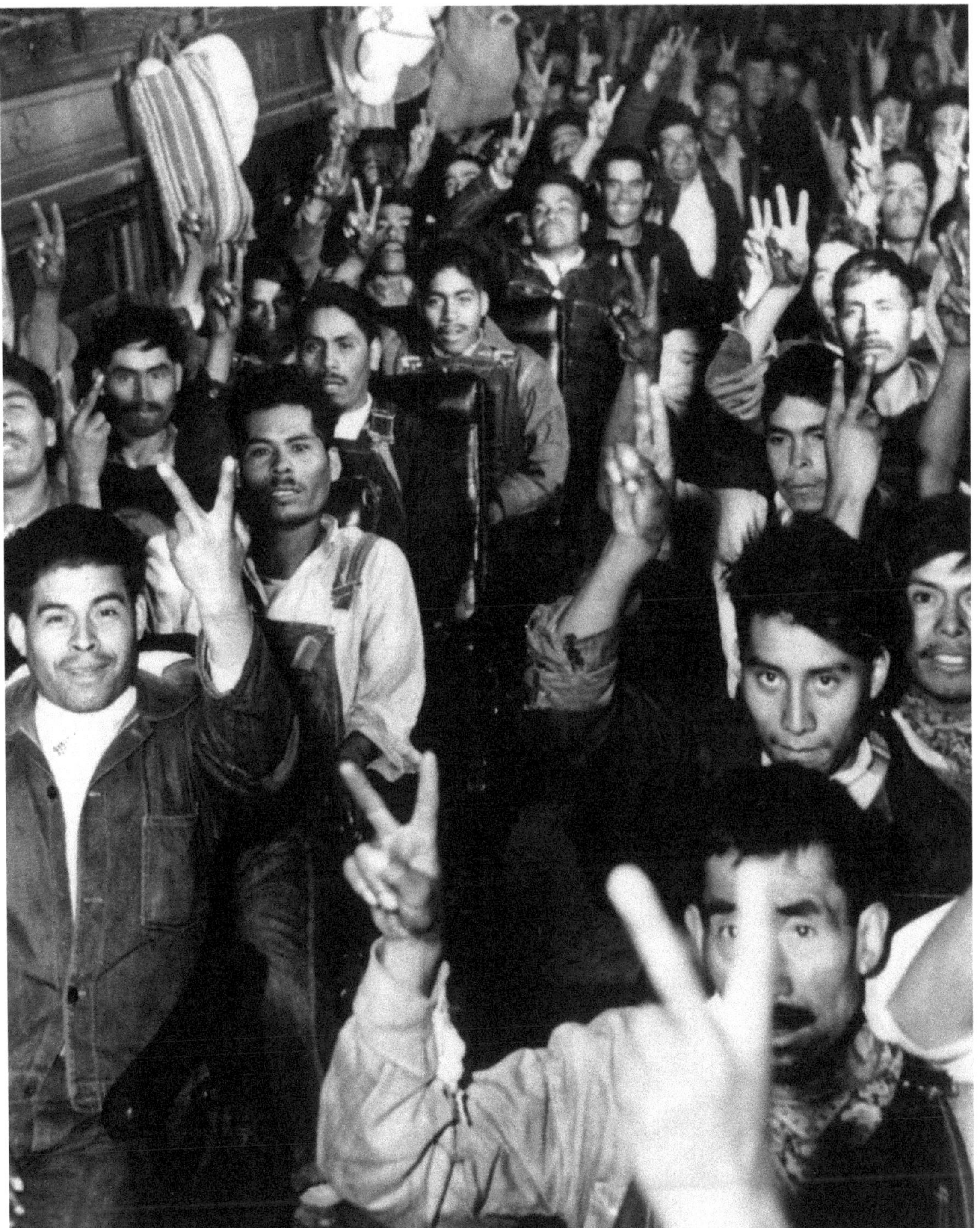

Mexican migrant workers sit in a railroad car and hold up their hands in the "V" for victory sign at the end of World War II.

Here the Brown Palace Hotel stands on the corner of 17th and Broadway in the Central Business District and the Midland Savings building is in the distance on the left. Bunting and banners that read "Welcome Rotary" hang over the street.

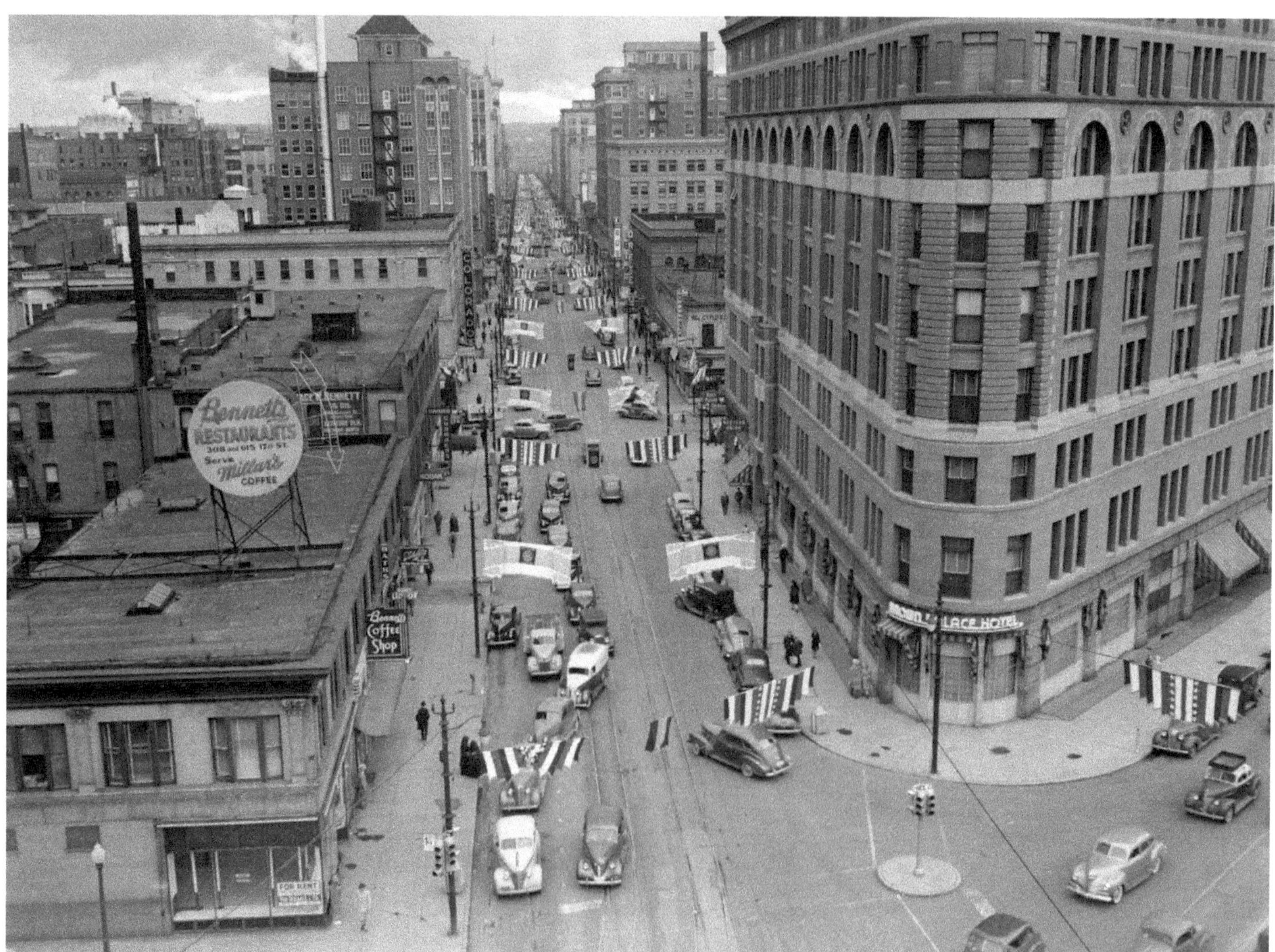

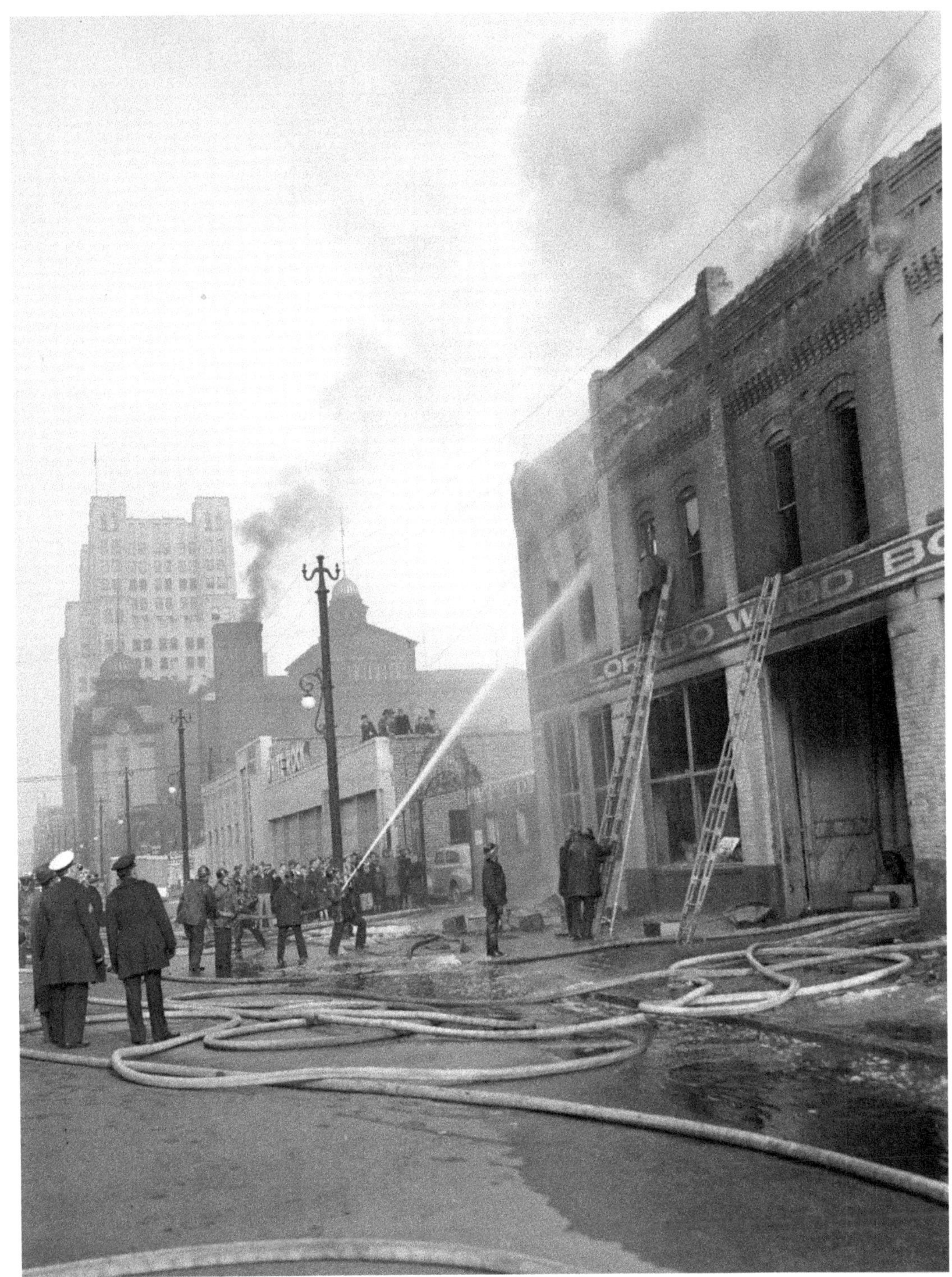

The Denver Fire Department fights a fire at the Colorado Wood Products Company, which was located in the 1200 block of Curtis Street.

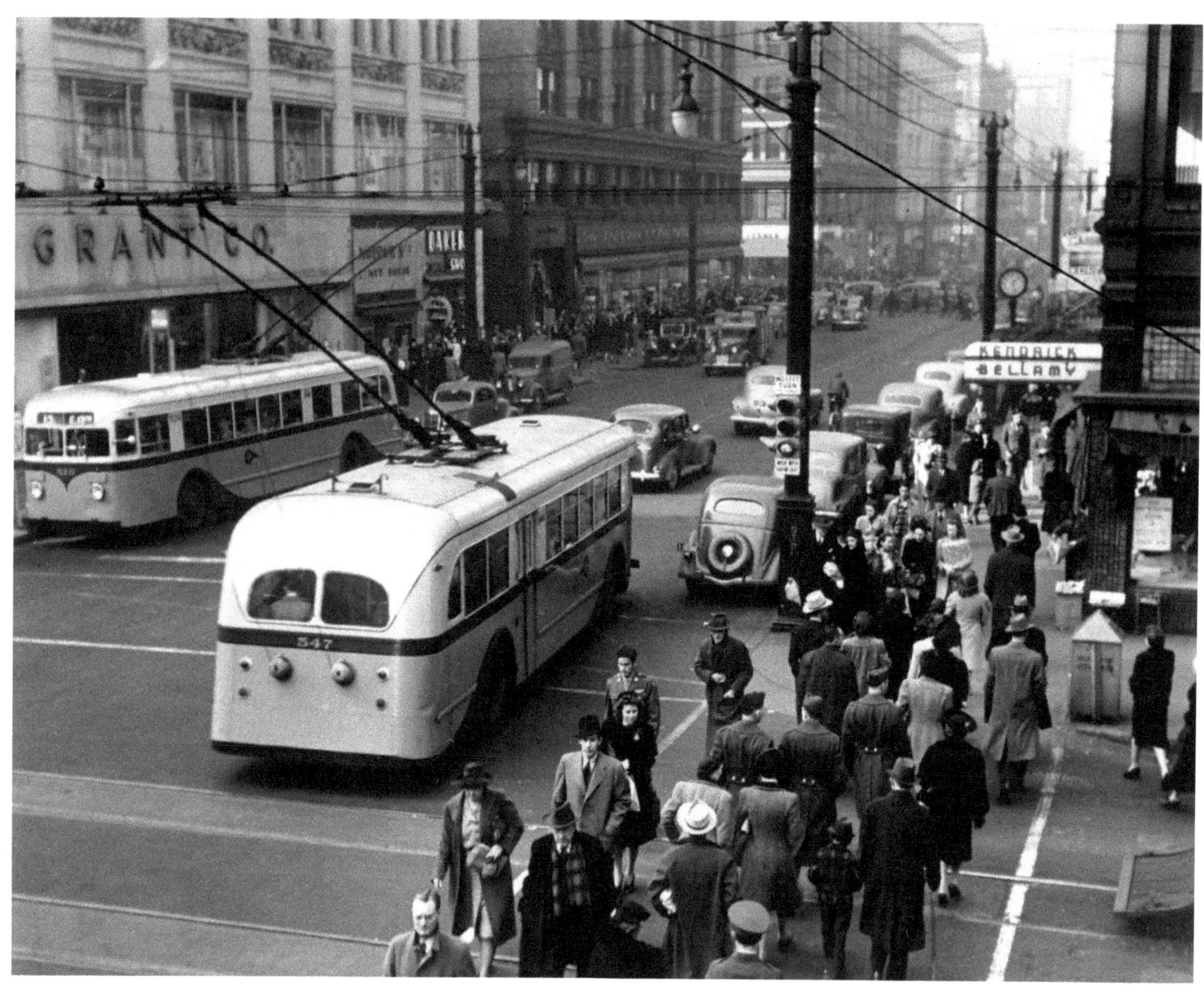

Pedestrians cross Stout Street in the Central Business District as two electric trolleybuses ply 16th Street. The Denver Tramway company trolleybuses were put in service in 1940.

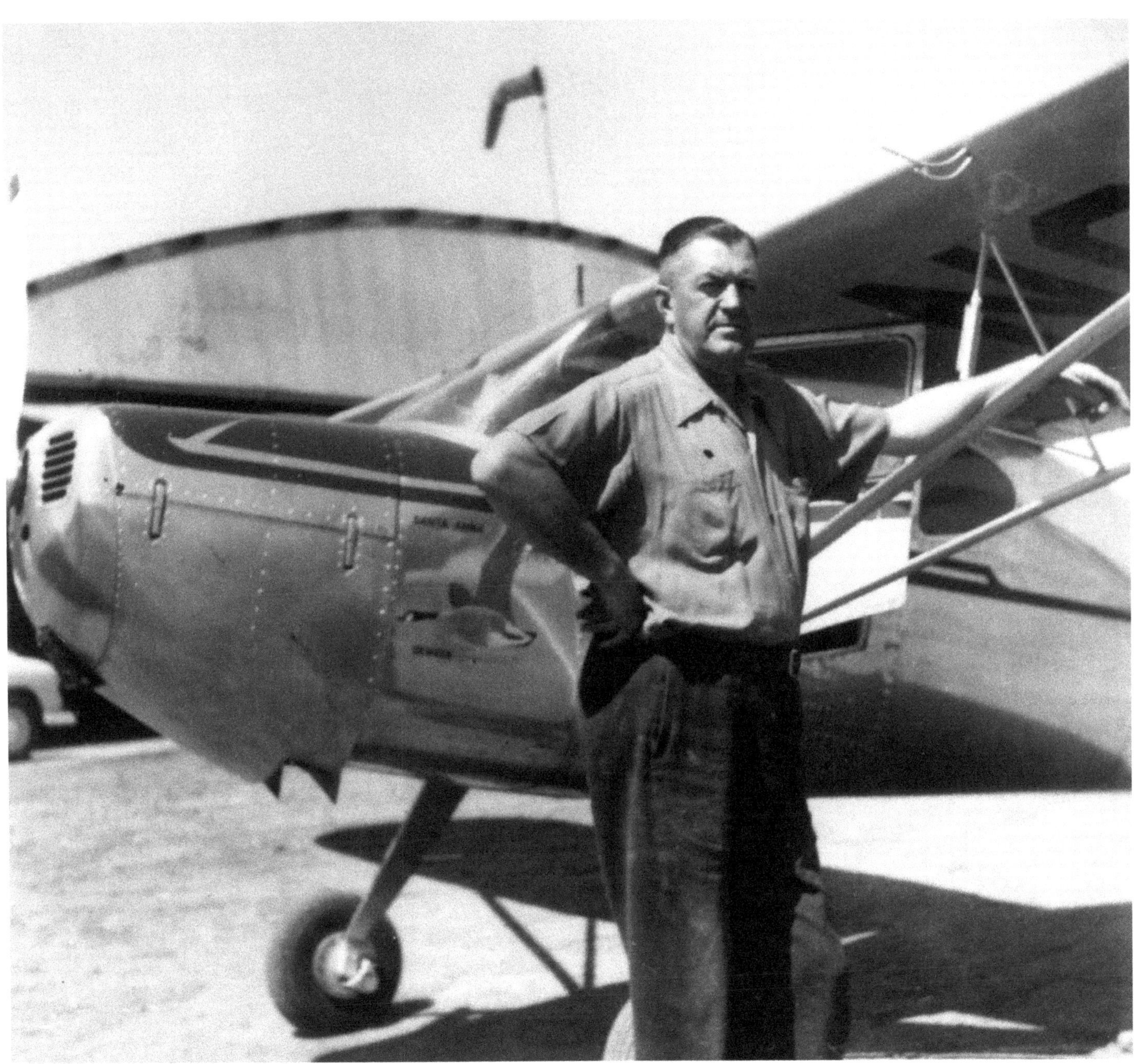

Louis Paul "Gus" Quinn was a well-known Colorado pilot and educator. Prior to World War II, he was a stunt pilot and barnstormer. During the war he served as a Cockpit Procedures Training (CPT) instructor for military pilots. Following the war, he and his wife, Hazel, championed general aviation in Colorado.

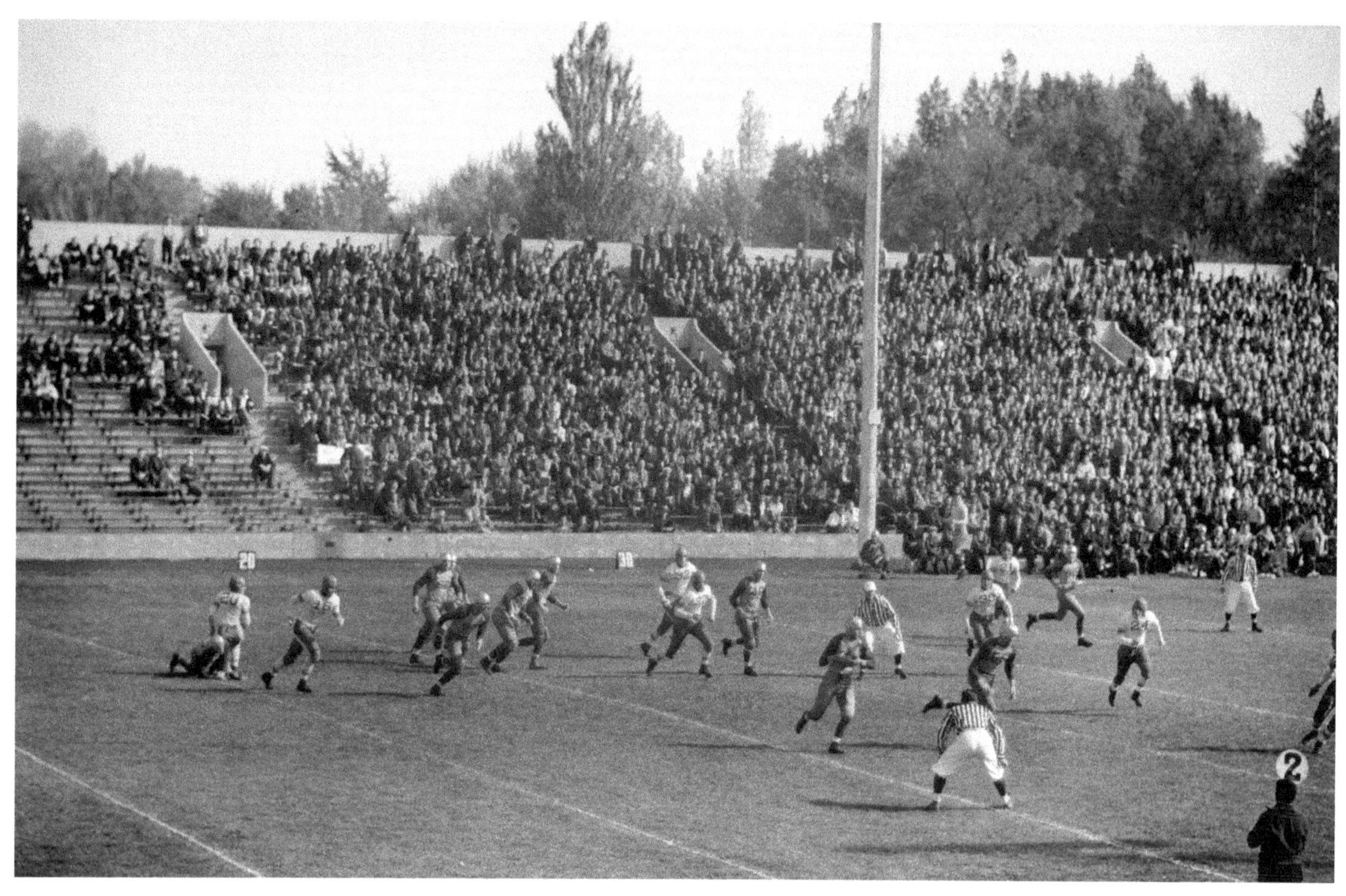

A crowd watches the University of Denver Pioneer football team at the 30,000-seat stadium, which was located on the DU campus from 1927 to 1974. The football program was discontinued in 1960.

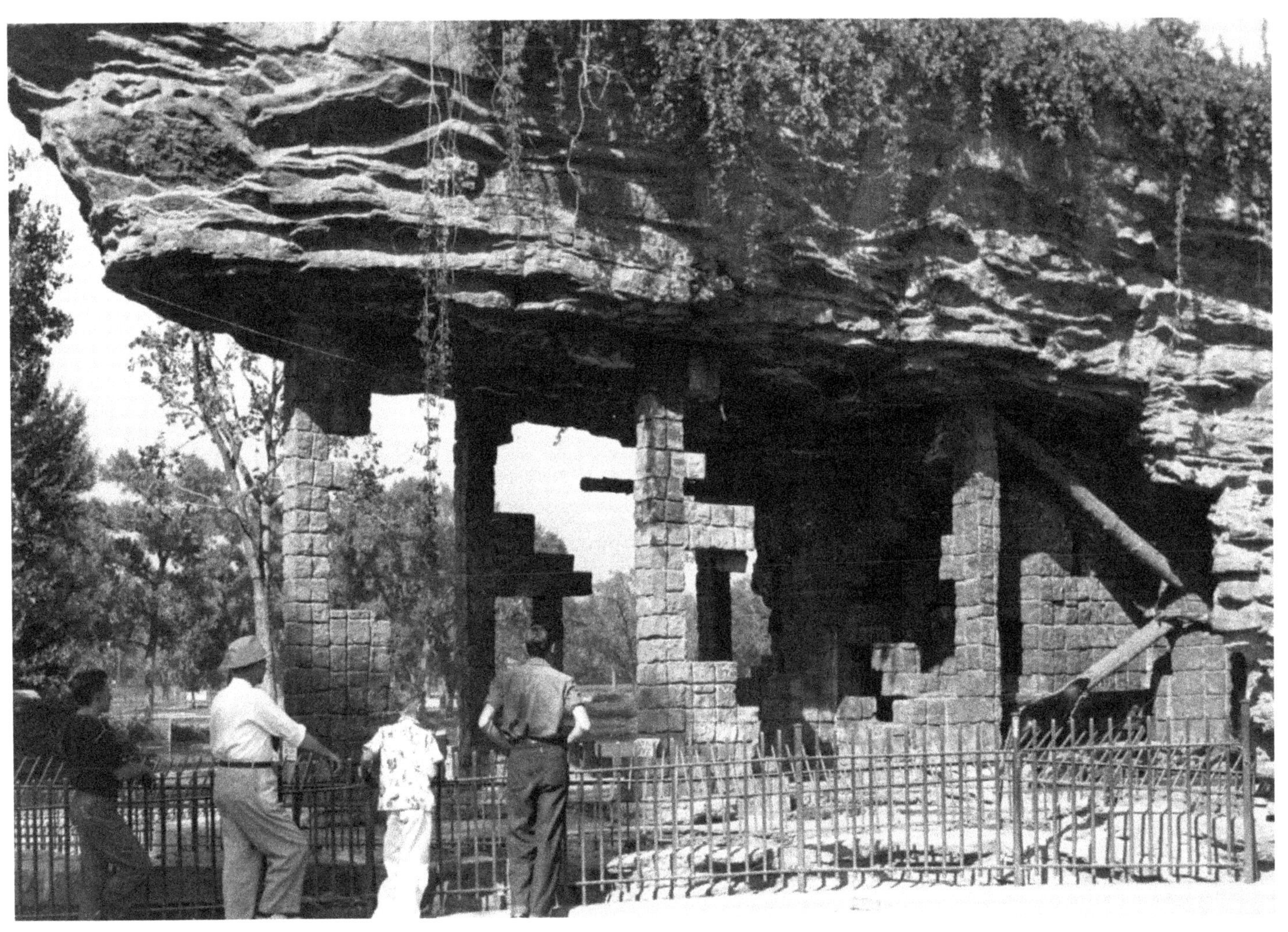

Bear Mountain, which opened in 1918 at the Denver Zoo, was the first natural habitat built in North America. Designed by Zoo Director Victor H. Borcherdt, the habitat was constructed of dyed and textured concrete, cast from natural rock formations. This cave, on the southern end of the habitat, was built to house monkeys, but because of their frequent escapes, it soon became home for the sea lions. Bear Mountain is now on the National Register of Historic Places and this section is used for the coati exhibit.

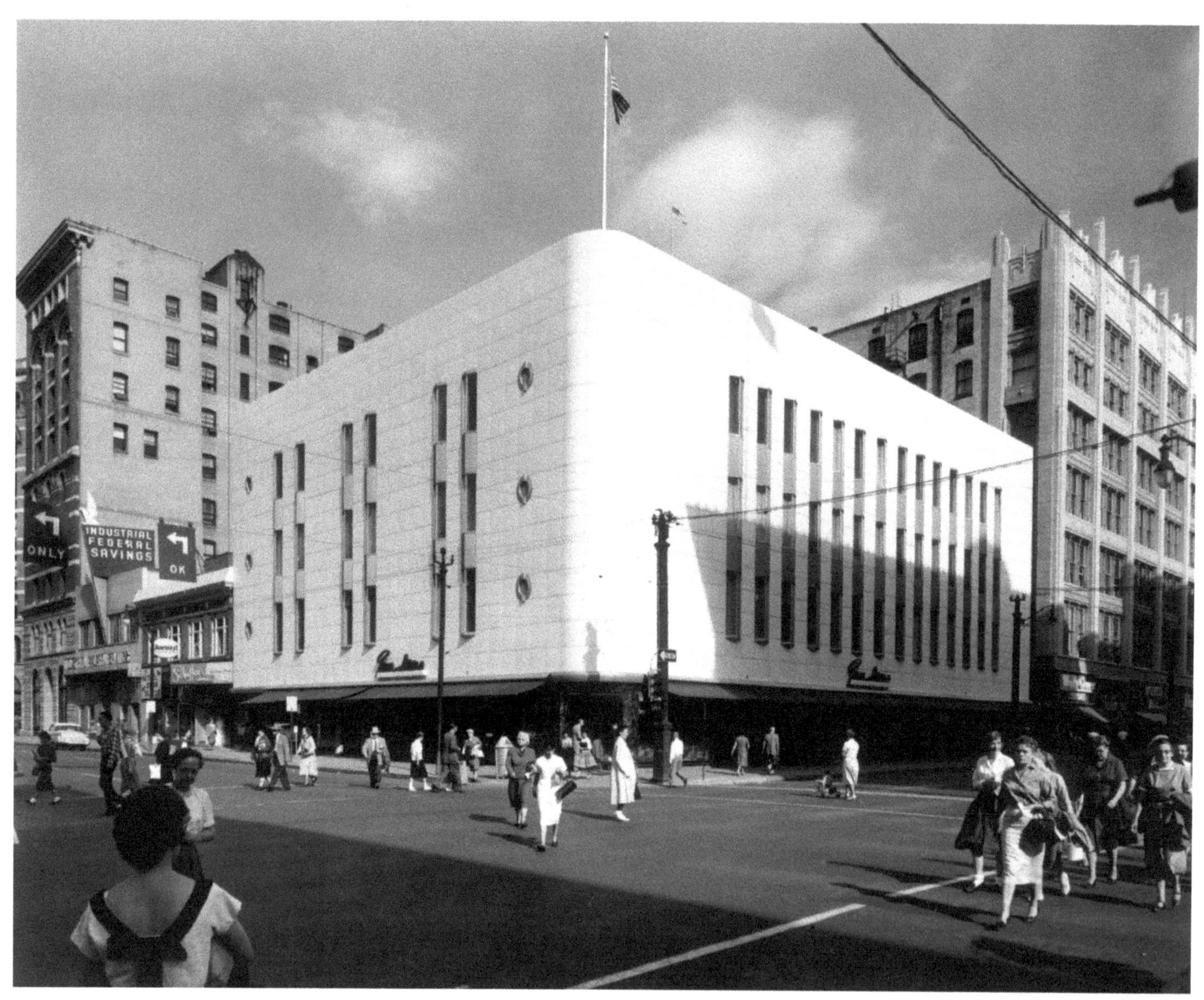

The Gano-Downs clothing company was an upscale men's store located on the corner of 16th and Stout. In the 1940s the company updated the building's facade to the moderne style.

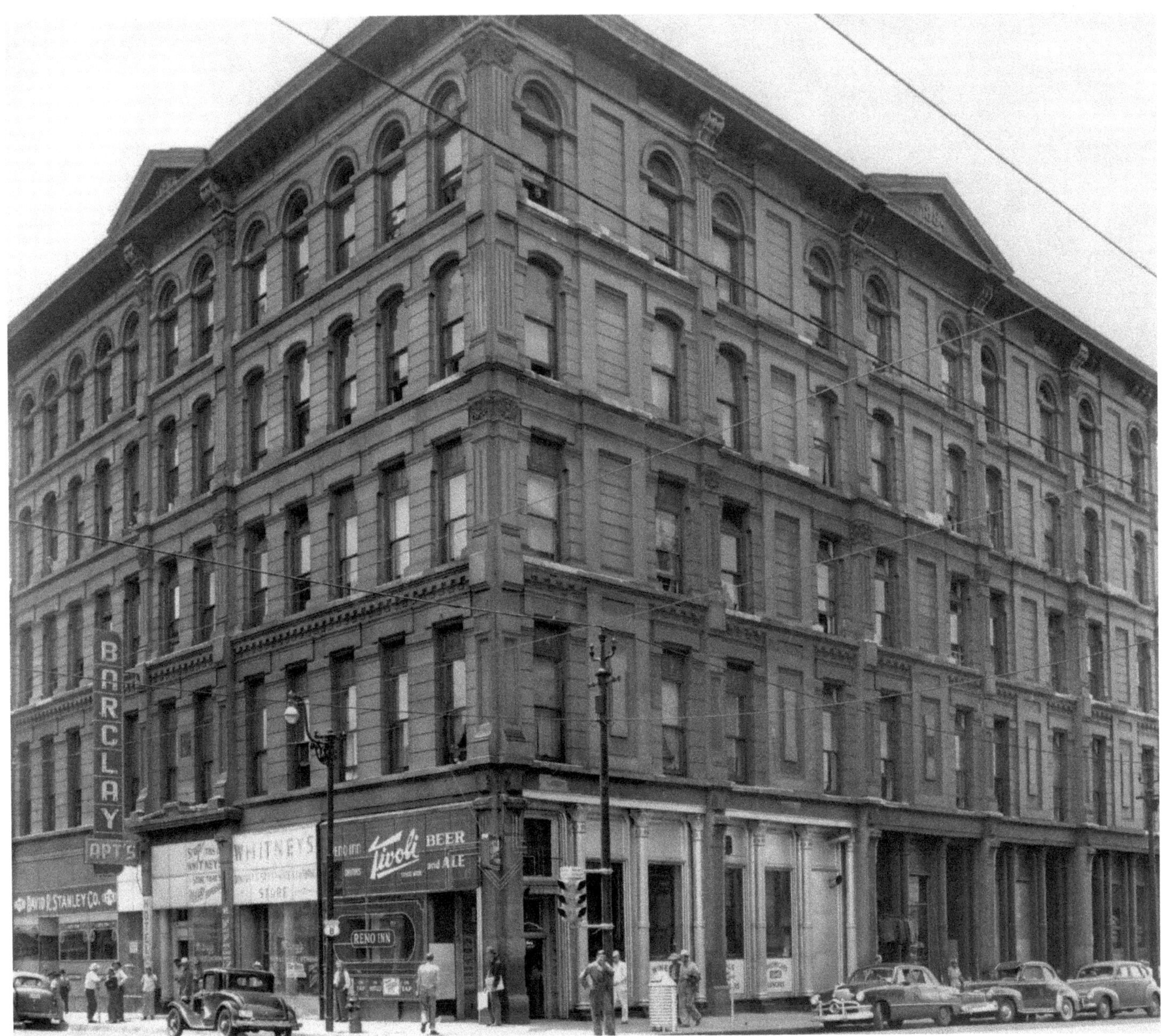

The Barclay Block, located at 18th and Larimer, was built as a business block and later became hotel apartments. In the late 1940s and early 1950s, the building reflected the overall economic decline in lower downtown Denver.

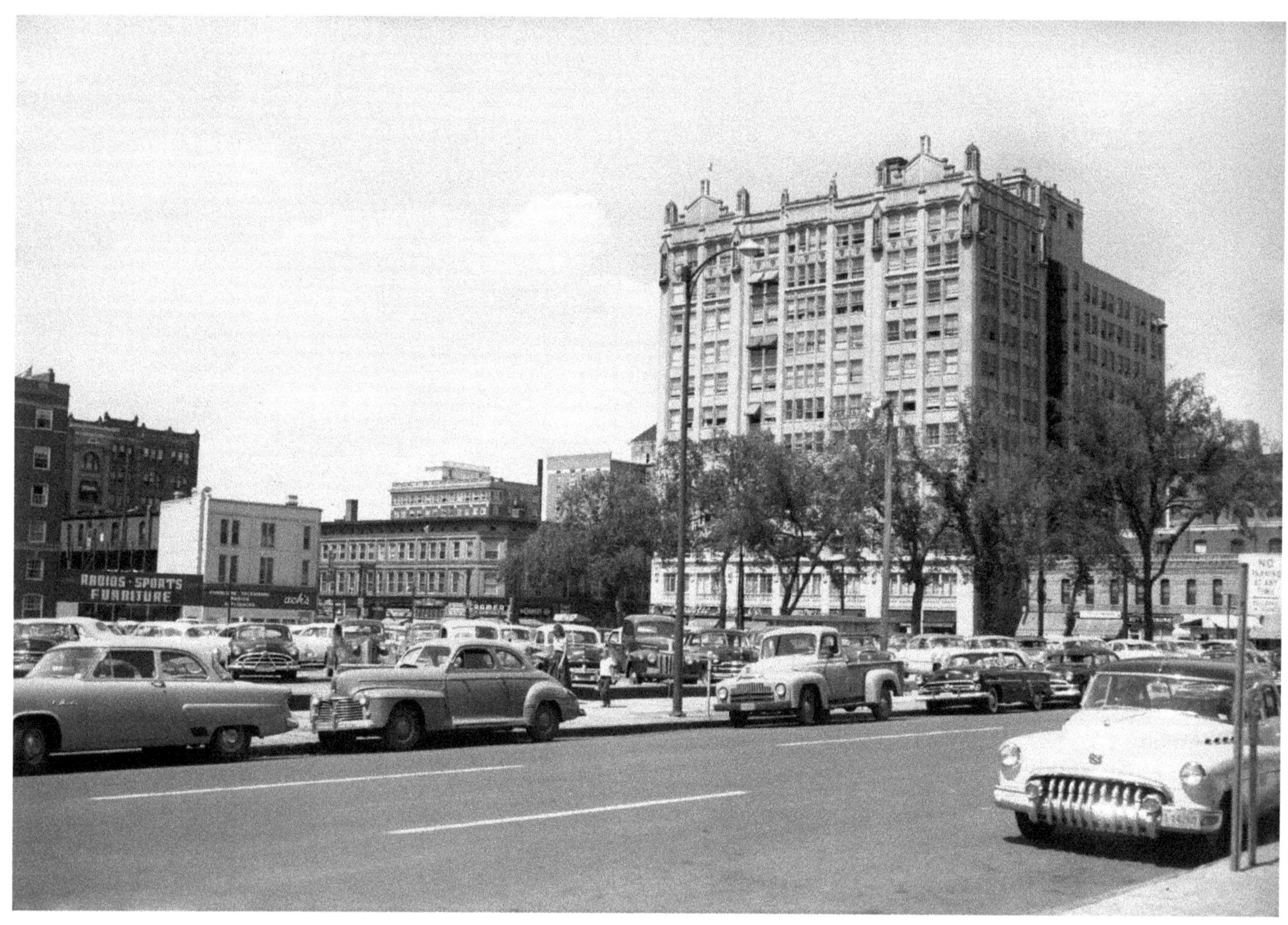

This parking lot was the site of the Arapahoe (later Denver) County Court House. After the building was razed in 1933, a small park was located on the site. By 1953 the park had been converted into a parking lot. In the late 1950s the May Company built a parabola-roofed addition, designed by architect I. M. Pei. The Republic Building, in the background, built in 1928, was located on 16th Street and was the tallest building in the city until 1953. It was demolished in the early 1980s to make way for the 56-story Republic Plaza.

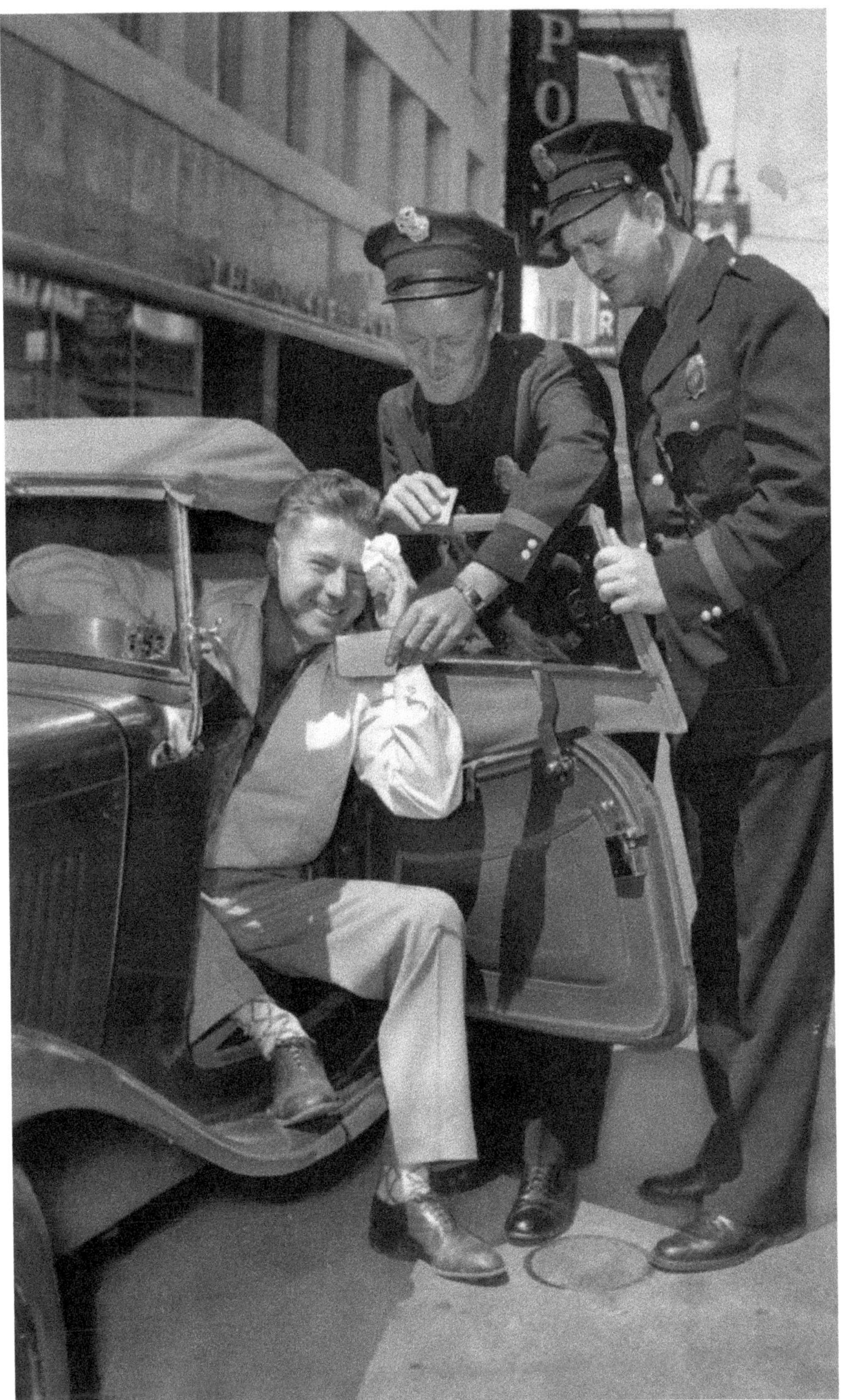

Denver police officers stop Walter R. Beaver in front of the Denver Post building, not for a traffic summons, but to give him a pair of tickets to the movie *Jeopardy*—part of a promotion sponsored by the Broadway Theater with the help of the Police Department.

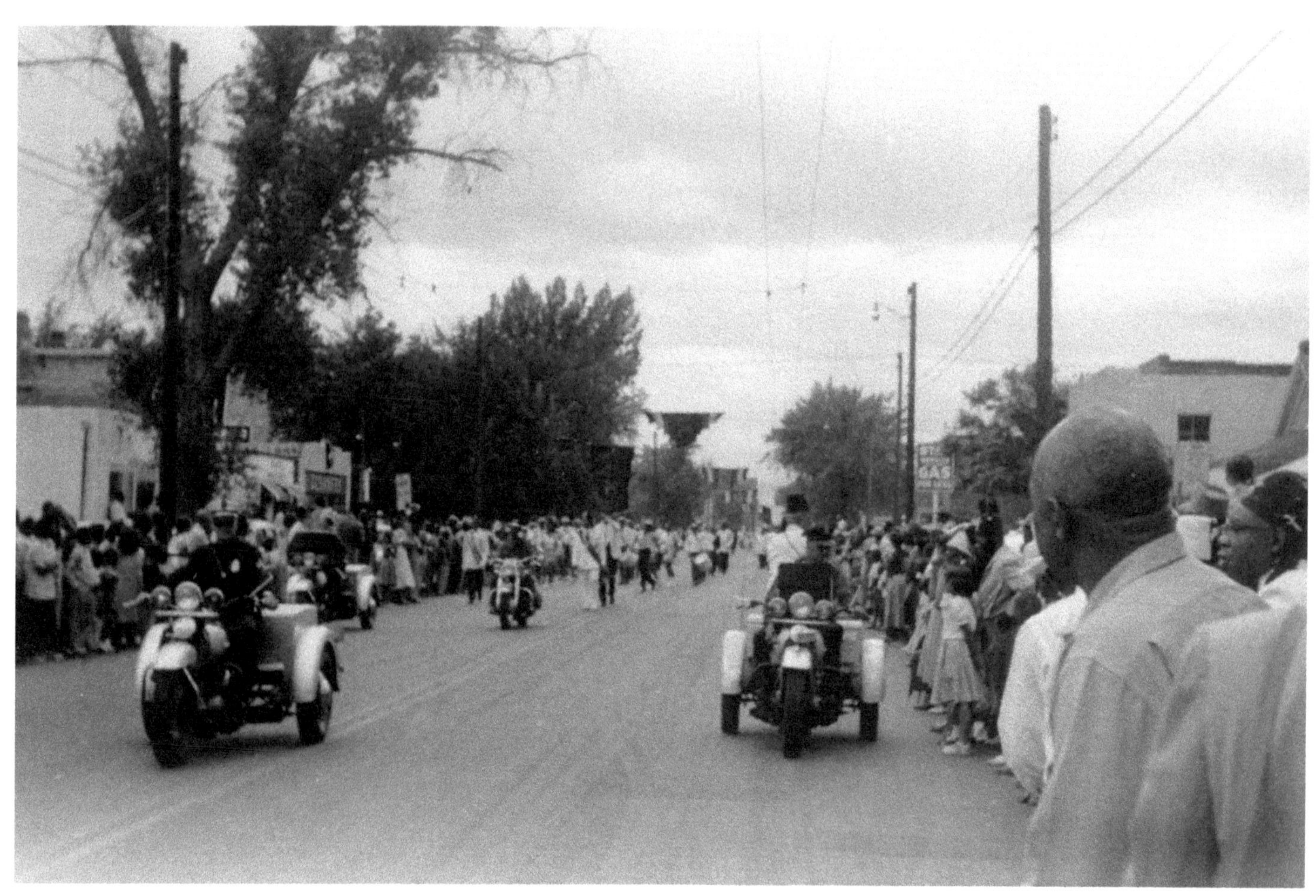

Policemen riding motorcycle trikes lead a Shriner's parade on Welton Street in the Five Points neighborhood. Members of Shrine 53 march in the parade.

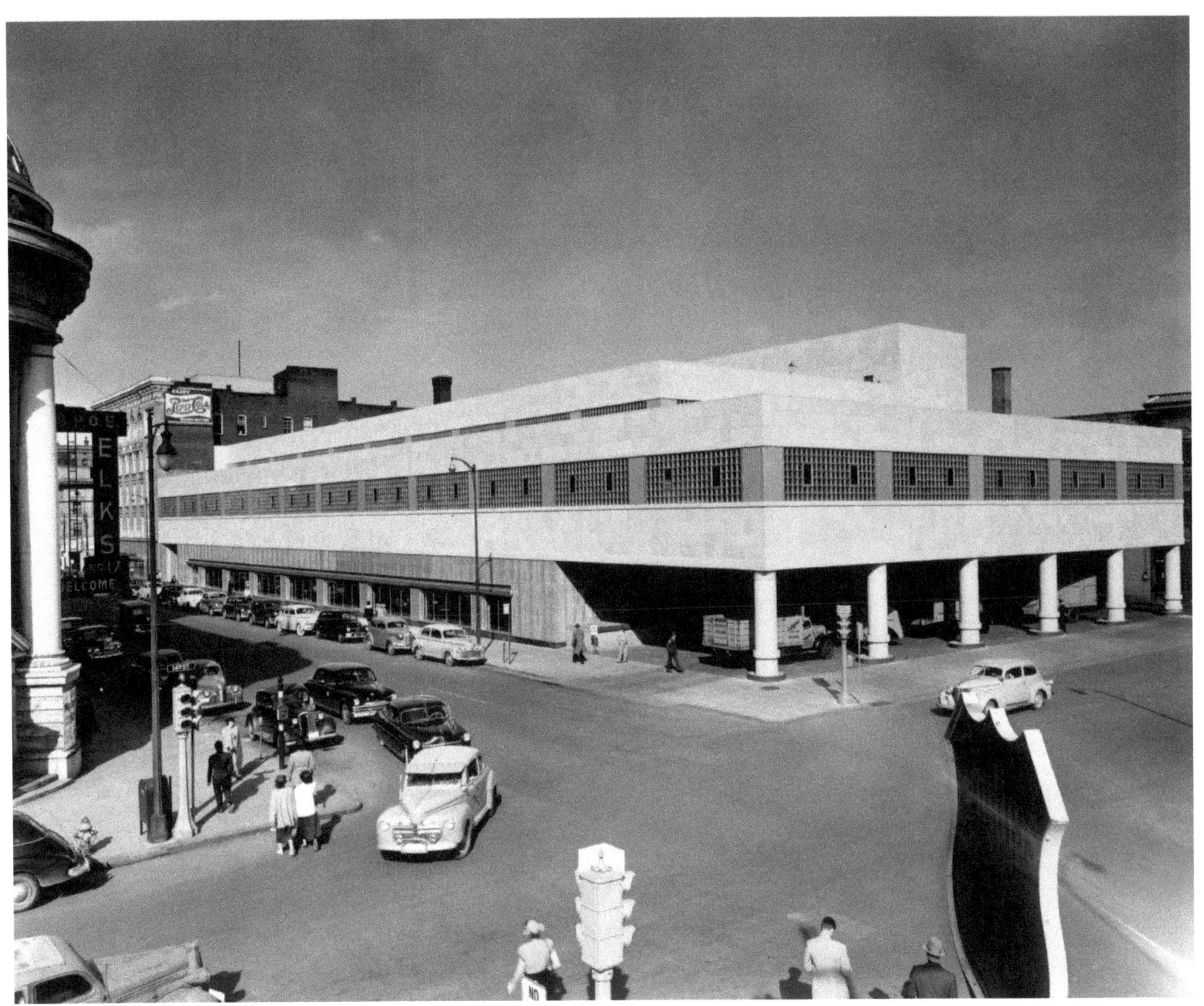

A view of the art-moderne Denver Post printing plant designed by Temple Buell, constructed of pink travertine, glass, and aluminum, and opened in 1950. The building was razed in 1998 and replaced first with a parking lot, and in 2005 with the Hyatt Regency Convention Center Hotel.

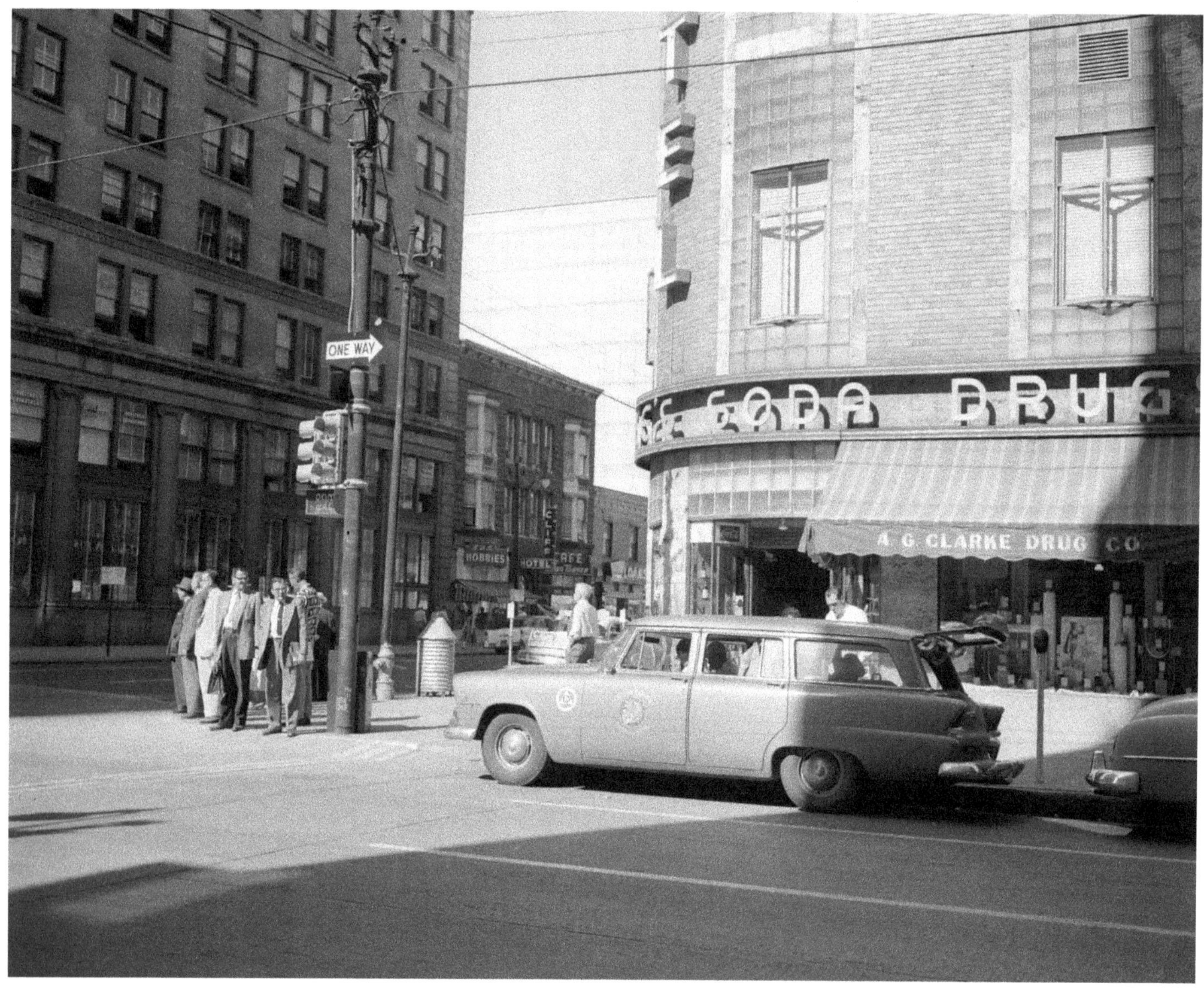

Men stand on the corner of 17th and Stout streets in front of the Albany Hotel. The hotel was remodeled in the 30s, given an art deco exterior and interior by architect Burnham Hoyt.

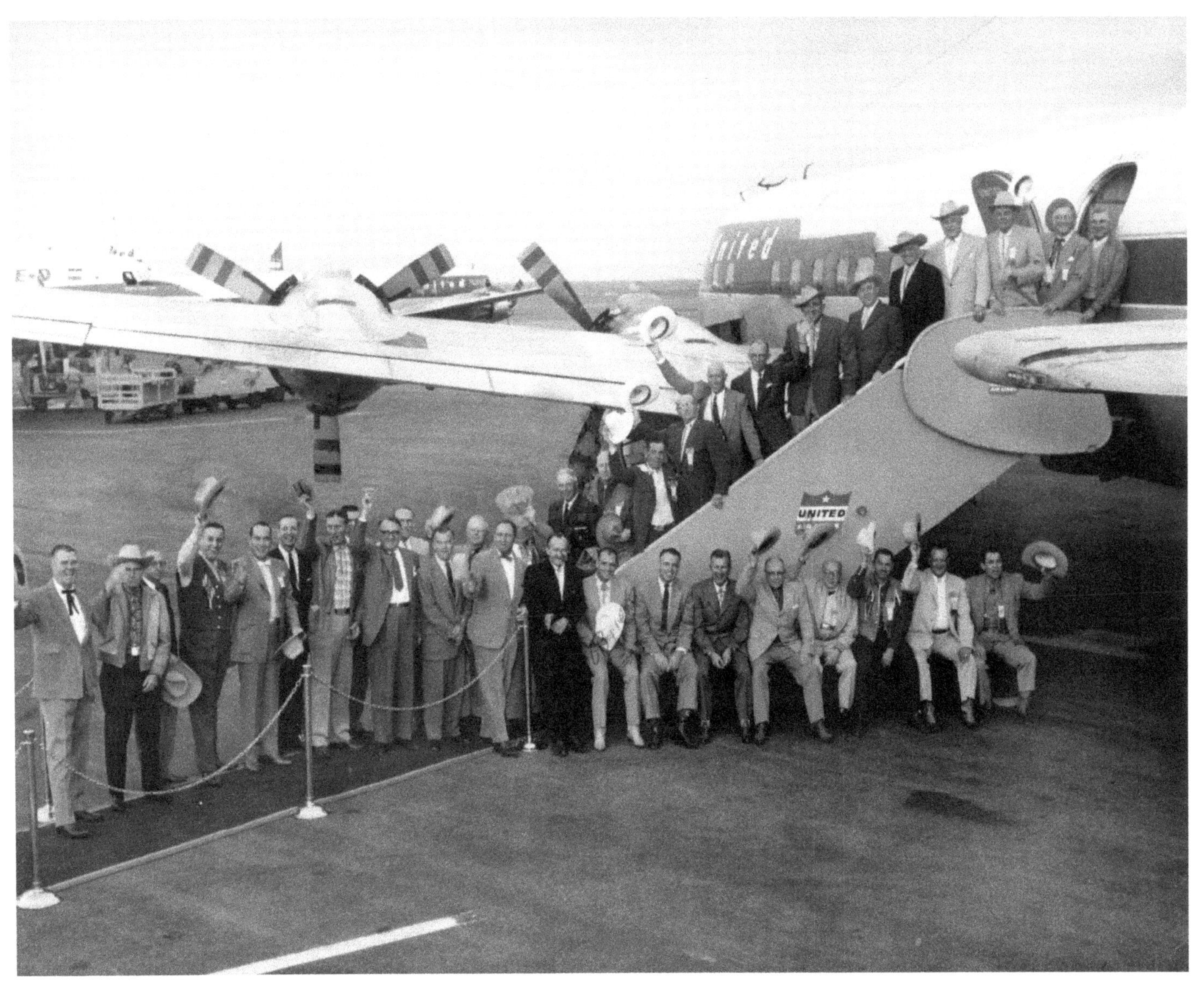

Members of the Roundup Riders of the Rockies, a private organization made up of prominent Colorado business and professional men, pose near a United Airline's charter plane at Denver's Stapleton Airport. Every year the members make a trail ride over the Continental Divide. The organization has a foundation dedicated to trail creation and improvement.

The Daniels and Fisher Department Store was located on the corner of 16th and Arapahoe streets and completed in 1912. The department store was for many years one of the city's finest retail establishments. The business was later sold to the May Company and became the May–D&F Store. This building was closed and razed in the 1970s. The Daniels and Fisher Tower was also slated for destruction, but was saved by preservationists and stands today.

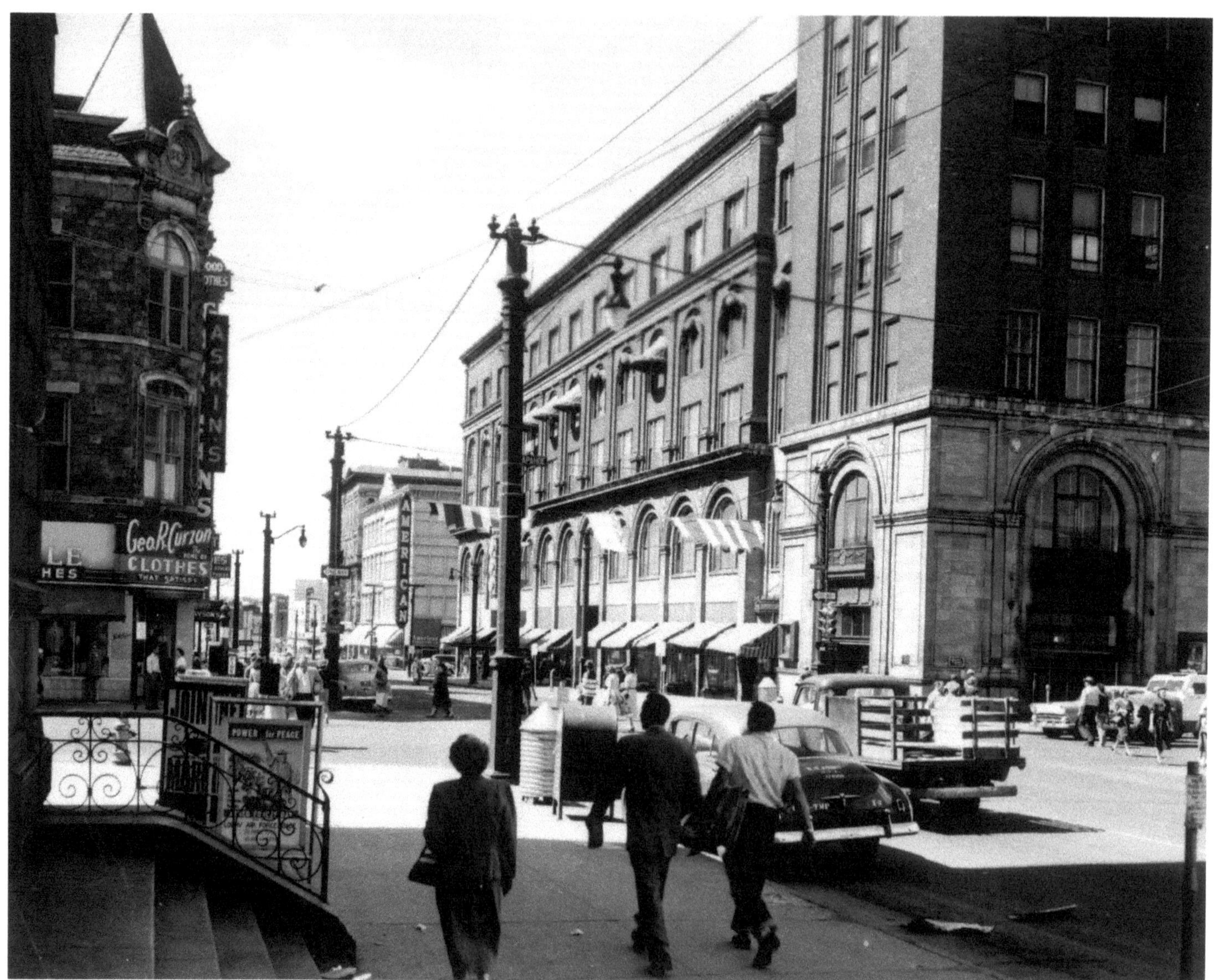

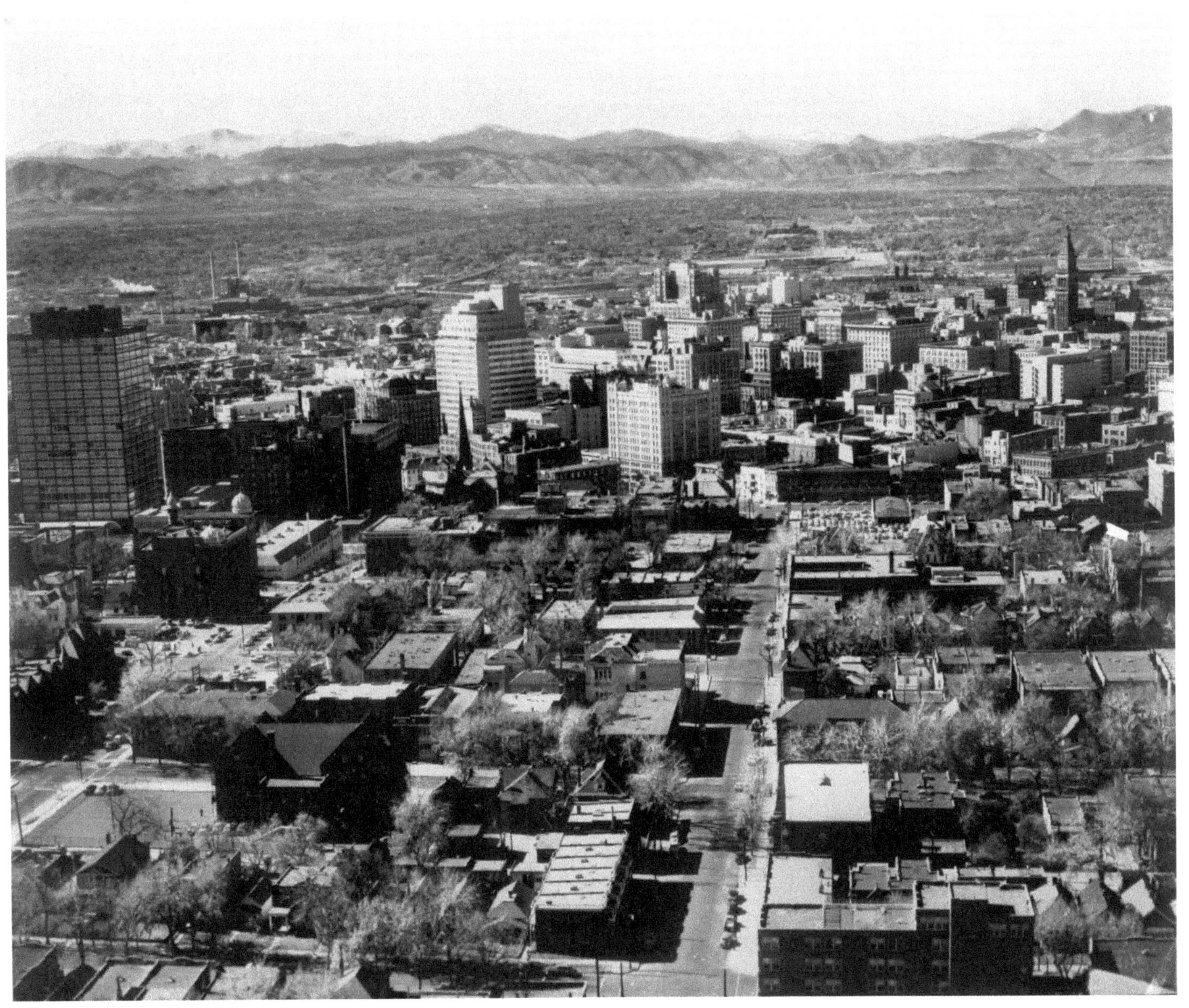

This aerial view of the city shows Denver's first modern high-rise building, Mile High Center, on the far left. Daniels and Fisher Tower, at this time still one of the city's tallest structures, is on the far right. The Front Range of the Rockies rises in the distance.

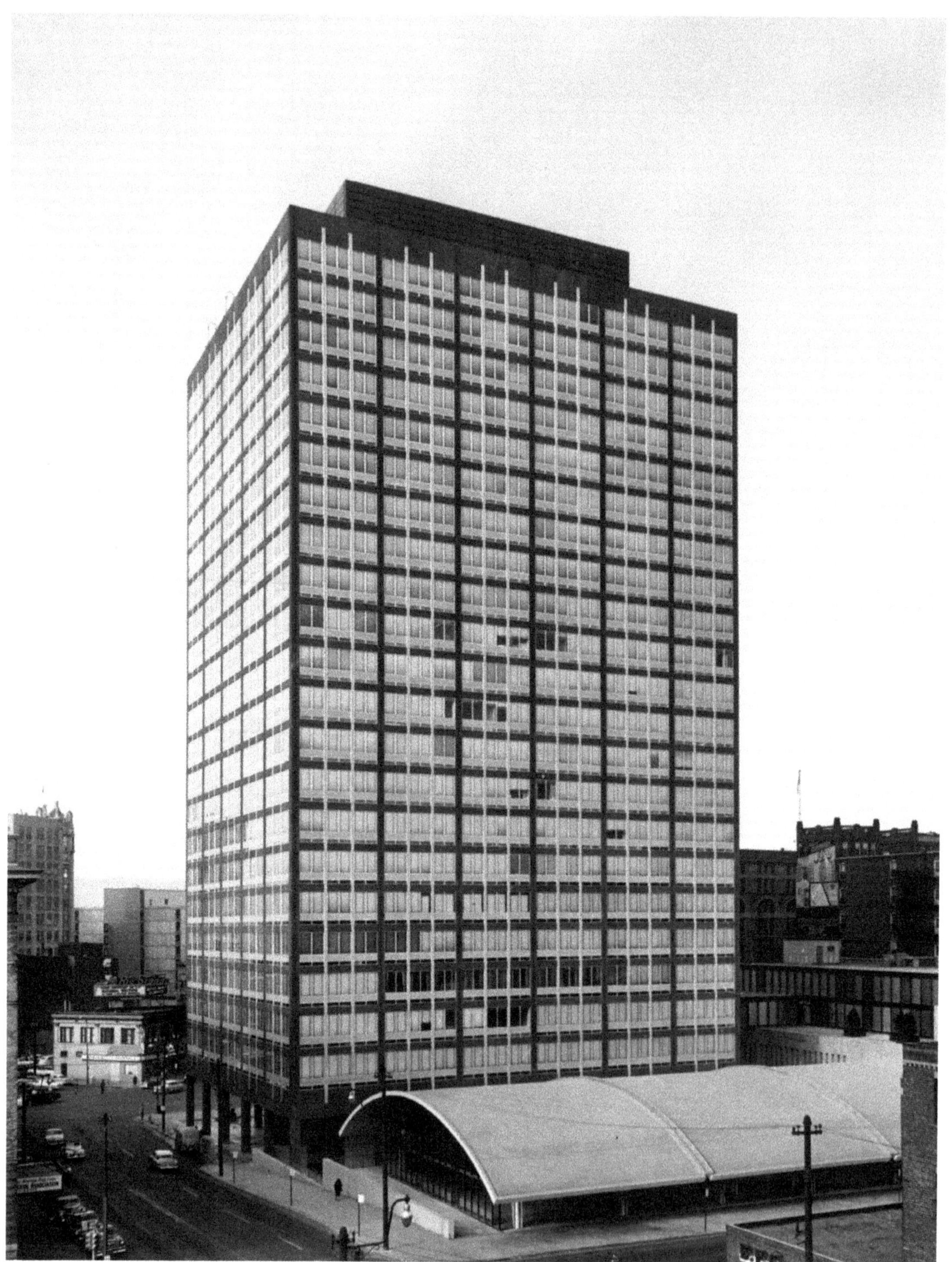

Mile High Center was designed by I. M. Pei and is considered to be Denver's first skyscraper. The wide-span concrete pavilion was designed as a foil to the geometric design of the tower.

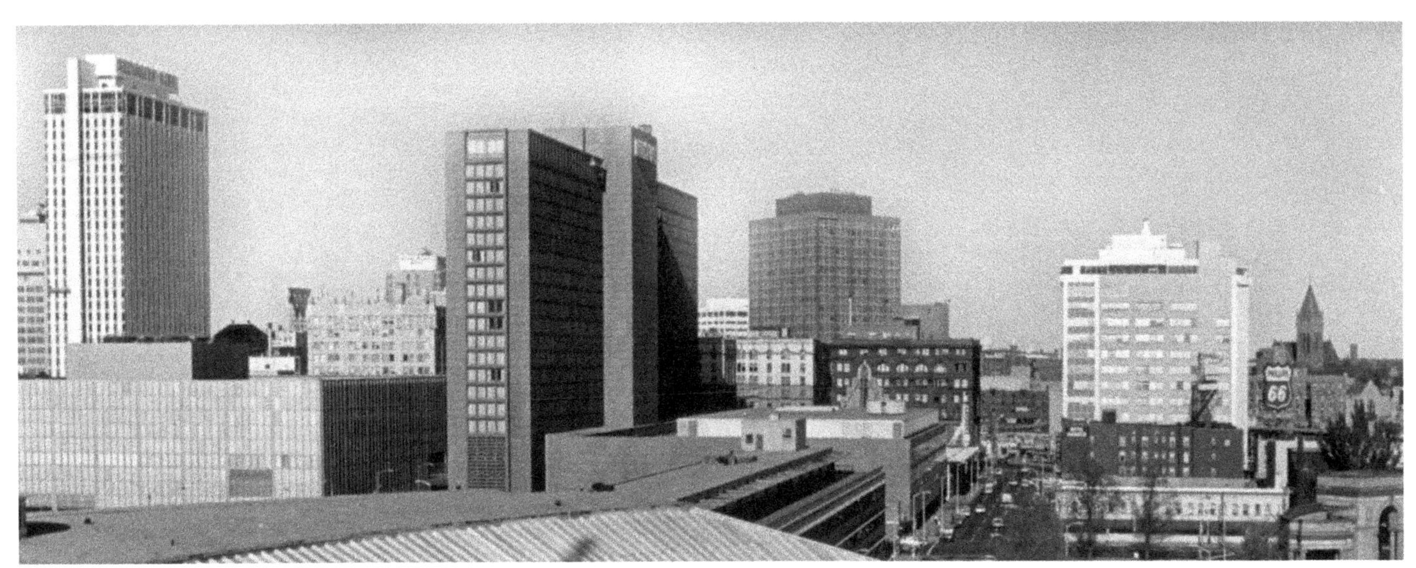

In this panoramic view of the Central Business District, three buildings built by the distinguished architect I. M. Pei are visible. Center left is the Hilton Hotel, and to the left of that the May-D&F Department Store. On the right of the Hilton, in the distance, is Mile High Center.

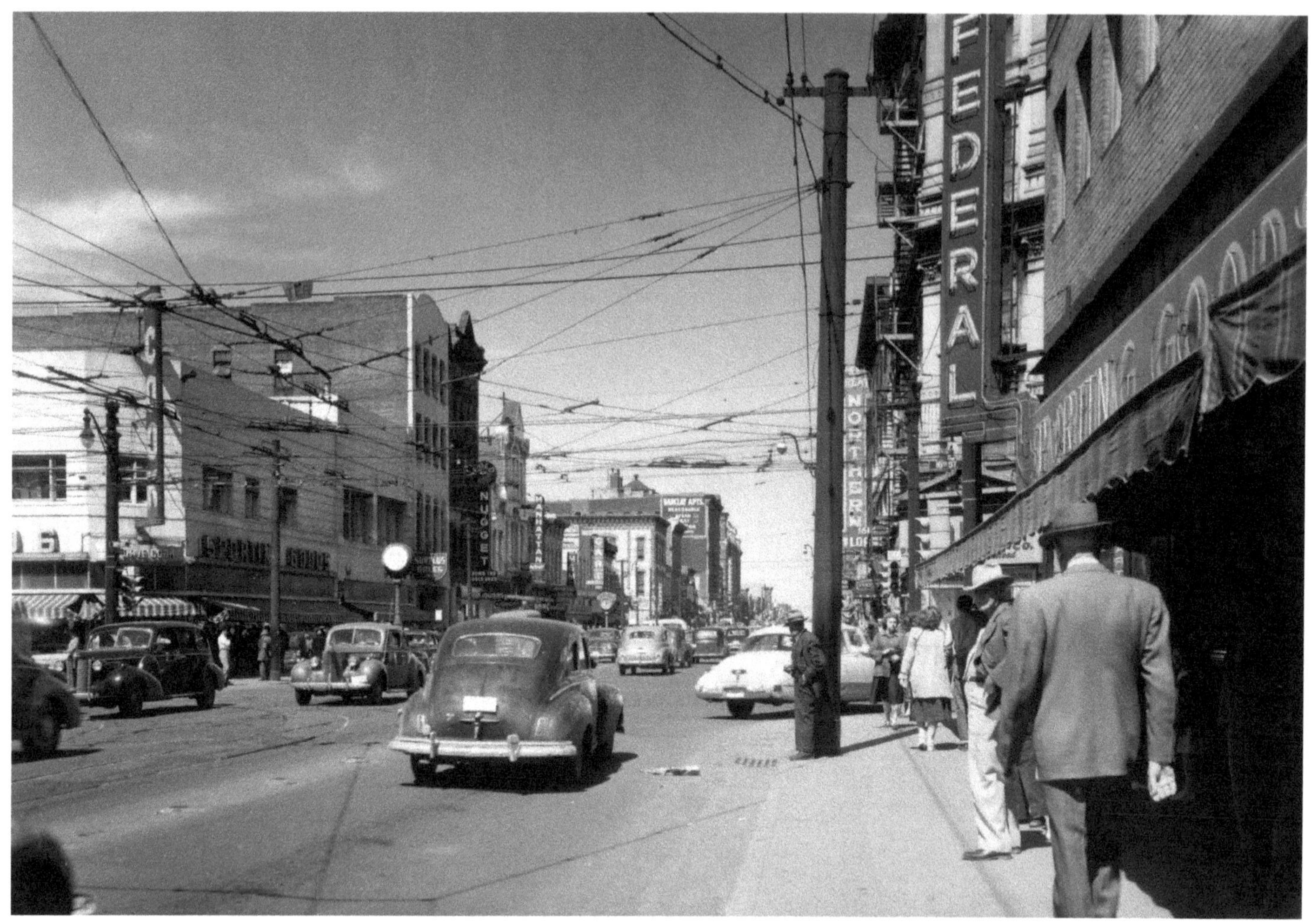

By the late 1940's Larimer Street had many bars and flophouses.

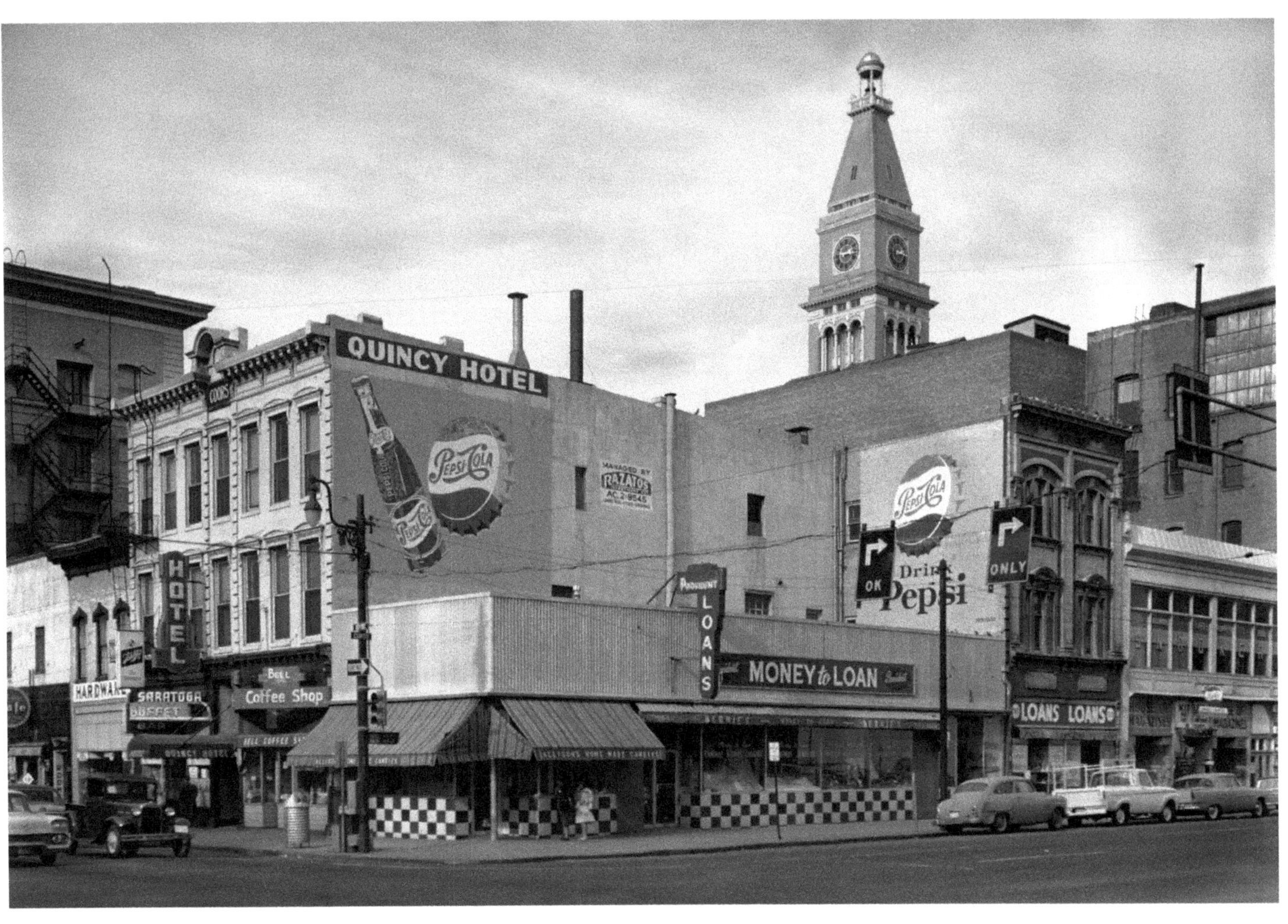

The Quincy Hotel was located in the Coors Block located on 15th Street near the corner of Curtis Street. A second Coors block was located around the corner, also on Curtis Street. The Daniels and Fisher Tower rises in the distance.

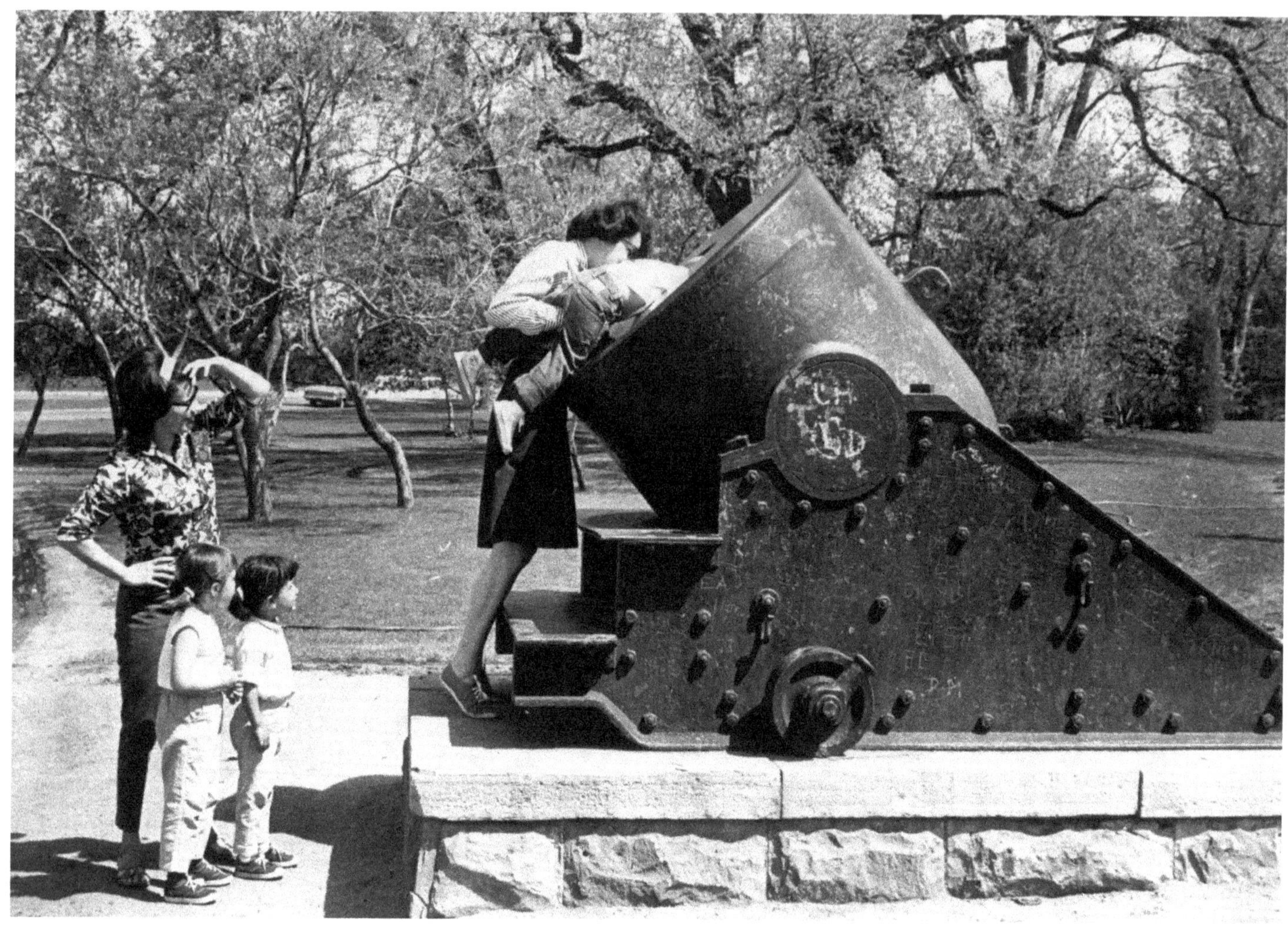

During an outing in City Park, this woman holds a young boy, who peers into a siege mortar.

Except for a one-block area known as Larimer Square, the Denver Urban Renewal Authority would eventually raze most of the historic buildings on Larimer Street. After the economic depression of 1893, few new buildings were built on the street, and by the mid twentieth century Larimer had become Denver's skid row, home to bars, liquor stores, and flop houses. In the late 1950s, Larimer Street was made famous by Jack Kerouac's book *On the Road.*

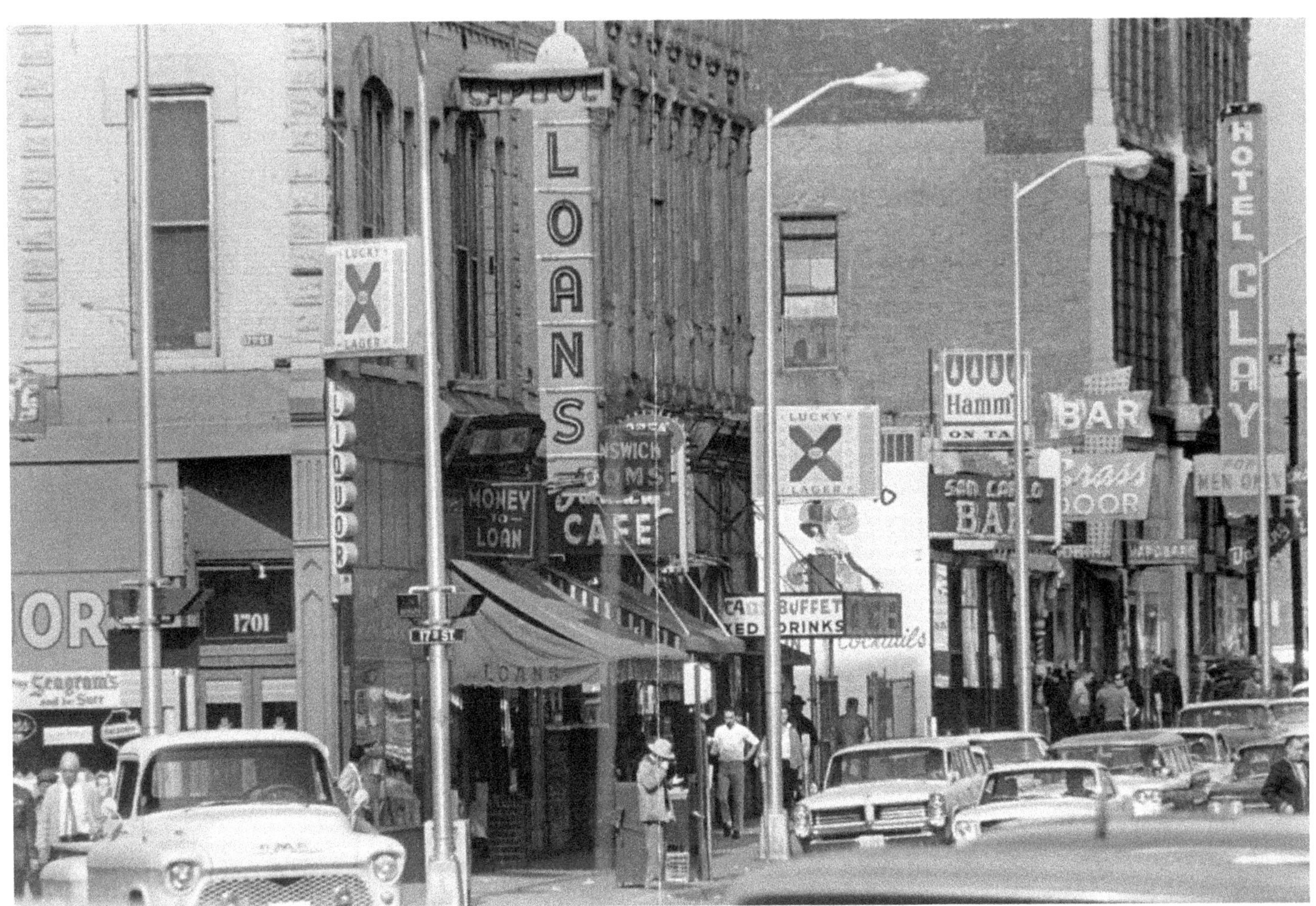

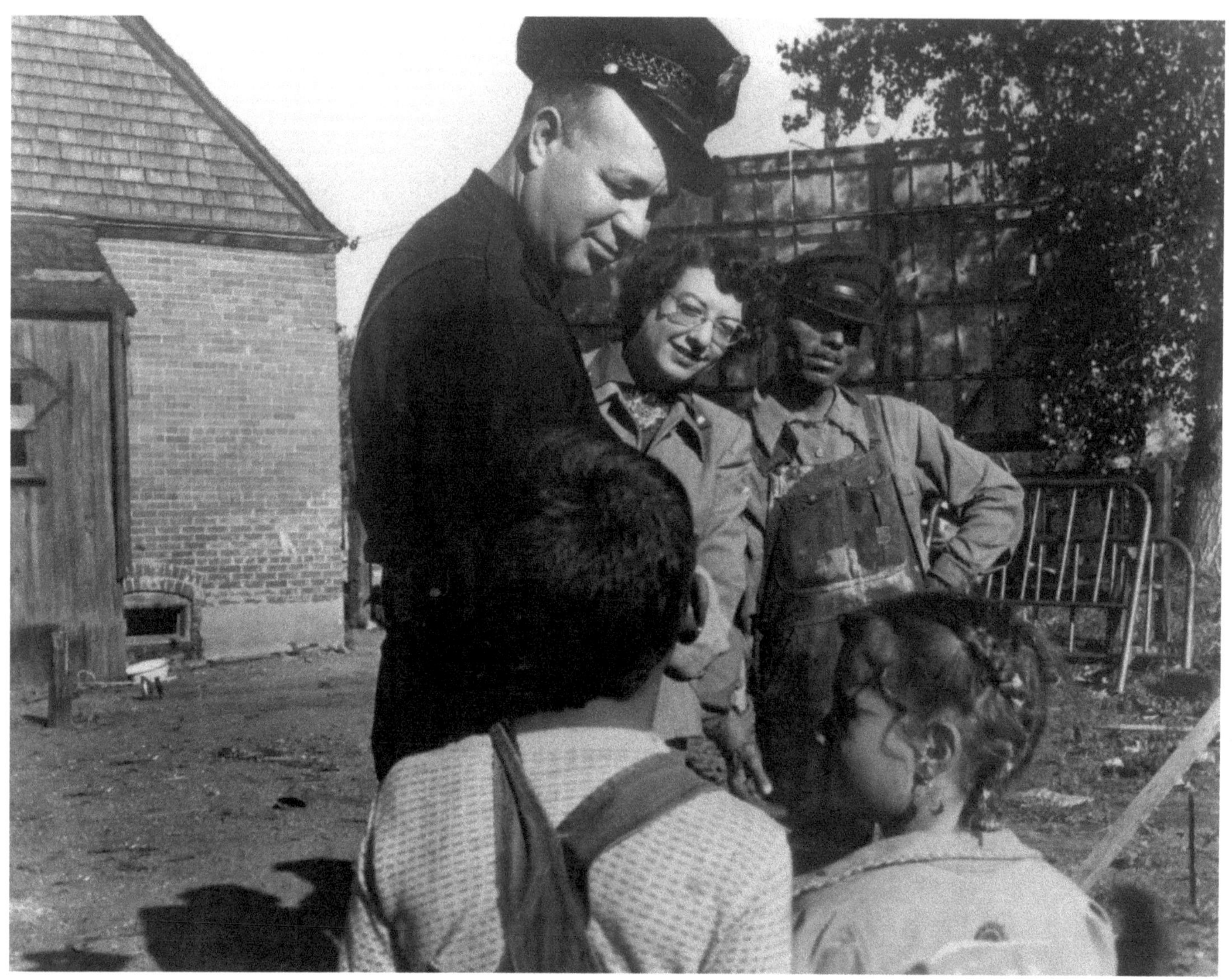

In 1948, Denver Mayor Quigg Newton established a committee to promote racial equality and to improve race relations. Here a member of the Committee on Human Relations and a Denver policeman pose with a man and his children, probably in Five Points.

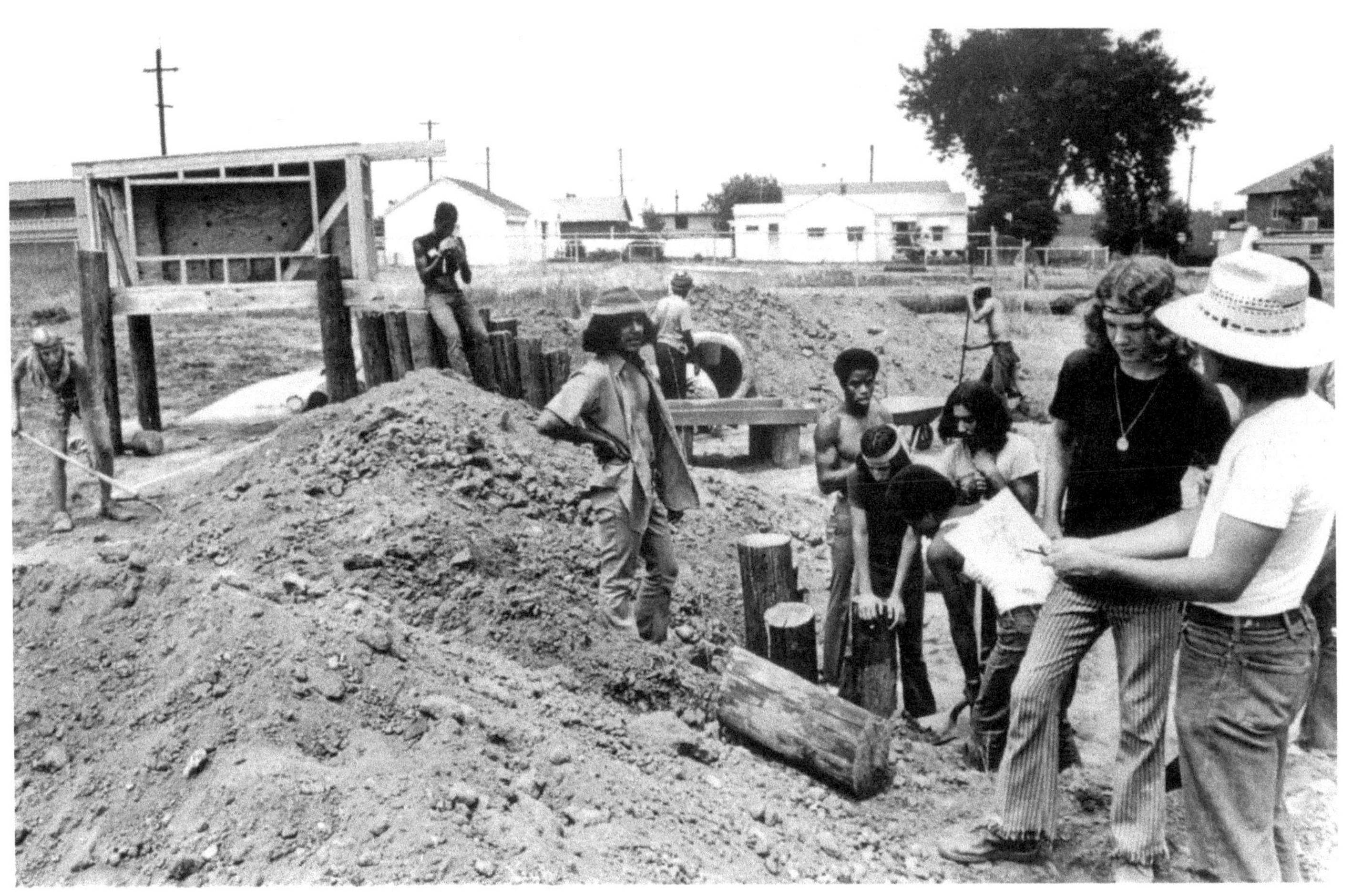

Students and volunteers help build a daycare center, probably in the Five Points neighborhood, in the late 1960s.

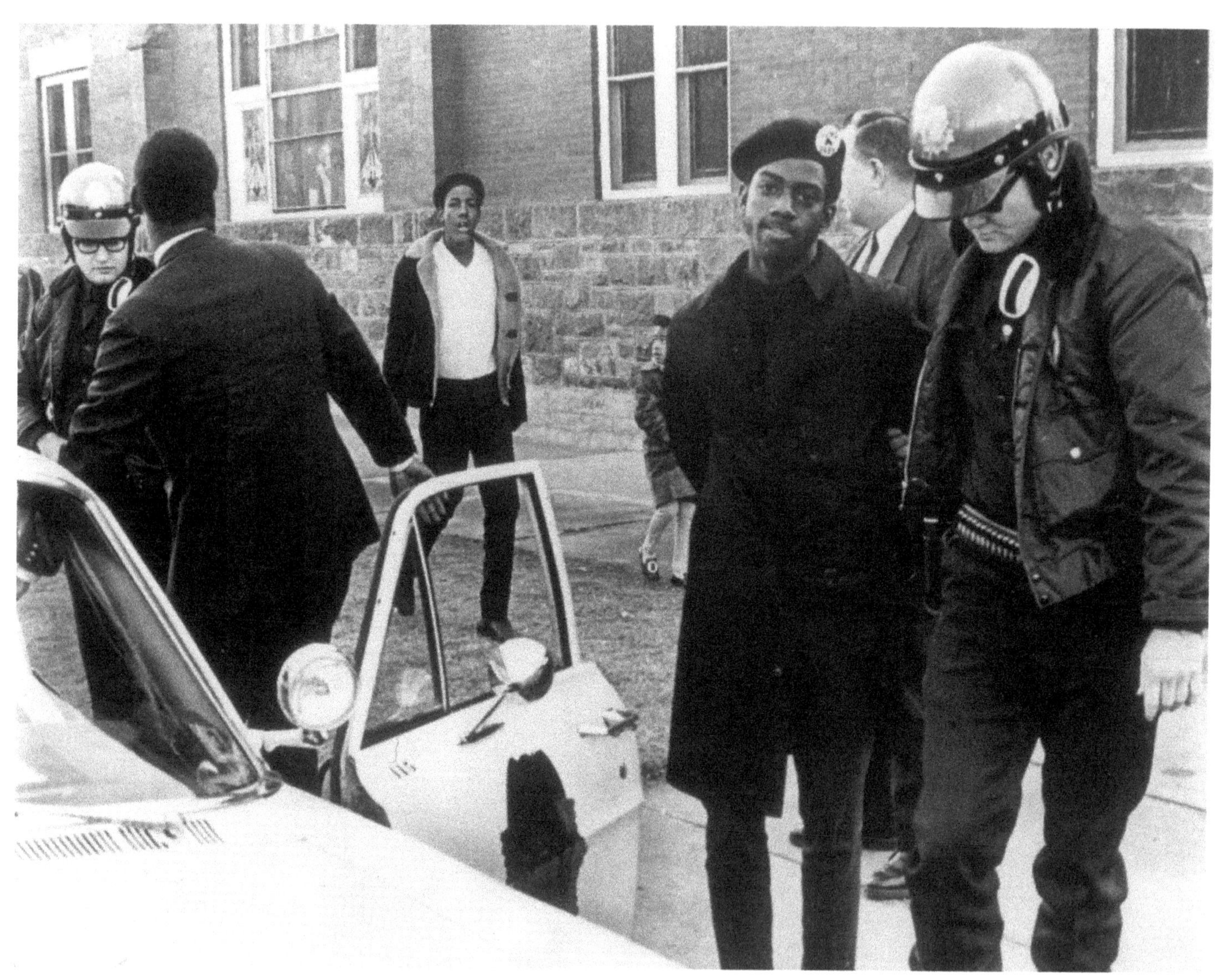

Black Panther member Chauncey Booker is arrested for contributing to the delinquency of minors, at Cole Junior High School, January 16, 1969.

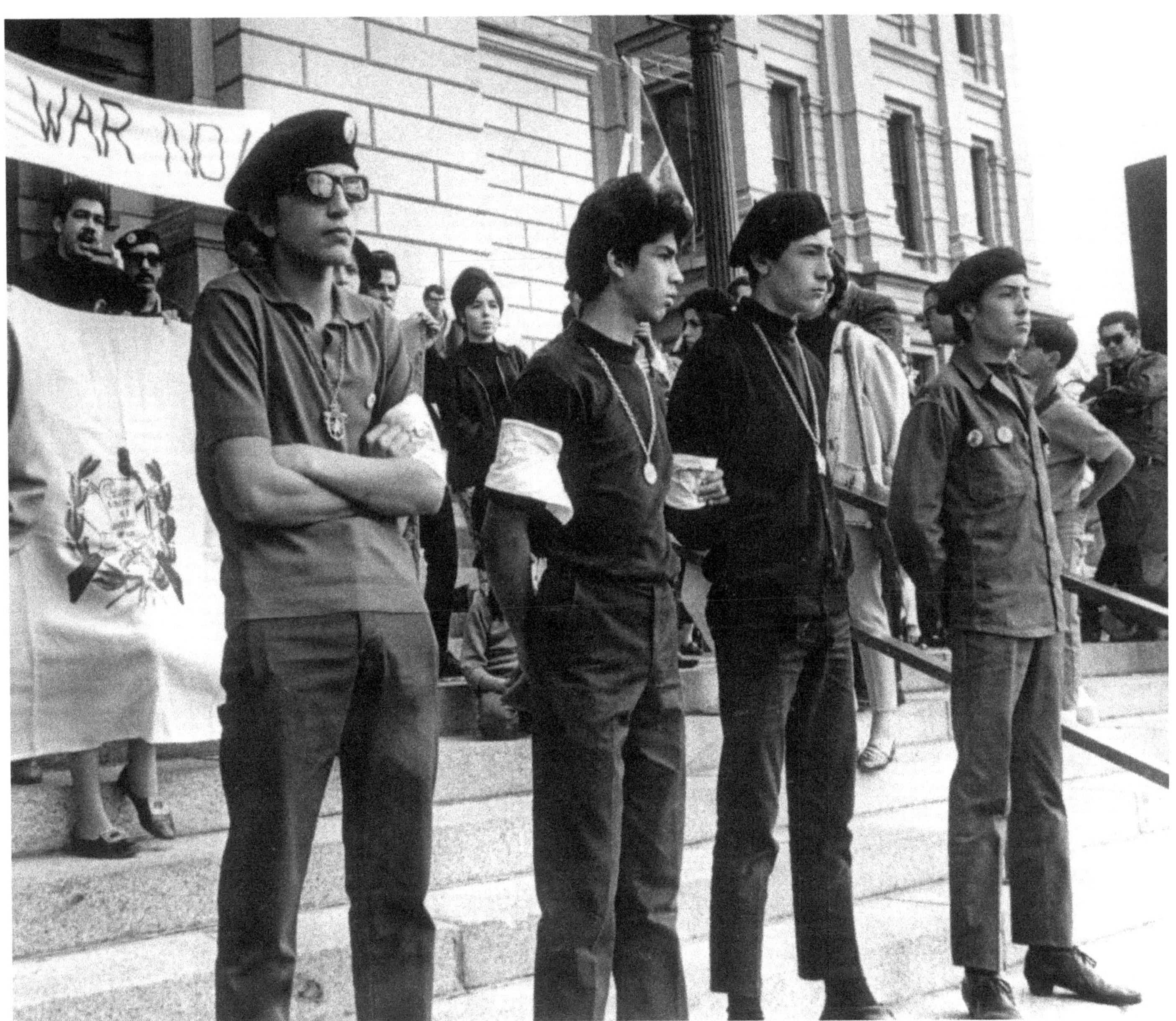

Corky Gonzales, a Chicano rights activist, addresses a crowd at an anti-war rally on the steps of the Colorado State Capitol building. He founded the urban civil rights and cultural movement called the Crusade for Justice, which advocated Chicano nationalism.

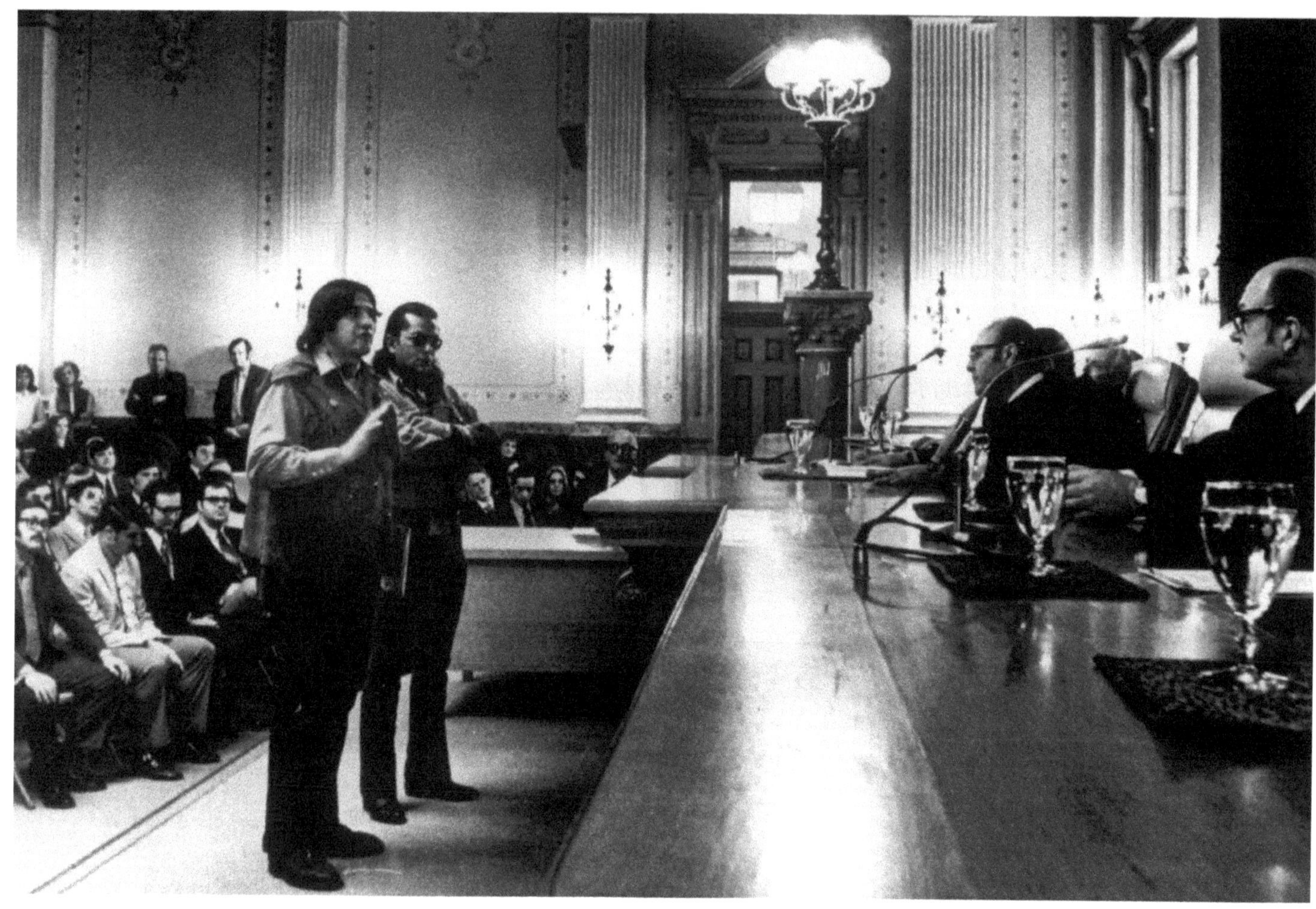

Two members of the American Indian Movement argue against what they perceive to be an anti–Native American bias in the Colorado State Bar exam.

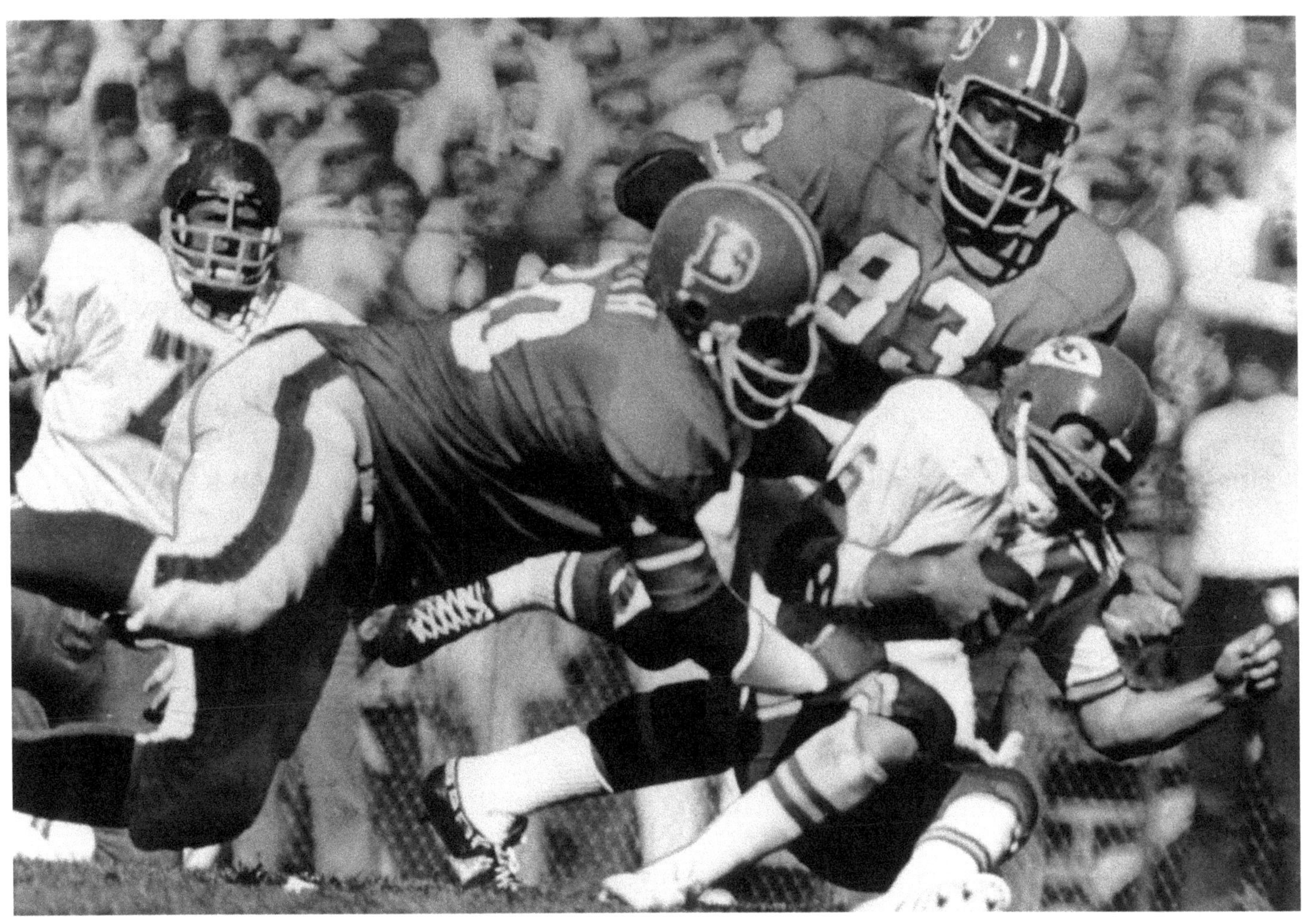

Denver Bronco Paul Smith tackles the Kansas City Chiefs' quarterback Len Dawson in a 1972 home game. The Chiefs won, 45 to 24.

Notes on the Photographs

These notes, listed by page number, attempt to include all aspects known of the photographs. Each of the photographs is identified by the page number, photograph's title or description, photographer and collection, archive, and call or box number when applicable. Although every attempt was made to collect all available data, in some cases complete data was unavailable due to the age and condition of some of the photographs and records.

II DENVER
Denver Public Library
MCC-1053

VI BROWN PALACE HOTEL
Denver Public Library
MCC-7

X POLICE REPORTERS
Denver Public Library
X-28852

02 ROCKY MOUNTAIN NEWS BEFORE THE CHERRY CREEK FLOOD
Denver Public Library
Photo by A. E. Rinehart
Z-1520

03 WEST DENVER DURING THE CHERRY CREEK FLOOD
Denver Public Library
X-29336

04 CITY JAIL
Denver Public Library
X-18658

05 SAM DUGAN HANGED BY VIGILANTES
Denver Public Library
Photo by Arundell C. Hull
Z-5786

06 DENVER CITY HOME GUARD
Denver Public Library
Z-3948

07 U.S. BRANCH MINT AT DENVER
Denver Public Library
Photo by Arundel Hull
Z-5788

08 15TH STREET BELOW LARIMER
Denver Public Library
X-23653

09 FIFTEENTH STREET
Denver Public Library
X-23701

10 FIRST NATIONAL BANK
Denver Public Library
X-23704

11 DUHEM BROTHERS PHOTO ART GALLERY
Denver Public Library
Photo by Duhem Brothers
X-18473

12 WOLFE HALL
Denver Public Library
Photo by Arundel C. Hull
Z-5787

13 LARIMER STREET
Denver Public Library
Photo by Charles Weitfle
X-23456

14 DENVER SCENES IN EARLY TIMES
Denver Public Library
Photo by William G. Chamberlain
X-19291

15 GERMAN METHODIST EPISCOPAL CHURCH
Denver Public Library
Photo by the Duhem Brothers Studio
X-18531

16 INTER-OCEAN HOTEL, DENVER
Denver Public Library
Photo by William G. Chamberlain
Z-8871

17 GRAND CENTRAL HOTEL
Denver Public Library
Photo by William Henry Jackson
WHJ-10140

18 FIRST BAPTIST CHURCH
Denver Public Library
Photo by William G. Chamberlain
X-27840

19 BUSINESS BLOCK, DANIELS & FISHER
Denver Public Library
Photo by the Duhem Brothers
X-18607

20 CHINESE FUNERAL PROCESSION
Denver Public Library
X-21496

21 **Panorama of Denver, no. 5.**
Denver Public Library
Photo by William Henry Jackson
WHJ-10450

22 **Corner of Larimer and 16th**
Denver Public Library
Photo by William G. Chamberlain
X-23443

23 **Beer Depot, Union Brewing Company**
Denver Public Library
X-22092

24 **Corner of 16th and Arapahoe Sts., Denver**
Denver Public Library
Photo by William Henry Jackson
WHJ-10474

25 **Larimer Street**
Denver Public Library
Photo by William Henry Jackson
WHJ-1029

26 **Tabor Opera House**
Denver Public Library
X-24749

27 **Courthouse, Denver**
Denver Public Library
Photo by Rose & Hopkins
H-257

28 **Larimer Street**
Denver Public Library
X-23444

29 **Post Office**
Denver Public Library
Photo by William Henry Jackson
WHJ-1573

30 **17th Street Looking N.W., Denver**
Denver Public Library
Photo by Rose & Hopkins
H-583

31 **Tennis Club, Corner of 14th Street and Curtis Place**
Denver Public Library
Z-1827

32 **Denver City Hall**
Denver Public Library
Photo by Rose & Hopkins
H-563

33 **Stout Street West, Denver**
Denver Public Library
Photo by Rose & Hopkins
H-580

34 **Ute Indians at the Denver Exposition**
Denver Public Library
Photo by William Henry Jackson
WHJ-101

35 **The Bethel Residence**
Denver Public Library
Photo by Rose & Hopkins
H-582

36 **15th and Lawrence, Denver**
Denver Public Library
Photo by William Henry Jackson
WHJ-10481

37 **Congregational Church and Denver Club**
Denver Public Library
Photo by Rose & Hopkins
H-250

38 **Wolfe Hall, Denver**
Denver Public Library
Photo by Rose & Hopkins
H-264

39 **Union Depot, Denver**
Denver Public Library
Photo from "Denver Picturesque and Descriptive"
X-18854

40 **North on Lawrence, From Fifteenth Street**
Denver Public Library
Photo from "Denver Picturesque and Descriptive"
X-18853

41 **Portrait of a Denver Police Officer**
Denver Public Library
Photo by Charles C. Wright
X-29674

42 **California & Equitable Buildings**
Denver Public Library
Photo by Rose & Hopkins
H-562

43 **Scandinavian House Saloon**
Denver Public Library
X-22489

44 **Coxey's Army**
Denver Public Library
X-21556

45 **Colorado Avenue and South Broadway**
Denver Public Library
X-27903

46 **Military Parade in Denver**
Denver Public Library
Photo by Harry M. Rhoads
Rh-234

47 **Masonic Temple**
Denver Public Library
Photo by Rose & Hopkins.
H-577

48 **Halt, Fix Bayonets, the City Hall War of 1894**
Denver Public Library
Photo by H. F. Peirson & Co.
X-22121

49 **1 P.M., Crowd at City Hall, City Hall War**
Denver Public Library
X-22118

50 **Equitable Building, Denver**
Denver Public Library
Photo by Rose & Hopkins
H-579

51 **Velocipede**
Denver Public Library
Photo by R. N. Ham
X-29761

52 **Turner Moving & Storage Company Vans**
Denver Public Library
X-24427

54 **Turner Moving & Storage Company**
Denver Public Library
Z-1021

55 **Manhattan Beach**
Denver Public Library
Photo by Frank Carruth
X-19530

56 **Ernest & Cranmer Building**
Denver Public Library
Photo by Rose & Hopkins
H-568

57 **Lobby in the Brown Palace Hotel**
Denver Public Library
Photo by Louis C. McClure
MCC-240

58 **Central Presbyterian Church**
Denver Public Library
Photo by Rose & Hopkins
H-259

59 **Cathedral of Saint John the Evangelist**
Denver Public Library
Photo by Rose & Hopkins
H-246

60 **Interior, Cathedral of St. John the Evangelist**
Denver Public Library
Photo by William Henry Jackson
X-25577

61 **Trinity Methodist Episcopal Church**
Denver Public Library
Photo by W. H. Lawrence & Co.
WHJ-1575

62 **City Park Pavilion**
Denver Public Library
X-27286

63 **Union Station**
Denver Public Library
Photo by L. C. McClure
MCC-283

64 **Festival of Mountain and Plain**
Denver Public Library
Photo by James B. Brown
X-33876

65 **Festival of Mountain and Plain Parade**
Denver Public Library
Photo by Charles D. Kirkland
X-25074

66 **Chinese Dragon, Festival of Mountain and Plain**
Denver Public Library
Photo by James B. Brown
X-18242

67 **Hotel Metropole**
Denver Public Library
Photo by Louis C. McClure
MCC-380

68 **Barbecue at the Denver Union Stockyards**
Denver Public Library
X-27812

69 **14th Street Viaduct Construction**
Denver Public Library
X-18015

70 **Unidentified Tavern**
Denver Public Library
X-25712

71 **Chamberlin Observatory**
Denver Public Library
Photo by George L. Beam
GB-7458

72 **Iliff School of Theology, University of Denver**
Denver Public Library
Photo by Joseph Collier
C-183

74 **Denver Skyline Looking Down 16th**
Denver Public Library
Rh-667

75 **Gano Clothing Company**
Denver Public Library
X-23949

76 **Harry Vardon About To Tee Off**
Denver Public Library
X-19893

77 **Auditorium**
Denver Public Library
Photo by Louis C. McClure
MCC-1027

78 **Denver Democratic Convention Welcome Arch**
Denver Public Library
X-23093

79 **Snow from the Moffat Road**
Denver Public Library
Z-5691

80 **Larimer Street Drunk Tank**
Denver Public Library
X-22125

81 **Daniels and Fisher Store**
Denver Public Library
X-22939

82 **Daniels and Fisher Cash Boys on the Roof of the Store**
Denver Public Library
X-22837

83 **J. J. Brown Residence**
Denver Public Library
Photo by P. Balsiger & Co.
X-26041

84 **Colorado Building**
Denver Public Library
Photo by Louis C. McClure
MCC-1269

85 **16th Street from Champa Looking North West**
Denver Public Library
X-23357

86 **Big Splash, White City**
Denver Public Library
Photo by Louis C. McClure
MCC-892

87 **Rough Riders**
Denver Public Library
Rh-700

88 **Manual High Teacher's Baseball Team**
Denver Public Library
X-28471

89 **Daniels and Fisher Tower at Night**
Denver Public Library
X-22930

90 **Larimer Street**
Denver Public Library
X-23472

91 **President Roosevelt on 17th Street**
Denver Public Library
Photo by Harry M. Rhoads
Rh-87

92 **Albany Hotel**
Denver Public Library
Photo by Louis C. McClure
MCC-849

93 **16th and Broadway**
Denver Public Library
Photo by Louis C. McClure
MCC-1260

94 **Nast Photo, 16th & Curtis**
Denver Public Library
X-23354

95 **Traffic Control Officer**
Denver Public Library
X-23634

96 **Female Swimmers at Washington Park**
Denver Public Library
Photo by Harry M. Rhoads
Rh-724

97 **Great Storm**
Denver Public Library
X-28965

98 **16th Street from Arapahoe**
Denver Public Library
Photo by Louis C. McClure
MCC-636

99 **Sixteenth Street**
Denver Public Library
Photo by Rocky Mountain Photo Company
X-23055

100 **Prisoner**
Denver Public Library
Photographer Harry M. Rhoads
RH-1770

101 **Car Flipped Over in Cherry Creek**
Denver Public Library
Photo by Harry M. Rhoads
Rh-1855

102 **Mining Exchange Building**
Denver Public Library
X-25109

103 **President Taft in Denver**
Denver Public Library
Photo by Harry M. Rhoads
Rh-654

104 **Princess Theatre**
Denver Public Library
Photo by L. C. McClure
MCC-1399

105 **The Benedict Transfer and Storage Co.**
Denver Public Library
Photo by Louis C. McClure
MCC-4199

106 **J. P. Fink's Block**
Denver Public Library
Photo by Louis C. McClure
MCC-4185

107 **Moving Picture Row**
Denver Public Library
Photo by Louis C. McClure
MCC-1901

108 **Foot Race**
Denver Public Library
X-29790

109 **Mounted Policemen**
Denver Public Library
X-29694

110 **Denver County Jail**
Denver Public Library
X-29712

111 **Auto Camp in City Park**
Denver Public Library
X-27190

112 **Sulky Races, City Park Race Track**
Denver Public Library
Photo by Harry M. Rhoads
RH-462

113 **Sailors and Soldiers Relax at a Red Cross Canteen**
Denver Public Library
Photo by Harry M. Rhoads
Rh-5903

114 **World War I Recruits**
Denver Public Library
Photo by Harry M. Rhoads
Rh-465

115 **Red Cross Trainees at Loretto Heights Service Camp**
Denver Public Library
Photo by George L. Beam
GB-7545

116 **World War I Recruits Depart for Europe**
Denver Public Library
Photo by George L. Beam
GB-565

117 **Ushers of the Broadway Theatre, Seasons 1916–1917**
Denver Public Library
Z-10

118 **Denver General Hospital**
Denver Public Library
X-28546

119 **Speer and Lincoln Avenues**
Denver Public Library
Photo by Ford Optical Company
X-22674

120 **Rocky Mountain Park**
Denver Public Library
X-27719

122 **Champion Boxer Jack Dempsey and His Wife, Estelle Taylor**
Denver Public Library
Rh-192

123 Colorado National Bank
Denver Public Library
Photo by Louis C. McClure
MCC-4302

124 Denver Tramway Strike
Denver Public Library
Photo by Harry M. Rhoads
Rh-5948

125 Auto Bandit Chaser
Denver Public Library
Photo by Ford Optical Company
X-29731

126 Holy Rosary Church
Denver Public Library
Photo by Rocky Mountain Photo Company
X-25369

127 Cathedral of the Immaculate Conception
Denver Public Library
X-25374

128 Roller Coaster at Elitch Gardens
Denver Public Library
Photo by Mile High Photo Company
X-27385

129 16th Street
Denver Public Library
Photo by Louis C. McClure
MCC-67

130 Continental Oil Building
Denver Public Library
Probably by Oscar E. Lindevall
X-24934

131 Packing House
Denver Public Library
Photo by Louis C. McClure
MCC-2415

132 Pergola, Civic Center
Denver Public Library
Photo by Louis C. McClure
MCC-2753

133 Curtis Street
Denver Public Library
X-2261

134 U.S. Post Office
Denver Public Library
Photo by Clark Blickensderfer
X-19824

135 Cheesman Pavilion
Denver Public Library
Photo by Louis C. McClure
MCC-2916

136 Sunken Gardens and West High School
Denver Public Library
Photo by Louis C. McClure
MCC-2966

137 Champa Street at 17th
Denver Public Library
X-22542

138 United States Mint and Colfax Avenue
Denver Public Library
X-27453

139 A & B Block
Denver Public Library
Photo by Rocky Mountain Photo Company
X-24853

140 Hendrie & Bolthoff Manufacturing and Supply Company
Denver Public Library
X-24273

141 Ku Klux Klan Parade, Larimer Street
Denver Public Library
X-21543

142 Y.W.C.A., Glenarm
Denver Public Library
X-29172

143 Denver Watches the World Series
Denver Public Library
X-28828

144 Colorado General Hospital
Denver Public Library
X-28543

145 Charles Lindbergh
Denver Public Library
Photo by Harry M. Rhoads
Rh-76

146 Traffic Officer on 16th Street
Denver Public Library
Photo by Harry M. Rhoads
Rh-171

147 Lita Grey Chaplin at Denver Union Airport
Denver Public Library
Photo by Colorado Photo Company
X-27504

148 Fingerprint and Mug Shot Room
Denver Public Library
Photo by Rocky Mountain Photo Company
X-29686

149 William L. Ford
Denver Public Library
Photo by William L. Ford
X-24484

150 S. H. Kress Building
Denver Public Library
Photo by the Denver National Company
X-22611

151 Mayan Theater
Denver Public Library
Photo by Rocky Mountain Photo Company
X-24683

152 Golden Eagle Dry Goods Company
Denver Public Library
Photo by Harry M. Rhoads
Rh-398

153 Colorado National Guard
Denver Public Library
Photo by Harry M. Rhoads
Rh-657

154 1933 Cherry Creek Flood
Denver Public Library
X-29286

155 16th and Wazee Streets After the Cherry Creek Flood
Denver Public Library
Photo by Charles E. Eyser
X-29311

156 16th Street, October 13, 1933
Denver Public Library
X-23348

157 Governor Johnson and Football Star Byron R. White
Denver Public Library
Photo by Harry M. Rhoads
Rh-1277

158 Echo Lake Park
Denver Public Library
Photo by Denver Photo Company
X-24003

159 Max Baer in Denver
Denver Public Library
Photo by Harry M. Rhoads
Rh-1183

160 President Roosevelt Visits Denver
Denver Public Library
Photo by Harry M. Rhoads
Rh-1299

161 Sixteenth Street
Denver Public Library
X-23350

162 Shanty Town, State Capitol in Distance
Denver Public Library
Photo by William L. Fick
Z-2735

163 Walker Castle
Denver Public Library
X-24961

164 Hook and Ladder Truck on Training Run
Denver Public Library
Photo by Oscar E. Lindevall
X-29571

166 Cleveland Place
Denver Public Library
X-22555

167 Painting No-Parking Zone
Denver Public Library
Photo by Rocky Mountain News
X-27890

168 Mead & Mount Construction Company
Denver Public Library
X-27538

169 Lowry Field
Denver Public Library
Photo by Harry M. Rhoads
Rh-1274

170 Lowry Field Federal Works Agency
Denver Public Library
Photo by Highton
Z-5633

171 Workers Day, World War II
Denver Public Library
Z-836

172 17th Street
Denver Public Library
X-23048

173 Fire at 12th and Curtis Streets
Denver Public Library
X-22609

174 16th Street
Denver Public Library
X-23364

175 Gus Quinn
Denver Public Library
X-21967

176 University of Denver Football Game
Denver Public Library
Photo by Harry M. Rhoads
Rh-4581

177 Bear Mountain, Denver Zoo
Denver Public Library
X-20118

178 Gano-Downs Company
Denver Public Library
X-24025

179 Barclay Apartments
Denver Public Library
Photo by Cloyd Teter, staff photographer, Denver Post
X-29220

180 Former Court House Square
Denver Public Library
X-23379

181 Broadway Theater Promotion
Denver Public Library
Photo by Albert Moldvay, staff photographer, Denver Post
X-24577

182 Shriner's Parade, Five Points
Denver Public Library
Photo by Clarence F. Holmes
X-22323

183 Denver Post Printing Plant
Denver Public Library
X-28804

184 Albany Hotel
Denver Public Library
X-23044

185 Roundup Riders of the Rockies
Denver Public Library
Z-4416

186 Daniels and Fisher Building
Denver Public Library
Z-120

187 Aerial View of Denver
Denver Public Library
Photo by a Rocky Mountain News staff photographer
X-29117

188 Mile High Center
Denver Public Library
Photo by the Mile High Photo Company
X-25084

189 Panoramic View of the City
Denver Public Library
X-29123

190 Continental Oil Company Building
Denver Public Library
X-24935

191 QUINCY HOTEL
Denver Public Library
Photo by Jackson C. Thode
X-29785

192 MORTAR IN CITY PARK
Denver Public Library
X-27196

193 LARIMER STREET IN 1967
Denver Public Library
X-23478

194 MEMBER OF COMMITTEE ON HUMAN RELATIONS AND DENVER POLICEMAN
Denver Public Library
X-28755

195 UNIVERSITY STUDENTS HELP BUILD A DAYCARE CENTER
Denver Public Library
X-21626

196 BLACK PANTHER CHAUNCEY BOOKER BEING ARRESTED
Denver Public Library
X-28764

197 CORKY GONZALES ADDRESSES WAR RALLY
Denver Public Library
Photo by John Gordon
X-21617

198 A.I.M. BEFORE THE COLORADO SUPREME COURT, OCTOBER 7, 1971
Denver Public Library
X-32084

199 DENVER BRONCOS VS. KANSAS CITY CHIEFS
Denver Public Library
Z-107

HISTORIC PHOTOS OF DENVER

By the late nineteenth century, the city of Denver was a vibrant cultural center of the West. Through changing fortunes, Denver has continued to grow and prosper by overcoming adversity and maintaining the strong, independent culture of its citizens.

Historic Photos of Denver captures this journey through still photography selected from the finest archives. From the Arapaho Tribe to the election of Mayor Robert Speer, the construction of Red Rocks Amphitheatre to the completion of the Remington Ordnance Plant, *Historic Photos of Denver* follows life, government, education, and events throughout the city's history.

This volume captures unique and rare scenes through the lens of hundreds of historic photographs. Published in striking black and white, these images communicate historic events and everyday life of two centuries of people building a unique and prosperous city.

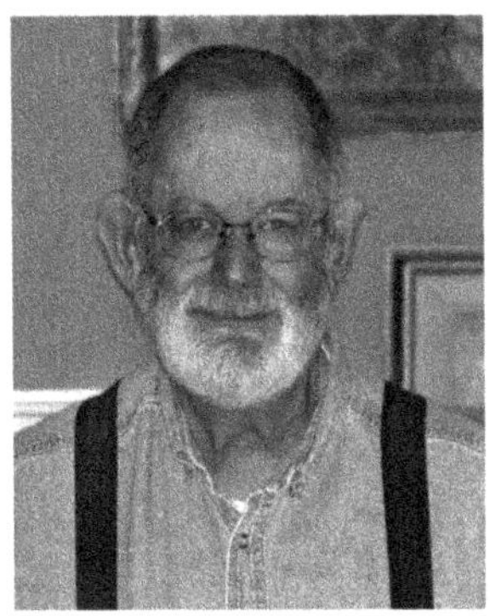

Myron Vallier has worked for more than seven years as librarian cataloging visual materials for photoswest.org, the web site for the Denver Public Library's Western History and Genealogy Department. During this time he has developed a great appreciation for the photographers and photography of the American West.

Myron was raised in Taos, New Mexico, and took an early interest in the arts. He served as a Peace Corps volunteer in Caracas, Venezuela, as a social worker and counselor, and once ran an antique business. With advanced degrees in history and library science, he has worked as a librarian in academic, public, and state libraries.

Myron lives in Conifer, Colorado, located in the foothills outside Denver, with a friend and Forrest, a large husky.

WWW.TURNERPUBLISHING.COM

www.ingramcontent.com/pod-product-compliance
Lightning Source LLC
LaVergne TN
LVHW060609110826
845154LV00003B/60

* 9 7 8 1 6 8 3 3 6 9 3 4 9 *